Home is Where the Heart Is

Home is Where the Heart Is

Studies in Melodrama and the Woman's Film

Edited by Christine Gledhill

BFI Publishing

First published in 1987 by the
British Film Institute,
127 Charing Cross Road, London WC2H 0EA
© British Film Institute 1987
© Introduction and editorial matter:
Christine Gledhill
© All previously published material:
original source
Sources are quoted at head of each article
© Previously unpublished material:
author 1987
Stills courtesy of Twentieth Century-Fox,
Rank, MGM and Warner Bros.
Cover still: from *Now, Voyager* (Irving Rapper, 1942),
courtesy of the Kobal Collection
Frontispiece: from *Way Down East* (D. W. Griffith, 1920)
Set in Linotron Sabon by
Fakenham Photosetting Limited,
Fakenham, Norfolk
and printed in Great Britain by
Anchor Brendon Ltd, Tiptree, Essex

British Library Cataloguing in Publication Data

Home is where the heart is: studies in
    melodrama and the woman's film.
    1. Moving-pictures – History and criticism
    2. Melodrama – History and criticism
    I. Gledhill, Christine Ann
    II. British Film Institute
    791.43′52   PN1995.9.M4/

ISBN 0–85170–199–X
ISBN 0–85170–200–7 Pbk

Contents

for Beverle

Acknowledgments

THE process of building this anthology was shared by three groups of students to whom I am much indebted. In early Summer 1981, TA 222 – post-graduate seminar at UCLA – contributed an energy and enthusiasm to my first exploration of this new field which is materially represented in essays gathered here. RTF 302 – final year undergraduates at Temple University, Philadelphia – presented me, during the early, snowy months of 1985, with lively, challenging, sometimes painful response to the materials and ideas emerging from the evolving anthology. Finally, the passage from Autumn 1985 to Spring 1986 brought the support of London University Extra-Mural Diploma students, whose love of melodramatic films and commitment to the knottier historical and theoretical questions of the form accompanied the concluding stages of this project and continues in the planning of a season of Hollywood melodramas and women's pictures at the National Film Theatre, scheduled for Spring 1988.

Individuals I want to thank for their encouragement and help are Ed Buscombe and Roma Gibson at the BFI, and Jeannie Allen, Jackie Byars, John Caughie, Richard Dyer, Jane Gaines, Beverle Houston, Ann Kaplan, Maria LaPlace, Janet Walker and Linda Williams, for support and many helpful conversations and/or correspondences. I want also to acknowledge the valuable work of the many pioneers and contributors to this developing field of study for whom, sadly, there was not space. Lastly I must thank Matthew, Luke and Richard for tolerating my many absences in pursuit of this project.

Introduction

THIS volume spans over a decade of film criticism, which, from the early 70s on, set out to put melodrama on the cinematic map. It represents the history of this critical endeavour and its problems, for engagement with melodrama goes beyond mere delineation of a newly discovered genre. Running through these essays is the double-sided question, *what is melodrama – what critical framework does it demand?* Feminism, in particular, given melodrama's long relegation as a women's cultural domain, claims a stake in critical reappropriation of the form and introduces the problem of the 'woman's film' which, it has been assumed, represents a sub-set of melodrama.

A central problem is melodrama's status not just as a cinematic genre, but as a mode with formative roots in the nineteenth century, rivalling realism in its claim to found the popular cinema. Many of these essays touch on nineteenth-century influences in film melodrama. However, once outside the cinematic, definitional possibilities proliferate. Melodrama exists as a cross-cultural form with a complex, international, two-hundred-year history. The term denotes a fictional or theatrical kind, a specific cinematic genre or a pervasive mode across popular culture. As a mode melodrama both overlaps and competes with realism and tragedy, maintaining complex historical relations with them. It refers not only to a type of aesthetic practice but also to a way of viewing the world. Thus, it is claimed, melodrama at its nineteenth-century peak informed two systems of thought underlying twentieth-century cultural analysis – Marxism and Freudian psychoanalysis (Wylie Sypher, 1965; Peter Brooks, 1976). And the phenomena it constructs range beyond art or entertainment to include religious and civic ceremony, politics and informational forms such as broadcast news or the popular press (Stuart Cunningham, 1981).

This collection does not attempt to represent such historical and cultural profusion, but seeks to clarify the issues at stake within a limited field: white, Anglo-Saxon cinema, based with one exception in Hollywood. This limitation is partly dictated by available material but is also historically strategic. Questions about the significance of melodrama in contemporary Western popular culture start with Hollywood and its huge international influence. For historical investigation leads to American culture, and Hollywood in particular as the place where European melodramatic traditions were re-

1

moulded in such a way that they could return in the twentieth century – their Victorian, national and class specificities transformed – to found both international and local popular film and televisual cultures.

As regards television, soap opera is commonly seen as the last resort of melodrama. But soap opera, like the woman's film, has an affiliation with women's culture, the elision of which with melodrama should not be assumed. In view, then, of Hollywood's importance to this investigation, and in the interests of concentrated rather than diffuse focus, work on television and soap opera has been put to one side. Nevertheless its presence can be felt in several of these essays as the new concepts it generates raise questions for assumptions about the film text and gendered spectatorship.

Melodrama is discussed in terms of gender and class, but only recently in relation to race and ethnicity. Emerging questions concern both the role of ethnicity in Western melodrama, and the function of melodrama for ethnic minority cultures (Jane Gaines, 1987). Some studies have been made of the adoption of the melodramatic mode by nationalist cultures emerging from neo-colonialism – for instance Brazilian *telenovelas* (Ana Lopez, 1985). How far the melodramatic aesthetic extends to non-Western cultures such as those of Japan or India is a matter of debate. These questions demand clearer definition of melodrama as mode and genre, of its historical and international lines of affiliation. Moreover, certainty that the term 'melodrama' constitutes legitimate categorisation rather than superficial resemblance requires parallel historicisation of non-European fictional forms (see, for example, Ashish Rajadyaksha, 1986).

If the ethnic voice is missing from this collection, the feminist presence all but dominates. This, however, does not indicate an intention to produce one more 'women and ...' anthology, but reflects where recent work has largely come from. The significance of feminist analysis of melodrama is not simply that it brings a 'woman's area' into critical view, but that it poses wider questions about gender and culture. At stake are the categories used to demarcate art from entertainment, the serious from the trivial, the tragic and realist from the melodramatic – demarcations which determine how the relationship between ideology, popular culture and pleasure is conceptualised.

The organisation of this volume is dictated partly by history, partly by conceptual questions. My preliminary 'investigation' of the melodramatic field which follows attempts a ground-clearing and mapping exercise, setting up some historical and contemporary signposts so that the overlaps and differences between the anthology's individual contributions can be located in a wider historical, critical – and polemical – arena.

Part One: Starting Out collects three critical moments in the constitution of melodrama within film studies, whose influence has been pervasive. Although these pieces by Thomas Elsaesser, Geoffrey Nowell-Smith and

Laura Mulvey come from different positions and use different concepts, they are marked by major shifts in film theory during the 70s. It is important to acknowledge this context, for melodrama's point of entry into film studies gave it a particular slant which I shall argue current analysis is struggling to supersede. The value of these early contributions lies in the questions they provoke which push beyond the parameters of initial interest in film melodrama. The work that followed these influential beginnings, while generally taking a narrower focus by concentrating on particular generic sub-sets, periods or texts, has opened out the historical and methodological questions they implied. The remaining contributions to this anthology, then, are gathered under heads representing different areas and methods of inquiry.

Part Two: With Woman in Mind deals with the production and consumption of different sub-sets of melodrama and the woman's film from the 30s to the early 60s. A central theme is the symbolic place of 'woman' and the maternal in melodrama in relation to the changing position of women – a relationship explored through the social, ideological and cultural discourses which bear both on the role of women in society and the representation of 'woman' by the film industry. Between them these essays examine three major sites of transformation and negotiation in melodrama's construction of 'woman': one, the shift from nineteenth- to twentieth-century, and from European to American, melodrama; second, the shifting relations between the patriarchal film industry and a 'circuit of women's culture' (Maria LaPlace) which, existing on the margins of the mass media, is drawn into genres seeking female audiences; and third, the relation between Freudian psychoanalysis, its Americanisation and Hollywood's changing constructions of 'woman', the 'maternal' and the 'feminine'. Sue Harper's study of a cycle of costume melodramas produced by the British studio, Gainsborough, during the 1940s, contributes a national and historical comparative dimension to this section's focus on the gendered negotiations of melodramatic production and consumption.

Part Three: Hollywood's Family Romances addresses issues of desire, pleasure, fantasy, aesthetics and ideology in relation to the melodramatic hero. Freudian ideas are central to these essays: the 'libido' and 'pleasure principle', driving force both of the hero's and melodrama's visceral, non-conceptual aesthetic energy (Elsaesser); the 'family romance', source of narrational subjectivity in classic Hollywood cinema and of plot structures which express the public as the private (Browne and de Cordova, respectively); the Oedipal equation of masculine desire with power and authority (Lesage and Rodowick); and popular Freudianism, itself a mechanism for rationalising the failure of contemporary melodrama to rearticulate Victorian identification of paternal authority with moral order (Rodowick). Finally, Julia Lesage interrogates the role of racial imagery in *Broken*

Blossoms's fantasies of rape and incest within the patriarchal family, and the perverse – ideological – pleasures of such fantasies for female audiences.

Part Four: What do Women Want? focuses debates in feminist textual analysis about how to read the woman's film and its female representations. In this respect it offers a counterpart to Part Two, which approaches texts through their social and discursive contexts. A central question, clarified in Annette Kuhn's concluding essay, is the relation between the female spectator as a set of textual positions and the social audience constructed by gender, class and race. At issue is the cine-psychoanalytic model of spectatorship which, if it appears to account for male pleasure in the fetishised or voyeuristically objectivised figure of the woman, does not fit the female audience's 'recognition' so neatly. Mary Ann Doane uses psychoanalysis to expose the patriarchal workings of classic narrative, arguing that, in the woman's film, which cannot simply reproduce the heroine as patriarchal fantasy, narrative is forced into a series of convoluted strategies to deny the figure automony. Drawing on feminist revisions of psychoanalysis, Linda Williams and Tania Modleski offer alternative constructions of the woman's film – Williams arguing of *Stella Dallas* the different subjectivities and spectatorial positions open to the female audience and Modleski, of *Letter from an Unknown Woman*, the different functions for male and female audiences enacted by melodrama's embodiment of the 'repressed feminine'.

These essays, chosen for their distinctive development of earlier positions or for their introduction of new directions, do not cohere into a linear or consistent argument about melodrama and the woman's film. Rather they both overlap and diverge, their ideas bouncing off one another to open the field to further pleasures of investigation.

The Melodramatic Field: An Investigation

CHRISTINE GLEDHILL

1 Melodrama and Cinema: The Critical Problem

> The initial success of romantic tearjerkers reflected their collective capacity to stroke the emotional sensibilities of suburban house-wives, but recent analysts suggest that the 50s melodramas are actually among the most socially self-conscious and covertly 'anti-American' films ever produced by the Hollywood studios.
>
> Thomas Schatz, 1981, pp. 224–5

FROM the turn of the century through to the 60s melodrama had been conceived in predominantly pejorative terms. As drama it represented debased or failed tragedy, demarcating an empty period in nineteenth-century dramatic history; in fiction it constituted a fall from the seriousness and maturity of the realist novel, relegating authors such as Dickens and Hardy to the second rank. In this respect melodrama was at the beginning of the century constituted as the anti-value for a critical field in which tragedy and realism became cornerstones of 'high' cultural value, needing protection from mass, 'melodramatic' entertainment.

Melodrama and Film Criticism

It was partly its association with melodrama that inhibited the acceptance of cinema as a serious object of study. In literary criticism it was not until the 60s, with the establishment of theatre studies and a growing concern with the history of theatricality and performance[1] that melodrama received any serious attention. Paradoxically, however, while literary criticism sought to recover melodrama as popular and ephemeral form (Booth, 1965; Rahill, 1967; Grimstead, 1968) film criticism was concerned to demonstrate the Shakespearean or Mozartian qualities in the oeuvres of Howard Hawks, John Ford or Alfred Hitchcock. Auteurism dominated 60s film studies, subjecting the extravagances of Hollywood *mise en scène* – later to be analysed as the basis of melodramatic rhetoric – to metaphorical interpretation as authorial vision. Popular films were validated not as melodrama but as exemplars of a humanist-realist tradition.

It may seem surprising that the rise of genre criticism at the turn of the 60s

5

in acknowledgment of cinema's industrial and popular base, while rehabilitating the notion of convention and typing, did little to recover melodrama. However, the generic enterprise was marked by defensiveness. It focused on discrete genres that could clearly be demarcated from each other and went to those genres which could boast already admired auteurs or prestigious connections with national tradition and history – the western or 'classic' gangster film for example (Cook, 1985). Melodrama was at best a fragmented generic category and as a pervasive aesthetic mode broke genre boundaries. In so far as it had a visible generic existence in the family melodrama and its lowly companion, the woman's film, melodrama could offer neither the thematic and evolutionary coherence exhibited by, say, the western, nor sufficient cultural prestige to appeal to the cognoscenti – condemned as it was by association with a mass and, above all female, audience.

When melodrama finally came into critical view it was in the context of an entirely different debate, when at the end of the 60s, Anglo-Saxon film criticism opened up to French structuralist and neo-Marxist aesthetics, dramatically reconstituting the critical field. In particular the relation between 'art' and 'popular culture' was reconceived. The efforts of the 60s to extend the values of a humanist-realist tradition to Hollywood were critiqued as misconceived liberalism, which ignored capitalist commodity production of both high and mass culture and the intimate connection between signification and ideological reproduction. The aesthetic value of realism was reversed in arguments about its bourgeois underpinnings, auteurism was critiqued for its ideological naïveté and a nascent genre criticism stagnated before melodrama had become an issue.

What allowed melodrama to emerge with full force into this reconstituted critical field was a new emphasis on the operation and ideological effectivity of aesthetic form. The *mise en scène* criticism of the 60s had prepared the way, particularly in certain French variants which had valued stylistic flamboyance for an aesthetic significance of its own, not needing thematic justification[2]. A convergence now occurred between this concern, which had fostered a Franco-American strand of formalist or 'pop-art' appreciation of Hollywood style, and a newly militant ideological criticism that looked to formal analysis in order to assess the complicity or subversiveness of a work. Whereas the realist-humanist tradition had privileged aesthetic coherence as the embodiment of authorial vision, the neo-Marxist perspective looked to stylistic 'excess' and narrative disjuncture for their 'exposure' of contradictions between a mainstream film's aesthetic and ideological programmes. Formal contradiction became a new source of critical value because it allowed apparently ideologically complicit films to be read 'against the grain' for their covert critique of the represented status quo.[3]

Enter Douglas Sirk

Many established Hollywood auteurs and genre practitioners were revalued according to this perspective, but some new ones came into view. Significant for melodrama was neo-Marxist reappraisal of the films of Douglas Sirk. Already subject to a camp following, Sirk was now constructed as a Brechtian director, who, constrained by the Hollywood studio system, had lighted on a popular genre – melodrama and with it the woman's film – for the access it gave to the neuralgic centre of Eisenhower's America, which through a range of 'distanciation' devices he exposed in a formal and ironic critique. In the arguments of Paul Willemen (1971) and Jon Halliday and Sirk (1971) melodrama was not itself the object of analysis, but the use Sirk made of it to disclose the distortions and contradictions of bourgeois – or petit bourgeois – ideology. According to Halliday and Willemen, Sirk's formation as a left-wing intellectual and theatre director in 30s Weimar Germany and his experience making film melodramas at UFA when the Nazis came to power gave him particular understanding of the contradictions hidden in the formal and ideological operations of melodrama. And in America, the grossness and vulgarity of the cliché-ridden plots handed him by the studios made the Hollywood genre particularly susceptible to formal criticism through parody and stylistic excess.

From Sirk to Melodrama

Although the goal of this approach was to demonstrate a 'critical' dimension in Sirk's Hollywood films, it also drew attention to and validated pleasures less ideologically pure. For there occurred a slippage of the 'subversion' argument from its attachment to Sirk as 'author' to melodrama itself. The visibility of Sirk in the early 70s, and the centrality of his high bourgeois family melodramas to a growing concern with ideology, had the effect of reorganising the cinematic field of authorial *mise en scène*. Through discovery of Sirk, a genre came into view. The works of directors, whose exploitation of colour, widescreen, camera movement, had previously been valued for humanist-realist thematics, were now seen as overwrought examples of the bourgeois family melodrama. Stylistic excess had no longer to be defended or justified as the correlative of a coherent vision. It became a positive value, passing from an authorial to a generic trademark and under this rubric the films of Minnelli, Ray, Ophuls, Cukor and Kazan came to stand alongside Sirk to mark the parameters of a new critical field. The problem that followed was precisely what kind of field melodrama offered – genre? style? mode? ideology?

The critical constitution of melodrama in the 70s was substantially determined by larger movements within film theory itself. Thomas Elsaesser's 'Tales of Sound and Fury' (1972) was the earliest, and remains the most comprehensive, account of film melodrama, attempting to come to terms not only with the melodramatic nature of Hollywood aesthetics, but with the place of cinema in the total field of European melodramatic forms. Perhaps because arriving early in the decade, it is also a transitional piece, poised between the auteurist and *mise en scène* approaches of the 60s and the ideological concerns of the 70s: its emphasis is formal, posing melodrama as 'a problem in style and articulation' (below, p. 43). However, the historical reach of the essay takes *mise en scène* analysis beyond a residual auteurism, to suggest the constitution of American cinema in a melodramatic tradition and the melodramatic basis of Hollywood's aesthetic, emotional and cognitive effects.

70s Neo-Marxism – Classic Realist/Narrative Texts

That the issue of melodrama as a formative cinematic mode was not pursued and that Elsaesser's seminal essay has waited more than ten years before appearing in three anthologies almost simultaneously, is, perhaps, accounted for by the development of post-structural and cine-psychoanalytic approaches to ideology and aesthetics in the mid-70s. To have pursued Elsaesser's line of investigation would have meant rethinking, rather than dismissing, the 'great tradition' of humanist realism which the *mise en scène* debates of the 60s inherited from literary criticism. In particular it would have meant rethinking both realism and the nineteenth-century novel in their relationship with melodrama.[4] However, structuralist neo-Marxism, in critiquing the notion of 'popular art', identified 'realism' as the anti-value, in which could be exposed at once literary critical tradition, bourgeois ideology and the manipulations of the capitalist culture industries. Paradoxically, then, neo-Marxist film criticism took the extension of the 'great tradition' to cinema at face value and condemned Hollywood for its perpetuation of the practices of the nineteenth-century – realist – novel. From this, now pejorative, alignment rose the 'classic realist text' as the model which linked the novel, Hollywood films and television programmes.

Classic realist texts, it was argued, reproduce bourgeois ideology because they implicate the spectator in a single point of view onto a coherent, hierarchically ordered representation of the world, in which social contradictions are concealed and ultimately resolved through mechanisms of displacement and substitution. In this process the spectator is 'interpellated' as the 'individual subject' of bourgeois ideology.[5] Clarification of the Lacanian psychoanalytic underpinnings of these arguments in the mid-70s produced a second line of attack on mainstream cinematic forms: the critique of the patriarchal subject. This Oedipal construct links the child's perception of sexual difference as the woman's castration or 'lack' with the acquisition of language and gendered identity. Repressing this traumatic knowledge, the (male) child achieves in the same process mastery of the symbolic codes of language and unified, stable identity. The price is 'femininity', the sign of difference, recalling counterva-

8

lent linguistic and psychic realities – the unbridgeable gap between words and meanings, between 'I' and self, which, operating through the unconscious, subtend illusions of the subject's command of language and its world. The 'classic narrative text', refining the earlier realist model, describes patriarchy's obsessive return to this founding scenario, analysing in the processes of narrative disruption and resolution, and in textual play round the figure of 'woman', mechanisms of identification which evoke the desire and at the same time resecure the homogeneous identity of a patriarchal subject.[6]

The subversive construction of Sirk and the dominance of the classic realist/narrative text from the mid-70s on influenced subsequent approaches to film melodrama. A central concern was to establish the nature of melodrama's radical potential. The critique of realism meant anti-realist excess came to be highly valued, while cine-psychoanalysis found in 50s family melodrama, which drew on the popularisation of Freudian ideas, self-consciously Oedipal screenplays. It remained a question, however, whether a Sirkian capability could be legitimately attributed to melodrama as a whole, or, whether Sirk constituted a special case in relation to other 50s melodramas.[7]

Psychoanalysis and Melodrama
Geoffrey Nowell-Smith's intervention (1977) drew the anti-realist and psychoanalytic strands together. Pointing out the historical relation of realism and melodrama and drawing on the Freudian concept of 'conversion hysteria', his generic rather than authorial analysis rearticulated melodrama's disruptive relation to the classic realist/narrative text. As a bourgeois form, melodrama is constrained by the same conditions of verisimilitude as realism. If the family melodrama's speciality is generational and gender conflict, verisimilitude demands that the central issues of sexual difference and identity be 'realistically' presented. But these are precisely the issues realism is designed to repress. Hence the syphoning of unrepresentable material into the excessive *mise en scène* which makes a work melodramatic. From this perspective the radical potential of melodrama lies less in a Sirkian critique of bourgeois life style and values than in the possibility that the 'real' conditions of psychic and sexual identity might – as symptoms of a 'hysterical text' – press too close to the surface and break the reassuring unity of classic realist narrative. 'Ideological failure', built into the melodramatic programme, results in the breakdown of realism.

While this generic approach disposed of the 'Sirk factor', a second problem emerges with the construction of the genre itself on the basis of the 50s family melodrama – a profile soon to become sufficiently solidified to warrant a chapter in Thomas Schatz's *Hollywood Genres* (1981). Not only did this perspective inhibit exploration of melodrama's affiliations across a range of melodramatic cycles of earlier and later decades, it obscured the relation between family melodrama and the woman's film – a major, if disdained,

9

production category of the 30s and 40s, which the former happily pillaged in a series of remakes and adaptations. This became a crucial question for feminist consideration of the form.

Melodrama and the Woman's Film

Feminist writing about melodrama and the woman's film has confronted a paradox. The crux of the classic realist/narrative text – the function of the female figure as a representation both of the threat of castration and ultimate goal of desire – produces a contradictory scenario in which 'woman' is subjected alternately to voyeuristic punishment or fetishistic idealisation. From this stems the feminist argument that female figures in mainstream cinema do not represent women, but the needs of the patriarchal psyche.[8]

However, where film theory saw in melodrama's exposure of masculinity's contradictions a threat to the unity of the (patriarchal) realist/narrative text, feminists found a genre distinguished by the large space it opened to female protagonists, the domestic sphere and socially mandated 'feminine' concerns. The fact that the home and personal relationships provide common ground to the family melodrama and woman's film has given substance to the assumption that the latter constitutes a sub-set of melodrama, tailored specifically for female audiences. However, subversive construction of melodrama begs the question whether 'subversion' works in the same way for both forms.

Laura Mulvey's essay on Sirk and melodrama (1977/8) examined this question in terms of the intersection of gender with genre. Noting the intense recognition felt by many women of the emotional and ideological dilemmas played out in Sirk's woman's films, she questioned the construction of melodrama as a form which exposes *hidden* contradiction. Pointing out that ideology is always and necessarily contradictory, Mulvey argued that patriarchal culture has consistently turned to domestic conflict as a safety valve for social problems arising from the over-valuation of masculinity. In this respect a similar function is performed by Greek tragedy and Victorian melodrama. By extension, the rise of the 50s family melodrama out of remakes of 30s women's pictures could equally be understood as attempting reconstruction of heterosexual relations and gender roles in a post-war rapprochement with the 'feminine'.

However, if contradictions arising from the sexual and social positioning of men and women in relation to each other are hidden from the male in the accommodations Western culture makes to the symbolic functioning of masculinity – for example the western or gangster film with their codes of action, honour, success and failure – they are part of the daily lived experience of the female audience, who have little need to practise subversive reading in order to perceive them. From this position Mulvey proposed the influential distinction between male and female point-of-view melodrama, demarcating the 'tragically' inclined family melodramas of Minnelli and Sirk from Sirk's work in the more humble sphere of the woman's film, centring on female protagonists.

Re-thinking Anti-realism
By drawing attention to the differentially gendered evaluations of melodrama and the woman's film and to the contradiction between participant recognition and ironic distanciation in Sirk, Mulvey's argument invites reconsideration of the subversive construction of Sirkian irony.[9] For if melodrama can be a radically 'critical' form, what then is being critiqued and for whom? In Brechtian interpretation of Sirkian strategies the object of parody is bourgeois wish-fulfilment, an identification supported by the high production values of 50s family melodrama which focused on upper-middle-class homes crammed with lavish furnishings and consumer goods, celebrating the life-style of a class 'basking complacently under Eisenhower, while already disintegrating from within' (Halliday, 1971, p. 10). This assumes not only that particular 'fantasies' belong to particular classes, but that a film's fantasy is a reflection of its audience's fantasies:

> ... the world the audience wants to see (an exotic world of crime, wealth, corruption, passion, etc.) is a distorted projection of the audience's own fantasies to which Sirk applies a correcting device, mirroring these very distortions. (Willemen, 1972/3, p. 130)

However, while this assumption might be justified in the case of Brecht's intervention into the bourgeois theatre of Weimar Germany (from which the argument is extrapolated), its application to Sirk's position in Hollywood sidesteps the question of the mass audience and its differential composition by class, gender, race, age. If we grant the appeal of 50s family melodrama to the upwardly mobile ambitions of Hollywood's petit bourgeois or working-class audiences, the question still remains how the material goods and marital scenarios supposedly fantasised by one class function in the fantasy of another class.

Irony and parody operate between two secure points: the position which we who perceive the irony occupy and that which, held at a distance, is critiqued. The 'radical readings' of the 70s belonged to the critics, made at the expense of the naïve involvement of American 'popular' audiences in the 1950s.

The problematic identification of melodrama with bourgeois fantasy was compounded by another commonsense identification of melodrama with women. This is evident in accounts of Sirk's 'mastery' of what would otherwise be dismissed as Hollywood's lowliest form, the woman's weepie.

In *Imitation of Life* Sirk is fighting – and transcending – the universe of Fannie Hurst and Ross Hunter (not to mention Lana Turner, John Gavin, and Sandra Dee) ... On the surface, *Heaven* is a standard women's magazine weepie – mawkish, mindless, and reactionary. Yet just beneath the surface it is a tough attack on the moralism of petit bourgeois America. (Jon Halliday, 1971, pp. 9–10)

An intelligent director confronting the world of Fannie Hurst or of Lloyd C. Douglas, confronts not only banality but an even more virulent kind of falsity; the self-deceptions and consoling lies about life and human character that the tearjerking mode exists to supply us with. (James Harvey, 1977/8, p. 54)

The designation of the family as a bourgeois institution, the perceived materialisation of bourgeois ideology in these films in a sphere conventionally assigned to women – the home, family relations, domestic trivia, consumption, fantasy and romance, sentiment – all imply equivalence between the 'feminine' and bourgeois ideology. The two audiences for Sirkian irony can be further specified: one which is implicated, identifies and weeps, and one which, seeing through such involvement, distances itself. The fact that, across all classes, the first is likely to be female and the other male was not remarked on. Nor was the recourse of 50s family melodrama to the 30s woman's film as a source of patriarchal renewal investigated. To take a well known example, Fannie Hurst's *Imitation of Life*: John Stahl's version (1934), however myopic it may be on the issue of race, is thoroughly a woman's film, suppressing the male role to the margins in the interests of an all female household. Sirk's remake turns the story into a problem of the absent husband and father and obtains his critique of white values at the cost of turning poor, struggling Lana Turner into a 'bad mother' – a judgmental temptation few Sirkian commentators have been able to resist, despite the possibility within the logic of the 'Sirkian system' for ironically exposing ideologies of motherhood. Ironic value in this context has an implicitly misogynist edge.

Melodrama and the History of Cinema
The constitution of melodrama as family melodrama and as a genre that 'disrupts' the classic realist/narrative text not only obscured its relation to the woman's film, but made it difficult to pursue its connections with the nineteenth-century melodramatic forms which, it has been suggested, constitute a founding tradition of Hollywood as a whole. What, for instance, is the justification confining melodramatic categorisation to films about domestic situations and 'feminine' conditions? Why are the shoot-out, the lone treck through the wilderness, the rituals of horse and gun, any less excessive

12

than a family conflict about – taking an example from Minnelli's *The Cobweb* – curtains destined for a psycho-therapeutic clinic? But if melodramatic rhetoric informs westerns, gangster and horror films, psychological thrillers and family melodramas alike, how tenable is it to constitute melodrama in a critical, disruptive relation to the classic realist/narrative text?[10]

A different Marxist tradition, which should be acknowledged, reverses the aesthetic values adopted by the post-structural ideological project. For example, Raymond Williams's discussion of melodrama's defeat of English naturalism (1977), Charles Eckert's analysis of *Marked Woman* (1973/4) and Chuck Kleinhans's account of family melodrama (1978), all deploy the concept of displacement to suggest melodrama's mystifying resolution of 'real' social conflicts – which realism would seek to lay bare – at the surrogate level of family and personal relations. What is valued as critical irony by the anti-realist school represents merely an evasive ambivalence, seeking to accommodate all possible audiences. This reversal of aesthetic/ideological value, however, is no more satisfactory a mode of categorisation, for it suggests that the 'real' lies in a set of socio-economic relations outside the domestic and personal sphere, to which issues of sexual relations, of fantasy and desire are secondary.

A major issue, then, in the exploration of melodrama is the relationship and difference between melodrama and realism. Is one the ideological undoing of the other, or do they constitute different projects?

Some Questions about Melodrama
In this survey of the development of melodrama criticism in the 70s, several points of tension have surfaced. The first is the identification of melodrama with bourgeois ideology as opposed to its sub-cultural use, particularly by women. A second concerns the relation of melodrama as either a founding mode of Hollywood cinema, or a particular, if mobile and fragmentary, genre, specialising in heterosexual and family relations. A fourth tension emerges around gender, as concerns critical value, genre (the relation of the woman's film to melodrama) and representation (where melodrama's investment in 'woman' as patriarchal symbol conflicts with the unusual space it offers to female protagonists and women's concerns). Finally, melodrama raises issues of pleasure, fantasy, ideology and their role in 'popular' culture.

These are areas which cannot be examined within the parameters of film studies alone because they pose pressing questions of a wider history of cultural institutions. Nor can they be covered within the scope of an introductory piece like this. But in what follows, drawing on a variety of writings in theatrical history, literary and film criticism, I attempt to sketch a contexting framework in which such questions can be pursued.

II Historicising Melodrama

> When we look at the emergence of the modern melodrama about 250 years ago ... everyone can clearly understand its class nature as drama of and for a specific class poised against another class.
>
> Chuck Kleinhans, 1978, p. 40

> Melodrama always sides with the powerless.
>
> Martha Vicinus, 1981, p. 130

> Melodrama is a notoriously bourgeois aesthetic.
>
> Wylie Sypher, 1965, p. 267

> Melodrama itself was essentially entertainment for the industrial working class ... its basic energy was proletarian.
>
> Michael Booth, 1965, p. 52

> Melodrama as echo of the historically voiceless ...
>
> David Grimstead, 1971, p. 80

Like the novel, melodrama is frequently associated with the bourgeoisie – in the eighteenth century a European bourgeoisie, struggling for ascendency over a decadent aristocracy, or, two hundred years later, a bourgeoisie 'decaying from within' in Eisenhower's America. However, between these two periods of bourgeois 'crisis' lies the intervening generalisation of 'crisis' and 'mode' across social classes and cultural forms which made melodrama both a central nineteenth-century paradigm and a formative influence in twentieth-century mass culture. A crucial factor in these shifts is the role played by emergent working-class audiences and 'popular' tradition in the early formation of melodrama.

Melodrama and Class Struggle
The conditions for the emergence of melodrama, many histories suggest, were created when, during the eighteenth century, the bourgeoisie took power from the aristocracy by assimilation or revolution and manoeuvred for cultural hegemony in the name of 'ordinary citizens'. Although the common alignment of melodrama with the theatre and realism with the novel is misleading, nevertheless the theatre constituted an important site of contestation in this struggle, the institutional and aesthetic forms of which would be central to the development of melodrama.

In eighteenth-century England and France, royal patents granted to two or three theatres monopoly over the 'official' repertoire and rights of censorship over all other forms of 'illegitimate' or 'Minor House' entertainment. Thus protected, and drawing dramatists from the ranks or associates of their aristocratic audience, the Patent Theatres were the social centre of the ruling elite and therefore a stake in bourgeois struggle to redefine reality and aesthetic value. For in opposition to aristocratic theatrical monopoly, rapid urban growth, consequent on capitalist expansion, produced broadening audiences drawn from newly emerging middle, lower-middle and proletarian classes. Since the monopoly of the Patent Theatres was vested in the performances of 'plays', defined by their use of spoken dialogue, consolidation of an 'illegitimate' theatre depended on the entrepreneurial development of former folk and popular entertainment traditions for their capacity to evade official restrictions: dumb show, pantomime, harlequinade, ballets, spectacles, acrobatics, clowning, busking, the exhibition of animals and freaks, and, above all, musical accompaniment and song.

In Paris the entrenchment of the aristocracy, to be removed only by revolution at the end of the century, and the grip of an outworn aristocratic neo-classic tradition over the official repertoire, led to the thriving institutionalisation of alternative entertainments (Rahill, 1967, pp. 16–17, and Brooks, 1976). In England, on the other hand, the bourgeoisie, having gained power earlier in the century by assimilation rather than revolution, perceived these developments as cause of deteriorating 'dramatic standards' in the Patent Houses themselves. This judgment, compounded by the growth of political satire, led to the legal codification of former aristocratic restrictive practices in the Licensing Act of 1737, designed to control the minor theatres and police the pleasures of newly emerging 'popular' audiences (Loftis, 1963).

Paradoxically these attempts to control a developing theatrical culture drove the 'illegitimate' theatre still further into elaboration of spectacular traditions and the consolidation of an alternative dramatic rhetoric, which eventually risked lines of spoken dialogue to clarify increasingly complicated plots. Box-office receipts outweighed the problems of police harassment. In consequence the English Patent Houses, unable to survive on the drawing power of the official repertoire, were forced into competition for the new audiences such entertainments attracted, interlacing the 'official' repertoire with 'box-office pullers' stolen from the illegitimate theatre.

In France, the Revolution legalised such entertainments, removing all but political aesthetic restriction. For several critics (notably, Peter Brooks, 1976), French post-Revolutionary theatre is central to the codification of melodrama as a distinct theatrical genre. The violent accession of the bourgeoisie, the extreme constraints of an outworn neoclassicism and the oppositional consolidation of a vigorous 'illegitimate' popular theatre meant that Revolution and the end of restriction brought a more complete break with aristocratic culture than occurred in England and a more flourishing alternative in the theatrical explosion that followed. However, although French melodrama was distinguished by strong internal coherence and wide international influence, it was not a purely national product. Rather the institutional and ideological conditions of French theatre at the turn of the century made it a crucible in which a wide range of European fictional and dramatic currents, popular traditions, and an extremist form of bourgeois demand met.[11]

Forging a Melodramatic Aesthetic: Two Cultural Trajectories

Contradictions between cultural monopoly and economic expansion opened spaces for the insertion and development of popular traditions and laid the institutional basis for the emergence of melodrama out of a convergence between bourgeois and 'popular' cultural trajectories.

Melodrama's bourgeois inheritance   Many dramatic histories locate the inception of melodrama in the degeneration of bourgeois tragedy. Raymond Williams' study, *Modern Tragedy* (1966), by historicising the *category* of tragedy as well as its form, opens up the implications of this perception, suggesting how bourgeois appropriation altered the aesthetics of tragedy in ways that both contributed to melodrama and eventually led to its critical repudiation.

Contrary to common belief, Williams argues, the significance of the Greek tragic hero was not his status as an individual. The term itself indicated membership of a group, not the unique and isolate personality suggested in modern usage. Society in ancient Greece and medieval Europe was organised in visible hierarchies – from the king down to the peasant and upwards to the gods or God. Tragedy turned on actions of momentous social import. If the hero were a king or head of a ruling household, his actions, through a web of hierarchical interconnections, had significance for society at large. The representative role of the tragic hero is demonstrated in the fact that, contrary to modern conceptions, pre-bourgeois tragedy did not end in the death of the hero but 'with the affirmation made possible and informed by the death' (p. 54).

Neoclassicism had made significant inroads into the social representativeness of early tragic forms by appropriating the tragic hero in the image of a ruling minority. Rank now stood not for a network of feudal social and spiritual relations and responsibilities, but a source of aristocratic class style. The tragic action was increasingly internalised as individual error, to which rank conferred tragic value in so far as the hero, conforming to elite codes of decorum, displayed dignified and noble endurance of his fate (p. 26). While the moral dimension of decorum and notions of individual error appealed to the bourgeois sensibility, the investment of tragic value in a person of rank was both meaningless and intolerable to its democratic ideals. Eighteenth-century bourgeois culture abandoned the aristocratic trappings of neoclassic tragedy: 'From Lower Life we draw our Scene's Distress – Let not your Equals move your Pity less' (quoted in Williams, p. 91).

With elimination of the hero's rank, went also the fatalistic emphasis on 'dignified endurance' of fate as an acceptable tragic stance. In its place emerged the notion of 'poetic justice' and a new moral mission for the theatre. Tragedy must demonstrate not only that suffering arises from moral error, but also that happiness rewards steadfast virtue and moral reform. The theatre took on an educative role through the power of example and appeal to the 'sympathetic emotions' of what was understood to be an essentially benevolent human nature. The protestant conscience identified with the heart. A sentimental dramaturgy emerged, demanding a new kind of spectatorial response of recognition and identification with familiar characters in affecting circumstances. Poetic justice was the morality of feeling: 'the tragic catastrophe either moves its spectators to moral recognition and resolution, or can be avoided altogether, by a change of heart' (Williams, p. 31). Sentimentalisation, stress on the individual, appeals to the personal, all supported the shift in the social terrain of bourgeois fiction and drama from feudal and aristocratic hierarchies to the 'democratic' bourgeois family – arena of personal, moral and social conflict, and support of the triad, heroine/villain/hero, which became a dominant dramatic structure from thereon.

However, eighteenth-century sentimental drama failed either to create enduring forms or to command the new audiences congregating in the cities. Nor, though bequeathing a repertoire of character types, plot devices, rhetorical structures, dramatic conflicts drawn from the central image of the family, did it of itself produce melodrama. Despite the stress on the 'sympathetic emotions', argues Wylie Sypher (1965), eighteenth-century culture produced largely 'mental fictions' (p. 260). In Peter Brooks's view (1976), bourgeois sentimental forms lacked 'the heroic dimensions, overt excitement and ... cosmic ambition which melodrama would yield' (p. 83). Frank Rahill (1967) adds 'violence' as another missing element. For these, melodrama would draw on popular traditions brought to a high degree of sophistication in the illegitimate theatre.

Popular traditions Prohibition on spoken dialogue opened the way to the development of earlier traditions in at least three areas of major significance to melodrama. First, if illegitimate entertainments were to become a viable economic and professionalised concern, *spectacle* provided that element which could be most fully developed without running the risk of falling into the forbidden category of the 'play'. This led to increasingly sophisticated productions with elaborate and varied costuming, exotic sets, spectacular enactments and special effects (Rahill, 1967, p. 23). Spectacle in its turn demanded and developed earlier *performance* traditions such as dumb show, pantomime, harlequinade, tumbling, acrobatics and balladry.

Music constituted a third non-verbal dimension of meaning and link to

17

popular tradition. For, although – apart from the French neoclassic stage – music had always had a place in the theatre (David Mayer, 1981), it was for 'illegitimate' theatre both a legal and aesthetic means of existence. The use of song also permitted the undercover insertion of a verbal element. However, mimed dumb show and pantomime offered other means to this end. According to Peter Brooks (1976) the display of placards with explanatory information was common, as was the unfurling of flags and banners at appropriate moments to reveal written inscriptions. Beyond this, pantomime had evolved a whole repertoire of non-verbal signs or 'visible emblems' such as meteors, rainbows, lightning, spectres, crosses in flames, rising tombs and the like, which would instantly tell the audience the nature of a particular situation, or a character's moral standing (pp. 63–4). Elaborating such traditional techniques, the illegitimate theatre had by the end of the eighteenth century consolidated a sophisticated theatrical *mise en scène*.

The Socio-Cultural Formation of Melodrama

Bourgeois and popular cultural trajectories were brought together by the peculiar social and institutional circumstances of theatrical entertainment from the mid-eighteenth to mid-nineteenth century. Under such conditions earlier folk and current 'popular' traditions overlaid, or coalesced with, 'establishment' dramaturgical and fictional structures.

From institutional to aesthetic intertextuality   Shifting class formations and the increasingly mixed social composition of the audience (Grimstead, 1968; Douglas Reid, 1981) gave rise to a number of theatrical practices aimed at attracting a wide range of social groups. Programming was lengthy and heterogeneous. For example, at Covent Garden in the early nineteenth century, *Romeo and Juliet* was paired with *Puss in Boots*, and *Hamlet* with *The Miller and His Men*, a popular melodrama (Frank Rahill, 1967, p. 114). Such programming initiated audiences into a range of cultural forms, both 'legitimate' and 'illegitimate' and prepared the way for aesthetic transmutation between genres and modes – for a welding of fantasy, spectacle and realism – which would be crucial to the melodramatic aesthetic as a cross-class and cross-cultural form.

Melodrama arose to exploit these new conditions of production, becoming itself a site of generic transmutation and 'intertextuality'. Based on commerce rather than cultural monopoly, melodrama multiplied through translation, adaptation, and, in the absence of copyright laws, piracy. Literary and dramatic classics – including Shakespearean tragedies, popular fiction, Romantic poetry and operatic libretti, newspapers and topical events, police journals and penny dreadfuls, paintings and etchings, popular songs and street ballads all provided material for melodrama (Michael Booth, 1965, pp. 50–1 and 1981; Frank Rahill, 1967, p. 115).

18

Heterogeneous programming also created conditions for intertextuality in production style and performance mode. Not only might the same company perform melodrama, Shakespearean tragedy, opera, eighteenth-century comedy or fairy-tale plays (Grimstead, 1968, p. 107), but in one evening's entertainment a single actor would perform acrobatic numbers and comic dance routines, sing ballads and double in pantomime, melodrama, or Shakespeare (Louis James, 1981, p. 11). In this context older traditions and new ideas converged at the level of performance. On one hand, many nineteenth-century actors had acquired acrobatic and miming skills through experience in circus or travelling troupes (James, op. cit.). On the other, melodramatic performance modes relate to eighteenth- and nineteenth-century treatises codifying the language of bodily gesture, facial expression and intonation (Peter Brooks, 1976 and James, 1981). These theories were of widespread general interest, passing into the popular Victorian science of phrenology and providing the basis of widely used French and English acting manuals – for instance the Delsarte method. The control over gesture and facial expression which dumbshow and acrobatics taught the actor merged with such theories to produce a precise but versatile body language (see James, 1981; Susan Roberts, 1986).

Music offered another site of coalescence. The dependence of illegitimate theatre on music was not only legal. Apart from the inclusion of popular songs and ballads, music, 'often written and performed with great care ... to clarify the action and enhance the dramatic effect', was integral to Minor House entertainments (Rahill, 1967, p. 24; Mayer, 1981) and led to the emerging genre's appropriation of the French term, 'mélo-drame'. In fact this had been coined by Jean Jacques Rousseau in the early 1770s, to distinguish his 'scène lyrique', Pygmalion, from Italian opera. In the belief that French was 'too harsh a language to be sung', Rousseau experimented with new verbal and musical relations in which – prefiguring melodramatic usage – 'words and music, instead of going together, are heard alternately and where the spoken phrase is ... announced and prepared by the musical phrase' (quoted in James Smith, 1973, p. 1). 'Music-drama' as such had a relatively short life, but the term achieved lasting currency as a designation for melodrama, a form which embedded words in music, song and dance, in a way that imparted a musical dimension to every other register – verbal and visual.

Melodrama as a Nineteenth-Century Paradigm
Despite the pressures of aesthetic restriction, a socially broadening audience, and a heterogeneous repertoire, neither legal enforcement nor the contingencies of programming were alone responsible for the emergence of melodrama as a pervasive aesthetic mode. Other forces operating in nineteenth-century culture brought pressures to bear under which the new aesthetic became a central cultural paradigm.

19

The manichean outlook If eighteenth-century sentiment produced only 'mental fictions', by the mid-eighteenth century countervailing tendencies came into play, notably in the rise of gothic fiction in England and the *Sturm und Drang* movement in Germany. Several commentators point to the importance for melodrama of gothic fiction (Booth, 1965; Rahill, 1967; Brooks, 1976). Arguably, in its widespread popularity, bourgeois and popular traditions met on equal terms and to their mutual profit. English gothic fiction, succumbing to Germanic influence and in its turn highly influential in France, reintroduced a metaphysical dimension to moral conflict, facilitating the gradual slide from bourgeois sentiment to the sensation, spectacle and violence of melodrama, from the ancient routines of dumb show, pantomime and balladry to a consolidated melodramatic rhetoric. Moral drama, the conflict of manichean opposites, and spectacle converged. Illegitimate theatrical entertainments such as pantomime drew on the gothic fiction of Mrs Radcliffe and Monk Lewis in what for many constitute the first melodramas. According to Wylie Sypher (1965) melodrama's conflict of polar opposites provided an epistemological and imaginative paradigm across nineteenth-century culture and thought. Darwin, Freud and Marx were all products of the melodramatic imagination.

Melodrama and social change Nineteenth-century society, subject to rapid change consequent on industrialisation, experienced class similarly as polarisation rather than as hierarchical relationship – polarisation dramatised in revolution, the growth of Chartism, trade unionism and Communism. Oppositions in wealth, education and welfare became a highly visible feature of rapidly industrialising and expanding cities, while imperial conquest brought home contrasts between ethnic mores and life-styles.

With the passing of hierarchical social relationships went also the traditional values and ways of life that had given society its cohesion. Because of its multi-valency, this loss was shared by new entrants to the middle class, the emerging working class, the rural labourer and by women across classes (Grimstead, 1971; Vicinus, 1981). Arguably such social extensiveness served to modify the complacency of eighteenth-century sentimental fiction and open up the heroine/villain/hero triad – which heretofore had articulated the triumph of the bourgeois victim over an aristocratic villain – to the pessimistic ironies of folk tradition, with their implication that 'the losers are not always those who deserve it most' (Elsaesser, p. 4; see also Louis James, 1981).

The family, the country and the past Where eighteenth-century sentimental fiction, in rejecting the public arena of aristocratic social relations, had found in the private bourgeois family a compensatory source of moral and social order, the family itself came under increasing social and symbolic pressure in the nineteenth century. The separation of work and home, consequent on industrialisation and the withdrawal of married middle-class women from production, combined with philanthropic struggles around the employment of working-class women and children in factories, brought the family into new social and emotional configurations (see Grimstead, 1971; Kleinhans, 1978; Vicinus, 1981; Kaplan in this volume).

Despite current association of melodrama with the domestic, it could (and arguably still can – see below, p. 23) be created out of almost any topic. Nevertheless melodrama's invariable deployment of familial values across sub-genres attests to a psychic overdetermination in the conjunction of social and personal, charging the idea of home and family with a symbolic potency. This surfaces in a persistently nostalgic vein. As David Grimstead and Martha Vicinus note, melodrama's challenge lies not in confronting how things are, but rather in asserting how they ought to be. But since it operates within the frameworks of the present social order, melodrama conceives 'the promise of human life' (Grimstead, p. 28) not as a revolutionary future, but rather as a return to a 'golden past': less how things ought to be than how they should have been. The Edenic home and family, centring on the heroine as 'angel in the house' and the rural community of an earlier generation, animate images of past psychic and social well-being as 'moral touchstones' against which the instabilities of capitalist expansion and retraction could be judged and in which both labourer and middle-class citizen could confront the hostilities of the modern world.

Within this nostalgic structure it was possible for melodrama to shift its sympathies from the struggle for bourgeois ascendency to the victims of its success. 'Melodrama', Martha Vicinus states, 'sides with the powerless', while evil is associated with 'social power and station' (pp. 130, 132). Powerlessness regains moral power in its association with a family or social position that should command protection: that of the child, the daughter or mother, the ageing parent, the labouring poor. Through such 'moral touchstones' the contradictions of capitalism are negotiated: the apparently powerless, who by their persevering endurance win through, defeat the logic of capitalism, for reward comes through 'wholly noncompetitive virtues and interests' (Grimstead, 1971, p. 90). At the same time innocence and villainy construct each other: while the villain is necessary to the production and revelation of innocence, innocence defines the boundaries of the forbidden which the villain breaks. In this way melodrama's affective and epistemological structures were deployed, within the constraints of dominant socio-economic frameworks, to embody the forces and desires set loose by, or resisting, the drives of capitalism.

Nineteenth-century picture stories   The energy and ambivalence of the melodramatic imagination found their aesthetic release in an expanding culture of the visible. Eighteenth-century Minor House dependency on spectacle met with a growing emphasis on the visual across a range of cultural forms, as a generalised shift took place from verbal exposition towards visual demonstration: eventually 'visual proofs … substituted for dramatic proofs' (Vardac, 1949, p. 96). This was intensified in the nineteenth century by developments in optical science and technology and in the rise of mass consumer markets and visual media. Aside from the toys and spectacles which anticipated cinema, Michael Booth (1981) cites the building of art galleries and museums, the development of lithography and the craze for illustrated editions of the 'classics', the invention of the plate-glass window and electric lighting which introduced store fronts and the shopping arcade as sites of spectacle and consumption, and the architecture of the city itself with its public monuments and mercantile and industrial structures, constituting visual evidence of the spoils of commerce and imperialism. 'The world', he comments, 'was saturated with pictures' (p. 8).

This stress on visual address meant that when theatrical restrictions were lifted (1843 in England, 1789 in France) and spoken dialogue universally permitted, the theatre did not abandon its spectacular practices. Rather, increasingly sophisticated technology led to their elaboration. At the vortex of such diverse pressures, melodrama became a model for the nineteenth-century imaginative enterprise, in which narrative enactment of manichean moral conflict meshed with an aesthetics of the visible. Nicholas Vardac (1949), John Fell (1974), Peter Brooks (1976) and Michael Booth (1981) show how pressure towards visual narrativisation brought painting, the novel and theatre onto the same terrain. While many Victorian genre painters drew on acting manuals and theatrical tableaux for codes of gesture in order to tell pictorial stories of human nature caught in climactic moments (Booth, 1981; Louis James, 1981), theatrical *mise en scène* strove to attain the condition of painting, often deploying artists to execute scenery, or dramatising well known pictures (Booth, 1981). The proscenium arch became a picture frame. Cinema emerged from this common pictorial and narrative impetus: 'what is interesting … is the very nonuniqueness of the movies' techniques' (John Fell, 1974, p. xii).

Melodrama and the archaeology of the movies If 'theatricality' were part of a melodramatic aesthetic shared across cultural forms, nineteenth-century melodramatic theatre laid institutional and aesthetic foundations from which cinema would draw – specifically: techniques for 'cinematic' narration; a 'studio'-type system of generic production; and a model of circuit distribution.

Nicholas Vardac's pioneering study, *From Stage to Screen* (1949), charts the development of techniques bent on the narrativisation of action through 'telling' gestures, incidents or situations and an episodic, pictorial mode of narration which dispensed with dialogue and conventional 'dramatic' construction. Problems of continuity were solved by an increasingly sophisticated

22

stagecraft which anticipated, either by mechanically moving scenery and stages, or by gas and later electric lighting, many cinematic effects. Dissolves and fades eliminated the disruptive curtain drop, permitting swift changes in locale or time, or of 'vantage point within a given scene' (p. 65). Combined with a complex system of traps, bridges and moving scenery or stage structures, such techniques achieved what were effectively tracking shots, allowing movement from interior to exterior locations, or, the 'parallel editing' between different actions that was integral to melodramatic suspense. Rolling panoramas suggested the passage of time or movement of stage, ships, horses, trains, etc. The pictorialisation of the nineteenth-century stage produced what were effectively 'moving pictures'.

Such techniques dispensed with the expression of character through dialogue, relying on 'effective situations and telling *mise en scène*' (p. 52), 'actiontableaux' and episodic narration to externalise the inner states of characters. Vision effects, exploiting the 'dissolve' – deploying projection devices and combined with 'parallel editing' techniques – could shift 'the scene from what the character was doing to what he (sic) was thinking' (p. 35), while character itself was carried in 'external visual values' such as costume, makeup, gesture and facial expression. Louis James (1981) describes melodramatic acting as at once pictorial and dynamic, capable of producing shifts in the state of being or 'personae' of a single character or between the moods of alternating scenes.

The potentially amorphous diversity of the melodramatic mode was stabilised in a range of generic sub-divisions which picked up on historical, national and regional variations, many of which found new life in Hollywood genres: for example, gothic and eastern melodrama, heroic or nationalist melodrama, aquatic melodrama deploying great tanks of water, equestrian melodrama performed on horseback, nautical and domestic melodrama, the fallen woman melodrama, murder mystery, frontier and temperance melodrama, and so on (Booth, 1965; Rahill, 1967; Bradby et. al., 1981). Generic stability was promoted in the formation of stock companies, 'in which each member was hired to act a specific character type, performing it and no other', types which 'perpetuated generic conventions' (Booth, op. cit., p. 65).

In the system of production that evolved with melodrama the individual playwright vanished from the theatre. Two types of melodrama producer emerged: the actor turned showman, who combined a feeling for popular taste, a flair for inventive stagecraft and the financial sense of the entrepreneur; or the literary hack, often on contract to a particular theatre, who in order to make a living had to churn out a vast number of plays at great speed, and who consequently relied on adaptation and plagiarism. More important than the writer, however, were the large number of carpenters, scenery painters, gasmen and electricians, scene movers and special effects operators, whose efforts realised melodramatic *mise en scène*, spectacle and obligatory 'sensation scenes'. Often all that was required from the writer was a skeletal outline for action and situations as support for theatrical production values (Rahill, 1967).

Melodrama in America

Twentieth-century popular culture's melodramatic inheritance must be traced through the passage of European melodrama to America, for its transformation there was arguably a determining factor in the emergence of Hollywood aesthetics and its later international power.

David Grimstead's study of melodrama in nineteenth-century American theatre (1968) details how early puritan distrust of drama as diversionary or immoral gradually gave way to a post-Revolutionary desire to equal the cultural heritage of the 'old' country. Despite national ambition, however, the models of cultural achievement remained European and in a country where primary energies were still committed to expanding geographic, economic and political frontiers, drama constituted an importable commodity – especially when in the absence of copyright restrictions, already tried and tested material could be pirated with impunity at small cost (p. 144). Not only plays, but players too, came from England, considerably outweighing native production until towards the end of the nineteenth century (Rahill, 1967, p. 225).

Nevertheless melodrama's adaptation to the different socio-political conditions of American culture was transformative. First there was no already situated landed aristocracy against which a rising bourgeoisie had to struggle. The dominant ideology was republican and democratic, the evils of class inequality and injustice associated with a European yoke recently thrown off. American drama's national specificity was initially confined to expression of a democratic sensibility. The compatibility of melodrama with this form of nationalism was a major reason, David Grimstead (1971) suggests, for its centrality to the nineteenth-century American stage.

American adaptation of melodrama began to dismantle the class oppositions of European melodrama. In the first instance, melodrama's stress on unpremeditated feeling as an index of moral status and social value functioned for American nationalism as a 'great equaliser', bypassing inequalities of class and education (Grimstead, 1971, p. 88). Secondly, the expression of class oppositions in European melodrama were, in American versions, often transposed into country/city oppositions. In early American melodramas the villain was associated with the city, and its growing divisions between rich and poor. He often sported European airs, thus further demarcating national boundaries. The country, meanwhile, was invested with America's founding ideology, egalitarianism, and regeneration was found in its rural past (Grimstead, 1971, pp. 198–9; also Viviani in this volume, pp. 83–99). Melodrama's nostalgic mode, David Grimstead suggests, was strategic for a national identity convinced of its radicalism, acknowledging, but displacing into the past, the inequalities emerging with industrial-isation.

Arguably, these shifts in emphasis contributed to melodrama's later power as an international source of popular culture. An egalitarian ideology, inten-sified by the historical closeness of the social forms – the rural, extended domestic unit – in which one aspect of that ideal was rooted, produced an insistently populist address, that could make a cross-class and international appeal. And the ambivalent dynamic of the villain both acknowledged the pleasures, and at the same time judged the drives, of capitalism – aggression, acquisitiveness, competition, blatant individualism.

The delay, relative to European developments, in the maturing of a native melodrama was important to America's taking the form into the twentieth century. According to Frank Rahill (1967), truly American melodrama emerged only in the 1880s with a cycle of native civil war and frontier sagas. In his view these plays, working over issues of national identity made critical by the war, represented the sought for national drama. Coinciding with innova-tory theatrical technologies and a rising generation of inventive theatrical producers, these plays achieved a more sophisticated, if still spectacular, melodramatic rhetoric. While in Europe melodrama was waning, in America the melodramatic project gained new life, pushing theatrical technique still further in the direction of cinematic *mise en scène*, and into competition with the new medium.

But these developments were confined to metropolitan cities, where the size of middle-class audiences justified the capital outlay. Parallel to metropolitan culture, however, a new source of production arose in the growth of melo-drama houses in the lower-middle and working-class districts of urban centres and with the organisation of syndicated circuits devoted to the exclusive production and touring of melodramas of a simpler, more tra-ditional kind, which were patronised by provincial audiences. Melodrama became a theatrical industry, organised to produce and circulate standard-ised product, which would lay the basis for the film industry to come (see Pryluck, 1986).

Melodrama as Cultural Category
Cinema participated in a critical phase in the shifting composition of theat-rical audiences. As industrial expansion was followed by the pursuit of con-sumers, the middle classes were sought as up-market and lucrative audiences. As Raymond Williams (1977) notes of London theatres, 'new dividing lines appeared between the "respectable" and the "popular", and at the respect-able end there was an integration of middle-class and fashionable audiences and tastes' (p. 210). This integration was facilitated by a programme of theatre building and refurbishment, in which facilities were upgraded and performance times shortened and made later to suit the work hours and

social engagements of the middle class (Williams, op. cit.; Rahill, 1967; Grimstead, 1968; McCormick, 1981). Melodramatic intrigue went upmarket in 'sophisticated' drawing-room melodrama, or in technically ever more spectacular sensation melodramas. Alternatively it went underground into the new 'society dramas' of Jones and Pinero, or was displaced by opera and ballet. In America, melodrama's late flowering, resulting in a more 'plausible, adult and intellectually respectable' form, enabled it to hold onto the middle-class audience longer (Rahill, 1967, p. 268).

High art versus mass entertainment   Division of the audience into 'establishment' and 'popular' according to geographical location, ability to pay and sub-cultural taste was supported and contributed to the consolidation of the categories of 'high' and 'low' culture that have been crucial to twentieth-century evaluation of melodrama. Michael Booth (1965) has remarked on what he sees as the unprecedented 'detachment and isolation from the theatre of the great writers of the nineteenth century' (p. 47). The subordination of the word in favour of production values, the low fixed fee system of payment and lack of copyright, drove the potential dramatist to the more private forms of poetry and the novel. However, the emergence of a high-paying audience and consequently higher payments for plays, together with copyright legislation, encouraged the return of the dramatic 'artist' to the theatre. At the same time a minority intelligentsia supported an 'independent' theatre movement, promoting the 'new drama' of Ibsen, Shaw and Chekhov, while nascent cinematic entertainments competed for the popular audience. To this cultural divide the redefinition of the categories of tragedy and realism were crucial.

Redefining tragedy and realism   Despite his own antipathy to melodrama, Raymond Williams's *Modern Tragedy* (1966) is important for its historicisation of formal categories, showing how tragedy, far from attaining timeless universality, has been subject to appropriation and redefinition by successive social formations. His argument suggests how current conceptions of the tragic hero and tragic action, resulting from bourgeois redefinition of the form (see above, pp. 16–17), serve to demote melodrama.[12] Williams argues that Romantic endeavour to reinvent tragedy after its eighteenth-century demise did little to extend the social reach of the form initially promised by bourgeois cultural reform, but rather further narrowed the category to apply only to the inner conflict of a uniquely self-conscious individual, opposed to, or outside of society altogether, expressing an 'often minority attitude to life and contemporary experience' (p. 36). By the end of the nineteenth century, tragedy became an elite category by virtue of its distance from common life, so that, Williams suggests, events 'deep in the pattern of our own culture ... war, famine, work, traffic, politics' are not considered tragic (p. 49).

While tragedy had been effectively displaced from the theatre by the dominance of nineteenth-century melodrama – indeed often staged and even rewritten as melodrama – realism was at the heart of popular developments. Nicholas Vardac (1949) identifies three broad, inter-related trends in nineteenth-century theatrical aesthetics: spectacle, melodrama and realism – all constituted within what he defines as a 'realist-romantic movement' and existing in uneasy and uneven relationship to the end of the century. Vardac documents this paradox in the history of nineteenth-century theatrical staging. However romantic the dramatic conception, the producer, carpenters and set painters, the lighting and special effects personnel, were committed to as realistic a materialisation of the 'romantic idea' as possible. Thus melodrama could bring together the grandiose and the banal.

Nevertheless, realism, along with tragedy, emerged at the end of the century as a criterion of elite cultural value. According to Vardac, theatrical realism gained its edge as a cultural touchstone when the technologies for realistic staging became too cumbersome for melodrama's need of speedy, episodic narration. With the return of the 'literary' dramatist to the theatre, greater value was placed on dialogue, character analysis and naturalist performance. Realism became a singular goal on its own account, and the hallmark of metropolitan 'high culture', while melodrama was relegated to entertainments for popular and/or poorly equipped provincial theatres. The separation out of a middle-class audience, the impact of 'new drama' and the reformed categories of tragedy and realism led to melodrama's derision.

Melodrama and Cinema
The emergence of cinema made a significant intervention into this cultural field, setting up new relations of competition and influence between different branches of the growing culture industries. Nicholas Vardac's account of the incompatibility of the staging demands of melodrama and realism suggests that part of cinema's success was its capacity to reweld the symbiosis of 'photographic realism' and 'pictorial sensationalism' which in the theatre had been breaking up. Technically the cinema solved the problems of the stage, and the verbal limitations of the novel, in their common search to realise the melodramatic imagination. Film offered the photographic naturalism to which audiences had become accustomed through the illustrated press and the new staging techniques of the metropolitan centres, while editing could reproduce at a fraction of the cost the narrative continuity which in the theatre demanded either complex and labour intensive machinery, or 'nonnaturalistic' sets and backdrops. Cinema, moreover, could bring the sophistication and spectacle of the metropolitan theatres to provincial and working-class audiences. It offered to twentieth-century society a renewed site of cultural cohesion. In its turn the melodramatic stage contributed to cinema both audiences prepared for visual narrative and a repertoire of

non-copyright material, 'pre-formed for pictorial illusion' (Vardac, op. cit., p. 173) for which there was known appeal and which film could better. More significant, perhaps, was the theatrical bequest of a range of staging and performance techniques tailored to the requirements of 'telling stories in pictures'.

Despite its melodramatic heritage the cinema's critical entourage was soon to constitute it as a singularly 'realist' medium (Vardac, p. 200). Characterisation was a central element in this claim. However, discursive analysis dialogue are a major source of realist character, while the melodramatic aesthetic had striven to eliminate or subordinate dialogue in favour of the demonstrative, musically co-ordinated gesture and action. If the film industry did not hurry to overcome the technical problems of synchronising sound and picture, this was perhaps because it had no need to; music and sound effects provided the aural resources that its melodramatic constitution required without the cost of technological research. In the cinema, however, as Griffith demonstrated, exteriorisation of character is not dependent on the large-scale gesture alone; the intimacy of the photographic close-up could register subjective states and relationships with an immediacy that lent credence to the perception of cinema as a naturalist medium, supporting the claim that all cinema required was synchronous sound in order to outgrow its melodramatic origins. Whether such cinematic subjectivity, however, constitutes 'psychological realism' or a basis for the renewed intermeshing of realism and melodrama in twentieth-century culture is an issue to be determined only by investigating melodrama's survival after the demise of the specifically Victorian form that dominated the theatre for nearly a century.

III Melodrama as Cultural Form

> It could not be more bluntly put that it was the bourgeoisie itself that invented for the people the popular myth of the melodrama ... serials in the popular press, cheap 'novels' ...
>
> Louis Althusser, 1969, p. 139

> Twentieth century critics have taught generations of students to equate popularity with debasement, emotionality with ineffectiveness, religiosity with fakery, domesticity with triviality, and all of these, implicitly, with womanly inferiority.
>
> Jane Tompkins, 1985, p. 123

How can the nineteenth-century melodramatic project be thought in a way that clarifies its passage into, and function for, twentieth-century mass culture?

Although constructed outside the immediate concerns of film theory, Peter

Brooks's recently influential study, *The Melodramatic Imagination* (1976), recasts many of the features of nineteenth-century melodrama in a way that is pertinent to the problems film theory has confronted. Because Brooks is concerned to justify the melodramatic as source of inspiration for Balzac and James, he is committed to re-evaluation of the form rather than to its critique; moreover, he has little interest in the ideological questions that inform contemporary cultural analysis. However, this allows him to investigate melodrama on its own terms and take seriously its appeal. This distinguishes his approach from many previous literary studies which, despite serious intentions of historical recovery, tend to dwell on entertaining curiosities and find it difficult to describe the plots and characters of Victorian melodrama without a smile of condescension at the 'popular' mind of our forbears (see especially Maurice Disher, 1949 and 1954). It also puts Brooks on a different footing from film theory which till recently either valued melodrama only if it could be shown, through analysis of covert operations not available to its audiences, to be 'symptomatically' ruptured; or critiqued the form as an instrument of the capitalist culture industries, which imposed on or mystified the mass audience. Brooks permits a look at melodrama outside the entrenched oppositions of such approaches: bourgeois/working-class; melodrama/realism; empathy/criticism.

Brooks investigates melodrama as a specifically modern mode, which evolves out of the loss of pre-Enlightenment values and symbolic forms, in response to the psychic consequences of the bourgeois social order, in which the social must be expressed as the personal. In this argument feudal societies derived cohesion, legitimation and self-perpetuation, through the 'Traditional Sacred' – in Brooks's terms, an 'evident, persuasive and compelling ... system both of mythic explanation and implicit ethics' (p. 18). He sees the passage from the Renaissance, through the 'momentary compromise of Christian humanism' to the Enlightenment as a slow process of desacralisation during which 'the explanatory and cohesive force of sacred myth lost its power, and its political and social representations [church and monarchy, ed.] lost their legitimacy' (pp. 15–16). Consequently post-sacred society needed to find both a secular system of ethics and a means of investing individual everyday lives with significance and justification.

In place of the 'traditional sacred', melodrama uncovers what Brooks calls the 'moral occult', 'the domain of operative spiritual values which is both indicated within and masked by the surface of reality' (p. 5). Expressed in such terms, the notion of a 'moral occult' suggests an idealist portmanteau for 'bourgeois ideology' and this would surely be the case if Brooks focused on specific contents. However this concept develops in his account as a generalised need for 'significance', the terms of which are historically relative, rather than as a set of specific ideological ideas. In melodrama an ideological meets a psychic need, needs that are not necessarily identical.

Central to this argument is the concept of repression, which in post-Englightenment, secular bourgeois society, characterised by the 'reductions of rationalism' (p. 19) and orientation to the 'reality principle', operates in codes of social behaviour, conventions of language and the structure of the psyche. At the same time the post-Enlightenment project stimulates demands for personal significance and value, and for acknowledgment of all that cannot be contained within the dominant order – anti-social desire, the 'numinous', the struggle of good and evil.

Melodrama's inheritance from popular tradition enabled it to apply 'pressure' to the conventional and repressive discourses of the post-Enlightenment order, breaking through 'everything that constitutes the "reality principle", all its censorships, accommodations, tonings-down' (p. 41). To this end melodrama utilises narrative mechanisms that create a blockage to expression, thereby forcing melodramatic enactments into alternative and excessive strategies to clarify the dramatic stakes. Characteristically the melodramatic plot turns on an initial, often deliberately engineered, misrecognition of the innocence of a central protagonist. By definition the innocent cannot use the powers available to the villain; following the dictates of their nature, they must become victims, a position legitimated by a range of devices which rationalise their apparent inaction in their own behalf. Narrative is then progressed through a struggle for clear moral identification of all protagonists and is finally resolved by public recognition of where guilt and innocence really lie.

Melodrama's recourse to gestural, visual and musical excess constitutes the expressive means of what Brooks calls the 'text of muteness'. Devices such as dumb show, pantomime, tableaux and spectacle reach 'toward ... meanings which cannot be generated from the language code' (p. 72). The spectacle, moral polarisation and dramatic reversals for which melodrama is so often criticised serves the purpose of clarification, identification and palpable demonstration of repressed 'ethical and psychic' forces, which nevertheless constitute compelling imperatives (p. 36).

Thomas Elsaesser's analysis of pathos (see below p. 66) extends this view of melodramatic epistemology to Hollywood's domestic melodrama. Its central protagonists become objects of pathos because constructed as victims of forces that lie beyond their control and understanding. Nevertheless, the externalisation of conflict into narrative structures or *mise en scène* offers the audience signs of the protagonists' condition and the forces in play. Pathos, unlike pity, is a cognitive as well as affective construct. The audience is involved on a character's behalf and yet can exercise pity only by reading and evaluating signs inaccessible to the dramatis personae.

Melodrama's ethical conflicts, however, though symbolically rendered, are not produced as allegorical abstractions, since bourgeois culture insists that the moral is the personal. But neither is personalisation in melodrama a

30

mechanical reflection of the ideology of individualism. In the absence of a metaphysical system of transcendent value, the personality becomes the source of overriding imperatives, now 'identified with emotional states and psychic relationships, so that the expression of emotional and moral integers is indistinguishable' (p. 42). The family, with its ties of duty, love and conflict, the site where the individual is formed, and the centre of bourgeois social arrangements, provides a repertoire of such identities and the space for melodramatic enactments. Characters in melodrama 'assume primary psychic roles, father, mother, child and express basic psychic conditions' (p. 4). This leads Brooks onto Freudian terrain. The family, as an 'overdetermined' psychic institution locks into unconscious desires and forces. However, this does not mean that melodrama is about either the family or individual psychology, 'because melodrama exteriorises conflict and psychic structures, producing ... what we might call the "melodrama of psychology"' (pp. 35–6). For melodrama, working less towards the release of individual repression than towards the public enactment of socially unacknowledged states, the family is a means, not an end.

Ultimately Brooks's 'moral occult' shifts between the refiguring of Good and Evil in human life, demonstration of conflicting, unconscious forces in the psyche, and confrontation with the limits of language and the decentred subject exposed by modernism. The terms of this slippage suggest ways to re-pose the commonly assumed hostile relations of melodrama and realism.

Old-Fashioned Melodrama, Contemporary Realism

Nineteenth-century aesthetic history suggests the interdependent development of melodrama and realism. However, realism is not static. As the systems of explanation which ground realism change – sociology, Marxism, psychology, economics, phenomenology, existentialism, feminism and so on – the codes and conventions of realism shift in pursuit of new 'truth' and greater 'authenticity'. And as realism offers up new areas of representation, so the terms and material of the world melodrama seeks to melodramatise will shift. What realism uncovers becomes new material for the melodramatic project.

Despite, however, their orientation to similar material, the epistemological projects of the two modes diverge. Although there may be conflict between the systems of explanation different realisms draw on, by definition they assume the world is capable of both adequate explanation and representation. Melodrama, however, if Peter Brooks' view is right, has no such confidence, for it attests to forces, desires, fears which, though no longer granted metaphysical reality, nevertheless appear to operate in human life independently of rational explanation. Thus if realism's relentless search for renewed truth and authentication pushes it towards stylistic innovation and the

31

future, melodrama's search for something lost, inadmissable, repressed, ties it to an atavistic past.

Arguably the importance of the gothic to Victorian melodrama lay precisely in such a return, its medievalism providing a theatrically pictorial vocabulary – the castle, the towers and dungeons, the landscape and the elements – with which to construct a symbolic arena for the acts of figures in whom moral polarities could be invested without depending on either transcendental hierarchies or the constraints of realist discourse. In its turn the Victorian has provided for Hollywood – notably its 1940s cycle of gothic romances – exactly the same function: a past that could be recalled to reincarnate moral conflict contemporary society believed it had outgrown. In place of monks, nuns and abbeys, the literal or implied presence of Dr Freud – arch-Victorian, patriarch – offers scenarios which promise secret knowledge and hidden conflict.

Derision of melodrama frequently stems from such attachment to an outmoded past – to what seem simplistic Victorian personifications of Good and Evil, Innocence and Villainy. However, melodrama re-enacts for contemporary society the persistent clash of moral polarities by exploiting its shifting relations with the realism; for it deals in conditions of personal guilt and innocence which can be established in relation to any discourse that demarcates the desirable from the taboo. Thus if the good and evil personifications of Victorian melodrama no longer provide credible articulations of conflict, modern melodrama draws on contemporary discourses for the apportioning of responsibility, guilt and innocence – psychoanalysis, marriage guidance, medical ethics, politics, even feminism. In this respect Brooks argues that the greater psychological sophistication of modern genres – the police series, the western, or the hospital drama – indicates not an abandonment of melodramatic rhetoric but a fuller realisation of psychology's 'melodramatic possibilities' (p. 204). To take recent examples, *Coma* (1977), despite its recourse to topical public debates about the morality of organ transplants, its 'independent' heroine and reference to women's movement discourses, harbours a melodrama of hospital intrigue in which the chief surgeon attempts to discredit a female doctor's pursuit and disclosure of medical malpractice (see Pribram, 1987). *Witness* (1984) hides its nostalgic recreation of lost innocence hounded by the corruption of the modern technocratic police state behind claims to anthropological representation of the Amish. And in Steven Spielberg's adaptation (1984) of Alice Walker's feminist *The Color Purple* a victimised heroine denounces her persecutor-husband. These films, as different as they are in subject matter, emerge in direct line of descent from *Way Down East* (1920) in their drive to identify the good and the evil and in their scenarios of persecuted innocence.

Melodrama's survival rests in the fact that its conflicts are not tied to a particular moral outcome or content: they turn 'less on the triumph of virtue than on making the world morally legible' (Brooks, p. 42). In this respect melodramatic desire crosses moral boundaries, producing villains who, even as the drama sides with the 'good', articulate opposing principles, with equal, if not greater, power. In so doing it accesses the underside of official rationales for reigning moral orders – that which social convention, psychic repression, political dogma cannot articulate. Thus whether melodrama takes its categories from Victorian morality or modern psychology, its enactment of the continuing struggle of good and evil forces running through social, political and psychic life draws into a public arena desires, fears, values and identities which lie beneath the surface of the publicly acknowledged world.

Melodrama, realism, modernism Melodrama's pleasure in naming names, is, Brooks suggests, the pleasure of articulated identities: 'Desire cries aloud its language in identification with full states of being' (p. 41). This formulation touches recent debates in post-structural film studies, positioning melodrama in opposition to the modernist claim that the only verifiable reality is the surface of the signifier itself. Peter Brooks argues that writers like Flaubert, Zola, Kafka and Joyce confront an 'abyss' of the kind theorised by the post-structuralists: the endless play of the signifier, the decentred subject, the impossibility of perfect coincidence between speaker and utterance, the chimera of identity and meaning. The project of realism tips over into its obverse: if it is impossible representationally to flesh out the world, then deconstruction will reveal the bare bones. Melodrama marks out a third route into this post-Enlightenment terrain. Taking its stand in the material world of everyday reality and lived experience, and acknowledging the limitations of the conventions of language and representation, it proceeds to force into aesthetic presence identity, value and plenitude of meaning. The signifier cannot cover the possibilities of the signified; nor will the melodramatic subject accept the gap between the self, its words and meaning laid bare by the post-structural project. Melodrama is above all a 'language of presence and immediacy' (p. 67). While the drive of realism is to possess the world by understanding it, and the modern and post-modern explore in different ways the consequences of this ambition's disillusion, the central drive of melodrama is to force meaning and identity from the inadequacies of language, 'making large, but unsubstantiable claims on meaning' (p. 199). In the face of the limitations of realism exposed by post-structuralism, it operates on the level not so much of 'Yes, but ...' than of 'So what!'

Genre and gender: melodrama and women Re-thinking melodrama and realism illuminates the problematic relation of the woman's film to melodrama and questions about the representation of women in either.

Melodrama has frequently been identified as a woman's genre. However, this is arguably a retrospective categorisation, following the role played by gender in the delegitimisation of melodrama by realism and tragedy. David

Grimstead (1968) notes the centrality of emotion to nineteenth-century culture as a source of moral value: 'emotional sensibility was the real criterion for virtue, and crying became its testament' (p. 11). Because it produced contradictions for the ideology of masculinity, the realm of 'feeling' was assigned to women. The heroine, idealised as 'Angel in the House' and focus of the 'Cult of True Womanhood' (see Ann Kaplan, below, p. 113) was often of more significance to the drama than the hero in her capacity to evoke and legitimate emotion. The obverse side of idealisation was fascinated horror at the prospect of the heroine's fall and subsequent degradation. Victorian patriarchs could weep publicly over the female victim, in demonstration of renewed feeling and virtue.

Recovery of realism and tragedy at the turn of the century as categories demarcating high from popular culture coincided with a re-masculinisation of cultural value. Realism came to be associated with (masculine) restraint and underplaying. It eschewed flamboyant characterisation in favour of psychological analysis, carried in verbal discourse and dialogue. The gestural rhetoric of melodramatic acting was displaced by 'naturalist' performance styles. Tragedy and realism focused on 'serious' social issues or inner dilemmas, recentring the hero and claiming tragic value for the failure of heroic potential. Sentiment and emotiveness were reduced in significance to 'sentimentality' and exaggeration, domestic detail counted as trivia, melodramatic utopianism as escapist fantasy and this total complex devalued by association with a 'feminised' popular culture. Men no longer wept in public.

Melodrama initially survived in cinema's capacity to embed melodramatic sentiment and feminine idealisations in photographic realism. However, the pursuit by a growing industry of the middle-class audience, abetted by the critical apparatus which sprang up around the new medium (Vardac, 1949, p. 200), gave rise to an industrial ambivalence about a product which was geared both to prestige and 'popularity'. Very soon cinema was constituted as an inherently 'realist' medium and it has become a given of film history that while early cinema produced melodrama by default, the power of speech instituted a critical break between a cinema destined for realism and its melodramatic origins. At the same time genre divisions were consolidated, allowing melodrama a separate identity (Bourget, 1985) which facilitated critical boundary lines drawn by gender. The 'classic' genres were constructed by recourse to masculine cultural values – gangster as 'tragic hero'; the 'epic' of the West; 'adult' realism – while 'melodrama' was acknowledged only in those denigrated reaches of the juvenile and the popular, the feminised spheres of the woman's weepie, the romance or family melodrama. However, it is doubtful whether Hollywood's major genres veered from their melodramatic predispositions. Nick Roddick's study of Warners (1983), for instance, qualifies the reputation of its product for realism, pointing to the studio's pre-eminent concern to achieve the 'best [aesthetic] effect' (p. 25). Arguably, synchronous sound was exploited for the sensation it could bring to contemporary material – for example, the gangster film's screeching car tyres or machine-gun fire – as much as for verisimilitude. The industry recognised this pervasive melodramatic base in its exhibition categories – western melodrama, crime melodrama, sex melodrama, backwoods melodrama, romantic melodrama and so on.

In Hollywood, realism came to be associated with the masculine sphere of action and violence. Paradoxically it was the woman's film with its emphasis on talk rather than action, which really benefited from the new access to realism which dialogue allowed (Andrea Walsh, 1984), while codes of action and taciturnity perpetuated and justified the gangster and westerners' melodramatic rhetoric, disguised by prestigious critical labels. In contrast the woman's film was identified with melodrama, syphoning off this pejorative ascription from Hollywood's mainstream product.

Clarification of the relation between the woman's film and melodrama, however, means considering not only gendered critical categories, but the role of women as cultural producers and consumers. Maria LaPlace argues that the film industry, needing to formulate a genre to attract female audiences, drew on a 'circuit of women's discourse' circulating on the margins of the mass media and traversing women's fiction, pamphlets, magazines, journalism, and more ephemeral forms, much of which is generated by and for women. While such female cultural practices do not operate in some free 'feminine' space, they are produced from the different social and psychic positioning of women within an overall complex of social relations and discourses. Both Maria LaPlace and Ann Kaplan trace the historical affiliations of the woman's film with traditions of nineteenth-century female writing in order to investigate its relation to Victorian melodrama's investment in woman, on the one hand, and the historical conditions of women's reading, writing or spectating on the other.

Given that it organises the same terrain as realism, nineteenth-century melodrama could not evade the fact that its domestic and feminine idealisations were rooted in the daily, lived experience of women, and unwittingly provided ground for female colonisation. Melodrama's over-investment in the symbol, combined with the impossibility of actually living it, produced a complex, highly ambivalent field for women. Kaplan, LaPlace and others show how female writers and readers took both melodramatic and realist routes into the sphere of the domestic, in a series of sub-cultural and 'transvaluative' discourses. Melodramatic pathos could be turned to assertion: the victimised heroine proves 'weakness is strength' as the assaults of the villain draw out 'hidden talents and unrecognised virtues' (Martha Vicinus, 1981, pp. 135–6); the martydom of the 'fallen woman' produces 'posthumous vindication' (Sally Mitchell, 1977, p. 42); the 'villainess' gives rise to iconoclastic and symbolically vengeful fantasies (Showalter, 1976; Vicinus, 1981).

On the other hand, some writers, particularly in America, produced a domestic realism that more literally transvalued that realm, focusing on the minutiae of the daily life of the home and personal relationships as the site of wider social and political organisation and value (see Sally Mitchell, 1977; Nina Baym, 1978; Jane Tompkins, 1985 and Kaplan and LaPlace in this volume). In nineteenth-century culture, however, these two strands did not demarcate rigid boundaries because of the interdependence of melodrama and realism, and the fact that the symbolic values of the domestic and 'feminine' permeated the culture as a whole.

Twentieth-century remasculinisation of cultural value meant, as Mitchell, Baym and Tompkins argue, that women's domestic realism has scarcely been recognised as such, because its terrain was foreign to a male canon. So when 30s Hollywood took women's fiction – itself divided between realist and melodramatic strains – as sources for the woman's film, aesthetic conflict displaced inter-dependence. For instance, at the textual level, the novel *Now, Voyager* is a realist rather than melodramatic fiction, but subject to a melodramatic overlay in the film's organisation of incident, music and *mise en scène*, which conflicts with its articulate dialogue (drawn from the book), realist characterisation and performance. Confusion – or contest – is suggested by the range of permutations produced in the 30s between patriarchal melodrama and women's fiction, offering such sub-genres as maternal sacrifice, fallen woman and romantic melodramas alongside women's pictures.

Arguments that melodrama is the 'drama of articulation', or allows the return of repressed psychic conflict, may not apply to the woman's film when it draws heavily on women's cultural discourses which themselves struggle, as Tania Modleski suggests of *Letter From an Unknown Woman*, to force patriarchy to speak (below, p. 326). The distinction can be pursued by comparing Stahl's with Sirk's *Imitation of Life* (1934 and 1959), where the dialogue of the first functions as personal conversation and in the second – in true melodramatic fashion – as 'emotional utterance, outburst ... expressive cadenza' or 'scenic element' (Brooks, 1976, p. 63 and Elsaesser, below, p. 51). In the end there appears to be no absolute line of demarcation between melodrama and the woman's film but, rather, a contest between them over the construction and meaning of the domestic, of personal life, and the place of men and women in this.

Melodrama and ideological analysis The notion of contested meaning suggests a basis for ideological analysis of melodrama. Subject to diverse pressures and inputs and the meeting place of bourgeois and working-class cultural trajectories, melodrama contributed to the institutional and aesthetic formation of 'the popular'. Emerging with capitalist mass entertainment, this term defines a terrain in which different classes and social groups meet and find an identity. To this extent it is judged an ideological construction – in which class divisions and struggle are dissolved, displaced by compensatory wants more easily satisfiable by the capitalist culture industries. However, if the 'popular' is claimed as a point of social cohesion, it is also contested. The 'popular' is fraught with tension, struggles and negotiations.

In this context the heterogeneity of the melodramatic aesthetic facilitates conflict and negotiation between cultural identities. At issue from an analytical perspective is the degree to which the melodramatic text works both on an 'imaginary' level, internal to fictional production, and on a realist level, which refers to the world outside the text. If, as Peter Brooks contends, melodrama feeds a demand for significances unavailable within the constraints of socially legitimate discourse but for which there is no other language, it must invest in highly symbolised personages, events and relations. But equally, melodrama must conform to realism's ever shifting criteria of relevance and credibility, for it has power only on the premiss of a recognisable, socially constructed world. As the terms of this world shift so must the recognition of its changing audiences be continually re-solicited. As melodrama leaves the nineteenth century behind, whose moral outlook it materialised, these two levels diverge, and it becomes a site of struggle between atavistic symbols and the discourses that reclaim them for new constructions of reality. David Rodowick (below, p. 268) analyses one form of such negotiation in the 50s domestic melodrama.

In the twentieth century, gender representation has been a major source of such contest. The figure of woman, which has served so long as a powerful and ambivalent patriarchal symbol, is also a generator of female discourses drawn from the social realities of women's lives – discourses which negotiate a space within and sometimes resist patriarchal domination. In order to command the recognition of its female audiences, melodrama must draw on such discourses. Thus in twentieth-century melodrama the dual role of woman as symbol for the whole culture and as representative of a historical, gendered point of view produces a struggle between male and female voices: the symbol cannot be owned, but is contested.

Cultural negotiation, however, is not easily decided. Melodrama touches the socio-political only at that point where it triggers the psychic, and the absence of causal relations between them allows for a short-circuiting between melodramatic desire and the socially constructed world. As Martha Vicinus (1981) notes, 'archetypal and mythic beliefs' associate with 'time-specific responses' (p. 128). This suggests a disjointed relation between aesthetics, pleasure and ideology in melodrama. For as different social groups reclaim the image, melodrama strives to recover its sources of symbolic enactment. The power of the symbol is not always destroyed by its exposure as ideological construct, for, as Ien Ang (1984) has suggested, the pleasures of the one do not necessarily coincide with the functions of the other. The argument between the Amish and Hollywood over their representation in *Witness* exemplifies such contest.

Melodrama addresses us within the limitations of the status quo, of the ideologically permissible. It acknowledges demands inadmissible in the codes of social, psychological or political discourse. If melodrama can only end in the place where it began, not having a programmatic analysis for the future, its possibilities lie in this double acknowledgment of how things are in a given historical conjuncture, and of the primary desires and resistances contained within it. This is important for understanding not only what we want to change but the strengths and weakness of where we come from.

Notes

1. I am indebted to John Caughie for pointing out the role of theatre studies in the recovery of melodrama.
2. See Richard Roud, 'The French Line', *Sight and Sound*, vol. 29 no. 4, Autumn 1960, for negative British response to *Cahiers du Cinéma*'s practice of formalist *mise en scène* criticism, and Jim Hillier (ed.), *Cahiers du Cinéma: The 1950s – Neo-Realism, Hollywood, New Wave* (London: Routledge & Kegan Paul, 1985) for translations of some key examples.
3. A seminal exposition of this approach is Jean-Luc Comolli and Jean Narboni's 'Cinema/Ideology/Criticism', originally a *Cahiers* editorial (October/November 1969) and translated in *Screen*, vol. 12 no. 1, Spring 1971. This was followed by a translation of the *Cahiers* editorial board's equally influential analysis of *Young Mr Lincoln* in *Screen*, vol. 13 no. 3, Autumn 1972.
4. Thomas Elsaesser suggests this possibility in his piece on Minnelli (see below, p. 217) and Peter Brooks (1976) argues the inter-dependency of the novel and theatrical melodrama (pp. 75–8 and 83–4).
5. The British anti-realist critique began to emerge in a special issue of *Screen*, vol. 13 no. 1, Spring 1972. Colin MacCabe's 'Realism and the Cinema: Notes on some Brechtian theses', published in *Screen*, vol. 15 no. 2, Summer 1974, provided an influential formulation of the 'classic realist text'. The notion of 'interpellation' is derived from Louis Althusser, 'Ideology and Ideological State Apparatuses' in Brewster, Ben (trans.), *Lenin and Philosophy and Other Essays* (London: New Left Books, 1971).
6. The psychoanalytic underpinnings of the classic realist text were first signalled in a special issue of *Screen*, vol. 14 no. 1/2 Spring/Summer 1973, dealing with semiotics and cinema, and were developed by Colin MacCabe, in 'The Politics of Separation', and by Stephen Heath in 'Lessons from Brecht', both in *Screen*, vol. 15 no. 2, Summer 1974. In Heath's later influential writings the critical emphasis was shifted from the classic realist to narrative text; see *Screen*, vol. 16 no. 1, Spring 1975; vol. 16 no. 2, Summer 1975; vol. 17 no. 3, Autumn 1976, vol. 19 no. 3, Autumn 1978. *Screen*, vol. 16 no. 2, translated Christian Metz's 'The Imaginary Signifier' in a special issue on psychoanalysis and the cinema.

7. This question was raised in a sceptical aside by Peter Lloyd (1972) and pursued by Steve Neale (1976/7).

8. Claire Johnston's 'Women's Cinema as Counter-Cinema', *Screen* Pamphlet, no. 2, September 1972, is an early and influential exposition of this view. Laura Mulvey's 'Visual Pleasure and Narrative Cinema' in *Screen*, vol. 16 no. 3, Autumn 1975 provided an equally influential development of feminist cine-psychoanalysis. See also my 'Recent Developments in Feminist Film Criticism' in Doane, Mellencamp and Williams (eds.), *Re-Vision: Essays in Feminist Film Criticism* (Los Angeles: AFI, 1984) for an account of feminist engagement with anti-realism and psychoanalysis.

9. Steve Neale (1976/7) raised this question in cine-psychoanalytic terms, examining from the perspective of the spectator constructed by textual irony and parody, the different accounts of irony offered by Elsaesser and Willemen. But the question can also be asked – as I do – of the socially constructed audience.

10. To put the question more concretely, if we take together *River of No Return, Salt of the Earth* and *Written on the Wind*, does *Written on the Wind* constitute melodrama, as opposed to *River of No Return* and *Salt of the Earth*, representing classic realist/narrative texts? Or could a dividing line be drawn between *Salt of the Earth* and the other two as different kinds of melodrama, to be distinguished from a work of social realism?

11. Among the international sources of early melodrama cited by Michael Booth (1965) and Frank Rahill (1967) are: the sentimental tragedies of George Lillo and Edward Moore, comedies of Steel and Colley Cibber and fiction of Samuel Richardson; *drame sérieux*, theorised by Diderot, and attempted by Beaumarchais, Mercier, Sedaine and others; the work of English 'mortuary moralists', the Reverends James Hervey and Edward Young; Rousseau's cult of sensibility; English gothic drama and fiction by Horace Walpole and Anne Radcliffe; *Sturm und Drang* and *Ritterdrama* plays; Goethe and Schiller; Shakespeare; the bourgeois drama of August von Kotzebue; the Romantic narrative poems and fiction of Southey, Byron and Scott, Victor Hugo and the two Dumas, and so on.

12. Formal accounts of melodrama such as those offered by Eric Bentley (1967) or Robert Heilman (1968), while committed to its re-evaluation, locate the form on a continuum with tragedy which places it on the side of the extrovert, 'mono-pathic' character (Heilman) or the raw desires of the child and dreamer who confuses 'I want' with 'I can' (Bentley). Such a character is defined in opposition to the 'divided', introspective protagonist of tragedy, who reaches a 'higher' plane of human experience. Heilman argues that it is necessary to recover melodrama in order to preserve the category of tragedy from its commonsense and journalistic dilution.

PART ONE

Starting Out

Tales of Sound and Fury

Observations on the Family Melodrama

THOMAS ELSAESSER

From *Monogram* no. 4, 1972, pp. 2–15.

ASKED about the colour in *Written on the Wind*, Douglas Sirk replied: 'Almost throughout the picture I used deep-focus lenses which have the effect of giving a harshness to the objects and a kind of enamelled, hard surface to the colours. I wanted this to bring out the inner violence, the energy of the characters which is all inside them and can't break through.' It would be difficult to think of a better way of describing what this particular movie and indeed most of the best melodramas of the 50s and early 60s are about. Or for that matter, how closely, in this film, style and technique is related to theme.

My notes want to pursue an elusive subject in two directions: to indicate the development of what one might call the melodramatic imagination across different artistic forms and in different epochs; secondly, Sirk's remark tempts one to look for some structural and stylistic constants in one medium during one particular period (the Hollywood family melodrama between roughly 1940 and 1963) and to speculate on the cultural and psychological context which this form of melodrama so manifestly reflected and helped to articulate. Nonetheless this isn't a historical study in any strict sense, nor a *catalogue raisonné* of names and titles, for reasons that have something to do with my general method as well as with the obvious limitations imposed on film research by unavailability. As a consequence, I lean rather heavily on half a dozen films, and notably *Written on the Wind*, to develop my points. This said, it is difficult to see how references to twenty more movies would make the argument any truer. For better or worse, what I want to say should at this stage be taken to be provocative rather than proven.

How to Make Stones Weep

Bearing in mind that (whatever one's scruples about an exact definition) everybody has some idea of what is meant by 'melodramatic', any discussion of the melodrama as a specific cinematic mode of expression has to start from its antecedents – the novel and certain types of 'entertainment' drama – from which script-writers and directors have borrowed their models.

The first thing one notices is that the media and literary forms which have habitually embodied melodramatic situations have changed considerably in the course of history and, further, they differ from country to country: in England, it has mainly been the novel and the literary gothic where melodramatic motifs persistently crop up (though the Victorian stage, especially in the 1880s and 90s, knew an unprecedented vogue for the melodramas of R. Buchanan and G. R. Sims, plays in which 'a footbridge over a torrent breaks under the steps of the villain, a piece of wall comes down to shatter him; a boiler bursts, and blows him to smithereens');[1] in France, it is the costume drama and historical novel; in Germany 'high' drama and the ballad, as well as more popular forms like *Moritat* (street-songs); finally, in Italy, the opera rather than the novel reached the highest degree of sophistication in the handling of melodramatic situations.

Two currents make up the genealogy. One leads from the late medieval morality play, the popular *gestes* and other forms of oral narrative and drama, like fairy-tales and folk-songs, to their romantic revival and the cult of the picturesque in Scott, Byron, Heine and Victor Hugo, which has its low-brow echo in barrel-organ songs, music-hall drama, and what in Germany is known as *Bänkellied*, the latter coming to late literary honours through Brecht in his songs and musical plays, *The Threepenny Opera* or *Mahagonny*. The characteristic features for our present purposes in this tradition are not so much the emotional shock-tactics and the blatant playing on the audience's known sympathies and antipathies, but rather the non-psychological conception of the *dramatis personae*, who figure less as autonomous individuals than to transmit the action and link the various locales within a total constellation. In this respect, melodramas have a myth-making function insofar as their significance lies in the structure and articulation of the action, not in any psychologically motivated correspondence with individualised experience.

Yet, what particularly marks the ballad or the *Bänkellied*, that is, narratives accompanied by music, is that the moral/moralistic pattern which furnishes the primary content (crimes of passion bloodily revenged, murderers driven mad by guilt and drowning themselves, villains snatching children from their careless mothers, servants killing their unjust masters) is overlaid not only with a proliferation of 'realistic' homely detail, but also 'parodied' or revitalised by the heavily repetitive verse-form or the mechanical up-and-down rhythms of the barrel organ, to which the voice of the singer adapts itself (consciously or not), thereby producing a vocal parallelism that has a distancing or ironic effect, to the extent of often criss-crossing the moral of the story by a 'false', or unexpected, emphasis. Sirk's most successful German melodrama, *Zu neuen Ufern*, makes excellent use of the street ballad to bring out the tragic irony in the court-room scene, and the tune which Walter Brennan keeps playing on the harmonica in King Vidor's *Ruby Gentry* works in a very similar way. A variation on this is the use of fairgrounds and carousels in films like *Some Came Running* and *Tarnished Angels*, or more self-consciously in Hitchcock (*Strangers on a Train*, *Stage Fright*) and Welles (*Lady from Shanghai* and *The Stranger*) to underscore the main action and at the same time 'ease' the melodramatic impact by providing an ironic parallelism. Sirk uses the motif repeatedly in, for instance, *Scandal in Paris* and *Take Me to Town*. What such devices point to is that in the melodrama the *rhythm* of experience often establishes itself against its value (moral, intellectual).

Perhaps the current that leads more directly to the sophisticated family melodrama of the 40s and 50s, though, is derived from the romantic drama which had its heyday after the French Revolution and subsequently furnished many of the plots for operas, but which is itself unthinkable without the eighteenth-century sentimental novel and the emphasis put on private feelings and interiorised (puritan, pietist) codes of morality and conscience. Historically, one of the interesting facts about this tradition is that its height of popularity seems to coincide (and this remains true throughout the 19th century) with periods of intense social and ideological crisis. The pre-revolutionary sentimental novel – Richardson's *Clarissa* or Rousseau's *Nouvelle Héloise*, for example – go out of their way to make a case for extreme forms of behaviour and feeling by depicting very explicitly certain external constraints and pressures bearing upon the characters, and by showing up the quasi-totalitarian violence perpetrated by (agents of) the 'system' (Lovelace who tries everything, from bribing her family to hiring pimps, prostitutes and kidnappers in order to get Clarissa to become his wife, only to have to rape her after all). The same pattern is to be found in the bourgeois tragedies of Lessing (*Emilia Galotti*, 1768) and the early Schiller (*Kabale und Liebe*, 1776), both deriving their dramatic force from the conflict between an extreme and highly individualised form of moral idealism in the heroes (again, non-psychological on the level of motivation) and a thoroughly corrupt yet seemingly omnipotent social class (made up of feudal princes and petty state functionaries). The melodramatic elements are clearly visible in the plots, which revolve around family relationships, star-crossed lovers and forced marriages. The villains (often of noble birth) demonstrate their superior political and economic power invariably by sexual aggression and attempted rape, leaving the heroine no other way than to commit suicide or take poison in the company of her lover. The ideological 'message' of these tragedies, as in the case of *Clarissa*, is transparent: they record the struggle of a morally and emotionally emancipated bourgeois consciousness against the remnants of feudalism. They pose the problem in political terms and concentrate on the complex interplay of ethical principles, religious-metaphysical polarities and the idealist aspirations typical of the bourgeoisie in its militant phase, as the protagonists come to grief in a maze of economic necessities, *realpolitik*, family loyalties, and through the abuse of aristocratic privilege from a still divinely ordained, and therefore doubly depraved absolutist authority.

Although these plays and novels, because they use the melo-dramatic-emotional plot only as their most rudimentary structure of meaning, belong to the more intellectually demanding forms of melodrama, the element of interiorisation and personalisation of what are primarily ideological conflicts, together with the metaphorical interpretation of class-conflict as sexual exploitation and rape is important in all subsequent forms of melodrama, including that of the cinema. (The latter in America, of course, is a stock theme of novels and movies with a 'Southern' setting.)

Paradoxically, the French Revolution failed to produce a new form of social drama or tragedy. The Restoration stage (when theatres in Paris were specially licensed to play 'melodramas') trivialised the form by using melodramatic plots in exotic settings, and providing escapist entertainment with little social relevance. The plays warmed up the standard motif of eighteenth-century French fiction and drama, that of innocence persecuted and virtue rewarded, and the conventions of melodrama functioned in their most barren form as the mechanics of pure suspense.

What before the Revolution had served to focus on suffering and victimisation – the claims of the individual in an absolutist society – was reduced to ground-glass-in-the-porridge, poisoned handkerchiefs and last-minute rescues from the dungeon. The sudden reversals of fortune, the intrusion of chance and coincidence had originally pointed to the arbitrary way feudal institutions could ruin the individual unprotected by civil rights and liberties. The system stood accused of greed, wilfulness and irrationality through the Christ-like suffering of the pure virgin and the selfless heroism of the right-minded in the midst of court-intrigues and callous indifference. Now, with the bourgeoisie triumphant, this form of drama lost its subversive charge and functioned more as a means of consolidating an as yet weak and incoherent ideological position. Whereas the pre-revolutionary melodramas had often ended tragically, those of the Restoration had happy endings, they reconciled the suffering individual to his social position, by affirming an 'open' society, where everything was possible. Over and over again, the victory of the 'good' citizen over 'evil' aristocrats, lecherous clergymen and the even more conventional villains drawn from the lumpen-proletariat, was re-enacted in sentimental spectacles full of tears and high moral tones. Complex social processes were simplified either by blaming the evil disposition of individuals or by manipulating the plots and engineering coincidences and other *dei ex machina*, such as the instant conversion of the villain, moved by the plight of his victim, or suddenly struck by Divine Grace on the steps of Nôtre-Dame.

Since the overtly 'conformist' strategy of such drama is quite evident, what is interesting is certainly not the plot-structure, but whether the conventions allowed the author to dramatise in his episodes actual contradictions in society and genuine clashes of interests in the characters. Already during the Revolution plays such as Monvel's *Les Victimes cloîtrées* or Laya's *L'Ami des Lois*, though working with very stereotyped plots, conveyed quite definite political sympathies (the second, for instance, backed the Girondist moderates in the trial of Louis XVI against the Jacobins) and were understood as such by their public.[2]

Even if the form might act to reinforce attitudes of submission, the actual working-out of the scenes could nonetheless present fundamental social evils. Many of the pieces also flattered popular sympathies by giving the villains the funniest lines, just as Victorian drama playing east of Drury Lane was often enlivened by low-comedy burlesque put on as curtain raisers and by the servants' farces during the intermission.

All this is to say that there seems a radical ambiguity attached to the melodrama, which holds even more for the film melodrama. Depending on whether the emphasis fell on the odyssey of suffering or the happy ending, on the place and context of rupture (moral conversion of the villain, unexpected appearance of a benevolent Capucine monk throwing off his pimp's disguise), that is to say, depending on what dramatic mileage was got out of the heroine's perils before the ending (and one only has to think of Sade's *Justine* to see what could be done with the theme of innocence unprotected...), melodrama would appear to function either subversively or as escapism – categories which are always relative to the given historical and social context.[3]

In the cinema, Griffith is a good example. Using identical dramatic devices and cinematic techniques, he could, with *Intolerance*, *Way Down East* or *Broken Blossoms* create, if not exactly subversive, at any rate socially committed melodramas, whereas *Birth of a Nation* or *Orphans of the Storm* are classic examples of how melodramatic effects can successfully shift explicit political themes onto a personalised plane. In both cases, Griffith tailored ideological conflicts into emotionally loaded family situations.

The persistence of the melodrama might indicate the ways in which popular culture has not only taken note of social crises and the fact that the losers are not always those who deserve it most, but has also resolutely refused to understand social change in other than private contexts and emotional terms. In this, there is obviously a healthy distrust of intellectualisation and abstract social theory – insisting that other structures of experience (those of suffering, for instance) are more in keeping with reality. But it has also meant ignorance of the properly social and political dimensions of these changes and their causality, and consequently it has encouraged increasingly escapist forms of mass-entertainment.

However, this ambivalence about the 'structures' of experience, endemic in the melodramatic mode, has served artists throughout the 19th century for the depiction of a variety of themes and social phenomena, while remaining within the popular idiom. Industrialisation, urbanisation and nascent entrepreneurial capitalism have found their most telling literary embodiment in a type of novel clearly indebted to the melodrama, and the national liberals in Italy during the *Risorgimento*, for example, saw their political aspirations reflected in Verdi's operas (cf. the opening of Visconti's *Senso*). In England, Dickens, Collins and Reade relied heavily on melodramatic plots to sharpen social conflicts and portray an urban environment where chance encounters, coincidences, and the side-by-side existence of extreme social and moral contrasts were the natural products of the very conditions of existence – crowded tenement houses, narrow streets backing on to the better residential property, and other facts of urban demography of the time. Dickens in particular uses the element of chance, the dream/waking, horror/bliss switches in *Oliver Twist* or *Tale of Two Cities* partly to feel his way towards a portrayal of existential insecurity and moral anguish which fiction had previously not encompassed, but also to explore depth-psychological phenomena, for which the melodrama – as Freud was later to confirm – has supplied the dynamic motifs and the emotional-pictorial decor. What seems to me important in this form of melodrama (and one comes across a similar conception in the sophisticated Hollywood melodramas) is the emphasis Dickens places on discontinuity, on the evidence of fissures and ruptures in the fabric of experience, and the appeal to a reality of the psyche – to which the notions of sudden change, reversal and excess lend a symbolic plausibility.

In France it is the works of Sue, Hugo and Balzac that reflect most closely the relation of melodrama to social upheaval. Sue, for example, uses the time-worn trap-door devices of cloak and dagger stage melodrama for an explicitly sensationalist, yet committed journalism. In a popular form and rendered politically palatable by the fictionalised treatment, his *Mystères de Paris* were intended to crusade on such issues as public health, prostitution, overcrowding and slum housing, sanitation, black-market racketeering, corruption in government circles, opium smoking and gambling. Sue exploited a 'reactionary' form for reformist ends, and his success, both literary and practical, proved him right. Twenty years later Victor Hugo, who had learnt as much from Sue as Sue had picked up from *Nôtre-Dame de Paris*, produced with *Les Misérables* a super-melodrama spectacular which must stand as the crowning achievement of the genre in the novel. The career of Jean Valjean, from convict and galley slave to factory owner and capitalist, his fall and literal emergence from the sewers of Paris to become a somewhat unwilling activist in the 1948 Revolution, is staged with the help of mistaken identities, orphans suddenly discovering their noble birth, inconvenient reappearance of people long thought dead, hair-breadth escapes and rescues, multiple disguises, long-suffering females dying of consumption or wandering for days through the streets in search of their child – and yet, through all this, Hugo expresses a hallucinating vision of the anxiety, the moral confusion, the emotional demands, in short, the metaphysics of social change and urban life between the time of Waterloo and 1848. Hugo evidently wanted to bring together in a popular form subjective experiences of crises, while keeping track of the grand lines of France's history, and he succeeds singularly well in reproducing the ways individuals with different social backgrounds, levels of awareness and imaginations, respond to objective changes in the social fabric of their lives. For this, the melodrama, with its shifts in mood, its different *tempi* and the mixing of stylistic levels, is ideally suited; *Les Misérables*, even more so than the novels of Dickens, lets through a symbolic dimension of psychic truth, with the hero in turn representing very nearly the id, the super-ego and finally the sacrificed ego of a repressed and paranoid society.

Balzac on the other hand, uses melodramatic plots to a rather different end. Many of his novels deal with the dynamics of early capitalist economics. The good/evil dichotomy has almost disappeared, and the manichean conflicts have shifted away from questions of morality to the paradoxes of psychology and economics. What we see is a Schopenhauerian struggle of the will: the ruthlessness of industrial entrepreneurs and bankers, the spectacle of an uprooted, 'decadent' aristocracy still holding tremendous political power, the sudden twists of fortune with no-good parasites becoming millionaires overnight (or vice versa) through speculation and the stock-exchange, the antics of hangers-on, parvenus and cynical artist-intellectuals, the demonic, spellbinding potency of money and capital, the contrasts between abysmal poverty and unheard-of affluence and waste which characterised the 'anarchic' phase of industrialisation and high finance, were experienced by Balzac as both vital and melodramatic. His work reflects this more in plot and style than through direct comment.

To sum up: these writers understood the melodrama as a form which carried its own values and already embodied its own significant content; it served as the literary equivalent of a particular, historically and socially conditioned *mode of experience*. Even if the situations and sentiments defied all categories of verisimilitude and were totally unlike anything in real life, the structure had a truth and a life of its own, which an artist could make part of his material. This meant that those who consciously adopted melodramatic techniques of presentation did not necessarily do so out of incompetence nor always from a cynical distance, but, by turning a body of techniques into a stylistic principle that carried the distinct overtones of spiritual crisis, they could put the finger on the texture of their social and human material while still being free to shape this material. For there is little doubt that the whole conception of life in nineteenth-century Europe and England, and especially the spiritual problems of the age, were often viewed in categories we would today call melodramatic – one can see this in painting, architecture, the ornamentation of gadgets and furniture, the domestic and public *mise en scène* of events and occasions, the oratory in parliament, the tractarian rhetoric from the pulpit as well as the more private manifestations of religious sentiment. Similarly, the timeless themes that Dostoyevsky brings up again and again in his novels – guilt, redemption, justice, innocence, freedom – are made specific and historically real not least because he was a great writer of melodramatic scenes and confrontations, and they more than anything else define that powerful irrational logic in the motivation and moral outlook of, say, Raskolnikov, Ivan Karamazov or Kirilov. Finally, how different Kafka's novels would be, if they did not contain those melodramatic family situations, pushed to the point where they reveal a dimension at once comic and tragically absurd – perhaps the existential undertow of all genuine melodrama.

Putting melos into drama
In its dictionary sense, melodrama is a dramatic narrative in which musical accompaniment marks the emotional effects. This is still perhaps the most useful definition, because it allows melodramatic elements to be seen as constituents of a system of punctuation, giving expressive colour and chromatic contrast to the story-line, by orchestrating the emotional ups and downs of the intrigue. The advantage of this approach is that it formulates the problems of melodrama as problems of style and articulation.

Music in melodrama, for example, as a device among others to dramatise a given narrative, is subjective, programmatic. But because it is also a form of punctuation in the above sense, it is both functional (that is, of structural significance) and thematic (that is, belonging to the expressive content) because used to formulate certain moods – sorrow, violence, dread, suspense, happiness. The syntactic function of music has, as is well-known, survived into the sound film, and the experiments conducted by Hanns Eisler and T. W. Adorno are highly instructive in this respect.[4] A practical demonstration of the problem can be found in the account which Lillian Ross gives of how Gottfried Reinhard and Dore Schary re-edited John Huston's *Red Badge of Courage* to give the narrative a smoother dramatic shape, by a musical build-up to the climaxes in a linear order, which is exactly what Huston had wanted to avoid when he shot it.[5]

Because it had to rely on piano accompaniment for punctuation, all silent film drama – from *True Heart Susie*, to *Foolish Wives* or *The Lodger* – is 'melodramatic'. It meant that directors had to develop an extremely subtle and yet precise formal language (of lighting, staging decor, acting, close-up, montage and camera movement), because they were deliberately looking for ways to compensate for the expressiveness, range of inflection and tonality, rhythmic emphasis and tension normally present in the spoken word. Having had to replace that part of language which is sound, directors like Murnau, Renoir, Hitchcock, Mizoguchi, Hawks, Lang, Sternberg achieved in their films a high degree (well recognised at the time) of plasticity in the modulation of optical planes and spatial masses which Panofsky rightly identified as a 'dynamisation of space'.

Among less gifted directors this sensitivity in the deployment of expressive means was partly lost with the advent of direct sound, since it seemed no longer necessary in a strictly technical sense – pictures 'worked' on audiences through their dialogue, and the semantic force of language overshadowed the more sophisticated pictorial effects and architectural values. This perhaps helps to explain why some major technical innovations, such as colour, widescreen and deep-focus lenses, crane and dolly, in fact encouraged a new form of sophisticated melodrama. Directors (quite a sizeable proportion of whom came during the 30s from Germany, and others were clearly indebted to German expressionism and Max Reinhardt's methods of theatrical *mise en scène*) began showing a similar degree of visual culture as the masters of silent film-drama: Ophüls, Lubitsch, Sirk, Preminger, Welles, Losey, Ray, Minnelli, Cukor.

Considered as an expressive code, melodrama might therefore be described as a particular form of dramatic *mise en scène*, characterised by a dynamic use of spatial and musical categories, as opposed to intellectual or literary ones. Dramatic situations are given an orchestration which will allow for complex aesthetic patterns: indeed, orchestration is fundamental to the American cinema as a whole (being essentially a dramatic cinema, spectacular, and based on a broad appeal) because it has drawn the aesthetic consequences of having the spoken word more as an additional 'melodic' dimension than as an autonomous semantic discourse. Sound, whether musical or verbal, acts first of all to give the illusion of depth to the moving image, and by helping to create the third dimension of the spectacle, dialogue becomes a scenic element, along with more directly visual means of the *mise en scène*. Anyone who has ever had the bad luck of watching a Hollywood movie dubbed into French or German will know how important diction is to the emotional resonance and dramatic continuity. Dubbing makes the best picture seem visually flat and dramatically out of sync: it destroys the flow on which the coherence of the illusionist spectacle is built.

That the plasticity of the human voice is quite consciously employed by directors for what are often thematic ends is known: Hawks trained Lauren

Bacall's voice so that she could be given 'male' lines in *To Have and Have Not*, an effect which Sternberg anticipated when he took great care to cultivate Marlene Dietrich's diction, and it is hard to miss the psychoanalytic significance of Robert Stack's voice in *Written on the Wind*, sounding as if every word had to be painfully pumped up from the bottom of one of his oil-wells.

If it is true that speech in the American cinema loses some of its semantic importance in favour of its material aspects as sound, then conversely, lighting, composition, decor increase their semantic and syntactic contribution to the aesthetic effect. They become functional and integral elements in the construction of meaning. This is the justification for giving critical importance to the *mise en scène* over intellectual content or story-value. It is also the reason why the domestic melodrama in colour and widescreen, as it appeared in the 40s and 50s is perhaps the most highly elaborated, complex mode of cinematic signification that the American cinema has ever produced, because of the restricted scope for external action determined by the subject, and because everything, as Sirk said, happens 'inside'. To the 'sublimation' of the action picture and the Busby Berkeley/Lloyd Bacon musical into domestic and family melodrama corresponded a sublimation of dramatic conflict into decor, colour, gesture and composition of frame, which in the best melodramas is perfectly thematised in terms of the characters' emotional and psychological predicaments.

For example, when in ordinary language we call something melodramatic, what we often mean is an exaggerated rise-and-fall pattern in human actions and emotional responses, a from-the-sublime-to-the-ridiculous movement, a foreshortening of lived time in favour of intensity – all of which produces a graph of much greater fluctuation, a quicker swing from one extreme to the other than is considered natural, realistic or in conformity with literary standards of verisimilitude: in the novel we like to sip our pleasures, rather than gulp them. But if we look at, say, Minnelli, who has adapted some of his best melodramas (*The Cobweb, Some Came Running, Home From the Hill, Two Weeks in Another Town, The Four Horsemen of the Apocalypse*) from generally extremely long, circumstantially detailed popular novels (by James Jones, Irving Shaw *et al.*), it is easy to see how in the process of having to reduce seven to nine hours' reading matter to ninety-odd minutes, such a more violent 'melodramatic' graph almost inevitably produces itself, short of the narrative becoming incoherent. Whereas in novels, especially when they are staple pulp fare, size connotes solid emotional involvement for the reader, the specific values of the cinema lie in its concentrated visual metaphors and dramatic acceleration rather than in the fictional techniques of dilation. The commercial necessity of compression (being also a formal one) is taken by Minnelli into the films themselves and developed as a theme – that of a pervasive psychological pressure on the characters. An acute sense of claustrophobia in decor and locale translates itself into a restless, and yet suppressed energy surfacing sporadically in the actions and the behaviour of the protagonists – which is part of the subject of a film like *Two Weeks in Another Town*, with hysteria bubbling all the time just below the surface. The feeling that there is always more to tell than can be said leads to very consciously elliptical narratives, proceeding often by visually condensing the characters' motivation into sequences of images which do not seem to advance the plot. The shot of the Trevi fountain at the end of a complex scene where Kirk Douglas is making up his mind in *Two Weeks* is such a metaphoric condensation, and so is the silent sequence, consisting entirely of what might appear to be merely impressionistic dissolves, in the *Four Horsemen*, when Glenn Ford and Ingrid Thulin go for a ride to Versailles, but which in fact tells and foretells the whole trajectory of their relationship.

Sirk, too, often constructs his films in this way: the restlessness of *Written on the Wind* is not unconnected with the fact that he almost always cuts on movement. His visual metaphors ought to have a chapter to themselves: a yellow sports-car drawing up the gravelled driveway to stop in front of a pair of shining white doric columns outside the Hadley mansion is not only a powerful piece of American iconography, especially when taken in a plunging high-angle shot, but the contrary associations of imperial splendour and vulgar materials (polished chrome-plate and stucco plaster) create a tension of correspondences and dissimilarities in the same image, which perfectly crystallises the decadent affluence and melancholic energy that give the film its uncanny fascination. Sirk has a peculiarly vivid eye for the contrasting emotional qualities of textures and materials, and he combines them or makes them clash to very striking effect, especially when they occur in a non-dramatic sequence: again in *Written on the Wind*, after the funeral of Hadley Sr., a black servant is seen taking an oleander wreath off the front gate. A black silk ribbon gets unstuck and is blown by the wind along the concrete path. The camera follows the movement, dissolves and dollies in on a window, where Lauren Bacall, in an oleander-green dress is just about to disappear behind the curtains. The scene has no plot significance whatsoever. But the colour parallels black/black, green/green, white concrete/white lace curtains provide an extremely strong emotional resonance in which the contrast of soft silk blown along the hard concrete is registered the more forcefully as a disquieting visual association. The desolation of the scene transfers itself onto the Bacall character, and the traditional fatalistic association of the wind remind us of the futility implied in the movie's title.

These effects, of course, require a highly self-conscious stylist, but they are by no means rare in Hollywood. The fact that commercial necessities, political censorship and the various morality codes restricted directors in what they

could tackle as a subject has entailed a different awareness of what constituted a worthwhile subject, a change in orientation from which sophisticated
melodrama benefited perhaps most. Not only did they provide a defined
thematic parameter, but they encouraged a conscious use of style as meaning,
which is a mark of what I would consider to be the very condition of a
modernist sensibility working in popular culture. To take another example
from Minnelli: his existential theme of a character trying to construct the
world in the image of an inner self, only to discover that this world has
become uninhabitable because it is both frighteningly suffocating and in-
tolerably lonely (*The Long, Long Trailer* and *The Cobweb*) is transformed
and given social significance when joined to the stock melodrama motif of
the woman who, having failed to make it in the big city, comes back to the
small-town home in the hope of finding her true place at last, but who is
made miserable by mean-mindedness and bigotry and then suffocated by the
sheer weight of her none-too-glorious, still ruefully remembered past (*Hilda
Crane, Beyond the Forest, All I Desire*).[6] In Minnelli, it becomes an opportunity to explore in concrete circumstances the more philosophical questions
of freedom and determinism, especially as they touch the aesthetic problem
of how to depict a character who is not constantly externalising himself into
action, without thereby trapping him in an environment of ready-made symbolism (for example, the discussion of decor and decoration in *The Cobweb*).

Similarly, when Robert Stack shows Lauren Bacall her hotel suite in *Written on the Wind*, where everything from flowers and pictures on the wall to
underwear, nailpolish and handbag is provided, Sirk not only characterises a
rich man wanting to take over the woman he fancies body and soul, or the
oppressive nature of an unwanted gift. He is also making a direct comment
on the Hollywood stylistic technique that 'creates' a character out of the
elements of the decor, and that prefers actors who can provide as blank a
facial surface and as little of a personality as possible.

Everyone who has thought at all about the Hollywood aesthetic wants to
formulate one of its peculiar qualities: that of direct emotional involvement,
whether one calls it 'giving resonance to dramatic situations' or 'fleshing out
the cliché' or whether, more abstractly, one talks in terms of identification
patterns, empathy and catharsis. Since the American cinema, determined as it
is by an ideology of the spectacle and the spectacular, is essentially dramatic
(as opposed to lyrical; concerned with mood or the inner self) and not
conceptual (dealing with ideas and the structures of cognition and perception), the creation or reenactment of situations which the spectator can identify with and recognise (whether this recognition is on the conscious or
unconscious level is another matter) depends to a large extent on the aptness
of the iconography (the 'visualisation') and on the quality (complexity, sub-
tlety, ambiguity) of the orchestration for what are trans-individual, popular
mythological (and therefore generally considered culturally 'lowbrow') ex-

periences and plot-structures. In other words, this type of cinema depends on the ways 'melos' is given to 'drama' by means of lighting, montage, visual rhythm, decor, style of acting, music – that is, on the ways the *mise en scène* translates character into action (not unlike the pre-Jamesean novel) and action into gesture and dynamic space (comparable to nineteenth-century opera and ballet).

This granted, there seems to be a further problem which has some bearing on the question of melodrama: although the techniques of audience-orientation and the possibility of psychic projection on the part of the spectator are as much in evidence in a melodrama like *Home From the Hill* or *Splendor in the Grass* as they are in a Western or adventure picture, the difference of setting and milieu affects the dynamic of the action. In the Western especially, the assumption of 'open' spaces is virtually axiomatic; it is indeed one of the constants which makes the form perennially attractive to a largely urban audience. This openness becomes problematic in films that deal with potential 'melodrama' themes and family situations. The complex father–son relationships in *The Left-Handed Gun*, the Cain–Abel themes of Mann's Westerns (*Winchester 73, Bend of the River*), the conflict of virility and mother-fixation in some of Tourneur's Westerns (*Great Day in the Morning, Wichita*) or the search for the mother (-country) in Fuller's *Run of the Arrow* seem to find resolution only when the hero can act positively on the changing situations. Otherwise, resolution demands the price of self-destruction. By contrast, in Raoul Walsh's adventure pictures, as Peter Lloyd has shown,[7] identity comes in an often paradoxical process of self-confirmation and overreaching – but always through direct action, while the momentum generated by the conflicts pushes the protagonists forward in an unrelentingly linear course.

The family melodrama, by contrast, though dealing largely with the same oedipal themes of emotional and moral identity, more often records the failure of the protagonist to act in a way that could shape the events and influence the emotional environment, let alone change the stifling social milieu. The world is closed, and the characters are acted upon. Melodrama confers on them a negative identity through suffering, and the progressive self-immolation and disillusionment generally ends in resignation: they emerge as lesser human beings for having become wise and acquiescent to the ways of the world.

The difference can be put in another way. In one case, the drama moves towards its resolution by having the central conflicts successively externalised and projected into direct action. A jail-break, a bank-robbery, a Western chase or cavalry charge, and even a criminal investigation lend themselves to psychologised, thematised representations of the heroes' inner dilemmas and frequently appear that way (Walsh's *White Heat* or *They Died With their Boots On*, Losey's *The Criminal*, Preminger's *Where the Sidewalk Ends*).

The same is true of the melodrama in the *série noire* tradition, where the hero is edged on or blackmailed by the *femme fatale* – the smell of honeysuckle and death in *Double Indemnity, Out of the Past* or *Detour* – into a course of action which pushes him further and further in one direction, opening a narrowing wedge of equally ineluctible consequences, that usually lead the hero to wishing his own death as the ultimate act of liberation, but where the mechanism of fate at least allows him to express his existential revolt in strong and strongly anti-social behaviour.

Not so in the domestic melodrama: the social pressures are such, the frame of respectability so sharply defined that the range of 'strong' actions is limited. The tellingly impotent gesture, the social gaffe, the hysterical outburst replaces any more directly liberating or self-annihilating action, and the cathartic violence of a shoot-out or a chase becomes an inner violence, often one which the characters turn against themselves. The dramatic configuration, the pattern of the plot makes them, regardless of attempts to break free, constantly look inwards, at each other and themselves. The characters are, so to speak, each others' sole referent, there is no world outside to be acted on, no reality that could be defined or assumed unambiguously. In Sirk, of course, they are locked into a universe of real and metaphoric mirrors, but quite generally, what is typical of this form of melodrama is that the characters' behaviour is often pathetically at variance with the real objectives they want to achieve. A sequence of substitute actions creates a kind of vicious circle in which the close nexus of cause and effect is somehow broken and – in an often overtly Freudian sense – displaced. James Dean in *East of Eden* thinks up a method of cold storage for lettuce, grows beans to sell to the Army, falls in love with Julie Harris, not to make a pile of money and live happily with a beautiful wife, but in order to win the love of his father and oust his brother – neither of which he achieves. Although very much on the surface of Kazan's film, this is a conjunction of puritan capitalist ethic and psychoanalysis which is sufficiently pertinent to the American melodrama to remain exemplary.

The melodramas of Ray, Sirk or Minnelli do not deal with this displacement-by-substitution directly, but by what one might call an intensified symbolisation of everyday actions, the heightening of the ordinary gesture and a use of setting and decor so as to reflect the characters' fetishist fixations. Violent feelings are given vent on 'overdetermined' objects (James Dean kicking his father's portrait as he storms out of the house in *Rebel Without A Cause*), and aggressiveness is worked out by proxy. In such films, the plots have a quite noticeable propensity to form a circular pattern, which in Ray involves an almost geometrical variation of triangle into circle and vice versa,[8] whereas Sirk (*nomen est omen*) often suggests in his circles the possibility of a tangent detaching itself – the full-circle construction of *Written on the Wind* with its linear coda of the Hudson–Bacall relationship at the end, or even more visually apparent, the circular race around the pylons in *Tarnished Angels* broken when Dorothy Malone's plane in the last image soars past the fatal pylon into an unlimited sky.

It is perhaps not too fanciful to suggest that the structural changes from linear externalisation of action to a sublimation of dramatic values into more complex forms of symbolisation, and which I take to be a central characteristic of the melodramatic tradition in the American cinema, can be followed through on a more general level where it reflects a change in the history of dramatic forms and the articulation of energy in the American cinema as a whole.

As I have tried to show in an earlier article (*Monogram* no. 1), one of the typical features of the classical Hollywood movie has been that the hero was defined dynamically, as the centre of a continuous movement, often both from sequence to sequence as well as within the individual shot. It is a fact of perception that in order to get its bearing, the eye adjusts almost automatically to whatever moves, and movement, together with sound, completes the realistic illusion. It was on the basis of sheer physical movement, for example, that the musicals of the 30s (Lloyd Bacon's *42nd Street* being perhaps the most spectacular example), the gangster movie and the B-thriller of the 40s and early 50s could subsist with the flimsiest of plots, an almost total absence of individual characterisation and rarely any big stars. These deficiencies were made up by focusing to the point of exaggeration on the drive, the obsession, the *idée fixe*, that is to say, by a concentration on the purely kinetic-mechanical elements of human motivation. The pattern is most evident in the gangster genre, where the single-minded pursuit of money and power is followed by the equally single-minded and peremptory pursuit of physical survival, ending in the hero's apotheosis through violent death. This curve of rise and fall – a wholly stylised and external pattern which takes on a moral significance – can be seen in movies like *Underworld*, *Little Caesar*, *The Roaring Twenties*, *Legs Diamond* and depends essentially on narrative pace, though it permits interesting variations and complexities, as in Fuller's *Underworld USA*. A sophisticated director, such as Hawks, has used speed of delivery and the pulsating urgency of action to comic effect (*Scarface*, *20th Century*) and has even applied it to films whose dramatic structure did not naturally demand such a treatment (notably *His Girl Friday*).

This unrelenting internal combustion engine of physical and psychic energy, generically exemplified by the hard-boiled, crackling aggressiveness of the screwball comedy, but which Walsh diagnosed in his Cagney heroes as psychotic (*White Heat*) and a vehicle for extreme redneck republicanism (*A Lion in the Streets*), shows signs of a definite slowing-down in the 50s and early 60s, where raucous vitality and instinctual 'lust for life' is deepened psychologically to intimate neuroses and adolescent or not so adolescent maladjustments of a wider social significance. Individual initiative is perceived as problematic in explicitly political terms (*All the King's Men*), after having previously been merely stoically and heroically anti-social, as in the film noir. The external world is more and more riddled with obstacles which oppose themselves to personal ambition and are not simply overcome by the hero's assertion of a brawny or brainy libido. In Mann's Westerns the madness at the heart of the James Stewart character only occasionally breaks through an otherwise calm and controlled surface, like a strong subterranean current suddenly appearing above ground as an inhuman and yet somehow poetically apt thirst for vengeance and primitive Biblical justice, where the will to survive is linked to certain old-fashioned cultural and moral values – of dignity, honour and respect. In the films of Sirk an uncompromising, fundamentally innocent energy is gradually turned away from simple, direct fulfilment by the emergence of a conscience, a sense of guilt and responsibility, or the awareness of moral complexity, as in *Magnificent Obsession, Sign of the Pagan, All that Heaven Allows* and even *Interlude* – a theme which in Sirk is always interpreted in terms of cultural decadence.

Where Freud left his Marx in the American home
There can be little doubt that the post-war popularity of the family melodrama in Hollywood is partly connected with the fact that in those years America discovered Freud. This is not the place to analyse the reasons why the United States should have become the country in which his theories found their most enthusiastic reception anywhere, or why they became such a decisive influence on American culture, but the connections of Freud with melodrama are as complex as they are undeniable. An interesting fact, for example, is that Hollywood tackled Freudian themes in a particularly 'romantic' or gothic guise, through a cycle of movies inaugurated possibly by Hitchcock's first big American success, *Rebecca*. Relating his Victorianism to the Crawford–Stanwyck–Davis type 'women's picture', which for obvious reasons became a major studio concern during the war years and found its apotheosis in such movies as John Cromwell's *Since You Went Away* (to the Front, that is), Hitchcock infused his film, and several others, with an oblique intimation of female frigidity producing strange fantasies of persecution, rape and death – masochistic reveries and nightmares, which cast the husband into the rôle of the sadistic murderer. This projection of sexual anxiety and its mechanisms of displacement and transfer is translated into a whole string of movies often involving hypnosis and playing on the ambiguity and suspense of whether the wife is merely imagining it or whether her husband really does have murderous designs on her: Hitchcock's *Notorious* and *Suspicion*, Minnelli's *Undercurrent*, Cukor's *Gaslight*, Sirk's *Sleep My Love*, Tourneur's *Experiment Perilous*, Lang's *Secret Beyond the Door*, all belong

in this category, as does Preminger's *Whirlpool*, and in a wider sense Renoir's *Woman on the Beach*. What strikes one about this list is not only the high number of European émigrés entrusted with such projects, but that virtually all of the major directors of family melodramas (except Ray)[9] in the 50s had a (usually not entirely successful) crack at the Freudian feminist melodrama in the 40s.

More challenging, and difficult to prove, is the speculation that certain stylistic and structural features of the sophisticated melodrama may involve principles of symbolisation and coding which Freud conceptualised in his analysis of dreams and later also applied in his *Psychopathology of Everyday Life*. I am thinking less of the prevalence of what Freud called 'Symptomhandlungen' or 'Fehlhandlungen', that is, slips of the tongue or other projections of inner states into interpretable overt behaviour. This is a way of symbolising and signalling attitudes common to the American cinema in virtually every genre. However, there is a certain refinement in the melodrama – it becomes part of the composition of the frame, more subliminally and unobtrusively transmitted to the spectator. When Minnelli's characters find themselves in an emotionally precarious or contradictory situation, it often affects the 'balance' of the visual composition – wine glasses, a piece of china or a trayful of drinks emphasise the fragility of their situation – e.g. Judy Garland over breakfast in *The Clock*, Richard Widmark in *The Cobweb* explaining himself to Gloria Grahame, or Gregory Peck trying to make his girlfriend see why he married someone else in *Designing Woman*. When Robert Stack in *Written on the Wind*, standing by the window he has just opened to get some fresh air into an extremely heavy family atmosphere, hears of Lauren Bacall expecting a baby, his misery becomes eloquent by the way he squeezes himself into the frame of the half-open window, every word his wife says to him bringing torment to his lacerated soul and racked body.

Along similar lines, I have in mind the kind of 'condensation' of motivation into metaphoric images or sequences of images mentioned earlier, the relation that exists in Freudian dream-work between manifest dream material and latent dream content. Just as in dreams certain gestures and incidents mean something by their structure and sequence, rather than by what they literally represent, the melodrama often works, as I have tried to show, by a displaced emphasis, by substitute acts, by parallel situations and metaphoric connections. In dreams one tends to 'use' as dream material incidents and circumstances from one's waking experience during the previous day, in order to 'code' them, while nevertheless keeping a kind of emotional logic going, and even condensing their images into what, during the dream at least, seems an inevitable sequence. Melodramas often use middle-class American society, its iconography and the family experience in just this way as their manifest 'material', but 'displace' it into quite different patterns, juxtaposing stereotyped situations in strange configurations, provoking clashes and ruptures which not only open up new associations but also redistribute the emotional energies which suspense and tensions have accumulated in disturbingly different directions. American movies, for example, often manipulate very shrewdly situations of extreme embarrassment (a blocking of emotional energy) and acts or gestures of violence (direct or indirect release) in order to create patterns of aesthetic significance which only a musical vocabulary might be able to describe accurately, and for which a psychologist or anthropologist might offer some explanation.

One of the principles involved is that of continuity and discontinuity (what Sirk has called the 'rhythm of the plot'). A typical situation in American melodramas has the plot build up to an evidently catastrophic collision of counter-running sentiments, but a string of delays gets the greatest possible effect from the clash when it does come. In Minnelli's *The Bad and the Beautiful* Lana Turner plays an alcoholic actress who has been 'rescued' by producer Kirk Douglas giving her a new start in the movies. After the première, flushed with success, self-confident for the first time in years, and in happy anticipation of celebrating with Douglas, with whom she has fallen in love, she drives to his home armed with a bottle of champagne. However, we already know that Douglas isn't emotionally interested in her ('I need an actress, not a wife' he later tells her) and is spending the evening with a 'broad' in his bedroom. Lana Turner, suspecting nothing, is met by Douglas at the foot of the stairs, and she, at first too engrossed in herself to notice how cool he is, collapses when the other woman suddenly appears at the top of the stairs in Douglas' dressing gown. Her nervous breakdown in the car is conveyed by headlights flashing against her windscreen like a barrage of footlights and arc-lamps.

This letting-the-emotions-rise and then cringing them suddenly down with a thump is an extreme example of dramatic discontinuity, and a similar, vertiginous drop in the emotional temperature punctuates a good many melodramas – almost invariably played out against the vertical axis of a staircase.[10] In one of the most paroxysmic montage sequences that the American cinema has known, Sirk has Dorothy Malone in *Written on the Wind* dance on her own, like some doomed goddess from a dionysian mystery, while her father is collapsing on the stairs and dying from a heart-attack. Again, in *Imitation of Life*, John Gavin gets the brush-off from Lana Turner as they are going down the stairs, and in *All I Desire* Barbara Stanwyck has to disappoint her daughter about not taking her to New York to become an actress, after the girl has been rushing downstairs to tell her father the good news. Ray's use of the staircase for similar emotional effects is well-known and most spectacular in *Bigger than Life*, but to give an example from another director, Henry King, I'd like to quote a scene from *Margie*, a film following rather closely Minnelli's *Meet Me in St. Louis*, where the heroine,

Jeanne Crain, about to be taken to the graduation ball by a blind date (whom we know to be her father) since her poetry-loving bespectacled steady has caught a cold, comes tearing down from her bedroom when she hears that the French master, on whom she has a crush, has dropped in. She virtually rips the bouquet of flowers out of his hands and is overwhelmed by joy. With some embarrassment, he has to explain that he is taking somebody else to the ball, that he only came to return her papers, and Margie, mortified, humiliated and cringing with shame, has just enough time to get back upstairs before she dissolves in tears.

While this may not sound terribly profound on paper, the visual orchestration of such a scene can produce some rather strong emotional effects and the strategy of building up to a climax so as to throttle it the more abruptly is a form of dramatic reversal by which Hollywood directors consistently criticised the streak of incurably naïve moral and emotional idealism in the American psyche, first by showing it to be often indistinguishable from the grossest kind of illusion and self-delusion, and then by forcing a confrontation when it is most wounding and contradictory. The emotional extremes are played off in such a way that they reveal an inherent dialectic, and the undeniable psychic energy contained in this seemingly so vulnerable sentimentality is utilised to furnish its own antidote, to bring home the discontinuities in the structures of emotional experience which give a kind of realism and toughness rare if not unthinkable in the European cinema.

What makes these discontinuities in the melodrama so effective is that they occur, as it were, under pressure. Although the kinetics of the American cinema are generally directed towards creating pressure and manipulating it (as suspense, for example), the melodrama presents in some ways a special case. In the Western or the thriller, suspense is generated by the linear organisation of the plot and the action, together with the kind of 'pressure' which the spectator brings to the film by way of anticipation and *apriori* expectations of what he hopes to see; melodrama, however, has to accommodate the latter type of pressure, as already indicated, in what amounts to a relatively 'closed' world.

This is emphasised by the function of the decor and the symbolisation of objects: the setting of the family melodrama almost by definition is the middle-class home, filled with objects, which in a film like Philip Dunne's *Hilda Crane*, typical of the genre in this respect surround the heroine in a hierarchy of apparent order that becomes increasingly suffocating. From father's armchair in the living room and mother's knitting, to the upstairs bedroom, where after five years' absence dolls and teddies are still neatly arranged on the bedspread, home not only overwhelms Hilda with images of parental oppression and a repressed past (which indirectly provoke her explosive outbursts that sustain the action), it also brings out the characteristic attempt of the bourgeois household to make time stand still, immobilise life and fix forever domestic property relations as the model of social life and a bulwark against the more disturbing sides in human nature. The theme has a particular poignancy in the many films about the victimisation and enforced passivity of women – women waiting at home, standing by the window, caught in a world of objects into which they are expected to invest their feelings. *Since You Went Away* has a telling sequence when Claudette Colbert, having just taken her husband to the troop-train at the station, returns home to clear up after the morning's rush. Everything she looks at or touches – dressing-gown, pipe, wedding-picture, breakfast cup, slippers, shaving-brush, the dog – reminds her of her husband, until she cannot bear the strain and falls on her bed sobbing. The banality of the objects combined with the repressed anxieties and emotions force a contrast that makes the scene almost epitomise the relation of decor to character in melodrama: the more the setting fills with objects to which the plot gives symbolic significance, the more the characters are enclosed in seemingly ineluctable situations. Pressure is generated by things crowding in on them and life becomes increasingly complicated because cluttered with obstacles and objects that invade their personalities, take them over, stand for them, become more real than the human relations or emotions they were intended to symbolise.

It is again an instance of Hollywood stylistic devices supporting the themes, or commenting on each other. Melodrama is iconographically fixed by the claustrophobic atmosphere of the bourgeois home and/or the small-town setting, its emotional pattern is that of panic and latent hysteria, reinforced stylistically by a complex handling of space in interiors (Sirk, Ray and Losey particularly excel in this) to the point where the world seems totally predetermined and pervaded by 'meaning' and interpretable signs.

This marks another recurrent feature, already touched on, that of desire focusing on the unobtainable object. The mechanisms of displacement and transfer, in an enclosed field of pressure, open a highly dynamic, yet discontinuous cycle of non-fulfilment, where discontinuity creates a universe of powerfully emotional, but obliquely related fixations. In melodrama, violence, the strong action, the dynamic movement, the full articulation and the fleshed-out emotions – so characteristic of the American cinema – become the very signs of the characters' alienation, and thus serve to formulate a devastating critique of the ideology that supports it.

Minnelli and Sirk are exceptional directors in this respect not least because they handle stories with four, five or sometimes six characters all tied up in a single configuration, and yet give each of them an even thematic emphasis and an independent point of view. Such skill involves a particularly 'musical' gift and a very sensitive awareness of the harmonising potential contained in contrasting material and the structural implications of different characters' motives.

Films like *Home From the Hill*, *The Cobweb*, *Tarnished Angels* or *Written on the Wind* strike one as 'objective' films, since they do not have a central hero (even though there may be a gravitational pull towards one of the protagonists) and nonetheless they cohere, mainly because each of the characters' predicaments is made plausible in terms that relate to the problems of the others. The films are built architecturally, by a combination of structural tensions and articulated parts, and the overall design appears only retrospectively, as it were, when with the final coda of appeasement the edifice is complete and the spectator can stand back and look at the pattern. But there is, especially in the Minnelli movies, also a wholly 'subjective' dimension. The films (because the parts are so closely organised around a central theme or dilemma) can be interpreted as emanating from a single consciousness, which is testing or experiencing in dramatic form, the various options and possibilities flowing from an initially outlined moral or existential contradiction.

In *The Cobweb* John Kerr wants both total self-expression and a defined human framework in which such freedom is meaningful, and George Hamilton in *Home From the Hill* wants to assume adult responsibilities while at the same time he rejects the standards of adulthood implied in his father's aggressive masculinity. In the latter, the drama ends with a 'Freudian' resolution of the father being eliminated at the very point when he has resigned himself to his loss of supremacy, but this is underpinned by a 'Biblical' one which fuses the mythology of Cain and Abel with that of Abraham blessing his first-born. The interweaving of motifs is achieved by a series of parallels and contrasts. Set in the South, the story concerns the relations of a mother's boy with his tough father, played by Robert Mitchum, whose wife so resents his having a bastard son (George Peppard) that she won't sleep with him again. The plot progresses through all the possible permutations of the basic situation: lawful son/natural son, sensitive George Hamilton/hypochondriac mother, tough George Peppard/tough Robert Mitchum, both boys fancy the same girl, Hamilton gets her pregnant, Peppard marries her, girl's father turns nasty against the lawful son because of the notorious sex-life of his father, etc. However, because the plot is structured as a series of mirror-reflections on the theme of fathers and sons, blood ties and natural affinities, Minnelli's film is a psychoanalytical portrait of the sensitive adolescent – but placed in a definite ideological and social context. The boy's consciousness, we realise, is made up of what are external forces and circumstances, his dilemma the result of his social position as heir to his father's estate, unwanted because felt to be undeserved, and an upbringing deliberately exploited by his mother in order to get even with his father, whose own position as a Texan landowner and local big-shot forces him to compensate for his wife's frigidity by proving his virility with other women. Melodrama here becomes the vehicle for diagnosing a single individual in ideological terms and objective categories, while the blow-by-blow emotional drama creates the second level, where the subjective aspect (the immediate, and necessarily unreflected experience of the characters) is left intact. The hero's identity, on the other hand, emerges as a kind of picture-puzzle from the various pieces of dramatic action.

Home From the Hill is also a perfect example of the principle of substitute acts, mentioned earlier, which is Hollywood's way of portraying the dynamics of alienation. The story is sustained by pressure that is applied indirectly, and by desires that always chase unattainable goals: Mitchum forces George Hamilton to 'become a man' though he is temperamentally his mother's son, while Mitchum's 'real' son in terms of attitudes and character is George Peppard, whom he cannot acknowledge for social reasons. Likewise, Eleanor Parker puts pressure on her son in order to get at Mitchum, and Everett Sloane (the girl's father) takes out on George Hamilton the sexual hatred he feels against Mitchum. Finally, after his daughter has become pregnant he goes to see Mitchum to put pressure on him to get his son to marry the girl, only to break down when Mitchum turns the tables and accuses him of blackmail. It is a pattern which in an even purer form appears in *Written on the Wind*: Dorothy Malone wants Rock Hudson who wants Lauren Bacall who wants Robert Stack who just wants to die. *La Ronde à l'Américaine*. The point is that the melodrama dynamism of these situations is used by both Sirk and Minnelli to make the emotional impact 'carry over' into the very subdued, apparently neutral, sequences of images that so often round off a scene and which thereby have a strong lyrical quality.

One of the characteristic features of melodramas in general is that they concentrate on the point of view of the victim: what makes the films mentioned above exceptional is the way they manage to present *all* the characters convincingly as victims. The critique – the questions of 'evil', of responsibility – is firmly placed on a social and existential level, away from the arbitrary and finally obtuse logic of private motives and individualised psychology. This is why the melodrama, at its mst accomplished, seems capable of reproducing more directly than other genres the patterns of domination and exploitation existing in a given society, especially the relation between psychology, morality and class-consciousness, by emphasising so clearly an emotional dynamic whose social correlative is a network of external forces directed oppressingly inward, and with which the characters themselves unwittingly collude to become their agents. In Minnelli, Sirk, Ray, Cukor and others, alienation is recognised as a basic condition, fate is secularised into the prison of social conformity and psychological neurosis, and the linear trajectory of self-fulfilment so potent in American ideology is twisted into the downward spiral of a self-destructive urge seemingly possessing a whole social class.

This typical masochism of the melodrama, with its incessant acts of inner violation, its mechanisms of frustration and over-compensation, is perhaps brought most into the open through characters who have a drink problem (cf. *Written on the Wind, Hilda Crane, Days of Wine and Roses*). Although alcoholism is too common an emblem in films and too typical of middle-class America to deserve a close thematic analysis, drink does become interesting in movies where its dynamic significance is developed and its qualities as a visual metaphor recognised: wherever characters are seen swallowing and gulping their drinks as if they were swallowing their humiliations along with their pride, vitality and the life-force have become palpably destructive, and a phoney libido has turned into real anxiety. *Written on the Wind* is perhaps the movie that most consistently builds on the metaphoric possibilities of alcohol (liquidity, potency, the phallic shape of bottles). Not only is its theme an emotional drought that no amount of alcohol, oil pumped by the derricks, or petrol in fast cars and planes can mitigate, it also has Robert Stack compensate for his sexual impotence and childhood guilt feelings by hugging a bottle of raw corn every time he feels suicidal, which he proceeds to smash in disgust against the paternal mansion. In one scene Stack is making unmistakable gestures with an empty Martini bottle in the direction of his wife, and an unconsummated relationship is visually underscored when two brimful glasses remain untouched on the table, as Dorothy Malone does her best to seduce an unresponsive Rock Hudson at the family party, having previously poured her whisky into the flower vase of her rival, Lauren Bacall.

Melodrama is often used to describe tragedy that doesn't quite come off: either because the characters think of themselves too self-consciously as tragic or because the predicament is too evidently fabricated on the level of plot and dramaturgy to carry the kind of conviction normally termed 'inner necessity'. Now, in some American family melodramas the inadequacy of the character's responses to their predicament becomes itself part of the subject. In Cukor's *The Chapman Report* and Minnelli's *The Cobweb* – two movies explicitly concerned with the impact of Freudian notions on American society – the protagonists' self-understanding as well as the doctors' attempts at analysis and therapy are shown to be either tragically or comically inadequate to the situations that the characters are supposed to cope with in everyday life. Pocket-size tragic heroes and heroines, they are blindly grappling with a fate real enough to cause intense human anguish, which as the spectator can see, however, is compounded by social prejudice, ignorance, insensitivity on top of the bogus claim to scientific objectivity by the doctors. Claire Bloom's nymphomania and Jane Fonda's frigidity in the Cukor movie are seen to be two different but equally hysterical reactions to the heavy ideological pressures which American society exerts on the relations between the sexes. *The Chapman Report*, despite having apparently been cut by Darryl F. Zanuck Jr., remains an extremely important film partly because it treats its theme both in the tragic and the comic mode, without breaking apart, underlining thereby the ambiguous springs of the discrepancy between displaying intense feelings and the circumstances to which they are inadequate – usually a comic motif but tragic in its emotional implications.

Both Cukor and Minnelli, however, focus on how ideological contradictions are reflected in the characters' seemingly spontaneous behaviour – the way self-pity and self-hatred alternate with a violent urge towards some form of liberating action, which inevitably fails to resolve the conflict. The characters experience as a shamefully personal stigma what the spectator (because of the parallelisms between the different episodes in *The Chapman Report*, and the analogies in the fates of the seven principal figures of *The Cobweb*) is forced to recognise as belonging to a wider social dilemma. The poverty of the intellectual resources in some of the characters is starkly contrasted with a corresponding abundance of emotional resources, and as one sees them helplessly struggling inside their emotional prisons with no hope of realising to what degree they are the victims of their society, one gets a clear picture of how a certain individualism reinforces social and emotional alienation, and of how the economics of the psyche are as vulnerable to manipulation and exploitation as is a person's labour.

The point is that this inadequacy has itself a name, relevant to the melodrama as a form: irony or pathos, which both in tragedy and melodrama is the response to the recognition of different levels of awareness. Irony privileges the spectator vis-à-vis the protagonists, for he registers the difference from a superior position. Pathos results from non-communication or silence made eloquent – people talking at cross-purposes (Robert Stack and Lauren Bacall when she tells him she's pregnant in *Written on the Wind*), a mother watching her daughter's wedding from afar (Barbara Stanwyck in *Stella Dallas*) or a woman returning unnoticed to her family, watching them through the window (again Barbara Stanwyck in *All I Desire*) – where highly emotional situations are underplayed to present an ironic discontinuity of feeling or a qualitative difference in intensity, usually visualised in terms of spatial distance and separation.

Such archetypal melodramatic situations activate very strongly an audience's participation, for there is a desire to make up for the emotional deficiency, to impart the different awareness, which in other genres is systematically frustrated to produce suspense: the primitive desire to warn the heroine of the perils looming visibly over her in the shape of the villain's shadow. But in the more sophisticated melodramas this pathos is most acutely produced through a 'liberal' *mise en scène* which balances different points of view, so that the spectator is in a position of seeing and evaluating contrasting attitudes within a given thematic framework – a framework which is the result of the total configuration and therefore inaccessible to the protagonists themselves. The spectator, say in Otto Preminger's *Daisy Kenyon* or a Nicholas Ray movie is made aware of the slightest qualitative imbalance in a relationship and also sensitised to the tragic implications which a radical misunderstanding or a misconception of motives might have, even when this is not played out in terms of a tragic ending.

If pathos is the result of a skilfully displaced emotional emphasis, it is frequently used in melodramas to explore psychological and sexual repression, usually in conjunction with the theme of inferiority; inadequacy of response in the American cinema often has an explicitly sexual code: male impotence and female frigidity – a subject which allows for thematisation in various directions: not only to indicate the kinds of psychological anxiety and social pressures which generally make people sexually unresponsive, but as metaphors of unfreedom or a quasi-metaphysical 'overreaching' (as in Ray's *Bigger than Life*). In Sirk, where the theme has an exemplary status, it is treated as a problem of 'decadence' – where intention, awareness, yearning, outstrip performance – sexual, social, moral. From the Willi Birgel character in *Zu Neuen Ufern* onwards, Sirk's most impressive characters are never up to the demands which their lives make on them, though some are sufficiently sensitive, alive and intelligent to feel and know about this inadequacy of gesture and response. It gives their pathos a tragic ring, because they take on suffering and moral anguish knowingly, as the just price for having glimpsed a better world and having failed to live it. A tragic self-awareness is called upon to compensate for lost spontaneity and energy, and in films like *All I Desire* or *There's Always Tomorrow*, where as so often, the fundamental irony is in the titles themselves, this theme which has haunted the European imagination at least since Nietzsche, is absorbed into an American small-town atmosphere, often revolving around the questions of dignity and responsibility, how to yield when confronted with true talent and true vitality – in short, those qualities that dignity is called upon to make up for.

In the Hollywood melodrama characters made for operettas play out the tragedies of mankind which is how they experience the contradictions of American civilisation. Small wonder they are constantly baffled and amazed, as Lana Turner is in *Imitation of Life*, about what is going on around them and within them. The discrepancy of seeming and being, of intention and result, registers as a perplexing frustration, and an ever-increasing gap opens between the emotions and the reality they seek to reach. What strikes one as the true pathos is the very mediocrity of the human beings involved, putting such high demands upon themselves trying to live up to an exalted vision of man, but instead living out the impossible contradictions that have turned the American dream into its proverbial nightmare. It makes the best American melodramas of the 50s not only critical social documents but genuine tragedies, despite, or rather because of the 'happy ending': they record some of the agonies that have accompanied the demise of the 'affirmative culture'. Spawned by liberal idealism, they advocate with open, conscious irony that the remedy is more of the same. But even without the national disasters that were to overtake America in the 1960s this irony, too, almost seems to belong to a different age.

Notes

1. A. Filon, *The English Stage* (London, 1897). Filon also offers an interesting definition of melodrama: 'When dealing with Irving, I asked the question, so often discussed, whether we go to the theatre to see a representation of life, or to forget life and seek relief from it. Melodrama solves this question and shows that both theories are right, by giving satisfaction to both desires, in that it offers the extreme of realism in scenery and language together with the most uncommon sentiments and events.'
2. See J. Duvignaud, *Sociologie du Théâtre* (Paris, 1965), IV, 3, 'Théâtre sans révolution, révolution sans théâtre'.
3. About the ideological function of nineteenth-century Victorian melodrama, see M. W. Disher: 'Even in gaffs and saloons, melodrama so strongly insisted on the sure reward to be bestowed in this life upon the law-abiding that sociologists now see in this a Machiavellian plot to keep democracy servile to Church and State. (...) There is no parting the two strains, moral and political, in the imagination of the nineteenth-century masses. They are hopelessly entangled. Democracy shaped its own entertainments at a time when the vogue of Virtue Triumphant was at its height and they took their pattern from it. (...) Here are Virtue Triumphant's attendant errors: confusion between sacred and profane, between worldly and spiritual advancement, between self-interest and self-sacrifice...'. (*Blood and Thunder*, London, 1949, pp. 13–14.) However, it ought to be remembered that there are melodramatic traditions outside the puritan-democratic world view: Catholic countries, such as Spain, Mexico (cf. Bunuel's Mexican films) have a very strong line in melodramas, based on the themes of atonement and redemption. Japanese melodramas have been 'high-brow' since the Monogatari stories of the 16th century, and in Mizoguchi's films (*The Life of Oharu, Shin Heike monogatari*) they reach a transcendence and stylistic sublimation rivalled only by the very best Hollywood melodramas.
4. Hanns Eisler, *Composing for the Films* (London: Dobson, 1951).
5. Lillian Ross, *Picture* (Harmondsworth: Penguin, 1958).
6. The impact of *Madame Bovary* via Willa Cather on the American cinema and the popular imagination would deserve a closer look.
7. *Brighton Film Review* nos. 14, 15, 21.
8. Ibid. nos. 19, 20.
9. I have not seen *A Woman's Secret* (1949) or *Born to be Bad* (1950), either of

which might include Ray in this category, and the Ida Lupino character in *On Dangerous Ground* (1952) – blind, living with a homicidal brother – is distinctly reminiscent of this masochistic strain in Hollywood feminism.

10. As a principle of *mise en scène* the dramatic use of staircases recalls the famous *Jessnertreppe* of German theatre. The thematic conjunction of family and height/ depth symbolism is nicely described by Max Tessier: 'Le héros ou l'héroine sont ballotés dans un véritable scenic-railway social, où les classes sont rigoureusement compartimentées. Leur ambition est de quitter à jamais un milieu moralement dépravé, physiquement éprouvant, pour accéder au Nirvana de la grande bourgeoisie.... Pas de famille, pas de mélo! Pour qu'il y ait mélo, il faut avant tout qu'il y ait faute, péché, transgression sociale. Or, quel est le milieu idéal pour que se développe cette gangrène, sinon cette cellule familiale, liée à une conception hiérarchique de la société?' (*Cinéma 71*, no. 161, p. 46)

[The hero or heroine are tossed about in a social equivalent of a scenic railway, with rigorously compartmentalised classes. Their ambition is to get out, once and for all, of a milieu that is morally depraved and physically distressing, in order to gain access to the Nirvana of the grand bourgeoisie.... No family, no melodrama! For there to be melodrama, there first must be a lapse, sin, a social transgression, and what milieu is more ideally suited for the development of such a gangrene than the familial cell, tied as it is to a hierarchical conception of society? (Editor's trans.)]

Minnelli and Melodrama

GEOFFREY NOWELL-SMITH

From *Screen* vol. 18 no. 2, pp. 113–18.

W H A T this paper claims is that the genre or form that has come to be known as melodrama arises from the conjunction of a formal history proper (development of tragedy, realism, etc.), a set of social determinations, which have to do with the rise of the bourgeoisie, and a set of psychic determinations, which take shape around the family. The psychic and social determinations are connected because the family whose conflicts the melodrama enacts is also the bourgeois family, but a complexity is added to the problem by the fact that the melodrama is also a particular form of artistic representation. As artistic representation it is also (in Marxist terms) ideology and (in Freudian terms) 'secondary revision', but it cannot be simply reduced to either. As artistic representation it does not 'reflect' or 'describe' social and psychic determinations. Rather, it *signifies* them. This act of signifying has two aspects: on the one hand it produces a narrated or represented content, the life of people in society; and on the other hand it narrates and represents to and from a particular standpoint or series of standpoints, 'subject positions'. Now it might be thought that the former aspect, concerning the content, is a question for social (historical-materialist) analysis, and the latter, concerning the form, a matter for psychology or psychoanalysis. What I shall claim is that this is not the case and that the positions of the narrating are also social positions, while what is narrated is also psychical. The 'subject positions' implied by the melodrama are those of bourgeois art in a bourgeois epoch, while the 'represented object' is that of the oedipal drama.

Melodrama and Tragedy

Melodrama originally meant, literally, drama + melos (music) and this eighteenth-century sense survives in the Italian *melodramma* – grand opera. In its early form melodrama was akin to pastoral, and differentiated from tragedy in that the story usually had a happy end. Not much of the original meaning has survived into later – Victorian and modern – usages of the term, but the differentiation from tragedy has become, if anything, more marked. The principal differences are two, both of them the result of developments in art forms generally that began in the eighteenth century and were consolidated later. The first of these concerns modes of address and the second the representation of the hero(ine). At the time it should be noted that in many other respects the melodrama is the inheritor of many tragic concerns, albeit transposed to a new situation.

Melodrama as Bourgeois Form

One feature of tragic and epic forms up to (roughly) the eighteenth century is that they characteristically deal with kings and princes, while being written by, and for the most part addressed to, members of a less exalted social stratum. (The authors, even Homer, are broadly speaking 'intellectuals', while the audience is conceived of, however inaccurately, as 'the people'). With the advent of the novel (cf. Scarron's *Le Roman bourgeois*) and the 'bourgeois tragedy' of the eighteenth century, the situation changes. Author, audience and subject matter are put on a place of equality. As Raymond Williams has noted (*Screen* vol. 18 no. 1, Spring 1977), the appeal is directly to 'our equals, your equals'. Mystified though it may be, the address is from one bourgeois to another bourgeois, and the subject matter is the life of the bourgeoisie. This movement of equalisation generally goes under the name of (or is conflated with) realism, but it also characterises forms which in other respects are not conspicuous for their realism, such as the melodrama.

In so far as melodrama, like realism, supposes a world of equals, a democracy within the bourgeois strata (alias bourgeois democracy) it also supposes a world without the exercise of social power. The address is to an audience which does not think of itself as possessed of power (but neither as radically dispossessed, disinherited, oppressed) and the world of the subject matter is likewise one in which only middling power relations are present. The characters are neither the rulers nor the ruled, but occupy a middle ground, exercising local power or suffering local powerlessness, within the family or the small town. The locus of power is the family and individual private property, the two being connected through inheritance. In this world of circumscribed horizons (which corresponds very closely to Marx's definition of 'petty bourgeois ideology') patriarchal right is of central importance. The son has to become like his father in order to take over his property and his place within the community (or, in variant structures, a woman is widowed and therefore inherits, but the question posed is which man she can pass the property onto by remarriage; or, again, the father is evil and the son must grow up different from him in order to be able to redistribute the property at the moment of inheritance, etc., etc.). Notably, the question of law or legitimacy, so central to tragedy, is turned inward from 'Has this man a right to rule (over us)?' to 'Has this man a right to rule a family (like ours)?'. This inward-turning motivates a more directly psychological reading of situations, particularly in the Hollywood melodrama of the 50s.

Action and Passion

Aristotle defined History as 'what Alcibiades did and suffered'. Doing and suffering, action and passion, are co-present in classical tragedy, and indeed in most art forms up to the romantic period. There is then a split, producing a demarcation of forms between those in which there is an active hero, inured or immune to suffering, and those in which there is a hero, or more often a heroine, whose role is to suffer. Broadly speaking, in the American movie the active hero becomes protagonist of the Western, the passive or impotent hero or heroine becomes protagonist of what has come to be known as melodrama. The contrast active/passive is, inevitably, traversed by another contrast, that between masculine and feminine. Essentially the world of the Western is one of activity/masculinity, in which women cannot figure except as receptacles (or occasionally as surrogate males). The melodrama is more complex. It often features women as protagonists, and where the central figure is a man there is regularly an impairment of his 'masculinity' – at least in contrast to the mythic potency of the hero of the Western. It cannot operate in the simple terms of a fantasy affirmation of the masculine and disavowal of the feminine, but the way it recasts the equation to allow more space for its women characters and for the representations of passion undergone throws up problems of its own. In so far as activity remains equated with masculinity and passivity with femininity, the destiny of the characters, whether male or female, is unrealisable; he or she can only live out the impairment ('castration') imposed by the law. In their struggle for the achievement of social and sexual demands, men may sometimes win through, women never. But this fact about the plot structure is not just an element of realism, it reflects an imbalance already present in the conceptual and symbolic structure. 'Masculinity', although rarely attainable, is at least known as an ideal. 'Femininity', within the terms of the argument, is not only unknown but unknowable. Since sexuality and social efficacy are recognisable only in a 'masculine' form, the contradictions facing the women characters are posed in more acutely problematic form from the outset. For both women and men, however, suffering and impotence, besides being the data of middle-class life, are seen as forms of a failure to be male – a failure from which patriarchy allows no respite.

The Generation Game

To describe as patriarchy the law which decrees suffering and impairment (if only as motors for dramatic action) and decrees them unequally for men and for women, is also to raise the problem of generations. The castration which is at issue in the melodrama (and according to some writers in all narrative forms) is not an a-historical, a-temporal structure. On the contrary it is permanently renewed within each generation. The perpetuation of symbolic sexual division only takes place in so far as it is the Father who perpetuates it.

It is not just the place of the man relative to the woman, but that of the parent (male) relative to the children, which is crucial here. Melodrama enacts, often with uncanny literalness, the 'family romance' described by Freud – that is to say the imaginary scenario played out by children in relation to their paternity, the asking and answering of the question: whose child am I (or would I like to be)? In addition to the problems of adults, particularly women, in relation to their sexuality, the Hollywood melodrama is also fundamentally concerned with the child's problems of growing into a sexual identity within the family, under the aegis of a symbolic law which the Father incarnates. What is at stake (also for social-ideological reasons) is the survival of the family unit and the possibility for individuals of acquiring an identity which is also a place within the system, a place in which they can both be 'themselves' and 'at home', in which they can simultaneously enter, without contradiction, the symbolic order and bourgeois society. It is a condition of the drama that the attainment of such a place is not easy and does not happen without sacrifice, but it is very rare for it to be seen as radically impossible. The problems posed are always to some extent resolved. Only in Ophuls' *Letter from an Unknown Woman*, where Lisa dies after the death of her (fatherless) child, are all the problems laid out in all their poignancy, and none of them resolved.

Hysteria and Excess
The tendency of melodramas to culminate in a happy end is not unopposed. The happy end is often impossible, and, what is more, the audience knows it is impossible. Furthermore a 'happy end' which takes the form of an acceptance of castration is achieved only at the cost of repression. The laying out of the problems 'realistically' always allows for the generating of an excess which cannot be accommodated. The more the plots press towards a resolution the harder it is to accommodate the excess. What is characteristic of the melodrama, both in its original sense and in the modern one, is the way the excess is siphoned off. The undischarged emotion which cannot be accommodated within the action, subordinated as it is to the demands of family/lineage/inheritance, is traditionally expressed in the music and, in the case of film, in certain elements of the *mise en scène*. That is to say, music and *mise en scène* do not just heighten the emotionality of an element of the action: to some extent they substitute for it. The mechanism here is strikingly similar to that of the psychopathology of hysteria. In hysteria (and specifically in what Freud has designated as 'conversion hysteria') the energy attached to an idea that has been repressed returns converted into a bodily symptom. The 'return of the repressed' takes place, not in conscious discourse, but displaced onto the body of the patient. In the melodrama, where there is always material which cannot be expressed in discourse or in the actions of the characters furthering the designs of the plot, a conversion can take place

into the body of the text. This is particularly the case with Minnelli. It is not just that the characters are often prone to hysteria, but that the film itself somatises its own unaccommodated excess, which thus appears displaced or in the wrong place. This is the case both in the musicals (*The Pirate, Meet Me in St Louis*, etc.), which tend to be much more melodramatic than others from the same studio and where the music and dancing are the principal vehicles for the siphoning of the excess but where there may still be explosions of a material that is repressed rather than expressed; and in the dramas proper, where the extreme situations represented turn up material which itself cannot be represented within the convention of the plot and *mise en scène*.

It should be stressed that the basic conventions of the melodrama are those of realism: i.e. what is represented consists of supposedly real events, seen either 'objectively' or as the summation of various discrete individual points of view. Often the 'hysterical' moment of the text can be identified as the point at which the realist representative convention breaks down. Thus in the scene in *The Cobweb* where the lake is being dragged for Stevie's body there is no certainty either as to what is being represented (is the woman Stuart is talking to Meg or is it Karen?) or as to whose point of view, if anybody's, is being represented. The breakdown of the stable convention of representation allows such questions to be temporarily suspended in favour of what is, at one level, simple narrative confusion, but on another level can be seen as an enactment of a fantasy that involves all the characters whom the plot has drawn together. At the level of this collective fantasy, Stevie is Stuart's and Meg's 'child' and therefore the child Stuart could have had by Meg, did he not already have children by Karen (from whom he is estranged). The possibility of Stevie being dead brings this submerged fantasy to the surface, but not directly into the articulation of the plot. Realist representation cannot accommodate the fantasy, just as bourgeois society cannot accommodate its realisation.

Provisional Conclusion
Melodrama can thus be seen as a contradictory nexus, in which certain determinations (social, psychical, artistic) are brought together but in which the problem of the articulation of these determinations is not successfully resolved. The importance of melodrama (at least in the versions of it that are due to Ophüls, Minnelli, Sirk) lies precisely in its ideological failure. Because it cannot accommodate its problems, either in a real present or in an ideal future, but lays them open in their shameless contradictoriness, it opens a space which most Hollywood forms have studiously closed off.

Notes on Sirk and Melodrama

LAURA MULVEY

From *Movie*, no. 25, Winter 1977/78, pp. 53–6.

IT HAS been suggested (for example, by Paul Willemen in 'Distanciation and Douglas Sirk', *Screen* vol. 12 no. 2, and 'Towards an Analysis of the Sirkian System', *Screen* vol. 13 no. 4; and by Stephen Neale in 'Douglas Sirk', *Framework*, no. 5) that the interest of Hollywood 50s melodrama lies primarily in the way that fissures and contradictions can be shown, by means of textual analysis, to be undermining the films' ideological coherence, contradictions of a kind, whether on the level of form or of narrative incident, that seem to save the films from belonging blindly to the bourgeois ideology which produced them. This argument depends on the premise that the project of this ideology is to conjure up a coherent picture of a world by concealing the incoherence caused by exploitation and oppression. In this view a text which defies unity and closure is quite clearly progressive. Although this line of argument has been productive and revealing, there is a way in which it has been trapped in a kind of Chinese box quite characteristic of melodrama itself. Ideological contradiction is the overt mainspring and specific content of melodrama, not a hidden, unconscious thread to be picked up only by special critical processes. No ideology can even pretend to totality: it must provide an outlet for its own inconsistencies. This is the function of 50s melodrama. It works by touching on sensitive areas of sexual repression and frustration; its excitement comes from conflict not between enemies, but between people tied by blood or love.

If this view of melodrama as a safety valve for ideological contradictions centred on sex and the family seems to deprive it of possible redemption as progressive, it also places it in the context of wider problems. The workings of patriarchy, the mould of feminine unconscious it produces, have left women largely without a voice, gagged and deprived of outlets (of a kind supplied, for instance, by male art), in spite of the crucial social and ideological functions women are called on to perform. In the absence of any coherent culture of oppression, the simple fact of recognition has aesthetic importance; there is a dizzy satisfaction in witnessing the way that sexual difference under patriarchy is fraught, explosive and erupts dramatically into violence within its own private stamping ground, the family. While the Western and the gangster film celebrate the ups and downs endured by men of action, the melodramas of Douglas Sirk, like the tragedies of Euripides, probing pent-up emotion, bitterness and disillusion well known to women, act as a corrective.

Roughly, there are two different initial standpoints for melodrama. One is coloured by a female protagonist's dominating point of view which acts as a source of identification. The other examines tensions in the family, and between sex and generations; here, although women play a central part, their point of view is not analysed and does not initiate the drama. Helen Foley (in an article 'Sex and State in Ancient Greece' in *Diacritics*) provides a background to the second of these standpoints when she argues from the plays of Aeschylus that over-valuation of virility under patriarchy causes social and ideological problems which the drama comments on and attempts to correct: 'male characters ... overly concerned with military and political glory at the expense of domestic harmony and their own children', and 'the emotional, domestic sphere cannot be allowed direct political power and the wife must subordinate herself to her husband in marriage; but the maternal or domestic claims are nevertheless central and inviolable, a crucial check on bellicose male-dominated democracy.' For family life to survive, a compromise has to be reached, sexual difference softened, and the male brought to see the value of domestic life. As art and drama deal generously with male fantasy, a dramatic rendering of women's frustrations, publicly acting out an adjustment of balance in the male ego is socially and ideologically beneficial. A positive male figure who rejects rampant virility and opposes the unmitigated power of the father, achieves (at least by means of a 'happy end') the re-integration of both sexes in family life. The phallocentric, castration-based, more misogynist fantasies of patriarchal culture are here in contradiction with the ideology of the family, and in melodrama are sacrificed in the interests of civilisation and reaffirmation of the Oedipus complex. (Rafe, for instance, in *Home from the Hill* re-establishes the family and 'feminine' values on the grave of his over-bearing father.) But, as Sirk and critics have pointed out, the strength of the melodramatic form lies in the amount of dust the story raises along the road, a cloud of over-determined irreconcilables which put up a resistance to being neatly settled in the last five minutes.

Sirk, in the two films on which he had virtual independence (*Tarnished Angels* and *Written on the Wind*, both produced by Albert Zugsmith), dealt with the problems raised by this particular contradiction (the melodrama articulated by male Oedipal problems) with minimal attention to a standardised happy end. He turns the conventions of melodrama sharply in the direction of tragedy as he shows his pre-Oedipal adult protagonists Roger Shumann and Kyle Hadley (both played by Robert Stack) tortured and torn by the accoutrements of masculinity, phallic obsessions which caricature actual emotional dependence and fear of impotence, finally bringing death.

Death as used by Sirk, unlike the death of the patriarch devoured by his sons (see Freud's *Totem and Tabu*) does not produce a new, positive reconciliation but provides an extremely rare epitaph, an insight on man as victim in patriarchal society, pursued specifically by castration anxiety; castration anxiety not (as is common) personified by a vengeful woman but presented *dread*fully and without mediation. However, it is only in dealing with the male unconscious that Sirk approaches complexities nearing the tragic. His Universal movies deal more specifically with women and work more clearly within melodramatic conventions.

Significantly, discussions of the difference between melodrama and tragedy specify that while the tragic hero is conscious of his fate and torn between conflicting forces, characters caught in the world of melodrama are not allowed transcendent awareness or knowledge. 'In tragedy, the conflict is within man; in melodrama, it is between men, or between men and things. Tragedy is concerned with the nature of man, melodrama with the habits of men (and things). A habit normally reflects part of nature, and that part functions as if it were the whole. In melodrama we accept the part for the whole; this is a convention of the form.' (R. B. Heilman, *Tragedy and Melodrama*). The melodramatic characters act out contradiction, achieving actual confrontation to varying degrees and gradually facing impossible resolutions and probable defeats. However, the implications and poignancy of a particular narrative cannot be evoked wholly by limited characters with restricted dramatic functions – they do not fully grasp the forces they are up against or their own instinctive behaviour. It is here that the formal devices of Hollywood melodrama (as analysed by Thomas Elsaesser in this anthology, pp. 43–69), contribute a transcendent, wordless commentary, giving abstract emotion spectacular form, contributing a narrative level that provides the action with a specific coherence. *Mise en scène*, rather than undercutting the actions and words of the story level, provides a central point of orientation for the spectator.

Sirk allows a certain interaction between the spectator's perception of incident, channelled through an aspect of *mise en scène*, and its overt impact within the diegesis, as though the protagonists, from time to time, *read* their dramatic situation with a code similar to that used by the audience. Although this skilful device uses some aesthetic as well as narrative aspects of the film to establish points for characters on the screen as well as for the spectator in the cinema, it cannot cover elements such as lighting or camera movement, which still act as a privileged discourse *for* the spectator.

In the opening scene of *All that Heaven Allows*, Cary (Jane Wyman) first looks at Ron (Rock Hudson) with desire, and the emotion is carried through into the second scene by means of a transition to the autumn leaves he had given her, so that we, the spectators, share with Cary the secret importance he has, as the touch of nature he has left behind marks the opening seconds of her preparation for what is to prove a barren evening at the Country Club. The children comment on Cary's red dress, interpreting it, as we do, as a sign of newly awakened interest in life and love but mistaking its object as the impotent and decrepit Harvey, her date and their preferred future stepfather. The camera does not allow the spectator to make the same mistake, establishing in no uncertain terms the formal detachment with which Cary sees Harvey, in contrast to the way in which in the previous scene Ron had been subtly extracted from the background and placed in close face-to-face with Cary.

Lighting style clearly cannot be recognised within the diegesis, and in *All that Heaven Allows* it illustrates the basic emotional division which the film is actually about: Cary's world is divided between the cold, hard light (blues and yellows) of loneliness, repression and oppression and the warmer, softer light (red/orange) of hope, emotional freedom and sexual satisfaction. In keeping with the pace and emotion generated by a particular scene, Sirk occasionally changes lighting from one shot to the next: for instance, in order to use the dramatic potential of an intricate screen which dominates Cary's confrontation with her son Ned.

Although it is impossible to better Rainer Werner Fassbinder's plot synopsis of *All that Heaven Allows* (Halliday and Mulvey (eds.), 1972) it might be useful to bring out some different emphases. The story line is extremely simple, if not minimal (concocted specifically to repeat the success of *Magnificent Obsession*) and is told strictly from a woman's point of view, both in the sense of world view (the film is structured around female desires and frustrations) and point of identification (Cary, a widow with two college-age children and a standard of life in keeping with her late husband's elevated social and economic position). The narrative quickly establishes lack (her world is sexually repressed and obsessed simultaneously, offering only impotent elderly companionship – Harvey – or exploitative lechery – Howard). She then discovers love and a potentially physically and emotionally satisfying *country* way of life in Ron Kirby, her gardener (whose resonance shifts from that of the socially unacceptable in the Country Club world to that of the independent man in harmony with nature out by the old mill where he grows trees). Cary's transgression of the class barrier mirrors her more deeply shocking transgression of sexual taboos in the eyes of her friends and children. Her discovery of happiness is then reversed as she submits to pressure and gives Ron up, resulting in a 'flight into illness'. The doctor puts her on the road to success through self-knowledge and a happy end, but by an ironic *deus ex machina* in reverse, their gratification is postponed by Ron's accident (caused by his joy at seeing Cary in the distance) and a hidden shadow is cast implicitly over their perfect, joyful acceptance of love, although as the shutters are opened in the morning, the cold, hard light of repression is driven off the screen by the warm light of hope and satisfaction.

Jon Halliday points out the importance of the dichotomy between contemporary New England society – the setting for the movie – and 'the home of Thoreau and Emerson' as *lived* by Ron. 'Hudson and his trees are both America's past and America's ideals. They are ideals which are now unobtainable ...' The film is thus posited on a recognised contradiction within the American tradition. The contemporary reality and the ideal can be reconciled only by Cary moving, as it were, *into* the dream which, as though to underline its actual ephemeral nature, is then broken at the end by Ron's accident. How can natural man and woman re-establish the values of primitive economy and the division of labour when the man is bed-ridden and incapable? How can a mother of grown children overcome the taboo against her continued sexual activity in 'civilised society', when the object of her desire is reduced to child-like dependence on her ministrations?

In other films, particularly *All I Desire, Imitation of Life* and *Tarnished Angels*, Sirk ironises and complicates the theme of the continued sexuality of mothers. The women perform professionally (from the depths of Laverne's parachute jump in *Tarnished Angels* to the heights of Lora's stardom in *Imitation of Life*) and attract the gaze of men and the curious crowd. Their problems are approached with characteristically Sirkian ambiguity as they try to brazen out their challenge to conformity as best they can. Cary, on the other hand, has no heroic or exhibitionist qualities, and the gaze and gossip of the town cause her agonies of embarrassment. It is only very occasionally that the setting and the narrative move away from Cary, and, when they do, it is significant. The gaze of Cary's friends at Sara's party is established in a scene before Cary and Ron arrive. The camera takes in the prurient voyeurism which turns the sexual association of a middle-aged woman with a younger man into an act of public indecency (this view is then expressed and caricatured by Howard's drunken assault on Cary).

Melodrama can be seen as having an ideological *function* in working certain contradictions through to the surface and re-presenting them in an aesthetic form. A simple difference, however, can be made between the way that irreconcilable social and sexual dilemmas are finally resolved in, for instance, *Home from the Hill*, and are not in, for instance, *All that Heaven Allows*. It is as though the fact of having a female point of view dominating the narrative produces an excess which precludes satisfaction. If the melodrama offers a fantasy escape for the identifying women in the audience, the illusion is so strongly marked by recognisable, real and familiar traps that the escape is closer to a daydream than a fairy story. The few Hollywood films made with a female audience in mind evoke contradictions rather than reconciliation, with the alternative to mute surrender to society's overt pressures lying in defeat by its unconscious laws.

PART TWO

With Woman in Mind

Studies in Production and Consumption

Who is Without Sin?

The Maternal Melodrama in American Film, 1930–39

CHRISTIAN VIVIANI

From *Les Cahiers de la Cinémathèque*, no. 28, July 1979.

Translated by Dolores Burdick.

MELO must be moving, and thus it has recourse – not to the grotesque, as many believe – but to situations, feelings and emotions which everyone has experienced at one time or another. These elements are juxtaposed, telescoped, multiplied, in order to maintain the pathos at an intense level, simultaneously creating both an outer layer, which seems unreal by virtue of its excessiveness, and an inner core, which calls upon a collective experience of real life. Successful melo maintains the difficult equilibrium between its narrative form – often of a baroque complexity – and its emotional content of disarming simplicity.

In this perspective, it is only natural to grant a privileged place to maternal sentiment. Disconsolate, unworthy or admirable mothers were already populating the plays of the nineteenth century, touching the spectator by appealing to the 'Oedipus' in him which/who asked nothing better than to rise to the surface. Let us recall the incest theme in Hugo's *Lucrèce Borgia* or – in an entirely different key – the *Parfum de la dame en noir* by Gaston Leroux, to pick two works at random.

In cinema, the entire edifice of Italian melo finds one of its sturdiest foundations in the mother theme, as one can clearly see in the films of Rafaello Matarazzo, or in evocative titles such as *Le Fils de personne* (Matarazzo), *Le Péché d'une mère* (Guido Brignone), *Les Enfants ne sont pas à vendre* (Mario Bonnard).

French cinema, always lukewarm and somewhat soberly elegant (and a touch boring) in its treatment of melodrama, found in the mother theme a rare occasion to give free rein to the emotions: either by honouring tested literary classics, like *La Porteuse de pain* or *La Porchade*,[1] or by featuring an actress of magnitude. Gaby Morlay was the veritable queen of these films, rivalled for a while by Françoise Rosay, who did not last as long, but who had the distinction of starring in Jacques Feyder's French masterpiece of the genre, the near-perfect *Pension Mimosas*.[2]

The theme developed just as richly in Hollywood where any star worth her salt gave in at least once in her career to the ritual of maternal suffering; either totally, in a film conceived entirely around this idea, or episodically, in a film where the idea is introduced as a side issue. (One thinks of Greta Garbo in Edmund Goulding's *Love* [1928] and Clarence Brown's *Anna Karenina* [1935] or Marie Walewska in Clarence Brown's *Conquest* [1938].) A smooth lovely face, still untouched by age but where imploring eyes are ringed with pain and greasepaint furrows, the hair streaked with appropriate silver threads delicately traced by a master hairdresser – it was a kind of rite of passage, an ordeal whereby the actress proved she was a True Actress. And then the Oscars would rain down, and the moviegoers would line up at the box office.

This type of role was also a kind of guarantee for the actress' future; it assured her that the public was ready to accept her ageing. Starting with the silents, maturing actresses used this type of film as a bridge between playing the seductress and playing 'the heavy'. There were some rather sensitive psychological analyses (*Smoldering Fires* [1924] and *The Goose Woman* [1925] – both by Clarence Brown) or attempts at serious social analysis (Henry King's *Stella Dallas* [1925]). But much earlier Griffith had already made the mother one of the central figures of his universe and had dedicated to her the first, and perhaps the finest, classic of the genre: *Way Down East* (1921), to which he gave a unique and quasi-epic breadth (three hours of running time).

During the Forties, the theme flourished exceptionally well because of the high preponderance of female viewers during the war. Only slightly hidden under 'realist' wraps, the maternal melo was in its full glory in a filmic world where femininity was organised between two poles: the pin-up (Betty Grable, Rita Hayworth) and the mother (Greer Garson). The end of the war and the progressive evolution of social mores gradually weakened the importance of something which had already been constituted as a sub-genre. The 1966 version of *Madame X* (by David Lowell Rich) tolled its death knell. Things had come full circle since one could date the birth of the genre with the first version of *Madame X*, Frank Lloyd's film of 1920. Certainly the origins of the maternal melo lie deeper and tracing its cinematic prehistory would make an exciting narrative; but let us simply say that the first version of *Madame X* fixes a certain set of elements and influences which already existed in a somewhat disparate state, fixes them into a strongly structured scenario which will serve as thematic matrix to the films that follow.

'Madame X': Eve Expelled from the Bourgeois Eden
The different versions of *Madame X* mark off the various stages of the history of Hollywood's maternal melo. In 1920, Frank Lloyd directed Pauline Frederick. In 1929, Lionel Barrymore directed Ruth Chatterton. In

1937, Sam Wood directed Gladys George. In 1966, David Lowell Rich directed Lana Turner in a production lengthily prepared by Douglas Sirk.

Madame X is an adaptation of a French play by Alexandre Bisson who seems to have left scarcely any trace in [the French] theatre, but who became a veritable war horse on Anglo-Saxon stages. Until 1966, the theatricality and 'Europeanness' of the work will be fully assumed: stage actresses play the lead,[3] and the Parisian setting of the original is maintained. We must wait until 1966 to see *Madame X* played by a movie star – Lana Turner – who had no previous stage experience. In addition, this last version transposed the story to the US and – adding the character of a Machiavellian mother-in-law (Constance Bennett) – brought the archetypal melo into a typically American social context for the first time.

The commercial failure of the 1937 version, the only failure of the four, can be explained by the refusal of its creators to make their *Madame X* either 'cinematic' or 'American'. The two earlier versions had been smash hits, addressed to a public not yet caught in the double trauma of the Wall Street crash and the coming of talkies. Theatre stars still possessed a dignity and prestige which were denied to movie stars and which predisposed them to the playing of admirable-mother roles. One can only explain the immense popularity which the already mature Ruth Chatterton met in films at the beginning of the second era on the basis of the almost mystical reverence which then surrounded actors coming from the stage already loaded with fame.[4] The moral code of old Europe still exercised a profound influence on Americans. Audiences were able to accept the fact that Madame X's fall was traceable to her adultery, committed in a moment of frenzy and expiated in lifelong maternal suffering.

One could also wink at the nobly theatrical and studied character of her suffering which, in a way, seemed to set the pose for posterity. But 1929 jostled the mind-set. Under the pressures of necessity America strengthened its nationalism and isolationism: internal problems needed attention and the time was no longer right for an admiring tenderness towards Old Europe. Cinema reflected this changing politics.

A careful study of dates shows the American cinema progressively eliminating Europe from the majority of its films after 1930; Europe is only tolerated when described with the irony of comedy or when fixed in an historic past envisaged as a simple romantic setting. This Americanisation of Hollywood cinema, which had been cosmopolitan in the silent era and would go back to cosmopolitanism in the Forties, was particularly clear in the melo; we witness the close of Garbo's career and the end of Dietrich's 'serious' period. In this context, the *Madame X* of 1937, faithful to tradition, and played 'as though on stage' by Gladys George, seemed a prehistoric fossil. The critics took note of the old-fashioned nature of the film and the public stayed away. Moreover, so many maternal melos had bloomed between

1929 and 1937 which had created strong and valid causes for the mother's 'fall' other than her breaking of a rigoristic moral code that the plight of Gladys George's Madame X must have seemed totally disproportionate to her initial fault.

The influence of *Madame X* on the whole sub-genre it more or less launched is not of an ideological order: the failure of the 1937 version proves that much. This influence was rather of a structural and dramaturgical nature. A woman is separated from her child, falls from her social class and founders in disgrace. The child grows up in respectability and enters established society where he stands for progress (in *Madame X* he becomes a lawyer). The mother watches the social rise of her child from afar; she cannot risk jeopardising his fortunes by contamination with her own bad repute. Chance draws them together again and the partial or total rehabilitation of the mother is accomplished, often through a cathartic trial scene. Let us note that if the American films of the golden age often showed the story of a success and a rise to fame, *Madame X* and the maternal melos tended to show the reverse: the story of a failure and a descent to anonymity or oblivion. Happy endings in this genre are as common as unhappy endings, but the former often have a false or tacked-on quality, do not really affect the basic pessimism of the maternal melo and may be used by talented film-makers as an unconscious prolongation of the characters' desire. Think of the oneiric aspect of the ending of von Sternberg's *Blonde Venus* (1932), for example: a gleaming Dietrich, swathed in furs, repeating the fairy tale she had been reciting to her child at the opening of the film.[5]

Madame X had two lines of progeny. Its legitimate off-spring constitute a small, clearly delimited group of films in which we see the 'European' vein of Hollywood's maternal melo. The bastard offspring are much more numerous and varied and make up what we can call an 'American' line of the sub-genre.

The Children of 'Madame X'
The impact of the first two versions of *Madame X* was such that a good number of maternal melos went on to borrow from Bisson's play, even copied it outright, blurring the original's outlines with more or less skill. These films, direct descendants of the model, were generally characterised by a European setting, sometimes situated in a recent past (turn-of-the-century, early twentieth); the mother's fall from grace was symbolised by a tormented odyssey which marked an opposition to the permanence of the bourgeois household, veritable ideal of this thematic, totally impregnated by Victorian morality. This European vein of maternal melo developed before Roosevelt's coming to power, except for the *Madame X* of 1937, whose failure we discussed above, and certain films with Kay Francis made when her career was already declining.[6] (Joe May's *Confession* [1937] was a remake of a

German film starring Pola Negri.) In addition to the films of Kay Francis, which were already marked by a certain theatricality and Europeanness, this whole vein can practically be defined in five specific films. In *Sarah and Son* (Dorothy Arzner, 1930) Ruth Chatterton easily repeated her success of the previous year in Barrymore's *Madame X*. *East Lynne* (Frank Lloyd, 1931) was the nth version of an old British classic, treated in films since 1912. *The Sin of Madelon Claudet* (Edgar Selwyn, 1931) brought to Helen Hayes, great lady of the stage, the cinematic consecration of the Oscar. The *Blonde Venus* of the next year trafficked in traditional structures tinged with a certain intellectual perversity. *The Secret of Madame Blanche* (Charles Brabin, 1933) went back to the same materials with conscientious application.

At the outset of the story, one finds the bourgeois Eden: the home. Before the Fall, Ann Harding (*East Lynne*), Kay Francis (*House on 56th Street*, *Confession*) or Gladys George (*Madame X*) know a semblance of happiness in the lovingly preserved comfort of a great house dominated by an immense staircase,[7] filled with discreet and faithful servants and lit up by the presence of a child. *East Lynne* is the name of a house and *The House on 56th Street* (Robert Florey, 1933) tells the story of a house. *Blonde Venus* is quite different, since it starts out by isolating the married couple in a crowded, uncomfortable little apartment, thus operating a critique on the pettiness of this domestic ideal and the irony that lay in making it an ideal at the very moment when the economic crisis had made this kind of home truly mythic. This statement of frustration was further underscored by the recital of a fairy tale, mentioned earlier, which simultaneously betrayed both the need for an ideal and its lack. This petit-bourgeois couple tells a fairy tale which is in fact only an episode of their own past, prettified by nostalgia.

At the exact opposite of this idealisation, we find the dance hall and the furnished room at the opening of *Sarah and Son*, the music hall of *The Secret of Madame Blanche* and the painter's studio of *The Sin of Madelon Claudet* which establish a more realistic, more tawdry or desperate ambiance. In contrast, the music hall of *The House on 56th Street* is painted with affection and brilliancy, like some carefree paradise. But it is a derisory paradise, ready to crumble. The man, authoritarian and rigid, unquestioned master of the place, is assimilated to a wrathful, Biblical God-the-Father (Conrad Nagel in *East Lynne*, Warren William in *Madame X*): Eve commits the sin (adultery) in thought (*East Lynne*) or deed (*Madame X*) and what follows is nothing but a modern transformation of the myth of Eve's Fall. But the man can also be emotionally weak (Philip Holmes in *The Secret of Madame Blanche*, Neil Hamilton in *The Sin of Madelon Claudet*), physically weak (Herbert Marshall in *Blonde Venus*) or both (Ruth Chatterton's husband in *Sarah and Son*): then it is he, as a vulnerable Adam, who drags Eve down into the Fall. However, he often pays for his weakness with his life (Philip Holmes in *The Secret of Madame Blanche* and *Sarah and Son*, Gene Raymond in *The House on 56th Street*) and leaves the woman alone to bear a burden for which he is at least partly responsible.

There remains the child, whose mother is separated from him (*East Lynne, Madame X*) or who is quickly doomed to separation (*The Sin of Madelon Claudet, The Secret of Madame Blanche, Sarah and Son, The House on 56th Street*). Thus punished in her motherhood, the woman begins a downward trajectory which is often parallelled by a geographic odyssey 'toward the bottom'. Ann Harding, driven out of England, makes a long journey through Europe which will lead to her lover's death in Paris and an illness which will leave her blind (*East Lynne*). In the same way, Irene Dunne leaves England for France where she ends up running a bar for soldiers (*The Secret of Madame Blanche*). Gladys George leaves Paris for the Côte d'Azur where she finds momentary peace as a governess, then goes all the way to New Orleans where she becomes a prostitute (*Madame X*). New Orleans is also the scene of Marlene Dietrich's degradation; she becomes a streetwalker there and loses her child (*Blonde Venus*). But this latter film (like *Sarah and Son*, like *Comet Over Broadway* [Busby Berkeley, 1939] and *I Found Stella Parrish* [Mervyn LeRoy, 1935] both with Kay Francis) shows the woman's fall followed by her rise to success. Actress or singer, the woman pulls herself up by means of her talent to the pinnacle of money and fame, gaining weaponry with which to do equal battle against the society which has dispossessed her of her role as mother. Thus Ruth Chatterton rises from shady cabarets to the stage of the opera to finally be worthy of winning back her child (*Sarah and Son*). Marlene Dietrich goes by way of Paris and becomes a great music hall star, coming back in an extravagantly stylish outfit to take up her role as mother and bring back to Herbert Marshall part of the dream of which their marriage had been deprived (*Blonde Venus*). Kay Francis leaves second-rate night clubs to find fame and dignity as a dramatic artist on the English stage (*Comet Over Broadway*). These latter films, because of the personalities of their directors or their screenwriters, show – with a certain bitterness – that money alone can put a woman on an equal footing with the society that rejects her. Instead of showing us mothers burrowing into anonymity, undergoing their punishment and sacrificing themselves for the sake of their child, these films set up an opposite model of women who reconquer their dignity by coming *out* of anonymity.

One can isolate the case of Kay Francis, in whom one finds the insistent motif of the stage (*I Found Stella Parrish, Confession, Comet Over Broadway*), nostalgia for the bourgeois ideal of house and home (*The House on 56th Street* which parallels the moral decline of the woman with the physical decay of the house where she lived) and sacrifice for the daughter (Sybil Jason plays the daughter in both *Stella Parrish* and *Comet*). This last theme, the most clearly drawn, is exploited in a particularly troubling manner in *The House on 56th Street* and *Confession* where Kay Francis kills, or takes responsibility for a crime, in order to protect her daughter from falling into her own 'sin' (gambling in *House*, love of the same man in *Confession*). This treatment of the theme of motherhood corroborates the idea of a Christian vision of Eve's Fall as operating in the maternal melo, the daughter seeming ready to follow exactly the same degrading itinerary as her mother.

If Kay Francis was able to incarnate such a reactionary ideology as late as 1939,[8] it was because the outdated aspect of the plot was fortunately balanced by the cleansing speed and irony of the Warners professionals. But we must recognise that with a few exceptions here and there, the European vein of the maternal melo is eminently reactionary in the ideological perspective of the New Deal. Heroines who are submissive, resigned, sickly, even naive (Helen Hayes in *Madelon Claudet*), defenceless, lacking in energy or decisiveness were hardly good examples for the movie-going public of 1932 and 1933 who needed to be mobilised to face the economic crisis. The direct lineage of *Madame X* was an uncomfortable reminder of an earlier state of mind which had *led* to the Wall Street crash. If dramatic structures were efficient as models, it was imperative to people them with more stimulating, combative heroines, a type already implicit as the ideal of the New Deal. Already the slightly feminist coloration of *Sarah and Son*[9] and the devastating arrogance of Dietrich in *Blonde Venus* had shown the way. In 1932, with the elections coming up and with men like Darryl F. Zanuck and Philip Dunne – both rather close to Roosevelt – occupying key posts in the big studios, the American vein of the maternal melodrama was beginning to take form.

The Bastards of 'Madame X'

From Griffith on, the American cinema had been exploring an essentially American domain of film melodrama: *True Heart Susie* (1919) and *Way Down East* (1920) already contained a great number of elements which will be used again in the Thirties.

In addition to traditional elements such as the secret, the illegitimate child, the rejected woman, the seduction, the silent love, Griffith introduces the city/country dichotomy, the critique of prejudices no longer aristocratic but petit-bourgeois, even rural; the permanence of the earth, the counterpoint of the elements of nature unleashed – these are new motifs grafted onto an already constituted corpus of melodrama.

Of all these elements, the most important is doubtless the displacement of the action's social milieu. In order to become truly American, the melo had to be adapted to a society without a true aristocracy, where the moral ideal was represented by the petite bourgeoisie.[10] One can say that it was Griffith who accomplished this decisive transposition in 1918 when he made *True Heart Susie*, a rural American melodrama, and *Broken Blossoms*, a traditional melo of British origins.[11] *True Heart Susie* takes place in a context both rural and petit bourgeois, but contains no critique of the social milieu. We must wait for *Way Down East*; here the social milieu no longer serves as a mere setting, but takes on its own meaning by way of the film-maker's critical glance. Significantly, in this latter film it is an unwed mother who is in conflict with the society in power. By symbolically underscoring the struggle of Lillian Gish against the prejudices that overwhelm her, by creating the spectacular finale on the thawing river, Griffith brought out the tragic composition that maternal melo was to take in its American vein: a rejected and solitary individual who bravely tries to go against the current. All-powerful destiny has been replaced by all-powerful society.

Griffith did not have to wait long for followers. The combined influence of *Way Down East* and the first *Madame X*, both of 1920, engendered the American vein of maternal melo. Films like *So Big* (Charles Brabin, 1923), *The Goose Woman* (Clarence Brown) or *My Son* (Edward Sloman, 1925) quickly mined this lode with considerable public response. For convenience, we shall take as our initial milestone Henry King's *Stella Dallas* (1925).[12] Adapted from a popular novel by Olive Higgins Prouty, the great American specialist (along with Fanny Hurst) in lachrymose literature, *Stella Dallas* still remains a classic of the genre, thanks to the sincerity and honesty of King's treatment. He depicted the rural, petit bourgeois milieu he had already shown in the admirable *Tol'able David* (1920), a film already bearing that aftertaste of bitterness and disillusionment which was going to give such a particular tone to the great epic frescoes he was to make his domain (*Stanley and Livingstone* [1940], *Captain from Castile* [1947]). We can set *Stella Dallas* as a parallel to *Madame X* because of the presence of certain themes – maternal sacrifice, the descent into anonymity, the reinsertion of the child in the mother's life. In contrast, there are the new themes of prejudice, education, female understanding, the 'good marriage' of the children. Capital innovation: the moral sin of *Madame X* is replaced by the social error that Stella undergoes, but for which she is scarcely responsible. This new position will be quickly absorbed by the maternal melo and will be impressively fruitful after 1932, as soon as the ideals of the Roosevelt period are in the air.

To the precursor role of *Stella Dallas*, we must add the catalytic function played by *Back Street* (John M. Stahl, 1932). It is not a maternal melo, but this film started the rage for the story of 'the other woman'. This success seems almost a sociological phenomenon and is hardly surprising in a period where rejects and marginals, gangsters and fallen women, seemed to conquer instant public sympathy. Irene Dunne, playing Rae Smith, 'the woman in the back street', surely felt this when she said, in a 1977 interview with John Kobal, '*Back Street* was very popular with women. The number of letters I received from women who were living in the "back street" of a man's life, and who thought I could give them answers to their problems! Sometimes they signed their letters, but most often they didn't. They simply wanted someone to talk to....'[13]

After 1932, Frank Capra made *Forbidden*, really another version of *Back Street* with an illegitimate child added. The same remark holds true for *The Life of Vergie Winters* (Alfred Santell, 1934). In fact, if children were missing from *Back Street* (except for John Boles' legitimate children who caused many torments for poor Irene Dunne), the theme of frustrated motherhood was there: Rae, the woman condemned to the shadows, looked with envy and emotion at the children of others, legitimate children she could never hope to bear. It was easy to superimpose the figure of 'the other woman' on that of the unwed mother and even reinforce the sympathy of the (mainly female) audience for the heroine. From all these influences was born the American vein of the maternal melo. Unlike the European vein, it is rich and diverse; born a little before Roosevelt's rise to power, it would stay in favour for a very long time, up until a film like *My Foolish Heart* (Mark Robson, 1951). All the great female stars, from Bette Davis to Susan Hayward, would succumb to it.

In contrast with the weakly, pathetic heroine of the European cycle, symbolised by the little Helen Hayes of *The Sin of Madelon Claudet*, the American cycle of maternal melo proposed a decisive and energetic heroine, more liberated and autonomous, a type of which Barbara Stanwyck remains the archetype (in *Stella Dallas* [King Vidor, 1937] and especially in *Forbidden*, Frank Capra's great film). This new heroine was born around 1932, during Hollywood's period of relative freedom from censorship, which can explain the fact that in 1933 Margaret Sullavan, in her first film, gave the character its most perfect expression in the fine work of John M. Stahl, *Only Yesterday*, a film unfortunately eclipsed by the popularity of *Back Street*. In *Only Yesterday*, everything combines to exculpate the unwed mother, justifying her behaviour by her deep love for a man. She chooses anonymity of her own free will, refusing to marry a man who has forgotten her, preferring to keep a marvellous memory rather than chain him artificially through duty. She chooses to remain single, but is not abandoned. She finds honourable work and is not forced to degrade herself to support her son. When the time comes, she will even give herself once to the man she loves and who has forgotten her, accepting with a poignant vitality this chance to live only in the present moment.

Unlike what happened in the European vein, in the American vein the mother is generally *not* socially outcast, but accepted by way of her work life. Menial jobs are rather rare and usually occur only in pre-1932 samples of the genre: Constance Bennett in *Common Clay* (Victor Fleming, 1930) and Loretta Young in the remake of *Private Number* (Roy del Ruth, 1936) flee a troubled past by becoming chambermaids, but love will soon raise them from this lowly condition. Sylvia Sidney in *Jennie Gerhardt* (Mario Gering, 1935)

91

is, on the other hand, exploited because of her status as a domestic even if the critical plot, based on Dreiser, has been somewhat softened in the adaptation. Finally, poor Winifred Westover goes through a veritable calvary of the struggling, uneducated woman in *Lummox* (Herbert Brenon, 1930). In general the woman has an honourable job which makes use either of her aptitudes for devotion (a journalist in *Forbidden*, a nurse in *Born to Love* [Paul Stein, 1931], a secretary in *That Certain Woman* [Edmund Goulding, 1937]) or of her artistic gifts (a milliner in *The Life of Vergie Winters*, a decorator in *Only Yesterday* and in Gregory La Cava's *Gallant Lady* [1933] and Sidney Lanfield's remake, *Always Goodbye* [1938], a music teacher in *Wayward* [Edward Sloman, 1932]).

Socially accepted through her work, it is very rare that she becomes a prostitute like poor Clara Bow in *Call Her Savage* (John Francis Dillon, 1933) or that she doesn't work at all like Barbara Stanwyck in *Stella Dallas*. Integrated into the world of work, she unconsciously participates in the general effort to bring America out of the crisis; she is set up as an antagonist to a hoarding, speculating society, repository of false and outworn values. Often described acerbically, this society is rich but idle, thus sterile, and it is the sacrifice of 'the other woman' and the presence of her bastard child which, in a certain sense, end up placing society in the perspective of hope for social progress.[14]

If the woman is accepted in her environment through her work, morally she is still more or less rejected. We have here the residue of an outworn morality, dictated by the rich and idle society, stigmatised and swept away by the morality of these films. No film is clearer on this point than the fine *Stella Dallas*. Stella, to whom Barbara Stanwyck lends a moving mixture of strident vulgarity and overflowing sentiment, acts throughout the film as though she were guilty of something. The cowardice of John Boles has managed to convince her that she is guilty of having been born into a lower social class and for lacking either the means or the will to rise. Vidor, who seems never to have finished settling his accounts with a certain petit bourgeois American mentality,[15] makes the subject far more than a simple anecdote, and confers on it a burgeoning complexity found in few melodramas (except perhaps in Capra's *Forbidden*). He gives us the portrait of an uncultivated, generous woman, all emotion and impulse, who does not realise that the 'good society' she admires so much is injuring her, and who, in a tragic and absurd sacrifice, ends up stripping herself of everything in the name of that society which has cast her as an inferior. If Vidor's version lacks the padded softness of Henry King's (cf. Ronald Coleman's courting of Belle Bennett at the opening of the silent version), it has, on the other hand, added a stifled rage which makes the ending seesaw towards veritable tragic-grandeur: the wedding of Stella's daughter offered as a spectacle to anonymous passersby, whom a policeman disperses.[16]

In *Stella Dallas*, misfortune comes from the city. John Boles, ruined by bankruptcy, and then by his father's suicide, comes to work in a small town. With the promise of social betterment, he abandons Stella and their daughter, who are in his way, and returns to the rich heiress who incarnates his own easy and symbolically sterile ideal. Boles represents the false values of the city and is bearer of destruction (suicide, bankruptcy, sterility). Stanwyck represents the true values of the country – generosity, abnegation, fertility. She finds an unexpected ally in Barbara O'Neil, the rich heiress, who offers Stella's daughter the values of culture and civilisation which, added to the simple and basic values inculcated by the mother, will permit city and country to join in an ideal of progress of which Stella's daughter will be the heir and repository. In a philosophy one could compare with that of Joan Crawford's films of this era, the ideal of the New Deal is incarnated halfway between city and country at the cost of heavy sacrifice from each, and thanks to female solidarity.[17]

This idealisation of the country is already found in Griffith's *Way Down East*. *The Sin of Madelon Claudet* also suggested it through its idyllic depiction of Madelon's youth on a farm. But it is perhaps *So Big* (1932), William Wellman's fine remake of Charles Brabin's 1923 silent, which really puts the issue at the centre of the maternal melo. Made a year before Roosevelt's coming to power, *So Big* – like many Hollywood films of that crucial year – bears an ideal rather close to Roosevelt's (cf. Wellman's western epic *The Conquerors*) which would tend to confirm the theory of connections uniting Roosevelt to certain Hollywood personalities (mainly at Warners or Fox, like Darryl F. Zanuck, producer of *So Big*). In this Wellman film, a social itinerary doubled by a moral and philosophical one (Thoreau and Whitman are not far away) make Barbara Stanwyck move from the role of city woman to that of country woman through a series of losses (two widowings, a financial failure, the moral loss of her son who denies the 'heritage' of his mother), losses which lead her towards happiness and wisdom, close to the earth and happy in the success of a young man to whom she has become attached. Here Stanwyck incarnates an archetype of the eternal mother (which the script drives home by depriving her of a male companion) linked, naturally, to the earth envisaged as an inexhaustible and permanent source of riches. In this adjusting of the pantheistic philosophies of Thoreau and Whitman to the needs of the crisis, women, once again, play a central role. They are the keepers of true values, shown by the complicity linking Stanwyck to Bette Davis, fiancée of Stanwyck's son, a girl who is a double for the Stanwyck of the film's opening, and who gives us a gleam of hope for the young man's future. Finally, success is represented once more by a character 'between country and city', who, because he is an artist, has a privileged, quasi-mystical rapport with nature.

Perhaps *Call Her Savage* carries to its ultimate expression this theme of the return to the earth: Clara Bow, more 'American' than 'natural' in behaviour, after going through frightful vicissitudes worthy of Madame X, returns to the country of her Indian forebears and finds happiness with an attractive half-breed (Gilbert Roland); the half-breed motif is symbolic, of course, since Clara herself is depicted as the daughter of an upper middle-class woman and an Indian chief.

The symbolic child who carries within him the salvation and progress of a society which has just undergone a real-life setback – the mother often gives him up of her own free will, while in the European cycle, the child was *taken away* from her. The mother gives up her child to insure him an education, a moral training that only a well-placed family can provide him. The mother's first reaction to the birth of her child is to reject him (Helen Hayes in *Madelon Claudet*, Barbara Stanwyck in *Forbidden*, Ann Harding in *Gallant Lady*); she then accepts him briefly, then realises that her single state can only lead the upbringing process to failure. She allows herself to be convinced to give the child to a childless family which is often that of the natural father (*Forbidden, Vergie Winters, Give Me Your Heart*). In sum, the maternal melo plays – sometimes with a certain cunning – on two levels. It seems outwardly attached to the old moral code by making the mother pay for her 'sin'. But it implicitly condemns the old system of values represented by a sterile or unhappy couple, which is obliged to adopt the bastard child in order to offer up the image of a traditional family. The only notable exception: *Only Yesterday*, where Margaret Sullavan rears her child by herself. In general, the ruse comes out, as in *Vergie Winters*; or the death of the 'legitimate' wife ends it by permitting the constitution of another family, united by both love and blood (*Gallant Lady, Always Goodbye, That Certain Woman*).

Give Me Your Heart (Archie Mayo) pushes to the absurd the creation of a new family around the child: the illegitimate son of Patric Knowles and Kay Francis, adopted by the married couple Patric Knowles/Frieda Inescourt, unites, thanks to the plotting of the two women, two couples around him: Kay Francis/George Brent, the American couple, and Knowles/Inescourt, the English couple. The bastard is a carrier of life, destined to regenerate a paralysed society. This role is particularly obvious in *Only Yesterday* where, on learning of his paternity, John Boles – ruined in the Wall Street crash – decides against suicide and takes care of the child Margaret Sullavan leaves him upon her death.

These films recount the tale of a woman's loss due to a man's lack of conscience and show her reconquering her dignity while helping her child re-enter society thanks to her sacrifices. It is a clear metaphor for an attitude America could adopt in facing its national crisis. *Only Yesterday* is a case in point; the sentimental errors of John Boles are clearly associated with his financial errors, for his stock market speculations ruin him. The entire American vein of maternal melo reflects the era and describes a society in transition, coming close to tragedy in this twilight preoccupation (the end of a world), for melodrama is only the illegitimate child of tragedy.

Between the respectable family, which represents the dying world, and the mother, who represents hope for the future, we find the man. In these films, he is usually a strange and weak-willed character, rarely played by a great star, a person who hasn't the courage to make up his own mind and who relies on the family to make decisions. This sometimes turns into an Oedipal conflict between mother and son, as in *Wayward* which indeed treats the struggle between two women for the affection of a man – Nancy Carroll, his sweetheart, and Pauline Frederick, his mother.[18] The weapon of the decadent family being hypocrisy (*Wayward, Common Clay, Private Number, Give Me Your Heart, That Certain Woman*), it is often through a ruse that the 'real' mother regains her rights (*Gallant Lady, Wayward, Always Goodbye*), or else by accident (*That Certain Woman, The Life of Vergie Winters*). Indisputably, the entire genre tends to establish the recognition of the rights of the natural mother. A refusal of such recognition is rare and resounds in a particularly poignant manner. The pessimism of *Forbidden* is almost unique: the final action of Barbara Stanwyck tearing up the will that recognises her as the mother of Adolphe Menjou's daughter, and which leaves her the fortune, is not an ultimate sacrifice, but an act of revolt and refusal. Compare this attitude with the serenely assumed independence of Margaret Sullavan in *Only Yesterday* and the tragic absurdity of the ending of *Stella Dallas*.

One can find a separate fate for *The Old Maid* (Edmund Goulding, 1939), one of Bette Davis' greatest successes. Set in nineteenth-century America (George Brent dies in the Civil War, leaving Bette Davis pregnant), it explores an era and a society where the unwed mother cannot for a moment contemplate rearing her own child. In order to remain near her daughter, she is forced to undergo all the torments and humiliations caused by the sick jealousy of her horrible cousin (Miriam Hopkins, more viperous than ever) and to become an object of fear and ridicule in the eyes of her own child. It is significant that in order to show such a subject in 1939, one must have recourse to a rather considerable temporal distance. *The Old Maid* is different from the other American maternal melos because the heroine comes from 'good family', is not cast out of her social class because of her child, but rather chooses silence and anonymity. This very sentimental film is not however without tragic resonances in its depiction of a society tearing itself apart and has a crepuscular atmosphere that can lead us to consider it the final point of the maternal cycle as developed in the Thirties in Hollywood. In many points (female jealousy, sentimentality, the personality of Bette Davis) *The Old Maid* already announces the forms that maternal melo will take in the Forties with films like *The Great Lie* (Edmund Goulding, 1941) or *To Each His Own* (Mitchell Leisen, 1946).

The Old Maid, unlike the other maternal melos of the Thirties, is isolated in a sort of 'placeless timelessness'. In becoming Americanised, the maternal melo had become more and more inflected toward the social, except in this film. For proof we have only to look at *Jennie Gerhardt*, a rather mediocre film despite a still vibrant Sylvia Sidney, but which clearly presents the sorrows of the unwed mother in a perspective of class prejudice.[19] The moral sin of the 'European-style' melos is replaced by a social error, vestige of a bad system stigmatised by the film: Sylvia Sidney in *Jennie Gerhardt*, Constance Bennett in *Common Clay* or Loretta Young in *Private Number* are all more or less victims of a form of '*droit de cussiage*' ('groper's rights') because of their position as servants. On the other hand, women who do 'noble' work (decorators, journalists, secretaries) find in their work the strength to bear the ordeals and problems of their lives: a sort of independence, a way of balancing the unstable nature of their condition as unwed mothers. This stability is reinforced by the presence of a man, product of the world of work, who sustains the heroine and loves her in silence (Ian Hunter in a number of Kay Francis' films).

In short, work, a social value, redeems the moral fault by permitting the mother to hide both her guilty liaison and her child. The reactionary nature of these works seems scarcely dented by the switching of accent to the social, for the mother now pays for her fault no longer through a veritable degradation, but by being condemned to anonymity, the true curse in the Hollywood thematics of the Thirties, totally geared to the success story and the rise to fame. In this regard there is hardly any difference between films after Roosevelt's accession, and a film like *Lummox* (1930) where the heroine, a cleaning woman, pays for her motherhood with a life of humiliation and anonymity.

The maternal melo in its American vein is an apologia for total renunciation, total sacrifice, total self-abnegation. Melodramatic exaggeration, of course, but still transparent enough in a period when America really needed to mobilise good will and dedication without promise of immediate recompense; witness the numerous 'unhappy endings' one finds in the sub-genre. While scrupulously respecting established dramatic structures, conscientious craftsmen and talented film-makers made movies of high quality which it would be interesting to study anew and subject to critical appraisal: *Common Clay, So Big, Gallant Lady, Vergie Winters, That Certain Woman*. Others created masterpieces whose scope makes them transcend the simple limits of a genre: *Forbidden, Blonde Venus, Only Yesterday, Stella Dallas, The Old Maid*. These film-makers and stars worked in a strict form whose rules they respected. The case of George Cukor and Constance Bennett is somewhat different.

Between 1930 and 1933, Constance Bennett was extremely popular, and was thus able to command very high salaries. In addition, she was the only major star of the time who was not attached to a given studio and who negotiated her own contracts with a legendary shrewdness. She specialised in the wildest melodrama, which seems strange if we consider her aristocratic bearing, sophistication and witty cynicism, so out of keeping with her roles of simple shopgirls, and so much more in tune with comedy, in which she also excelled. Her personality seemed to allow her to act her way through the most extravagant situations with a sort of ironic detachment that resembled a wink of complicity at the audience: basically, it was a way of getting the viewer's sympathy as valid perhaps as the pure and simple 'identification' that happened with a Barbara Stanwyck, for example. Constance Bennett often worked with directors intelligent enough to make use of the very ambiguity of her persona: Gregory La Cava and George Cukor were among the decade's best comic directors and Victor Fleming had a great sense of humour. But there was a privileged relationship between Bennett and Cukor; she found in him her ideal director. For his part, Cukor was floundering a bit at the beginning of his film career, having difficulty getting rid of the influence of theatre. He was stimulated by his association with Bennett, and out of their meeting came his first major film, *What Price Hollywood* (1932), a first version of *A Star is Born*, far from the polished work of 1954, to be sure, but certainly far more than a simple sketch. Cukor's approach differs radically from that of other directors in that he managed when necessary to suppress the ironic distancing in Bennett and to weld her very artificiality into the character he gave her to play. Thus, in the role of a movie actress, she is credible and moving from start to finish in *What Price Hollywood*, or in *Our Betters*, where she plays cruel and bitter social comedy like a virtuoso.

Cukor and Bennett made their contribution to the maternal cycle (in which the actress had already participated with films like *Common Clay* or *Born to Love*) in a strange work which curiously mingles melo and comedy – *Rockabye* (1933). For an actress who had already played the suffering mother, *Rockabye* was a subtle, almost Machiavellian exposé of the workings of maternal melo. A successful actress and a frustrated mother, she is separated from her adopted child and then from the man in her life, because his wife is expecting a child. With nothing more than this Cukor was able to ironise the traditional structures: instead of bearing an unwanted child, Bennett here takes the trouble to go out and adopt! *She* is sterile, while the 'legal wife' gives birth. In addition, the Bennett character acts in a play called *Rockabye*, written by the man she loves and which seems a veritable parody of numerous contemporary melos like *Call Her Savage* or *Blonde Venus*: the abandoned mother finds herself walking the streets in order to earn her living and support her child! In this film the clichés are given as clichés: everything is false and the melodrama is nothing but a show, an indirect way of denouncing the illusionism of the genre. The miracle is that in spite of everything, *Rockabye* contains natural and moving scenes, and that the artificial calvary of this actress manages to be touching through attention to detail and truth of emotion.

The point of *Rockabye* was that the maternal melo was only convention and illusion. But that is exactly what melo had to be – an illusion destined to mobilise the public in a certain direction, an illusion that transposed the anguish of an era, an illusion – who can deny it? – knowingly grounded in eroticism. The attractiveness of the actress was important, of course, but also the Oedipal theme which runs like filigree throughout Hollywood cinema from 1930 to 1945, and which a film like *Random Harvest* (Mervyn LeRoy, 1942) will set forth in nearly Freudian terms. And besides, what male viewer has never dreamed of being fondled by a desolate and arousing mother with the face of a Constance Bennett, a Kay Francis, a Marlene Dietrich, an Ann Harding? What female viewer has not dreamed of herself looking like an Irene Dunne, a Barbara Stanwyck, a Sylvia Sidney? The melodramatic mythology of Hollywood is doubtless false, but it is nonetheless seductive for being illusory.

Notes

1. One can compare more recent versions of these classics: *La Porteuse de pain* (Maurice Cloche, 1963) and *La Pocharde* (Georges Combret, 1954).
2. One can wonder at the large number of paternal melos in French cinema, many more than one finds in Italy or in Hollywood, but comparable to certain German productions: *Nostalgie* (Tourjanski, 1937), *Le Coupable* (Raymond Bernard, 1937), or *Nuit de décembre* (Kurt Bernhardt, 1939) and even – why not? – Pagnol's trilogy, where César is certainly the central figure.
3. Pauline Frederick and Ruth Chatterton won movie stardom in their respective versions. Gladys George was less lucky, and found herself quickly relegated to secondary roles, despite the 'name' she made on the stage.
4. This may be the only way, for example, to explain the astonishing success of the already old George Arliss at the beginning of the talkies.
5. This fairy tale, in fact, transposed into legendary terms Herbert Marshall's meeting with Marlene Dietrich: a stalwart knight, he saves her from a terrible dragon. The final reprise of this interrupted legend is thus all the more oneiric.
6. Even if her melos were often set in the US, Kay Francis was marked by the European influence. Perhaps it was her slightly formal appearance? She was hired at Warners at the same time as Ruth Chatterton and in a certain way she prologues the universe of Chatterton.
7. The staircase, symbol of power, is one of the traditional motifs of melo; for example in *Written on the Wind* (Douglas Sirk, 1956).
8. Kay Francis began to lose her popularity around 1934–35. If she hung on after that, it was thanks to an ironclad contract that made her the highest paid star of the moment, even if her films had only middling success or if they were sometimes not much better than B pictures.

9. If Dorothy Arzner is interesting because she was the only woman director then working in Hollywood, her feminist hagiographers have based too much of their admiration on the ideas in her work, without really taking into account the rarity of fine films in her output. *Sarah and Son*, for example, is rather heavy handed. One exception: the excellent *Craig's Wife* (1936), well served by Sidney Buchman's brilliant script.

10. This was already the case in Josef von Sternberg's *Blonde Venus*, not without irony. The petit-bourgeois setting was already in place in the shorts of Griffith, like *The New York Hat* (1912).

11. Although it was made before *Broken Blossoms*, *True Heart Susie* was released immediately after. But Griffith remained faithful to traditional melo; for example in *Orphans of the Storm* (1922) or *Lady of the Pavements* (1929).

12. King Vidor's film follows quite faithfully the plot of Henry King's first version. Only their very different approaches help distinguish between the two films. [The issue of *Les Cahiers de la Cinémathèque* (no. 28) in which this article was originally published, contains an appendix featuring plot outlines of all the melodramas discussed in the issue, which is entirely devoted to materials on melodrama in cinema.]

13. In *Focus on Film* no. 28: 'Irene Dunne: A Conversation with John Kobal.'

14. This antagonism is emphasised by racial differences in *Madam Butterfly* (Marion Gering, 1932), a film one could easily include in the category of Hollywood maternal melo.

15. *Stella Dallas* is certainly a work marked by the personality of this very great director; its heroine has more than one point in common with those of *Beyond the Forest* (1949) and *Ruby Gentry* (1951).

16. The framing of the scene, its lighting, even the form of the bay window where the wedding ceremony is enacted, evoke in a troubling way a cinematic spectacle.

17. This solidarity is obvious in *The Shining Hour* (Frank Borzage, 1938), where Joan Crawford and Margaret Sullavan are bound together in a series of reciprocal sacrifices. Let us also mention *Give Me Your Heart* (Archie Mayo, 1936), where Kay Francis is united with her son, thanks to the sterile wife who has adopted him.

18. This theme is luminously treated in John Cromwell's remarkable film *The Silver Cord* (1933), where Irene Dunne violently denounces the abnormal character of Laura Hope Crews' love for her son Joel McCrea.

19. It is curious to note that the work of Theodore Dreiser, a socially committed novelist, can easily be reduced to a melodramatic structure – for example, in *Carrie* (William Wyler, 1951), a fine film, strangely neglected and underrated.

Censorship and the Fallen Woman Cycle

LEA JACOBS

[This] is undoubtably an unfortunate time to bring the kept woman on the screen again and we are doing our best to make the studio heads conscious of the fact that the piling up of sex stories at the present time may bring about a situation where it will be necessary to get the studio heads together and make an agreement to lay off this type of story such as occurred when the gangster films got too numerous.[1]

James Wingate to Will Hays, MPPDA

IN THE 1930s, in the context of conflict between the film industry and various reform groups, the fallen woman film was rather loosely defined as a type, called the 'kept woman story' or more commonly, 'the sex picture'. Like the gangster film with which it was sometimes compared, the type served as a focal point for public criticism of the film industry. And, as a consequence of such criticism, it was targeted for regulation by the Motion Picture Producers and Distributors Association (MPPDA), the industry trade association responsible for censorship. In my view the fallen woman cycle offers a fruitful example for the study of self-regulation because it posed interesting and important problems at the level of representation. The cycle occasioned much debate between film producers and the MPPDA and necessitated the elaboration of industry-wide policies concerning the representation of money, illicit sexuality and the family. Here, through an examination of both contemporary and more recent critical definitions of the type, I will show how these genre conventions were identified within the social context of the 1930s and indicate the problems they posed for the industry and the MPPDA.

Art historian Linda Nochlin and literary critic Nina Auerbach have discussed the stereotyped image of the fallen woman in nineteenth-century culture.[2] This work does not deal at length with censorship, although Auerbach makes references to examples considered scandalous or shocking in the period.[3] However, the work establishes, with some precision, a formal description of the image of the fallen woman and the highly conventionalised narrative sequence of the 'fall' which generates this image. The most extensive definition of the fall is given in Auerbach's *The Woman and the Demon*, a study of representations of women in Victorian England.[4] Auerbach argues that the fall has its archetype in Milton's *Paradise Lost*. The sequence is motivated by some transgression on the part of the woman, usually a transgresssion of sexual mores such as adultery or having sex before marriage. Auerbach points out however that in British literature the sexual trespass which motivates the fall is generally elided. Rather, the narrative sequence is composed of the woman's progressive abasement and decline. This progression usually takes the form of a spatial displacement – a movement from the domestic space of the family to the public space of the street. The movement is generally accompanied by a decline in the woman's class status. Alone on the streets, she becomes an outcast, often a prostitute, suffering various humiliations which usually culminate in her death. Sometimes however, the woman is reformed, and the sequence is resolved when the woman is brought back within the family.

One example of the fall cited by Auerbach is a trilogy of paintings by Augustus Egg which apparently shocked its first audience at the Royal Academy.[5] The trilogy graphically depicts the highly conventionalised downward trajectory. The first painting, entitled *Misfortune*, is set in a well appointed drawing room. The accused woman lies prostrate before her husband; two children play in the background. The second painting, *Prayer*, is set in a poor and rather bare apartment. The children of the initial scene are absent but the woman has a female companion. In the last painting, *Despair*, the woman is beneath a bridge, looking towards a river and a city sky-line. She is poorly dressed and alone except for a baby (by convention illegitimate) which, obscured by her body, is barely visible within the frame. The fall is precisely this movement from the bourgeois drawing room to the bridge by the river, implying a loss of both class and familial status.

There are, of course, films which deal with adultery or illegitimate children prior to the 1930s. However in the early 30s Hollywood produced a large body of films which utilised and to an extent transformed the nineteenth-century convention of the fall. Film critics have proposed several names for this cycle: the confession tale (Richard Griffith), the maternal melodrama (Christian Viviani) and the fallen woman cycle (Marilyn Campbell, Betsy McLane).[6] I have decided to retain the name fallen woman cycle in order to emphasise the importance of the fall for the progression of the narrative. Like their nineteenth-century antecedents, the Hollywood films initiate a displacement – a movement away from the domestic space of the family – and movement in class, though not necessarily a *decline*.[7] Some films of the period invert the downward trajectory, proposing a *rise* in class. Examples include *Blonde Venus* (Paramount, 1932), in which the heroine becomes rich as an actress, and *Baby Face* (Warners, 1933) and *Bed of Roses* (RKO, 1933), in which the stereotypical 'kept woman' or 'gold-digger' procures money

101

from a lover. It should be noted that the heroine does not necessarily enter respectable society. I use the term 'class rise' because the films set up clear differences in monetary status. There is usually an opposition between the heroine's initial poverty and her initiation into wealth via men. The possibility of movement upward is almost always emphasised by a sequence in which the heroine is visually transformed, dressed up and surrounded by objects – furs, automobiles, diamonds – which redefine her 'class' status.

Recent film critics have proposed an historical definition of the cycle. That is to say, the narrative sequences which I call the fall and rise are explained with reference to a specific social context, in this case the Depression. In *We're in the Money* Andrew Bergman discusses the cycle as a reflection of the financial difficulties experienced by middle-class woman.[8] He lists a number of films in which the fall is motivated by economic hardship. One example cited by Bergman is *Faithless* in which the heroine becomes a prostitute to provide for her husband and sick baby. The fallen woman often becomes rich. In *Hollywood's Fallen Women Features* Betsy McLane discusses a number of films in which the heroine acquires diamonds, furs and a pent-house, enacting the stereotype of the 'kept woman'.[9] According to Richard Griffith, in an article on Depression film cycles, these films addressed the wishes or fantasies of women denied material goods because of the Depression.[10] In an article on the fallen woman film at R K O, Marilyn Campbell does not see the cycle as a response to women's financial difficulties but more generally as a result of what she calls the familial 'dislocations' characteristic of the period. She defines the type in terms of a series of 'irregular' familial relationships: women with illegitimate children, adulterous couples, criminal or kept women who live with men for money.[11]

However, contemporary accounts of the cycle are important for they provide a very different picture of how the films relate to their social context. Historians Garth Jowett and Robert Sklar have documented the array of groups and individuals – women's and church groups, educators, even some newspapers – which confronted the industry in this period.[12] Many of these groups found the fallen woman cycle particularly offensive and made their objections known both to the industry and the general public. That is to say, the genre did not simply 'reflect' the social condition of women in general but marked a disjuncture between the historical conditions of film production and the conditions of reception. The films were the site of a conflict between the film industry and specific sectors of its audience. At issue in the contemporary writing on the genre are major concerns of the reform forces – Hollywood's influence on sexual mores, on crime and juvenile delinquency. Genre conventions are identified in terms of their putative effects on real spectators.

In the 30s there was much discussion of the heroine's sexual trespasses and, in particular, violations of the ideal of female chastity. Consider a column by the film critic of *The Nation* entitled 'Virtue in 1933':

It happens that the climaxes of the two pictures seen this week, one at New York's largest theater and the other at one of its smallest, hinge on the same problem of conduct in a young girl's mind. The problem, of course, is not a particularly new one. Long ago there was a picture called *Way Down East* in which Miss Lillian Gish was to be seen grappling with it.... The only reason that one calls attention to its recurrence as a major theme at this time is that it may serve to illustrate the profound change that has come over movie producers and audiences alike in their attitude towards this and similar problems. No longer is there a certain risk of sympathy in showing the hero in the arms of his mistress, the heroine having a child by someone other than her husband, the ingenue making a few mistakes before settling down to a closer observance of conventions.[13]

The Nation takes a relatively 'moderate' view: both the industry and the public participate in a general transformation of sexual mores. But other sources, more critical of the industry, argue that this film type affirms and indeed promulgates changes in sexual mores. Take for example a discussion of the cycle in the Payne Fund Studies, the first mass communications study on the effects of film viewing. In *The Content of Motion Pictures* Edgar Dale notes: '[C]olorful and attractive stars are commonly given roles depicting women who lose their virtue, who are ruined by men, lead profligate lives.'[14] This is a 'dangerous situation' according to Dale because the use of stars in such roles makes the violation of the 'current moral code ... desirable or attractive.'[15] Thus the narrative sequence which I call the fall was recognised as a recurring feature of the cycle by its contemporaries. And the films were criticised in so far as Hollywood did not elide the transgression which motivated the fall but appeared to promote sex outside of marriage for women by making it attractive.

While much commentary was directed at the representation of sexuality within the cycle there were also complaints about the representation of money. One finds references to films which show kept women 'living in luxury' or what was rather vaguely identified as 'glamour'. Here, for example, is a letter of complaint sent to Will Hays from an employee of the MPPDA:

> Recent pictures from *[So] This is Africa*, through *Temple Drake, Baby Face*, etc. down to Constance Bennett's latest *[Bed of Roses]*, which I saw the day I got back home, and which again is the story of a criminal prostitute's methods of wangling luxury out of rich men ... the constant flow of these pictures leaves me with mental nausea...[16]

An article in *Photoplay* also bemoans the trend with an article entitled 'Charm? No! No! You Must Have Glamour'.[17] The main objection to this aspect of the cycle is that the films encourage prostitution by the representation of luxury. One newspaper columnist refers to the 'flourishing crop of loose ladies on the screen' suggesting that such films constitute a temptation for women in that the heroine gets rich – 'practical lessons in sin'.[18] The point is discussed in an academic context in *Movies, Delinquency and Crime*, one of the Payne Fund Studies. Analysing the effects of movies on 'sex delinquent' girls, the authors discuss the frequent visual representation of wealth in films:

> The girl who witnesses smart fashionable gowns in settings of splendor and luxury may find in them, in contrast to her own often cheap, flimsy, and outmoded apparel ... an irresistible appeal. In many cases the desire for luxury expresses itself in smarter and more fashionable selection of clothes, house furnishings, etc., within the financial means of the girl; but, on the other hand, many of the girls and young women studied grow dissatisfied with their own clothes and manner of living and in their efforts to achieve motion picture standards frequently get into trouble.[19]

The authors argue that in some films the visual representation of luxury is accompanied by a suggestion of criminal means of attaining it, that is prostitution. They clearly refer to stories of kept women or gold-diggers or what I call the narrative sequence of class rise.

The contemporary accounts indicate that the fallen woman cycle was recognised, if somewhat loosely defined, as a type. And as a type it brought to the fore major concerns of the reform forces. The films were held to be in violation of what Edgar Dale called 'the current moral code', to undermine normative definitions of sexuality, especially female sexuality, and to promote crime or sexual delinquency among women. The point is not to verify these claims – to ascertain if in fact the fallen woman cycle motivated women to prostitution and adultery in the 1930s. The point is that those concerns about real spectators were focused on and through two highly conventionalised narrative sequences – the heroine's sexual/moral fall and her attendant rise in class. In this social context genre conventions themselves became an issue and were eventually targeted for industry self-regulation by the MPPDA.

The regulation of the fallen woman cycle may be described in terms of the relations between the major film production companies, the MPPDA and groups critical of Hollywood in general and this cycle in particular. The function of the MPPDA was to protect the long-run interests of its member companies, the major producer-distributors.[20] By instituting industry self-censorship it sought to forestall criticism of Hollywood in the popular press and undermine public support for legislative measures, such as a federal censorship board, proposed by the advocates of reform.[21] In my view, then, censorship was a *defensive* operation which aimed at preventing the release of films which could pose some threat to the industry's long-term political and economic interests. However, individual producers, acting in their own short-run interests, frequently resisted the MPPDA's efforts to regulate production. In the perspective of the short-run, no single film was likely to provoke sustained criticism or more drastic legislative action. Thus, there were grounds for conflict between producers and their trade association because individual firms did not need to respond to the threats which confronted the industry as a whole over time. Geoffrey Shurlock, an industry censor, sums up this situation quite succinctly:

> The man who makes a film wants to find out if anybody is going to see it. That's his first consideration: will anybody go? And my consideration: is anybody complaining about it? That's our problem but not his. His problem is to get them in there.[22]

Given the conflicts between the MPPDA and the studios, it is usually argued that censorship of the fallen woman cycle, among other films, did not become effective until after 1934, following the Catholic Legion of Decency campaign and the appointment of Joseph Breen as head censor.[23] Historians suggest that it was only in the latter part of the decade that the industry's Production Code – the basic policy statement which governed the representation of topics such as adultery and illicit sex – could be enforced.[24] But a review of correspondence between producers and industry censors reveals that even prior to 1934, Jason Joy and James Wingate of the MPPDA carried out correspondence with producers and effected some revisions of both films and scripts. Thus, I prefer to think of self-regulation as a process of negotiation between censors – seeking to minimise what they deemed potentially offensive elements – and producers – who sought to retain such sensational elements, presumably in an effort to maximise profits. When public pressure on the industry increased, as it obviously did in 1933 and 1934, censors were in a position to negotiate relatively more extensive revisions of films and scripts. But, throughout the decade, the administrators of the MPPDA addressed the problems or difficulties posed by the fallen woman cycle. And there is a clear continuity in the terms in which censors discuss the films.

My aim here is to specify the various ways in which the conventions of the fallen woman cycle were identified by industry censors and became points of negotiation, hence of 'difficulty'. I rely upon MPPDA memos and correspondence with producers,[25] which permit us to make some inferences about how the complaints and criticisms of external groups were taken up by the MPPDA and brought to bear upon the production process.

For the MPPDA, a frequent point of contention was the heroine's sexual transgressions. Unlike British literature of the 19th century, in which the woman's transgression was traditionally elided, the Hollywood films often included, and even elaborated upon, this aspect of the story. Censors were concerned with the explicitness of such scenes. For example, in *The Easiest Way* (MGM, 1931) the heroine (Laura) becomes mistress to a wealthy man (Brockton). In his review of the script, Jason Joy, of the MPPDA, sought with some success to eliminate direct references to this relationship. He proposed the deletion of lines in which Laura was said to be living with a man or which used the word 'mistress'. He also proposed the revision of scenes which unambiguously showed Laura living in Brockton's apartment. He complained to the producer that 'the frank indication ... that Laura is living in Brockton's apartment plainly portrays the relationship that is more or less only delicately suggested throughout the balance of the script.'[26] He asked the producer to invent ways to play scenes so as to leave open the possibility that the couple was not living together, for example Brockton appears fully dressed at breakfast time, as if he had stopped in to 'visit'.

Joseph Breen, able to win greater concessions from producers than previous administrators, also sought to avoid the direct representation of the woman's sexual transgressions. *Private Number* (Twentieth Century-Fox, 1936) is an interesting case, for here the problem centres on details of characterisation and decor rather than lines of dialogue. The heroine's fall is precipitated by a man who takes her to what the script calls a 'gambling house' where she is subsequently arrested on a morals charge. At no point in the script is the house referred to as a house of prostitution. The point of contention between Breen and Darryl Zanuck, the producer, was the degree to which the script, and by extension the film, could indirectly suggest the nature of the heroine's liaison. Breen's objection to the script lies in the following details:

> The house is operated by Grandma Gammon, a lady suggestive of an elderly madam. There is the trim colored maid who looks through a peephole before opening the door, Cokely's winking at the maid, the drinking of champagne in a private parlour and the painting of a voluptuous lady in a harem. All tend, in our judgement, to give this house the color and flavor of a house of ill fame.[27]

Thus, even though the word prostitution is not mentioned, Breen found this scene to be too explicit at the level of atmosphere.

In general, the MPPDA's correspondence with producers focuses on the formal means by which the heroine's transgressions may be portrayed. Under the administrations of Joy and Wingate a great deal could be suggested as long as it was not explicitly avowed. In contrast, Breen was less likely to be satisfied with even an indirect representation of scenes of prostitution, adultery, or illicit sexuality. However, in my view, the difference between the two administrations is substantially one of degree. Breen was in a position to require much more extensive revisions of scripts. Thus in the case of *Private Number*, his negotiations extend beyond questions of dialogue – the use of the word 'house' or 'prostitution' – to include visual aspects of the scene.

Although censors gave much attention to the representation of the heroine's transgressions, the fall as such – the woman's explusion from the setting of the family and decline in class – did not generally pose great difficulties. Indeed, after 1934, the fall was emphasised in accordance with Breen's so-called 'system of compensating moral values', which required some form of suffering or punishment to offset violations of moral codes. This system is clearly demonstrated in the case of the 1941 remake of *Back Street* (Universal, 1932, 1941). The 1932 version of the film had been very successful and Universal was eager to re-release it in 1938. However, the film had also been criticised by the reform forces at the time of its original release; in particular, it had been attacked by Catholics connected with the Legion of Decency.[28] The story, which concerns the heroine's affair with a married man, was said to generate sympathy for the adulterers and to undermine the normative ideal of marriage as monogamous. When Breen argued against a re-release of the 1932 version, Universal agreed to do a remake.[29] Not all of Breen's suggestions for the new script were adopted, nonetheless they are important because they indicate how he would have changed the story in accordance with the 'system of compensating moral values'. He proposed the following emendations:

1. In the 1932 version, the hero, Walter, dies peacefully in the company of his mistress, Rae. Breen suggests that Walter, a diplomat, 'on the eve of his departure for London and the great international conference, is recalled from his mission in disgrace, because of his scandalous conduct – his stroke of apoplexy which causes his death being indicated as the result of the news that he has been disgraced'.

2. The heroine, Rae, is separated from Walter at the moment of his death, unlike the 1932 version.

3. A montage sequence is to be added which shows Rae's gradual degeneration after Walter's death. Rae is shown to be 'a cheap hag of a gambler', and is to be discovered in a gambling house by Walter's son, who has previously denounced her conduct.

4. The 1932 version concludes with a reprise of an earlier scene which reunites the couple in memory/fantasy. Breen's version suggests that 'when she (Rae) recognises the son she rushes out of the gambling joint and hurries back to her miserable room in a side street, to which the son follows her and where will be played the scene in which the son offers to give her $200 a month'.[30]

Breen's alterations place great emphasis on the fall – by the insistence on separating Rae from Walter at the moment of his death, by the montage sequence and the revised ending. Even Walter undergoes a fall in the proposed sequence concerning his disgrace and death. Further, in Breen's version, the fall appears as the *necessary consequence* of the transgression of moral codes. The sequence of events suggests that Walter's death and Rae's humiliation are 'caused' by their adulterous relationship. The trajectory of the fall is thus exploited as a means of censoring the 1932 version of *Back Street*. While Breen does request the inclusion of scenes in which there are explicit statements of moral principles – e.g. 'adultery is wrong' – such scenes are seconded by the logic of the narrative action which would constitute an indirect and impersonal form of commentary on the scenes of adultery.

The example of *Back Street* indicates the extent to which the fall could be consonant with the aims and strategies of censorship. In contrast, much discussion and debate surrounded those films or sequences in which the heroine became rich. The MPPDA repeatedly warned producers that the heroine's rise in class would make a film vulnerable to public criticism. Administrators also found that such films were likely to be cut at the hands of foreign censor boards or by the state boards which in this period were active in New York, Massachusetts, Kansas, Ohio, Pennsylvania, Virginia and Maryland.[31] The MPPDA's concerns about state censorship are illustrated by *Baby Face* (Warners, 1933). Both the script and the completed film are preoccupied with class rise, the narrative revolving around various exchanges of sex for money. The heroine (Lily), a poor girl from a steel town, actively pursues a series of progressively richer men, acquiring furs, a penthouse and finally, a rich husband. In his review of the initial script, James Wingate advises the producers about the probability of state intervention: 'Censor boards throughout the country are likely to analyse this picture as the story of a girl, who, by her sensual attractiveness, goes through life from one man to another and finally succeeds in marrying the president of a bank.' Wingate also refers to a 'recent MGM feature' that resembles *Baby Face* (probably *Red Headed Woman*, 1932) that was severely cut by state boards in Pennsylvania, Ohio and Maryland as well as being rejected by foreign boards in Australia and several Canadian provinces. He concludes: '[I]t is exceedingly difficult to get by with the type of story which portrays a woman who by means of her sex rises to a position of prominence and luxury ...[32] Indeed, an initial version of *Baby Face* was rejected outright by the New York state censor board.

The later administration of censorship under Breen was relatively less concerned with anticipating the actions of the state boards. However, Breen seems to have agreed with his predecessors that class rise presented a problem for the industry. In a memo on *Baby Face* written after the film's release he notes: 'This picture even as it now is ought not to suggest any jubilation on our part ... It suggests the kind or type of picture which ought not to be encouraged ...'[33] In another memo on *Camille* (MGM, 1936) he advises more tersely that 'being a mistress' should not be made 'profitable'.[34] This stance is predictable given his insistence on 'compensating moral values'. In the case of class rise, wealth follows as a direct and necessary consequence of the woman's sexual transgressions. Thus, the logic of the narrative action works against the moral code.

In treating films such as *Baby Face* censors often considered the explicitness of the scenes of the sexual transaction. They favoured the elimination of shots of physical contact, and also lines of dialogue referring to money and shots in which money changed hands. Further, at least in some cases, the MPPDA administrators raised more general questions about the film's effect on its audience. The problem was not merely how to represent the sexual transaction, but more crucially, the spectator's disposition towards the heroine's actions. Thus Wingate warns that state censor boards will reason that the acquisition of luxuries makes 'vice' attractive, inviting emulation of the heroine.[35] Jason Joy adopts a similar line of argument. In a memo enumerating the complaints likely to be made against MGM's *Red Headed Woman*, he compares the gangster and the fallen woman cycle. According to Joy, a basic criticism of the gangster film was that while the gangster was often a 'rat', he achieved money, power and notoriety, becoming attractive to audiences. Since these same elements account for the 'glamour' attached to the gold-digger, Joy predicts they are likely to be met with criticism by the advocates of moral reform.[36] Clearly, from the perspective of the MPPDA, showing a character become rich was not, in and of itself, a point of difficulty. But much discussion centred on the putative 'attractiveness' of the gold-digger insofar as her movement in class united a certain image of money and power with illicit sexuality.

In such cases there was sometimes an effort to counter the attractiveness of the gold-digger by a more or less explicit level of commentary. The simplest (and most transparent) example of this would be the denunciation scene in which the actions of the heroine are explicitly criticised by another character, a figure of moral authority. Thus, in *Baby Face*, a grandfatherly cobbler repeatedly warns the heroine that she has chosen the 'wrong way' in life. But the MPPDA does not seem to have had a single fixed routine for dealing with the representation of 'luxury'; my research so far reveals a range of devices which can be said to take on the *function* of censorship while differing considerably in their form. What is clear however is that the fallen woman cycle was defined and discussed similarly outside of the industry – in popular and academic sources – and within the industry, by the MPPDA censors. All of these sources employ terms such as 'glamour' and 'luxury' and there is general agreement that the cycle undermines accepted moral/sexual norms through the heroine's rise to wealth.

From an historical perspective, the concept of genre is often seen as a way of explaining the relationship of texts to their social contexts. For the fallen woman cycle this relationship has been conceived entirely in terms of the conditions of *reception*. Recent writing on the cycle has posed the question of its popularity or appeal in the 1930s and argued that the needs or fantasies of the audience in effect determined the emergence of the type. But, in my view, the historical interest of the fallen woman cycle lies in the rather peculiar conditions of its *production*. Their status as a coherent and recognisable type made these films vulnerable to criticism, bringing to the fore basic concerns of the reform forces about Hollywood's impact on sexual mores and behaviour. For the industry, and for the M P P D A, this criticism posed problems of representation in the most literal sense. That is to say, the problem was how to enact or invoke the conventions of the fall and/or rise. Given this, one could pose the question of how the administration of censorship mediated narrative conventions. Further, it should be possible to analyse the successive instances of the cycle as attempts to work on and around the rules of the genre, shifting emphasis, motivations, rearranging the sequence of cause and effect. Thus, the idea of genre provides a way of registering – of reading – the operations of the industry at the level of the text. It offers a means of examining, in some detail, how the tensions, the conflicts, which characterised the sphere of production surfaced in film.

Notes

1. James Wingate, Letter to Will Hays, n.d., *Jennie Gerhardt* Case File, Special Collections, Academy of Motion Picture Arts and Sciences Library, Beverly Hills.
2. Nina Auerbach, *Woman and the Demon: The Life of a Victorian Myth* (Cambridge, Massachusetts: Harvard University Press, 1982); Linda Nochlin, 'Lost and *Found*: Once More the Fallen Woman', *Art Bulletin* 60, 1978.
3. See, for example, her discussion of Elizabeth Gaskell's *Ruth* and Thomas Hardy's *Tess of the d'Urbervilles*, p. 168. From the point of view of censorship, one of the most interesting examples is *Madame Bovary*. Auerbach does not discuss Flaubert's trial, but see Dominick La Capra, *'Madame Bovary' on Trial* (Ithaca: Cornell University Press, 1982).
4. I rely extensively on the chapter entitled 'The Rise of the Fallen Woman', especially pp. 150–65. The central point of Auerbach's argument is that the fallen woman is a demonic, powerful and potentially threatening figure. In making this argument she posits a split between the narrative line and the *image* of the woman, contrasting 'an explicit narrative that abases the woman, an iconographic pattern than exalts her ... (p. 168). My discussion focuses on the narrative pattern of abasement, or the fall.
5. Auerbach, pp. 154–9.

6. Marilyn Campbell, 'RKO's Fallen Women, 1930–1933', *The Velvet Light Trap*, no. 10, Fall 1973, pp. 13–16; Richard Griffith, 'Cycles and Genres', from 'The Film Since Then', an additional section of the book *The Film Till Now* by Paul Rotha (Feltham, Middlesex: Hamlyn, 1967); Betsy Ann McLane, 'Hollywood's Fallen Women Features', Masters Thesis University of Southern California 1978; Christian Viviani, 'Who is Without Sin? The Maternal Melodrama in American Film, 1930–1939', reprinted on pp. 83–99 of this anthology.

7. Even in nineteenth-century literature the fallen woman sometimes advances in social position; Auerbach cites Thomas Hardy's *Ruined Maid* (1866) and George Moore's *Esther Waters* (1899). But the American films of the 30s are distinctive in their emphasis upon this possibility.

8. Andrew Bergman, *We're in the Money: Depression America and Its Films* (New York: Harper, 1971), pp. 49–55.

9. See McLane, pp. 206–7, for example.

10. Richard Griffith, in Rotha, pp. 438–9.

11. Campbell, pp. 15–16.

12. Garth Jowett, *Film the Democratic Art* (Boston: Little, Brown and Company, 1976); Robert Sklar, *Movie Made America* (New York: Random House, 1975).

13. William Troy, 'Virtue in 1933', in a weekly column 'Films', *The Nation*, vol. 136, no. 3534, 29 March 1933, pp. 354–5.

14. Edgar Dale, *The Content of Motion Pictures* (New York: Macmillan, 1935), p. 108.

15. Dale, p. 107.

16. Alice Ames Winter, Letter to Will Hays, 10 July 1933, Hays Collection, Indiana State Library, Indianapolis.

17. 'Charm? No! No! You Must Have Glamour', *Photoplay*, September 1931.

18. Mildred Martin, of the *Philadelphia Inquirer*, 23 July 1933, as quoted in a public relations report to Will Hays from K.L. Russell, 26 July 1933, Hays Collection, Indiana State Library, Indianapolis.

19. Herbert Blumer and Philip M. Hauser, *Movies, Delinquency and Crime* (New York: Macmillan, 1933), pp. 96 and 98–9.

20. The *Film Daily Yearbook* for 1930 lists the following as members of the MPPDA: Bray Productions, Caddo Company, Christie Film Company, Cecil B. DeMille Pictures Corporation, Eastman Kodak Company, Educational Film Exchanges, Electrical Research Products, First National Pictures, Fox Film Corporation, D.W. Griffith, Inc., Inspiration Pictures, Buster Keaton Productions, Kinogram Publishing Corporation, Metro-Goldwyn-Mayer Distribution Corporation, Paramount Famous-Lasky Corporation, Pathe Exchange, Principal Pictures Corporation, RCA Photophone, RKO Distribution Corporation, Hal Roach Studios, Sono Art-World Wide Productions, United Artists Corporation, Universal Pictures Corporation, Vitagraph, Warner Brothers Pictures.

21. The Upshaw bill of 1926 proposed the formation of a federal censorship board. Garth Jowett discusses the groups which supported this measure in *Film the Democratic Art*, pp. 170–1. The Hudson bill (HR 9986) of 1930 also proposed a censorship board and would have outlawed the marketing practices of block-booking and blindselling. The Brookhart Bill (S1003) was similarly concerned with economic regulation of the industry.

22. James M. Wall. 'Oral History with Geoffrey Shurlock', Louis B. Mayer Library, American Film Institute, Los Angeles, California (AFI, 1975), p. 209.

23. See Robert Sklar, *Movie-Made America* (New York: Random House, 1975), pp. 173–4 and pp. 189–94.

24. The most extended discussion of censorship in terms of the 'enforcement' of the Production Code can be found in Raymond Moley's *The Hays Office* (New York: Bobbs Merrill, 1945), pp. 77–82. However, I find it unlikely that the Code was simply 'enforced' in the manner of a law, through the exercise of the power of restraint. In my view, the quasi-legal model of self-regulation cannot account for the intricate process of *negotiation* between producers and the MPPDA by which censorship was conducted.

25. Correspondence between producers and industry censors may be found in the MPPDA Case Files, Special Collections, Academy of Motion Picture Arts and Sciences Library, Beverly Hills, California. Some correspondence is also located in the studio production files which are available for Warner Brothers and RKO. This paper draws upon a review of 66 MPPDA case files.

26. Jason Joy, Letter to Irving Thalberg, 10 November 1930, *The Easiest Way* Case File, Academy of Motion Picture Arts and Sciences Library, Beverly Hills.

27. Joseph Breen, Letter to Darryl Zanuck, n.d., *Private Number* Case File, Academy of Motion Picture Arts and Sciences Library, Beverly Hills.

28. See Martin Quigley, *Decency in Motion Pictures* (New York: Macmillan, 1937), p. 33.

29. Joseph Breen, Memos 1 February 1938 and 23 March 1939, *Back Street* Case File, Academy of Motion Picture Arts and Sciences Library, Beverly Hills.

30. Joseph Breen, Letter to Maurice Rivar, 29 March 1940, *Back Street* Case File, Academy of Motion Picture Arts and Sciences Library, Beverly Hills.

31. The sphere of influence of the boards actually extended beyond these states as Ira Carmen notes in *Movies, Censorship and the Law* (Ann Arbor: University of Michigan Press, 1967), p. 129.

32. James Wingate, Letter to Darryl Zanuck, 3 January 1933 and Letter, 28 February 1933, *Baby Face* Case File, Academy of Motion Picture Arts and Sciences Library, Beverly Hills.

33. Joseph Breen, Memo to Will Hays, 8 June 1933, *Baby Face* Case File.

34. Written notes following a story conference on *Camille*, 16 May 1936, *Camille* Case File.

35. James Wingate, Letter to Darryl Zanuck, 28 February 1933, *Baby Face* Case File.

36. Jason Joy, Letter to William A. Orr, 14 June 1932, *Red Headed Woman* Case File.

Mothering, Feminism and Representation

The Maternal in Melodrama and the Woman's Film 1910–40

E. ANN KAPLAN

THE AIM of this project is to explore the interconnections between certain historical discourses about the Mother and the changing representation of the Mother in film forms addressed largely, but not exclusively, to women. I will argue that the traditions that shape Mother representations in film derive from the nineteenth-century stage melodrama, sentimental novel and the literature of domestic feminism. I first survey briefly nineteenth-century Mother articulations as these came to America from France (particularly through Rousseau), and then show how mainstream literary discourses position the Mother in ways that parallel Rousseau's conceptions. I look next at how the dominant twentieth-century Mother discourse – embedded in neo-Freudian psychoanalytic theory – perpetuates nineteenth-century positioning, although the emphases are different. Having looked briefly at the nineteenth-century literary forms that cinema later relied on, I examine Mother representations in select films. In concluding I assess the degree to which Mother representations continue to be bound by the neo-Freudian psychoanalytic discourse that dominates our period, and suggest that feminist Freudian revisions may provide tools with which to alter oppressive patriarchal constructs.

The Cult of True Womanhood

While Mother representations obviously have a long and complex history, and are shaped in western civilisation by Greek myths and the Old and New Testaments, I am here concerned with the conception of Motherhood in the modern period. The Industrial Revolution may be seen as solidifying modern conceptions, which resulted partly from the economically necessary transition of certain women out of their role as producers in the old pre-industrial economy into that as middle-class consumers in the bourgeois home.[1] The new Mother ideology accompanying this transition was to ensure the success of capitalism as it moved from its work-oriented stage to what would become its twentieth-century, consumer style.[2]

Rousseau's *Émile* (1762) first articulated modern Mother ideology in a comprehensive way. In France it was a radical text in terms of its discourse about child-rearing. It established a different conception of how child-rearing should be organised, introducing the notion of a long preparation for adulthood, carefully overseen personally by the parents. Before this, *childhood* had not been particularly valued, as a stage, although this is far from saying that the child him/herself was not valued.[3] If the custom of sending children out to wet-nurses seems strange to us today, it was a necessity for many urban working mothers in the 19th century.[4]

It is not so much that the child was considered worthless (evil or without reason) as Elisabeth Badinter argues, as that there were contradictory discourses about child-rearing. Some discourses continued Augustinian assumptions about the child as an imperfect being, weighed down by original sin – for example, Juan Luis Vives denounced mothers who were affectionate or playful – but contradictory discourses encouraging parent–child affection also existed.[5]

We have very little evidence about the actual quality of mother–child relations before 1762 and thus should assume that, as now, this varied enormously. What is important in Rousseau is his *description* of a regime of total attention to the child from an early age. His disapproval of wet-nursing was merely one of many ways in which he set up a new organisation of child-rearing.

In reversing earlier discourses about the child in France, Rousseau's *Émile*, written as capitalism was being put in place, introduces a new Mother discourse. The emergence of a new social class, the bourgeoisie, created the need to articulate appropriate male/female sex-roles for the changed situation. The child assumes a new importance for Rousseau because what happens to him will determine the kind of man/citizen he will make.[6] In requiring that the utmost attention be paid to his physical health and to his emotional and intellectual development, Rousseau created a different role for the Mother. It is the conception of raising children for adulthood that is new and that defines the Mother's tasks.

For Rousseau, it is only because the early education of man is in woman's hands that her education is important. The girl's biological processes shape her to be a mother and require a special attention that has no parallel for the boy. The very survival of the human race depends on the woman's function in cementing the family through her skills in emotions and relationships. 'Naturally' the complement, the pleasure and the Mother of man, woman should learn only what is 'suitable' for her given role.[7] Taking on an imaginary proponent of sexual equality (he was later to have a real one in Mary Wollstonecraft),[8] Rousseau concludes that 'Although here and there a woman may have few children, what difference does it make? Is it any less a woman's business to be a mother? And do not the general laws of nature and morality make provision for this state of things?'[9]

Rousseau again inscribes in cultural discourse a division of labour necessary for the development of modern capitalism.[10] He theorises the kind of public (male)/private (female) split that structures the separate spheres in the 19th and early 20th centuries, regardless of whether women actually worked or not.[11] Classic in Rousseau's articulation is the ascribing to 'nature' what is already cultural, and the assumption that the middle-class ethic is to be taken as the norm.

It is these ideas that came to shape what I call the Master Mother Discourse that dominated the 19th and early 20th centuries, and from which we are now only beginning to emerge. In America, the ideas were particularly easily assimilated since, as David Leverenz has shown, Puritan discourses about the Mother already valued tenderness, and wet-nursing was not a regular custom.[12] Nevertheless, the impact of the Industrial Revolution (happening in America about a hundred years later than in Europe) stimulated a far more elaborate and institutionalised articulation of the Mother's duties than had been evident before.

As Linda Kerber points out, the Industrial Revolution in America followed on the heels of the Revolution which had already had an impact on the whole society, including women:

> The domestic function of the preindustrial woman had not needed ideological justification; it was implicit in the biological and political economy of her world. Someone had to keep the spinning wheel turning and the open-hearth fire constantly tended, and the nursing mother who could not leave her infant was the obvious candidate. In the domesticity of the preindustrial woman there was no sharp disjunction between ideology and practice. But the Revolution was a watershed. It created a public ideology of individual responsibility and virtue just before the industrial machinery began to free middle-class women from some of their unremitting toil and to propel lower-class women more fully into the public economy. The terms of domesticity were changed, and the pundits could not bring back the past.[13]

What Kerber describes well is the way in which American women were at once permitted to enter the political sphere, under the influence of the Revolutionary rhetoric, but at the same time were severely restricted in their activities through the concept of the Republican Mother. 'Motherhood', says Kerber, 'was discussed almost as if it were a fourth branch of government, a device that ensured social control in the gentlest possible way.'[14] The Republican Mother, that is, combined domesticity with political values, at once permitting women a kind of 'political' function, but neatly confining it completely within the home.

This ideology could be taken in either conservative or progressive directions, as we'll see. The conservative side is reinforced by Rousseau's *Émile*, widely read in America at the time.[15] The four qualities of what has been called 'The Cult of True Womanhood' – piety, purity, domesticity and submissiveness – closely mimic qualities of Rousseau's Sophie. Nancy Cott shows how the identification of woman with 'the heart' in addition signalled the inequality between the sexes, since this was inextricably involved with their status as dependent on men:

> If women are considered dependent on others (men) for their protection and support, self-preservation itself demanded skill in personal relationships. Rousseau's portrayal in *Émile* was the most unequivocal and influential formulation for this reasoning in the 18th century ... (His) central meaning resonated through the decades as a description of women's social options and a prescription for their behaviour.[16]

More progressive implications of the new ideology have to do with the encouragement of women's education (after all, if the mother is to train future citizens, she must be well informed herself),[17] and with the new sense of vocation that women received. Domesticity, as an ideology, gave women a feeling of satisfaction as well as of solidarity with their sex, Nancy Cott notes, because it included all women and was endowed with social and political meaning.[18]

The new ideology of Motherhood thus contained contradictory elements in America: it served both to promote the Industrial era through the consumerism it involved for the white, middle class, and to reassure the proponents of industrialism that all was not lost. In a rapidly changing world – one that the male order was not sure was all to the good – the Mother was to uphold, continue and represent the old values in danger of being swept away by the tide of changes that seemed beyond control.[19]

Women's Writing and Domestic Feminism in Nineteenth-Century America
The new ideology of Motherhood is reflected in the Mother paradigms that are inscribed in dominant literary representations in Europe and America, as Industrialism gets under way. In the novel and short story – the genres that emerged with industrialism – the Mother, when not absent, is confined to the polarised paradigms of the saintly, all-nurturing, self-sacrificing 'Angel in the House' or the cruel Mother type who is sadistic and jealous. The few variations – such as the heroic Mother, the vain silly Mother, or the possessive, smothering one – are mere gradations from the basic figures.

Three other points are of interest: first, when the Mother is present, she is most often looked at from the point of view of the *child* rather than being presented from *her* subjective point of view. In the nineteenth-century European *bildungsroman*, the Mother is often suppressed and the (usually) male

116

protagonist's articulate struggle is against the Father; in novels by female writers like Jane Austen or the Brontës, the female protagonist is often orphaned and subject to the whims of sadistic mothers, like Mrs Reed in *Jane Eyre*, or sickly, neurotic ones, like Mrs Earnshaw in *Wuthering Heights*. Surrogate mothers abound in these fictions, and while occasionally nurturing, they more often fail to satisfy (cf. Nelly Dean in *Wuthering Heights*).

Second, when the Mother is central, it is because she has either transgressed her 'correct' position (in which case the work of the narrative is to punish her or re-position her safely subordinate to the Father's Law); or she is a 'bad' Mother (sadistic, jealous), when the work of the narrative is to liberate the child figure and bring about the Mother's downfall. It is significant that only the bad Mother is sexual – indeed, her sexuality often defines her evil.

Finally, dominant fiction is interesting in that most Mother–Child relationships are Mother–Son bondings which tend to be presented positively rather than Mother–Daughter ones which are often negative.[20]

Now, while these generalisations apply to Western fiction as a whole, classical American literature contains a misogynist bias that resulted in few female representations at all, and even fewer Mothers.[21] Female readers of American literature must, for the most part, have felt even more excluded from the realm of fiction than their European sisters, and it is perhaps not surprising that they created their own popular literature to fill the gap. I will look very briefly a women's writing between 1840 and 1880 in order to see what Mother articulations predominate and how these illuminate early film images.

Two types of novel, outside of the canon, have bearing on film representations. These texts cannot, of course, avoid patriarchal constructs since women could only work within their given discursive field. Thus, as we would expect, we find many patterns that duplicate those in male writing. But it is here that the distinction between the two types of women's writing is useful: both types compensate for the misogynist bias of classical American fiction, but the degree of subversion differs.

The first type, the sentimental novel written by middle-class women for their peers, is addressed to women living under the constraint of the cult of true womanhood and embodies the melodramatic. The form served the important function of providing a release for the sufferings and frustrations of middle-class women bound by the dictates of True Womanhood beyond which they could not think. Peter Brooks has argued that the melodramatic mode foregrounds, through familial relations, what the social order forbids and represses.[22] In line with this, I would suggest the woman's melodrama articulates women's deepest unconscious fears and fantasies about their lives in patriarchy. Some novels, for instance, speak to women's unconscious resentment at being positioned in negativity, focusing, as Ann Douglas points out, on 'a confrontation between feminine sanctions and man-made dictates.'[23] This pattern allows women vicarious satisfaction in winning at least some battles. Others turn passivity into heroism by having a protagonist too pure or naive to clear herself of a sin of which she has been accused. The pathos that results would presumably bring tears of recognition to female readers.

The maternal sacrifice sentimental novel stressed the pathetic sides to Mothering, and in so doing uncovered some of the suffering that women endured just because of the socially sanctioned, constraining cult. *East Lynne* (a British novel published in 1861, quickly reprinted and sold widely in America), is typical of the type: it deals with a woman who deserts her husband and children for another man, but at cost to herself. She finally returns, incognito, to live as a governess to her own children in the house of her now re-married ex-husband. After suffering the pain and humiliation of such a positioning, she is finally recognised and forgiven before she dies.

This narrative has power because it speaks to the issue of the Mother's sexual desire, repressed in the True Womanhood Cult. The mother here allows sexuality to divert her from her destined path of self-sacrifice and nurturance, giving the reader vicarious experience of such transgression. But the available discursive field means that even women writers could not imagine any ending other than one in which the woman is returned to the fold, or dies.

The patriarchal underpinning of such narratives is clear, so much so that they may be seen, in a sense, as male Oedipal dramas. I will say more about this when dealing with the parallel films, but clearly the narrative pattern foregrounds the male yearning for the lost Mother that mainstream fiction suppresses.

A different aspect of the Motherhood discourse is addressed by the second type of nineteenth-century woman's novel whose themes may have been influenced by the discourse of domestic feminism as it arose out of women's work in the cause of abolishing slavery, and is embodied in writings by Margaret Fuller, the Grimké Sisters and Elizabeth Cady Stanton.[24]

Domestic feminism takes a step further the view of women like Mrs Sigourney, together with a host of so-called male 'experts' on mothering,[25] which (building on Rousseau's advice to Sophie), insists on the importance of the Mother's role in educating sons for future greatness – a view which still ignores woman's own desire: she is merely the vessel for future heroes, absenting any other fulfilment.

Margaret Fuller on the other hand insisted that women achieve a degree of autonomy through combining Motherhood and Wifehood with intellectual pursuits. In a way that was anathema to the True Womanhood Cult, while still remaining within its overall constraints, Fuller asserted women's higher morality. Cleverly combining patriarchal definition of the Mother-as-example with Emersonian notions of self-reliance, Fuller created an image of the woman as leader/teacher seeking to 'save' civilisation through her superior values.[26]

Fiction influenced by this kind of domestic feminism does not, like the sentimental novel, focus on the pathetic aspects of Motherhood. Rather, it stresses its heroic dimensions. Now placed as central rather than peripheral, Mother figures dominate the narrative and transvalue the socially subordinate position of Motherhood in the Master Mother Discourse. A good example of a novel that contains elements of domestic feminism discourse is Harriet Beecher Stowe's *Uncle Tom's Cabin*.

Although aspects of the novel fit very much into the sentimental melodramatic tradition of much women's writing, there is clearly a new, potentially subversive note here. (It was the sentimental, melodramatic parts, for example Little Eva's Death, Uncle Tom's Death, that made *Uncle Tom's Cabin* an instant stage success, to be played all around America throughout the 1930s.) The subversive note is mainly in the transvaluing of the subordinate position that Motherhood is traditionally assigned in patriarchy. If Rachel Halliday's Quaker house embodied the ideal, Mother-centred community, other impressive figures are Aunt Chloe, Mrs Shelby, Mrs Bird, Eliza, Simon Legree's mother and Little Eva (as child-mother). Mrs Shelby and Mrs Bird in particular evidence superior morality to their husbands, who are co-opted into immoral actions by the corrupt male sphere to which they must conform.

Secondly, the text foregrounds the mother–daughter relations usually repressed in mainstream fiction. These are found most obviously in Emmeline and her Mother, and then Cassy (Surrogate Mother) and Emmeline. Interesting here is that while Stowe indeed takes up one of the familiar Mother paradigms – that of the 'good' Mother, the 'Angel in the House' – she includes no cruel, sadistic Mothers, the polar paradigm. The body of the text itself is that of the all-nurturing, protective, all-forgiving, saintly Mother type. Readers are made to position themselves within the *Mother's* fears of loss and separation as against the usual placing as the abandoned *child*.

Now while Stowe's hypostatisation of self-sacrifice and suffering is ultimately problematic for contemporary feminists because it leaves unquestioned patriarchy's relegation of women to this role, her text is, finally, transgressive in *transvaluing* the subordinate position that Motherhood is traditionally assigned in patriarchy. Morally superior to their male counterparts, her mother figures dominate the text. For Stowe, being correctly motherly is woman's true destiny, black or white, and her figures are rated on a scale according to this value.

But if the Mother figures embody the highest morality, Stowe's male figures are also made moral to the degree that they embody the feminine mother-ideal. Masculinity is either morally weak (ineffective humanistically) or sadistic and brutal. Standing in for Christ, Uncle Tom is the nurturing 'mother' par excellence, and here we see how Stowe's Christianity shapes her ideology of Motherhood. Literally Mothers, women rate high on the scale of a spirituality measured in terms of degree of self-sacrifice and suffering, but biological males can attain this, following Christ's model.

To make Motherhood a universal value is transgressive in that while patriarchy may have invented the Ideal Mother as a balance for excessive male drives, it never intended the essential male attributes of desire, ambition, self-actualising, on which capitalism depends, to be undermined. In the text, women's subversive bonding dislocates and renders powerless male ends; (examples are the escape of Eliza and her son, engineered by Mrs Shelby and Mrs Bird, and most obviously Cassy and Emmeline's destruction of Simon Legree). The women effectively undermine the male business of making profit out of human bodies.

Harriet Beecher Stowe was thus partially able to transgress patriarchal Motherhood ideology. The two main limitations of her vision (namely essentialism or female individualism, and utopianism) are an inevitable result of the semiotic field within which she had to work. But *Uncle Tom's Cabin* is important in the development of a tradition of female writing more subversive than the sentimental novel because engaged with the ideology of domestic feminism. This ideology made out of Motherhood, as defined by patriarchy, a higher moral sphere with important social functions, which, once delineated, allowed women to move out of the home into the public sphere.

This analysis of the two types of nineteenth-century women's novel provides a context within which to distinguish types of film about Mothering addressed to women.

Psychoanalysis and the Mother
The constant recurrence of the Mother-sacrifice theme cannot be accounted for solely in terms of economic/social discourses, particularly in the 20th century. The prevalence of the sacrifice theme, together with the increasing relegation of Motherhood to the margins of fiction, peripheral to central masculine pursuits, suggests that the Mother offers some threat at a different level. The psychoanalytic discourse is relevant here both as a product of the industrial era and as itself a shaping discourse. The absence of concern with the Mother as subject, not only in dominant literature but also in intellectual and scholarly pursuits, cannot be an accident. Significantly, until the work produced by the recent women's movement, there has been no history of Motherhood analogous to the work done on childhood, the family and sexuality. Continuing Rousseau's original perspective, scholars focused on the child rather than the Mother. Political scientists have neglected the Mother and Social Science research has mainly dealt with the infant's early development, looking at the Mother as she functions in the child's life, rather than at the psychic, social and emotional impact of Mothering on the woman.

Whatever psychic life may have been like before the Industrial Revolution, it is the institution of the nuclear family – as articulated in discourses like Rousseau's – that set in motion the psychic processes that Freud was later to articulate and develop into a theory. Freud's account of the processes within the nuclear family provides an explanation, on a level other than the economic, for the Mother's first being over-installed as symbolic Mother, then relegated to the margins of patriarchal culture. Freud's theory of the Oedipus Complex suggests psychic origins for the polarised paradigms of the Mother that dominate representations, and provides further evidence of the threat that the Mother assumes for both the male and the female child.

In Freud's theory, both the boy and the girl suffer a trauma on 'discovering' the Mother's castration, and turn away from her, but for different reasons. The boy must eliminate the 'feminine' in himself (because it implies castration) and identify with his father; while the girl must accept her 'bleeding wound', her lack, and remains angry with her mother whom she holds responsible.

It is important here to separate Freud himself from later neo-Freudian psychoanalytic discourse which applied Freud's theories to the level of lived experience. While Freud himself indeed often falls into this trap, his account of the *fort-da* game[27] offers the important insight that the child can only accomplish its necessary separation from the Mother through representing her symbolically, first via the cotton reel, and then through contrasting images of her. He constructs two symbolic Mothers – one good, one bad – in order to deal with the real Mother's alternate nurturing and punitive dimensions.

It was the Freud who understood the level of the symbolic that Lacan was later to build upon in order to account for the inscribing of sex difference in language and culture. Lacan's theory of the constitution of the subject at the very moment of loss of the Mother's body may be modified to account for the crisis over the Mother in the Master Discourse. The loss of the Mother is inevitable in human development, but it is the particular structuring of this loss at the time of the Industrial Revolution that is significant.[28] The child not only loses the Mother's body (a loss that is essential for subjectivity), but also enters a symbolic order structured around the phallus as signifier. The desire for the Mother's body is displaced into the desire for the phallus as a result of the organisation of the nuclear family in patriarchy. It is this repressed desire for the Mother in an order that relegates her to the periphery that underlies the representations in the Master Mother Discourse.

Thus, Freud's discourse, when read on the level of representation, duplicates the Mother paradigms in dominant fiction outlined earlier. The historic semiotic field produces similar literary and psychoanalytic discourses about the Mother because signifying practices in general are phallocentric. Psychoanalytic theory, as a representation of a representation, was bound to construct itself according to, as well as to account for, the binary opposites of the good and bad Mothers that the child creates at an early age. The love/hate polarity becomes inscribed in psychoanalytic discourse, as Monique Plaza has shown.[29] In addition, Freud parallels earlier theories in looking from the child position, and then mainly from that of the *boy* child; Freud did not discuss the Mother's representations of the mother–child interaction, or analyse the psychic consequences of mothering for the woman.

Two brief essays by Freud, 'Creative Writing and Day Dreaming' and 'The Family Romance', offer an outline of the psychic processes through which narratives very like those in popular sentimental women's forms come to be constructed. For Freud, story-telling is the means by which the child deals with its anxiety about sex differences, sibling rivalry and beings upon whom it is dependent, especially the mother. In 'The Family Romance', Freud outlines two different fantasies, those of the Bastard and of the Foundling, both having to do with the child's Oedipal relationship to the Mother, and with origins. As Marthe Robert has shown, both stories rely on the dual image of the good/bad Mother: the child's idealised early representation of the Mother is overlaid by the negative images when the child believes that the Mother has betrayed him either with his father or with some other man.[30]

Significantly, Freud's descriptions of the child's fantasies imply a *male* subject. And it is this focus on the *male* child's loss of the idealised Mother that is found in the maternal sacrifice theme, as we'll see. Although the Mother's conflicts between sex and motherhood are also stressed in the maternal sacrifice pattern, it is only the novel influenced by domestic feminism that begins to address the *girl's* longing for the pre-oedipal Mother.

Perhaps the most damaging aspects of Freudian theory as far as the Mother is concerned have been in its application by late psychoanalysts to the level of lived experience. If Freud intended to keep things to the Symbolic level, his texts lay themselves open to literal readings. Although Freud only discussed the girl's Oedipal complex briefly and belatedly, believing that it remained shrouded in mystery, an insoluble enigma,[31] inferences about the girl's social position could be drawn from Freud's suggestions about her unconscious processes. In Freud's view, the girl, angry at her Mother for being castrated, for preventing libidinal activity, for not suckling her long enough, and, at adolescence, for guarding the girl's chastity, turns to her Father, desiring to have a child by him with which to replace her longing for the penis. Her later marriage to a man like her father, and her bearing of the child, signify, for Freud, woman's attainment of the 'feminine' and triumph over her castration anxiety.

It was thus easy for later child psychiatrists and psychologists like Melanie Klein, John Bowlby, Winnicott and Selma Fraiberg, to equate the 'feminine' with Motherhood as woman's 'natural' *social* role. The qualities of passivity, narcissism and masochism which Mothering entailed were considered 'normal' for woman, and the child experts had no qualms in prescribing the all-nurturing, self-denying and self-abasing behaviour (considered vital for the *child's* psychic health) that in fact put an intolerable burden on the Mother *as woman*.

It is the very ease with which daily, burdensome, social tasks are demanded of the Mother that belies the phallocentrism in psychoanalytic and child development discourses. And it is here that twentieth-century, child-rearing discourses link up with those in the 19th century initiated by Rousseau. There is a shift in the *rationale* offered for the Mother's social positioning, but that positioning remains remarkably the same. While in the 19th century the Mother was to stay home to take care of the child's social and emotional growth, so as to create a productive citizen, following Christian moral dictates, in the 20th century it is specifically the child's *psychic* health that the Mother is responsible for. She is to be the ever-present vessel for the child's needs and desires, which, properly handled, will enable him to grow into a happy, well-adjusted adult. The Mother's own needs and desires have no place.[32]

Thus, looking back from the position of twentieth-century phallocentric psychoanalytic discourse, it is possible to see that, even in the 19th century, the maternal sacrifice theme was addressed to male needs, desires and fantasies, as much as (if not more than) to female desire. The realist conventions of the sentimental novel gave illusory veracity to the social institutions and the division of labour essential for the success of the Industrial Revolution, inscribing them in consciousness, but at the same time, the fiction functioned to satisfy first, unconscious male desires for the idealized pre-Oedipal Mother (the child in these novels is usually male), and second, unconscious wishes to punish the Mother for her sexuality evident in her betraying the child with another man.

The Maternal Melodrama and the Woman's Film 1910–1940

In the first half of the twentieth century, the dominant popular form through which both the maternal sacrifice theme and the more resisting discourse (analogous to that in the nineteenth-century novel inspired by the ideas of domestic feminism) continue to find expression is the classical Hollywood film. The invention of film at the turn of the century is part of a crucial change taking place already in the late 19th century with the advent of modern consumer culture and advertising. As Allon White notes, this change involved 'the displacement of pleasure into the realm of the signifier (form, style, association) and its disassociation from the "real", from the world of work and dreary production'.[33] White notes that 'this disassociation was a necessary correlative to the unfettering of commodity-centred, consumer capitalism ...', and that 'the creaming off of the signifier from the signified marked a new phase in the production of Western subjectivity in its long

123

march from Feudalism to a bureaucratic society of controlled consumption'.[34]

What happens is that a new self-consciousness is built into the subject's constitution. If the mirror phase had always been a necessary part of the subject's entry into the Symbolic, it now becomes an inherent part of cultural experience. Consumer culture hooks onto the subject's inevitable desiring mode, reinforcing and exploiting it by constant stimulation. Beginning with the department store and the stage melodrama,[35] the culture of the spectacle is fully inscribed in society with the development of the cinema as an apparatus. Film becomes the form that replaces the popular novel in the way it addresses desires invoked by the new consumer culture: its mode as spectacle dovetails with modes of consumer culture in a vicious circle. In other words film emerges at a certain stage of consumer culture, its modes increasing consumerism and encouraging upward class-striving through accumulation of consumer products now desired and signifying status. And while the popular novel continues, it is also affected by the culture of the spectacle, using description in a self-consciously 'cinematic' style. The other self offered by the mirror becomes part of society's cultural mechanisms, transforming the subject's ways of perceiving and desiring.

Popular narrative patterns in relation to the Mother continue to be circulated in the new commercial form. The two main nineteenth-century literary types that I have discussed give rise to what I will argue are two differing film forms: the maternal melodrama and the woman's film. This distinction between film forms focusing on women's concerns will clarify what have hitherto seemed contradictions. Each form establishes a different subject position for the spectator: the maternal melodrama is arguably a *male* Oedipal drama, while the woman's film more specifically addresses female spectators and resists dominant ideology. I will discuss film examples of each type to show their enunciative stances.

The maternal melodrama derives from the sentimental novel and the stage melodrama. Just as the stage melodrama drew upon the gothic and sentimental novel for its plots, so early film pillaged in stage melodrama for its subjects. *East Lynne*, for example, was very quickly staged as a play in Brooklyn in 1863, and, as Sally Mitchell notes, 'for more than forty years, some version of the drama inspired by Ellen Wood's book was probably seen by an audience somewhere in England or North America.'[38] It is then fascinating to find *East Lynne* being made into a film twice in the silent period and in 1931 into a sound film by Frank Lloyd.

The maternal melodrama appeals to both the male and the female spectator, but in different ways. The appeal to the male spectator is in the narrative's enactment of the little boy's fantasies about an adoring, beautiful Mother. In the films, the Mother often gives birth out of wedlock, sacrifices herself for the welfare of her (usually in this film type) *male* child, seeking to

124

elevate him in society or to return him to his noble lineage (through his Father), while debasing and absenting herself. Such Mother love obviously supersedes the woman's bond with Father or lover, giving the male spectator the vicarious satisfaction of having the Mother sacrifice all for his needs.

The appeal to the female spectator is Oedipal from the other direction, as it were, and relies on female internalisation of patriarchal constructs. It permits the Oedipal fantasy of replacing the lost penis with a *boy* child, and, in addition, vicarious identification wth an idealised Mother-figure which women, as historical subjects in the cinema, can never live up to. The female spectator also participates vicariously in the Mother-boy idyll that we have been reared to find so touching and desirable.

The director who establishes par excellence this type in early cinema is D. W. Griffith. His *Mothering Heart* (1913) featured Lillian Gish in what was to be a series of roles as a self-sacrificing, pure, passive Mother figure – for instance in *True Heart Susie* (1919) and *Way Down East* (1920). As always in Griffith, the good woman is equated with the ideal Mother type, whether married or not, with or without children, and almost regardless of age. Here Gish is seen already with a 'mothering heart' as a teenager, playing with puppies. Responding to her lover's demands to marry, out of her desire for children, we see her once married, totally devoted to 'mothering' her husband, embodying as she does so the nineteenth-century Cult of True Womanhood. Once pregnant, she fantasises having her child in remarkable scenes in which Gish cradles a baby gown. Discovering her husband's infidelity, Gish moves back to her Mother's house, where she is happy enough, the baby fulfilling her and taking the place of husband. The baby's death reunites her with her husband who now in turn replaces the baby. The moral is that the good woman is always a Mother, in classic nineteenth-century style, no matter with whom she is interacting.

As Christian Viviani shows, this type of maternal melodrama took on its prototype form in *Madame X*, made from a play by Alexander Bisson, a film that had several versions and spawned a series of imitations through the 30s.[39] But what Viviani ignores is the alternate tradition of the maternal narrative that I argue came down through the second type of woman's nineteenth-century novel, influenced by the ideology of domestic feminism; it is this tradition which I shall deal with from here on. However, it is significant that there is in film no set of texts written and directed by women to parallel women's fiction. The woman's film was directed mainly by men (women may have written the script), and the distinction is rather in hierarchy of genres – this being a scorned, inferior one compared with the main, powerful male genres (Western, Gangster).[40]

In its derivation from women's fiction the woman's film deals with the more heroic or subversive aspects of Mothering and is arguably addressed more specifically to the female spectator. The films speak more to the conflicts and ambiguities that follow from woman's Oedipal positioning than to male Oedipal drama. In this connection, it is significant that most of the maternal melodramas feature a Mother–son relationship while most of the maternal women's films feature a Mother–daughter relationship. This makes sense in that if the woman's film is characterised by more resistance to patriarchal constructs – more questioning of woman's position as Mother – then part of the subversion is to inscribe strong Mother–daughter relationships. For, as noted, that relationship is generally repressed in patriarchal culture – and for a reason: it is seen as potentially threatening. Investment in the pathos of lost Mother–son bondings keeps the maternal melodrama from straying too far from patriarchal mandates.

Now it is true that the woman's film rarely opens up new space for the Mother, or allows her to hold on to a subversive position. For instance, Mothers are rarely seen working (outside the home) or totally independent from men, and when they are, as we'll see, it is by force, not choice. The discursive field was still, even in the 20s and 30s, not such as to make the independent career woman a possible positive construct. But even if the transgressing Mother is safely relocated in her place as subordinate to the Father by the film's end, the attempt of the films to subvert the dominant male Oedipal drama, for much of their extent, makes them powerful experiences for women, and possibly disturbing to male spectators.

It is significant that in general the woman's film, by virtue of being a resisting form, shows more sensitivity to social concerns than does the maternal melodrama, which situates itself more firmly in the terrain of unconscious Oedipal needs, fears and desires. The woman's film on the other hand puts more stress on the cognitive/conscious level, often foregrounding sociological issues and dealing more frequently with social institutions.

Such texts, for instance, problematise the public/male, domestic/female split. Some transvalue these patriarchally constructed spheres, showing the Mother's strong, transcending qualities in a male public order that is either corrupt or inadequate. Here the films show remnants of discourse from the early 20s, namely the public debate over the female vote and discourses around women's work occasioned by World War One. In other words, the 'strong' Mother, who was moral and unwilling simply to endure her situation passively, figured in representations even though, paradoxically, such women rarely *worked*, or thought of working, outside of the home. Their sphere was defined as the domestic, but this sphere was shown, in the manner of domestic feminism, to engender values higher than the male public sphere, which was implicated in consumer capitalism and the culture of the spectacle.

To varying degrees, two 20s films illustrate some of these generalisations. Lois Weber's *The Blot* reveals the female director's special sensitivity to the domestic sphere that could only come from inside knowledge and identifica-

126

tion. While not exactly a 'strong' Mother-figure, Mrs Griggs is (at least to a modern viewer) the most powerful and poignant figure in the film, far superseding in interest and attention the ostensible hero, Phil West, and heroine, Amelia, played by Louis Calhoun and Claire Windsor. The central 'couple' is indeed rather Mrs Griggs and her daughter Amelia, whose relationship is tenderly handled, emphasising their close-bonding. The camera re-inforces their bonding, intercutting fequently between them as it rarely does, for instance, between Mr and Mrs Griggs. The emotional climax of the film – the chicken-stealing scene – occurs, as I will show, not around the heterosexual couple, but around Mrs Griggs and Amelia.

Far from being relegated to the periphery of the narrative, Mrs Griggs becomes the central focus. The spectator is positioned so as to see from her point of view. Shots of the tired, depressed-looking Mrs Griggs, wife of an underpaid professor, are intercut with what she sees around her – the worn carpet, threadbare chairs, thin curtains and skeletal cat, driven to plunder the garbage can of the well-fed, financially secure Olsen family next door. We see her frustrations and distress over Phil West's visit to her sick daughter. Having settled the rich suitor in her daughter's room, her next task is to find the wherewithal to give him tea and cake. Her purse being empty, she pawns her aged Mother's last jewels and is seen excitedly preparing a tea tray complete with flowers. She launches proudly into the room only to discover that Phil has been replaced by Amelia's other suitor, the poor Vicar.

Weber's sensitivity to domestic detail is extended to her view of male characters – for example in the cutaways from what is going on in the daughter's room to the Vicar preparing to visit Amelia. In the first instance, as Phil West sits making love to Amelia, we have inserts of the chair he's on, caught in a hole in the carpet. In the second, we see the Vicar, unable to clean his shoes because out of shoe polish, resort to goose grease. While this does the job, it also attracts Amelia's cat when the Vicar visits her.

The climactic chicken-stealing scene positions us with Mrs Griggs in her distress at not having money to feed Amelia the food she needs to get well. She tries to buy a chicken on credit, only to be refused. On returning home, the camera shows her in her kitchen unable to avoid seeing the fat chickens that Mrs Olsen next door is preparing for her family. Repeated intercutting follows, indicating Mrs Griggs' increasing distress and subsequent temptation to steal one of the chickens left on the window ledge. The intensity of the Mother's struggle over this temptation shows her caught between two equally strong dictates: on the one hand to feed her family in genteel style; on the other, to be specially moral as an example to her children. The climax occurs when Amelia sees her Mother apparently about to steal a chicken, and, not waiting to see that she immediately returns the bird, is utterly disillusioned and disappointed.

Mrs Griggs' heroism consists in her complete dedication to the needs of her family, no matter what the personal cost to herself. She will never complain to her husband about the situation or ask him for anything. She understands her role as to make the best of things, to suffer in silence, and to deprive herself so that the family has sufficient. She is forced to put on a false front out of shame that she cannot manage, and thus without too much effort, the spectator is able to see what an impossible and thankless task she has.

The contrast with the prosperous Olsen family next door underscores the point. Mrs Olsen carries Mother functions to excess, over-cooking, over-preparing, over-indulging her family, and then behaving sadistically to her impoverished neighbour, refusing to allow even the cat to get what it can out of the garbage. Mrs Olsen over-Mothers to the degree that her husband can barely stand to be in the house, and here again one senses the film's implicit critique of a role that allows so little breadth that the Mother becomes suffocating out of excess energy, out of the very constraints of her placing. The critique extends to excessive consumption as symbolising status. For the Olsens, desire is channelled into consumer products to the detriment of their familial and social relations. Meanwhile, the film makes clear the analogous wastefulness of the wealthy upper class, who dine on rarified gourmet dishes offered as stimulus to a bored, satiated palate. The film indicates that the ease with which the ruling class can quench desire for pleasure through food and sex alters their relationship to desire. Juanita is thus surprised to find that she cannot simply possess Phil West, whom she desires as well as Amelia.

The camera's interest in the relation of the two mothers is clear in the constant visual connections that are established. The series of looks is structured primarily around Mrs Olsen looking at Mrs Griggs, and vice versa, rather than on male/female looking, and parallels the interchange of the female look between Mrs Griggs and her daughter. Only the brief sequence between Amelia and Phil show the kind of intercutting that classical Hollywood relies upon. This visual linking of the female characters is particularly interesting in that the main narrative issues indeed lie in the romance between Phil and Amelia, and in the social problem of the differential pay of a professor and of a small business man. Claire Windsor and Louis Calhoun are the film's stars, well-known from other Weber films, and the film obviously expects them to be the main attraction. The social message about the underpaid intellectual is characteristic of Weber films, as is her condemnation of the idle rich who waste money on trivialities – clothes, food, drink, cigarettes – while the Professor's family barely have enough to survive.

But Weber's politics do not move towards an analysis of class relations. Rather, she advocates benevolent individualism. The rich Phil West, won over by the pretty Amelia, persuades his Father to improve the salaries at the Professor's college, and to cap everything, asks Amelia to marry him. The film thus ends with Mrs Griggs rendered happy, since her two disinterested ends in life – her husband's happiness and comfort, and her daughter's happy marriage into money – have been achieved.

Weber's text, like Stowe's, thus works with the domestic/public-sphere split on the social level. Assuming the division of spheres, she validates the female sphere even though her narrative is apparently about the male sphere. If Amelia is coded for sexual desire, passive object of the male gaze, Mrs Griggs is coded for action, within her defined realm. The film looks at the way institutions of the family, marriage and Motherhood function and at how class determines life-style and values. Unlike Stowe's text, the film does not permit any dislocation of male ends, although the values of the domestic sphere do function to create a conscience in the hitherto rich and careless Phil West that ultimately leads him to disinterested action (or at least, actions against his class interests if in accord with his sexual desire!). But while refusing to question the place of the Mother or the structure of the nuclear family, *The Blot* does unwittingly (when read against the grain), reveal the pain and suffering of the Mother role and its 'heroic' possibilities in a sensitive, sympathetic way. It functions to release women's frustrations about their positioning by permitting articulation of the constraints of Mothering, while at the same time satisfying needs for fantasy 'solutions' not in fact available to spectators.

While Weber's film reveals a sensitivity to the female sphere that can only come from inside knowledge and identification, Harold Brennan's *Dancing Mothers* (1926), working more from the outside, argues provocatively and aggressively through comedy to expose the double standard. The film reveals the falsity of the myths that underlie the notion of the all-nurturing, self-abnegating Mother, showing that such blanket submission to others amounts to an unhealthy denial/subjugation of self.

Dancing Mothers offers surprising violation of the Master–Mother discourse in that the hitherto passively victimized Mother-figure not only moves out of the home to enter the night-life, but in addition falls in love with her daughter's boyfriend. In keeping with the drawing room drama style of play from which the film was taken, *Dancing Mothers* does not underscore the obvious Oedipal issues (Father and daughter are incestuously involved in each other's love affairs as well as Mother and daughter entering into erotic competition for McNaughton, the 'surrogate' Father/Son male figure); it rather carries it all off nonchalantly, and for largely entertaining ends.

But the film does have its serious side in its representation of the Mother, Ethel's, position. In a reversal of expected imaging, the Mother who seeks autonomy is not seen as 'bad'; rather, it is the Father and daughter who are shown to be 'lacking' in the way that they relate to Ethel. Dismayed by the revelation of the love between Ethel and McNaughton, Father and daughter try to persuade Ethel to stay, since they realise they need her. But Ethel, whose duty, she says, 'is now to herself', understands that they are still only

129

thinking of themselves in needing her. The last shot of the film shows her car leaving the house – whether to join McNaughton or not is unclear and perhaps unimportant. The point is that she walks out of her victimised position, refusing any more to be simply the silent figure in the background, keeping all together by her very passivity and self-abnegation.

While Weber's film shows the daily heroism of Mothering in patriarchy, Brennan's work focuses more explicitly on sex-roles, and on the working of the upper-class nuclear family. Far less moralising and propagandistic than Weber, Brennan is also less politically aware. Both reflect the lack of in-depth psychological development of characters typical of 20s films that often went together with a greater social concern about women's roles. Arguably this concern was a result of the discourses, initially of the First World War and of the Suffragette movement, and in the 20s, of the so-called New Woman whose departures from tradition created much debate about 'the woman question'.[41]

As we move into the 30s, we find gradual changes in the discourses that structure Motherhood in the woman's film, resulting first from changes in Hollywood as an institution, and second from historical changes, particularly the Depression. As Hollywood perfected the codes of linearity and illusionism in the early 30s, so the whole apparatus of classical cinema fell into place with its twin mechanisms of voyeurism and fetishism. As mechanisms for the most part serving the male unconscious, these entailed a different representation of the female body from that in the 20s. Naturally we are not talking about a sharp break but rather about a slow evolution towards ever-increasing eroticisation of woman's image. The 30s represent a transitional decade in which the areas opened up in the 20s in relation to women's roles continued to be explored while at the same time the psychoanalytic mechanisms of cinema undercut the surface narrative concerns.

Psychoanalysis as an explicit discourse was not to enter film narratives fully until after World War Two, when, as a result of war psychiatry and the post-war need to help veterans adjust to 'normal' life the discourse was drawn into the dominant culture. But 30s filmic narratives already show increased attention to the Mother's *responsibility* for the child's *psychic*, as against *social*, health. The emphasis shifts in an interesting way from the 20s focus (carried over from nineteenth-century ideology) on the Mother as moral (Christian) teacher, to the greater burden of creating happy, well-adjusted and fulfilled human beings. Instead of being the agent for shaping the public, external figure (the man/citizen), the Mother is now to shape the internal, psychic self. By the 40s, aberrations in the grown-up child are her fault.

The 30s represent the transition between these two emphases as may be seen in Stahl's *Imitation of Life* (1934) and Vidor's *Stella Dallas* (1937). Both, despite other narrative trends, ultimately focus on the daughters' *psychic* health and the Mother's need to sacrifice herself for it. But it is important, in line with comments above, that both films involve close Mother–daughter bondings, and violate the Master Mother discourse in addition by showing the Mother stepping outside of her allotted place. The films, that is, open up the terrain of the single Mother, who also becomes sexual.

But they do this in an ambivalent manner: as might be expected, the dislocation of traditional sex-roles during the Depression created social anxiety about the Mother-figure. As long as the traditional division of male/female spheres remained essentially unchallenged, as it arguably was through the 20s, despite superficial, female liberation (which did not involve women entering the public professions in large numbers), patriarchy could accept the discourse of the Mother's higher moral function. But when it was no longer economically feasible for the middle-class Mother to remain at home (or when the War made change in her function necessary), then the Mother becomes a source of trouble. Narratives in the 30s reflect this dis-ease by showing the Mother stepping out of her allotted place, but also revealing the disruption this causes, which entails either the Mother's return to her place safely under patriarchal law, or her separation from her child. Psychoanalytic discourse provides the justification for such insistence in that, as noted, what takes precedence is the *daughters'* psychic and social needs as against the *Mother's* desires.

But this very formulation exposes the difficulty of separating the Mother's desire from the daughter's needs. Mothers who are closely bonded positively with their daughters often identify their own desires with what is good for the daughter, as that has been defined by patriarchal culture and as they perceive it out of their sensitivity to their daughter's feelings. Occasionally, as in *Stella Dallas* (1937) these two levels do not cohere, in which case the Mother is in extreme conflict; she will, however, most likely choose in terms of what patriarchy deems appropriate rather than what both she and the daughter might actually desire.

John Stahl's *Imitation of Life* (1934) embodies the contradictory discourses about the Mother in 30s representations. The film is particularly important for what it shows about American society's occlusion of class distinctions – its myth of the 'melting pot', of classlessness, and about film's involvement in consumerism and the culture of the spectacle. Claudette Colbert, driven to make money to provide for her daughter, is very quickly positioned as a glamorous object in a luxurious upper-class setting. She and her house become (like the department store window, with its idealised mannequins) objects that embody the spectator's desire. Colbert's shimmering gowns and suave business outfits signify her success and are the things that attract Stephen to her.

The linking of women as a homogenous group across class lines by the Cult of True Womanhood had the ideological effect of masking essential class differences. This fits in with the ability of American culture to mask class distinctions in general due to the ease with which upward mobility could take place, in contrast to more rigid class distinctions in Europe.

What is significant is the way the text cannot confront the powerful race issues that underlie the narrative. The black and white Mothers embrace, while simultaneously denying, their class and race differences. Both apparently agree that blackness is something 'terrible' (viz. Colbert's admonition to Jessie when she accuses her mother of being black, 'How could you say such a thing to her [Peola]?'), and proceed to pretend the difference is not there. Peola is the only one who keeps on inserting the issue, disrupting the complicity of Colbert and Beavers. Colbert enjoys being 'Mothered' (viz. the foot-massaging scenes), while Beavers sees no humiliation in her position, finding it rather quite congenial. Colbert is differently positioned as a single Mother, however, in that her going out to work is made necessary by her husband's death. Since she is white and middle-class, working would not have been an automatic part of her experience, as it is for Louise Beavers who is poor and black.

But what is interesting is that in both cases, despite the women's situations as single, working Mothers, there is no lessening of the Master–Mother discourse. Both are supposed to fulfil the ideal Mother role while working. And both Mothers are seen to fail their daughters, at least in part because of their unorthodox living arrangements.

Colbert unintentionally pushes her daughter, Jessie, into the female Oedipal complex by taking on a handsome, youthful lover, Steven, whom Colbert asks to 'take care' of her daughter when she cannot be around. Jessie falls in love with Steven, creating a complex problem for the two adults. Colbert decides to break off her relationship with Steven (at least temporarily) for the sake of her daughter's happiness. In this case, the Mother–daughter bonding is 'safe' for patriarchy because the Mother wants something else as well, namely Steven Archer (unlike Stella Dallas who only *pretends* to want it).

Significantly, however, in the case of Peola and Delilah, the Mother–daughter bonding is complicated and intensified by cultural constructs of race and class. The white woman is required to shoulder motherhood and its burdens as a kind of duty. The very concept of the maternal *sacrifice* embodies the implicit (and patriarchally recognised) admission that many women do not want *only* to mother, and must relinquish personal desires for their 'higher' calling. But no such tension adheres to the black Mother, who is maternity personified. What else was there for the black woman to be in the 30s and beyond?

Delilah is thus not asked to sacrifice anything in the same way as Colbert is. Since archetypal mother is the only role society offers her (she plays this role no matter what her ostensible labour may be), there is no need to 'bring

132

her into line' in this respect. In fact, paradoxically, the film is forced by its own discourses of race and class (that take precedence over the inhibiton of a close Mother–daughter bonding) to bring Mother and daughter together. The film cannot allow Peola to continue rejecting her mother and passing for white, and thus *requires* that Peola return to her mother. Delilah's death is necessary to bring about the film's climax; Peola's rescinding her demand to be white.[42]

A comparison with *Stella Dallas* exposes the difference that the racial issues causes for the Mother–daughter discourse. Since there is no race issue in *Stella Dallas* the film puts the white mother in the sacrifice position by privileging upward mobility over close Mother–daughter bonding. Laurel is allowed to move up the social ladder, using her Father for legitimacy; but Peola is not allowed to use her white Father in a similar way. *Stella Dallas* uses class to keep mother and daughter separate, while *Imitation of Life* uses race to insist on keeping mother and daughter together.

Nevertheless, *Stella Dallas* offers an image of a Mother in a more deliberately resisting position than *Imitation of Life* while, paradoxically, the film contains perhaps more elements of the maternal melodrama in its sentimental appeal than other woman's films discussed. It is both the strong Mother–daughter relationship in the film, and Stella's refusal of the patriarchal Mother position which the film tries to impose on her, that puts the film in the 'woman's film' category.

Stella's resistance takes the form, first, of literally objecting to Mothering because of the personal sacrifices involved (mainly sensual pleasures); second, of expressing herself freely in her eccentric style of dress and being unabashedly sexual; finally in growing too attached and needful of her daughter. The film punishes her first by turning Stella into a 'spectacle' produced by the upper-class, disapproving gaze (a gaze that the audience is made to share through camera work and editing), but secondly, and most devastatingly, by bringing Stella to the recognition that she is an unfit Mother for her daughter. It is here that once again the issue of consumer culture intrudes. Stella has to learn that her values are not adequate for her daughter who awaits insertion into the upper-class 'department store window', surrounded by the appropriate *mise en scène*, in contrast to the inappropriate one that Stella's home offers. Within the film's value system, the daughter cannot get the nurturing, care and opportunities for material advancement if she stays with Stella. But, looking from outside the system, it is clear that in this case the Mother–daughter separation was necessary first because enjoyed too much by the participants, and second because it was outside of male control.

In keeping with psychoanalytic theory, then, 30s maternal narratives show both the necessity for the Mother to subordinate her desires to the daughter's needs and that, to be healthy, the daughter must turn away from the Mother and discover identity through marriage – that is, through subordination to the male. But, in all this, the Mother is represented as a basically 'good' figure – well-meaning, competent, able to stand alone, articulate if not intelligent. The Mothers are made central and their problems are the ones with which the spectator is made to identify. The contrast with mother figures in the maternal melodrama is clear, for in that narrative pattern the Mothers do not either resist their positioning or apparently find satisfaction in a life without men (as do Stella Dallas, and the Mothers in the first part of *Imitation of Life*). Rather, they are seen as seduced away from conventional places through force or weakness; their frailty, vulnerability or moral laxity is the issue, not any determination to fulfil their desires. Their failure is often through compliance with *evil*, rather than *good*, male demand.

In the post-war period both the maternal melodrama and the woman's film undergo marked changes. Indeed, the maternal sacrifice theme may be said to have all but exhausted itself, its essentially nineteenth-century ideology being finally archaic. In its place, we have a different kind of male Oedipal drama that focuses either, as in film noir, on the threat of female sexuality (now seen as extremely dangerous), or on the Mother's inadequacies, especially her inability to foster psychic health. *Mildred Pierce* and *Now Voyager* may be seen as setting the pattern for 50s and later films in their portrayals of the alternately masochistic and sadistic Mother. Close Mother–daughter bonding is now seen not merely as 'unhealthy' but as leading either to evil, or to neurosis.

Late 40s and 50s films (especially those by Fritz Lang and Alfred Hitchcock) now use neo-Freudian theory to expose the Mother's responsibility for the psychopathic protagonists that interests them. The Mothers in these films are blatantly monstrous, deliberately victimising their children for sadistic and narcissistic ends, and thereby producing criminals. Often the process of these films involves a kind of psychoanalysis of the sick protagonist (viz. Lang's *Secret Beyond the Door*, or Hitchcock's *Marnie*) in the course of which the protagonist is freed of the evil doings of the Mother.

The reasons for this change in the Mother discourse in the post-war period are complex and take us beyond the scope of this paper. Let me merely note in passing that the 'monstrous Mommie' image is prevalent in 80s representations (*Mommie Dearest, Frances*) which, as Fina Bathrick has argued, themselves seem to comment on 40s Hollywood Mother depictions in being *about* Hollywood stars. In the wake of the recent women's movement, America is once again in a crisis over who is to do the Mothering, analogous to the period following World War Two, if for very different reasons.

Feminist theory and art has begun to address the issue of Mothering on a variety of levels. Within the psychoanalytic framework, important work has been done in both America and Europe on revising traditional Freudian theory. Juliet Mitchell and Adrienne Rich have, in different ways, pointed out the phallocentrism of Freudian theory, and Mitchell, Dorothy Dinnerstein and Nancy Chodorow have begun to rewrite the Oedipal process from the girl's point of view so neglected by Freud. French feminist theorists have, in turn, used Lacanian psychoanalytic theory to understand the problem that subjectivity presents for the Mother positioned in negativity (that is, as the one lacking the penis) in a Symbolic system organised around the phallus as signifier.

Hopefully this new feminist psychoanalytic discourse will provide the tools for understanding how it is that the Mother has been positioned as either absent or peripheral in culture and representation, or locked into oppressive polarised paradigms. If the 19th century, following Rousseau, chose to hypostasise the 'good' Mother, the 20th century has increasingly foregrounded her polar opposite 'monstrous' Mother. It is the reasons for this shift within the Master Mother Discourse as well as the perpetuation of the Discourse well into the 20th century that we need to understand better as we confront in our daily lives the contradictions, ambivalencies and complexities of Mothering.

Meanwhile, feminist art has begun to focus on the Mother's experiences of ambivalence and contradictory demands. We need more films that address the girl's Oedipal drama, exploring the conflicts of love/hate for the Mother, and of separation/individuation from her. Such representations, once inscribed in cultural discourse, will begin to counteract the limited traditional Mother paradigms that patriarchy has for so long kept intact.

Notes

1. Cf. Barbara Welter, 'The Cult of True Womanhood: 1820–1860', in *American Quarterly*, vol. 18, Summer 1966, pp. 151–74; and Nancy Cott, *The Bonds of Womanhood: Woman's Sphere in New England, 1780–1835* (New Haven and London: Yale University Press, 1977). For a synthesis of scholarship on these issues, see Carl N. Degler, *At Odds: Women and the Family in America from the Revolution to the Present* (New York: Oxford University Press, 1980).

2. For recent theories about changes in consciousness in twentieth-century capitalism, see Rachel Bowlby. *Just Looking: Consumer Culture in Dreiser, Gissing and Zola* (London: Methuen, 1985).

3. Elisabeth Badinter's provocative book, *The Myth of Motherhood: An Historical View of the Maternal Instinct* (London: Souvenir Press, 1980), overstates the case of both mothers' indifference and the absence of value for the child prior to Rousseau.

4. Cf. George D. Sussman, 'Parisian Infants and Norman Wet Nurses in the Early Nineteenth Century: A Statistical Study', in *Journal of Interdisciplinary History*, VII: 4, Spring 1977, pp. 637–653.

5. For evidence of contradictory discourses about childbearing in Puritan America see David Leverenz, *The Language of Puritan Feeling: An Exploration in Litera-*

ture, Psychology and Social History (New Brunswick, NJ: Rutgers University Press, 1980), especially Chapter Three.

6. Cf. discussion of this in Linda Kerber, *Women of the Republic: Intellect and Ideology in Revolutionary America* (Chapel Hill: University of North Carolina Press, 1980), pp. 23–6.

7. Jean-Jacques Rousseau, *Émile*, trans. Barbara Foxley (London: Dent, 1911; reprint 1974), pp. 325–8; 348–9.

8. Cf. Cora Kaplan, 'Wild Nights: Pleasure/Sexuality/Feminism', in *Formations of Pleasure* (London: Routledge and Kegan Paul, 1983), pp. 15–30, for discussion of Wollstonecraft's response to Rousseau.

9. Rousseau, *Émile*, p. 328.

10. Clearly, the concept of private and public spheres was not new in the 18th century (cf. for example, Richard Goldthwaite, *Private Wealth in Renaissance Florence*, Baltimore: John's Hopkins University Press, 1969); but I am arguing that the conception of the two spheres took on new resonances with Rousseau.

11. Working-class women, of course, always fell outside of the rhetoric of Mother Ideology since they usually worked out of necessity. Nevertheless, the discourses held sway and influenced all classes.

12. Leverenz, *Language of Puritan Feeling*, pp. 158–61.

13. Kerber, *Women of the Republic*, p. 231.

14. Ibid., p. 200.

15. Cf. Cott, *Bonds of Womanhood*, pp. 166–7. See also Jay Fliegelman, *Prodigals and Pilgrims, The American Revolution Against Patriarchal Authority, 1750–1800* (Cambridge University Press, 1982), p. 275, f.n. 52.

16. Ibid., p. 167.

17. Ibid., pp. 84–98.

18. Ibid., pp. 98–100.

19. Welter, *Cult of True Womanhood*, pp. 151–2.

20. It is significant that in a collection of short stories, edited by Frederick Ungar (*To Mother With Love*, New York: Stephen Daye Press, 1950), not one story (even those by women writers) contains a mother–daughter relationship.

21. The most famous articulation of this bias is Leslie Fiedler's *Love and Death in the American Novel* (New York: Criterion Press, 1960).

22. Peter Brooks, *The Melodramatic Imagination: Balzac, Henry James, Melodrama and the Mode of Excess* (New Haven: Yale University Press, 1976), pp. 35–6.

23. Ann Douglas, *The Feminization of American Culture* (New York: Alfred A. Knopf, 1977), pp. 71–2.

24. Cf. Margaret Fuller's *Women in the Nineteenth Century* (New York: 1845); Sarah Grimké's series of essays in *The Liberator*, 26 January 1838; and Elizabeth Cady Stanton's *The Women's Bible* (New York: 1895), for examples of this literature.

25. Cf. Mrs Sigourney's *Letters to Mothers* (New York: 1838), and for summaries of the child care literature generally stressing the point, Cott, *Bonds of Womanhood*, Chapter 2; Degler, *At Odds*, Chapters 4 and 5; Maxine Margolis, *Mothers and Such: Views of American Women and Why They Changed* (Berkeley, Los Angeles: University of California Press, 1985), Chapter 2.

26. Fuller, *Woman in the Nineteenth Century*.

27. Sigmund Freud, 'Beyond the Pleasure Principle', *The Standard Edition of the*

Complete Psychological Works of Sigmund Freud, (ed.) James Strachey (London: Hogarth Press, 24 vols., 1953–74), vol. 18, pp. 14–15.

28. Cf. Kaja Silverman, *The Subject of Semiotics* (New York: Oxford University Press, 1983), pp. 192–3, for the suggestion that we need to read both Freud and Lacan's 'models of the subject in relation to the dominant discursive practices which defined their immediate context, and which still largely prevail'.

29. Monique Plaza, 'The Mother/The Same: Hatred of the Mother in Psychoanalysis', *Questions féministes*, no. 7, February 1980; reprinted in *Feminist Issues*, Spring 1982, pp. 75–99.

30. For full discussion of Robert's book about Freudian creativity, cf. Sandy Flitterman, 'That "Once-Upon-a-Time ..." of Childish Dreams', *Cine-Tracts*, no. 13, Spring 1981, pp. 14–26.

31. Cf. Freud's essay, 'Female Sexuality' (1931), reprinted in *Sexuality and the Psychology of Love*, (ed.) Philip Rieff (New York: Collier Books, 1963), pp. 194–212.

32. The most notorious example is John Bowlby. See his *Maternal Care and Mental Health* and *Deprivation of Maternal Care* (Geneva: World Health Organisation, 1951; reprinted New York: Schocken, 1966).

33. Cf. Janice Doane and Devon Leight Hodges, 'Looking for Mrs Goodmother: D. W. Winnicott's "Mirror-Role of Mother and Family in Child Development"', *Enclitic*, vol. 6, no. 2, Fall 1982, pp. 51–7, for full discussion of this issue. The authors develop and expand issues dealt with in Juliet Mitchell, *Psychoanalysis and Feminism* (London: Allen Lane, 1974; New York: Random House, 1975).

34. Allon White, 'Why Did the Signifiers Come Out to Play?' (unpublished paper, 1983), p. 8.

35. Ibid., p. 9. Cf. also Jacques Lacan, *Écrits: A Selection*, trans. Alan Sheridan (New York: W. W. Norton & Co., 1977), especially Chapter One on 'The Mirror Stage as Formative of the Function of the I', and Chapter Four, 'The Freudian Thing'. For analysis of Lacan, cf. Kaja Silverman, *The Subject of Semiotics* (New York: Oxford, 1983); and Anika Lemaire, *Jacques Lacan* (London: Routledge, Kegan and Paul, 1977).

36. Cf. Rachel Bowlby, *Just Looking*.

37. Cf. Brooks, *The Melodramatic Imagination*, pp. 86–7.

38. Sally Mitchell, 'Introduction' to Mrs Henry Wood's *East Lynne*, (ed.) Sally Mitchell (New Brunswick, NJ: Rutgers University Press, 1984), pp. vii–xviii.

39. Christian Viviani, 'Who is Without Sin? The Maternal Melodrama in American Film, 1930–39' (reprinted in this volume, pp. 83–99).

40. Viviani's article lists numerous titles in the maternal melodrama category. To the woman's films which I discuss could be added: *Applause* (Mamoulian, 1929); *A Bill of Divorcement* (Cukor, 1932); *The Women* (Cukor, 1932); *Mother Wore Tights* (Walter Lang, 1947); *Mother Is a Freshman* (Lloyd Bacon, 1949); *Dinner at Eight* (Cukor, 1933); Mrs Miniver (Wyler, 1942); *The Best Years of Our Lives* (Wyler, 1946); *Little Women* (Cukor, 1933).

41. Cf. for example, Lois Banner, *Women in Modern America: A Brief History* (New York: Harcourt Brace, 1974), Chapter 4. Banner is useful in that she explores advertising and film in commenting on new developments.

42. I am indebted to Christine Gledhill for many points in this reading of *Imitation of Life*.

Producing and Consuming the Woman's Film

Discursive Struggle in *Now, Voyager*

MARIA LAPLACE

FOR FEMINISTS interested in how cinema constructs female subjectivity and female desire, it is necessary to move away from a purely formal analysis of the internal workings of a film text to a more historically specific analysis of the relation of text to context, that is, to examine film as an historical process of intertextuality. Only then can the complexities of patriarchal ideology and female resistance to it become clear.

One way to begin such an analysis is to explore how a film articulates the complex of discourses which structure its narrative, *mise en scène* and mode of address. This approach presumes spectators already knowledgeable in a variety of cultural and social dicourses, gendered spectators, historical spectators in existence at the moment of the film's production. The analysis then becomes, in part, a project of film history. Historical analysis offers feminist film theory a way in which to complicate questions about the 'positioning' of female spectators and the construction of 'femininity' by classic (Hollywood) film. Ahistorical readings often miss much of the complexity of these films' textual and ideological operations; lost are elements of contradiction, discursive struggle and subversive signification which throw up barriers to closure and patriarchal hegemony. Thus, my analysis of *Now, Voyager* is an attempt to contribute to an historical understanding of the woman's film and its functioning for female spectators.

As a production category, the woman's film occupied an important place in the Hollywood studio system by virtue of its immense popularity and profitability – during the 30s and 40s such films were churned out at a fantastic rate at both the A (quality) and B (low-budget) levels. According to *Hollywood Looks at Its Audience* (Handel, 1950), a summary of twenty years of Hollywood's own market research, studio executives were convinced (whatever the actuality) that women made up the majority of the film audience. The studios conducted gender-differentiated surveys to discover what it was that women (supposedly) wanted to see. Based on the results, a set of criteria were developed for attracting women to the movies: it was concluded that women favoured female stars over male, and preferred, in order of preference, serious dramas, love stories, and musicals. Furthermore, women were said to want 'good character development', and stories with 'human interest'. In one sense, the woman's film can be viewed as the attempt to cover as much of this territory as possible.

The woman's film is distinguished by its female protagonist, female point of view and its narrative which most often revolves around the traditional realms of women's experience: the familial, the domestic, the romantic – those arenas where love, emotion and relationships take precedence over action and events. One of the most important aspects of the genre is the prominent place it accords to relationships between women. A central issue, then, in any investigation of the woman's film is the problematic of female subjectivity, agency and desire in Hollywood cinema. A dominant argument is that masculinist discourses inevitably (re)position the woman's film for patriarchy. However, by looking at the genre as the intersection of different discourses bearing on women in the 1930s it is also possible to take into account the existence of the margins of dominant patriarchal culture of a circuit of female discourse which, although mediated by patriarchal institutions (such as publishing companies), is largely originated *by and for women*. This circuit consisting of mass female audience novels and non-fiction books, stories and articles in women's magazines, and even women's associations, is a major source and context of the woman's film: the literature was often the basis for the screenplays and the circuit provided the space in which the woman's film as a genre could be approached and read by female spectators. That patriarchal institutions profit from this circuit is unquestioned; what is open to debate is how this circuit, almost completely ignored by patriarchal scholarship, has functioned for women. Has this subordinate 'women's culture' in any way promoted discourse that is subversive to patriarchy? I would argue that it can do, as I attempt to show in my analysis of *Now, Voyager* but that this can only be perceived clearly by opening up these texts to historical, social, culture and specifically female metaphysical considerations.

To this end I identify three discourses privileged by *Now, Voyager*[1] and by the material which marketed it: *consumerism*, the *image of the female star*, and *women's fiction*. These are also among the main constituents of the woman's film genre, providing many of its terms and conventions.

Consumerism
Consumerism can be defined broadly as the ideology of fetishised commodity consumption in twentieth-century capitalism. Particularly in relation to film, consumerism can be seen as the locus of a capitalist attempt to co-opt the early demands of feminism and the needs of the expanding female workforce, through the creation of a new 'female market'; women's desires for sexuality, power, freedom and pleasure could be channelled into the passive purchase and consumption of mass-produced commodities.

The discourse of consumerism was well in place by the end of the 1920s.

Stewart Ewen argues that the advertising industry of the teens and 20s developed a strategy to advance the new phase of capitalism based on the surplus of goods made by mass production.[2] As mass production came to manufacture many of the goods once produced by women in the home (either individually or collectively), it became necessary and desirable to substitute buying and consuming as worthy and significant activities. Women were seen as the ideal targets for indoctrination into the idea that these activities were life's ultimate gratification.

Ewen describes a two-pronged scheme of attack directed at women. One strategy was to continue to address women as housewives and mothers, even though it was well-known that a relatively large percentage of women were working outside the home from World War One onward. Advertising tried to keep women identified with the home, but redefined 'home' to meet the demands of consumer capitalism, creating a new role for women as 'administrators of the home ... directing ... consumption by her selection of the goods and services that society was producing' (Ewen, p. 168).

The ideas of freedom and equality for women, widely disseminated by feminists in the 1900–1929 era, were consciously incorporated into the rhetoric of advertising as an additional weapon in its arsenal (Ewen, p. 169). Research into advertising trade journals shows that, for instance, advertisers were aware that cigarette-smoking was a symbol of emancipation for women and played on that association in their advertisements. Cigarettes were offered as aspects of freedom – and a new market for the tobacco industry was constructed. Choice and freedom for women in the ads became synonymous with the mass-produced goods of the market, robbing them of their connotation of structural social change. Nevertheless, the effects of the idea that freedom and choice were legitimately desirable for women could not be entirely contained by Big Business. This contradictory aspect of consumer capitalism, which, in its ceaseless search for raw materials and new markets, recruits potentially subversive ideologies, has bearing on every discourse pertaining to the woman's film.

The other major strategy of advertising aimed at women exhibits similar goals and themes, but concentrates on a different part of 'femininity', women's physical appearance, and uses the rhetoric and techniques of the then emerging fields of ego and social psychology.

While the ideology of beauty was not new, twentieth-century advertising introduced the notion that beauty was not a natural given (either present or absent), but achievable by any women – though *only* through the use of the correct goods: cosmetics, grooming aids, fashion. Advertisements continually reiterated to women that their ability to win and keep a husband was contingent on the acceptability of their looks. Seizing on the concept of the 'social self' developed by social psychology (the idea that identity was based on the reactions of others), ads represented women as surrounded by watching, hostile, critical eyes that searched out the flaws which would cause social ostracism. Only the use of the designated product could prevent disaster. 'Women were being educated to look at themselves as things to be created competitively against other women, painted and sculpted with the aids of the modern market ... the survival tactic of allurement became their most conspicuous form of self-definition' (Ewen, p. 172).

The way this ideology is taken up by the Hollywood cinema and the actual connection between the film and advertising industries is discussed by Charles Eckert.[3] Hollywood cinema, especially in the 1930s, was structured, in part, around the presentation of women as glamorous objects to be emulated and consumed, and around the creation of a *mise en scène* that 'fetishises' consumer objects and a consumerist lifestyle. Eckert links these modes of representation to the practice of advertising and product 'tie-ins' between manufacturers and Hollywood studios. Significantly, the main industries involved in tie-ins – the display of products in films and of stars in product advertisements – are all aimed mainly at female consumers: fashion, cosmetics, home furnishings and appliances.

The consumerist discourse, then, with its message that happiness for women depends on their self-creation as desirable objects through the consumption of mass-produced products was, by the end of the 1930s, very much a part of the contemporary flux of ideas and images.

'Now, Voyager' and Consumerism
The narrative of *Now, Voyager* revolves around the cure of an intelligent but highly neurotic and repressed young woman, Charlotte Vale.[4] In depicting her neurosis, the film clearly plays on many of the terms of consumerism, especially in its first half (up until the time Charlotte returns home from a convalescent cruise). The primary sign that she is 'sick' is the way she looks: dowdy, overweight, ungroomed and unmadeup; it is a source, as well as a symptom, of her neurosis. And the first phase of her cure is both figured by and a result of a glamorous transformation of her appearance which in turn brings about the next step forward, the love of a good man. It is this level of the film that the studio seizes on in its marketing approach. The attempt to rewrite the film's other stucturing discourses – the Bette Davis image, and the genre of women's fiction – in terms of consumerism is evident in the *Now, Voyager* Press Book,[5] a collection of featurettes, photos, advertisements and suggestions for local publicity meant for use by (male) exhibitors. Headlines on the featurettes read: 'Bette Shows How Not To Be Glamorous in New Film', 'Tailored Classics Score as Favorites in *Now, Voyager* wardrobe for Bette Davis'. Pictures of Davis adorn 'Proper Coiffure is Key to Beauty Success' and 'Time, Place and Climate Determine Proper Dress'.

A central strategy here is the promotion of the film as a how-to-be-beautiful guide with Davis as chief instructor. This is to be furthered with tie-in campaigns with local and national businesses: 'Cosmetics Chart Gets Your Message To The Gals; An Easy Way to Sell the Ladies: Print Locally and Distribute in Beauty Shops and Cosmetics Counters.'

The title of the film is to be linked to consumer activities and businesses:

> Window displays in shops catering to femme clientele should be a must in your campaign: Clothing Shops: special windows showing travelling ensembles and accessories – Banner line, 'Now Voyager, Buy Wisely ... Now!' Beauty Shops: for window displays and newspaper ad, 'Now Voyager, Sail Thou Forth to Seek and Find ... Beauty.'

The Press Book proposes inundating communities with a welter of material aimed to induce women not only to see the film – for its beautiful clothes, glamorous stars, and romantic locales – but also to fulfil their function as consumers.

At the film's beginning, Charlotte is sick, neurotic, on the verge of a nervous breakdown. Because she is deviant in her femininity – she is 'ugly', she is a 'spinster' – others make her the object of their definitions, their scrutiny. Her mother describes her to Dr Jacquith before we see her as 'my ugly duckling ... a late child. Of course, it's true such children are marked.' Dr Jacquith is 'the foremost psychiatrist in the country' brought in by Lisa, her sister-in-law, to observe Charlotte. But their – and our – observation of Charlotte is delayed, building suspense and fascination around the question 'how awful does she look?', 'she' being not only Charlotte, but Davis: will our pleasurable recognition of her be withheld? The first shots of her tease along this suspense: they are of fragmented body parts: hands carving an ivory box put down their tools, reach and put out a cigarette and carefully hide the butt and ashes. Heavy legs in dark stockings and orthopaedic Oxfords walk slowly down the stairs and almost walk back up. Something is clearly wrong with this body; it is furtive, faceless, disjointed. Charlotte's body is finally seen in its entirety in a long shot framed in an archway, from Dr Jacquith's point of view. We share with him the shock of her appearance: the horror of her dumpy figure, ridiculously old-fashioned, matronly dress and hairdo, her rimless glasses and those shoes. The unsuitability of her garb is underscored when Lisa walks into the shot to greet Charlotte. Lisa is the feminine ideal: chic, elegant, up-to-date; by contrast, Charlotte is hideously Victorian. This is immediately followed by the second shock of a closeup: Davis's face, shot in hard, flat lighting, has exaggeratedly thick eyebrows, is wan and tight. This, coupled with her pathologically shy manner (complete absence of feminine charm), add up to a spectacle of ugliness inducing in the spectator a kind of horrified fascination and pity.

Charlotte barely speaks: others speak of her, to her, for her; she can only react. Being unattractive means having no voice, means being the butt of abuse and ridicule, the object of a medical and controlling gaze. Charlotte's niece, June, continually taunts her, 'You look ravishing! New dress?', 'What's got into you – 'Fess up, a romance?' This interaction is reminiscent of the 'social self' concept used in advertising – the notion that identity is defined by the opinions of others, whose approval and disapproval create the self, and that these judgments are based primarily on a woman's appearance. June is the feared other who is always watching, criticising women's looks and behaviour, ready to reject and ostracise for not measuring up to conventional standards. Charlotte's self-deprecating comments throughout the first half of the film indicate that she engages in the self-critical self-scrutiny encouraged by consumerism. But, in keeping with its logic, 'ugliness' is only the condition of not doing the proper things to the body; grooming, dieting, makeup, fashion can make any woman 'attractive'. And being attractive (if not beautiful) is the prerequisite to self-esteem, for self-esteem is based on being desirable to people, women as well as men. 'Popularity' signifies happiness.

Now, Voyager stresses the relation between beauty and commodities in a flashback to Charlotte's youth. In terms of the narrative it is, in a sense, anomalous. It occurs very early on in the film, erupts into the text as a privileged moment of enunciation, narrated by Charlotte's voice-over and seen from her point of view; and disappears, the only true flashback in the entire film. But, in terms of the consumerist discourse, it provides important information. For in the flashback Charlotte is no ugly duckling, nor is she rejected by men, repressed, nor completely dominated by her mother. Instead, she is pretty, well-dressed, charming, passionate, defiant of her mother. The flashback figures what Charlotte's dialogue afterward will reinforce: she is 'naturally' attractive (and passionate) – it is her mother who has forced ugliness upon her by not allowing her to follow consumerist dictates on diet, shoes, glasses.

After the flashback ends, Charlotte cries out to Jacquith, 'What man would ever look at me and say I want you? I'm fat – my mother doesn't approve of dieting. Look at my shoes – my mother approves of sensible shoes ... My mother, my mother, my mother!!' Charlotte knows what is necessary to achieve the correct appearance and that the point of looking attractive is to be desired by men – she is knowledgeable in the consumerist discourse. The film implies that no man *would* want her as she looks. Her own self-designation, 'Miss Charlotte Vale, spinster', is a saying of the unspeakable. To be a woman rejected by men, unable to marry and assume the proper role of wife, is to be without value, cursed, driven to madness. Charlotte is an object lesson for women. (This is explicitly stated in the Press Book where Davis is quoted as saying, 'What an object lesson I am. It should make all women rise and run to their beauty parlours.')

The flashback serves the further purpose of interjecting the Bette Davis image and discourse into the film early on. The spectator is released into recognition of the accustomed 'attractive' Davis, movie star glamour intact, albeit a bit toned down to a very youthful 'natural' look. And thus we are prepared for the metamorphosis to come.

When it does happen, it is structured exactly like Charlotte's first appearance: she is talked about, others are waiting to see her, she is an enigma whose meaning cannot be grasped merely by being seen. The other passengers on the cruise comment as they wait for her so they can begin their first shore trip, 'I think she's been ill', 'She looks pale but interesting', 'Shh, here she comes.' Again a full body shot is delayed and we see her legs walk hesitantly on the gangplank and pause. This is followed by a slow pan up to her face – this time the body is unified, connected and whole. The shoes are fashionable, the legs are slim, the outfit perfectly accessorised with bag, gloves, hat. Charlotte's face is now elegantly made up (and shot with all the conventions of glamour photography). She not only looks like Bette Davis again, she looks like an extremely chic version of the Davis image. In place of the spectacle of ugliness, there is the spectacle of the metamorphosis – the thrill of 'before and after' so beloved of advertising directed at women. The spectator is offered an unmediated view of this spectacle, invited to dwell on this body, and there is a pleasurable erotic charge to the moment.

The cruise sequence represents the apotheosis of the consumerist discourse in the film. Charlotte's physical transformation is continually emphasised in the narrative and *mise en scène*. She is framed 'to be looked at', centred, radiantly lit and wears a different, dazzling ensemble in every scene. Her evening clothes are sequined and beaded to catch the light and cut to flatter and reveal her body. Her day outfits are just as eye-catching – striking hats with veils, matching accessories, jewellery and corsages. The many changes and the plethora of detail keep the spectator focused on and fascinated by Charlotte's body, her beauty, her surface.

In terms of the narrative, the metamorphosis is part of her cure. She looks better, which means she *is* better (although, very importantly, she is not yet 'well'). It is also what makes the next stage of her cure possible; it opens up to her the healing powers of love, romance, admiration and popularity.

The film makes it clear that Charlotte's appearance is a necessary part of Jerry's infatuation. He continually compliments her looks and clothes, and when he sees a photo of the 'old' Charlotte, he doesn't recognise her: 'Who's the fat lady with the heavy brows and all the hair?' Evidently she could never have won him looking as she used to.

Although Charlotte is self-abasingly grateful for Jerry's love and attention – a position which reaches its extreme in her words to him: 'I'm such a fool, such an old fool. These are an old maid's tears of gratitude for the crumbs offered her. No one ever called me darling before' – it is Jerry who exhibits his love for Charlotte and not the other way round. Jerry falls madly in love with Charlotte without any effort on her part; she is never seductive or flirtatious; he makes all the advances, all the requests to spend time together, speaks extravagant words of love to her: 'I'm head over heels in love with you', 'I can't get you out of mind or heart.' Charlotte never even tells Jerry she loves him.

This serves an important purpose. The stress of this part of the narrative is that *he* loves *her* – that is the meaningful thing. Charlotte cannot gain her sanity without clear-cut male approval; she must be seen, desired and pursued as an attractive and sexually viable woman. When Charlotte returns to Boston, she returns in triumph, even though she and Jerry have had to part in mid-cruise. At the dock, Charlotte is surrounded by admirers male (especially) and female. 'There was no lady on this cruise as popular as you', the cruise director tells her. Lisa and June are dumbfounded by the change not only in her looks but in her status as desirable object. June is completely won over: 'You look simply gorgeous, Aunt Charlotte! I love your new dress', and 'can you ever forgive me?' The rewards of stylishness and good grooming seem to be universal love and admiration.

If the film were to consider Charlotte cured by her physical transformation and the finding of true heterosexual love, one could hardly claim the film speaks a woman's discourse. However, this is not the case. In the first place, not even consumerism is seamless; as it is articulated both in the wider culture and in *Now, Voyager* it addresses, on one level, the empowerment of women, for the appeal is to female desire itself, to wants and wishes, to (libidinal) pleasure, sexuality and the erotic, and a species of economic decision and choice. What consumerism attempts to do is to liberate these forces through the creation of a female market, only to contain them in the service of patriarchy and capitalism. In *Now, Voyager* these more subversive aspects of consumerism surface through their interaction with the two other major discourses – those of the star, Bette Davis, and of women's fiction – which are more closely involved in the circuit of 'women's culture'. These structure the film with equal force, putting into question the consumerist placement of women, and causing an unresolvable tension in the text.

Stars and the Star-System
In the woman's film the star-system and the female stars who are associated with the genre have an especially important function for it is in the articulation of the patriarchal dichotomies of private/public and domestic/social that the conventions of the star-system mesh with those of women's fiction, consumerism and the woman's film itself to form a powerful constellation of forces addressing and engaging the female spectator on a variety of levels.

The star-system exists as both a marketing tool in the selling of films and as an institution which solicits the psychic mechanisms of identification. It does so in a variety of ways, one of the most important being the 'dramatisation of the private realm', with particular emphasis on the 'spectacle of consumption' (de Cordova, 1982 and Dyer, 1979).[6]

More precisely, the star is an actress/actor whose private life takes on as much significance as her/his acting of roles. The discourse of the star goes beyond professional considerations of competence, artistry, career; the star's private life is a major arena of discourse. Who the star is as a 'real person' plays a large part in the circuit of cinema-related texts: fan magazines, gossip columns, articles in main-stream magazines and the 'news' section of news-papers, star biographies and general books on Hollywood, newsreels, radio programmes.

Thus, any single viewing of the star in a film is imbued with an accumula-tion of significance made up not only of former roles, but of everything the spectator knows about the star as a 'real person'. This 'personal knowledge' of the star becomes a means to identify with her/him and possibly to emulate his/her personality and lifestyle.

What is particularly interesting is how much of this material is not only directed at women but is also written by them: most of the fan magazine articles I have seen are authored by women, and the three top Hollywood gossip columnists were women: Hedda Hopper, Louella Parsons and Sheilah Graham. Fan magazines have always been weighted towards articles about women stars, featuring descriptions of their home lives, clothes, entertaining and romantic relationships. Additionally, there are beauty advice columns, home decorating tips, fashion spreads, advice to the lovelorn (often 'written' by a woman star) and even recipes. This is a realm of discourse clearly marked as female, even when male stars are being discussed, and its themes, preoccupations and conventions are very similar to those of the woman's film and women's fiction.

On one level, the star-system can be taken as part of the larger effort of consumer capitalism to create and win a female market/audience. But on another level this construct cannot contain its effects, just as consumerism and advertising cannot. Certain ideas and pleasures are introduced into the realm of the public and legitimated with unpredictable consequences. The discourse of the star and the star-system can offer a validation of the values of the personal and the domestic (love, feelings, relationships), which stands in contrast to masculinist values of dominance, 'honour' and competition. And it offers a representation of female power in the social world which contests the confinement of women to the family: the female star is visibly a woman whose work earns her large amounts of money and public acclaim. The latter is especially powerful in films which call on the subversive signi-fications of their stars in narratives in which there is a particular heightening of discursive contradictions, as in the case of Bette Davis in *Now, Voyager*.

From 1938–43, Bette Davis was one of the ten top-grossing stars in Holly-wood and the most popular and critically acclaimed female star. She appeared almost exclusively in the woman's film and was popularly thought to appeal mainly to women spectators. What was Davis's fascination for female spectators?

In *Stars* (BFI, 1979), Richard Dyer maintains that stars become identified with or are constructed along the lines of various social types and cultural stereotypes. Certain of these can function for (rather than against) the groups they represent, especially in the case of social outgroups (women, gays, racial and ethnic minorities) and have the potential to be 'subversive or oppositional ... to dominant ideology' (p. 38). For women one such stereotype is the Independent Woman. In cinema the Independent Woman falls into two categories: one is the 'good' strong woman, noble, generous, sympathetic; the other is 'evil', aggressive, domineering, sexual, 'neurotic'. Both convey strength and take action.

Davis's film roles are almost all one or the other Independent Woman. Some of her most famous early roles are the latter type – 'bitches' Dyer calls them: *Of Human Bondage* (1934), *Dangerous* (1935, Oscar for Davis), *Jezebel* (1938, Oscar for Davis), and *The Little Foxes* (1939). In this incarnation, Davis plays 'headstrong' women, snappy, sharp-witted, wilful, selfish and sexy, who often come to a bad end (or turn noble and sacrifice themselves). In the years just preceding *Now, Voyager*, there were a growing number of 'good' women; courageous, intelligent, competent, who persevere with dignity in the face of difficulties: *Marked Woman* (1937, actually a combination of the two types), *The Sisters* (1939), *Dark Victory* (1939), and *All This and Heaven, Too* (1941).

What links these roles is Davis's performance style. Characterised by a high level of intensity, energy and charged emotionality, it conveys a specific 'personality' that interacts with each film role. The Davis style consists in a deliberate, clipped vocal inflection; darting eye movements and penetrating stares; a swinging, striding walk; gestures such as clenching fists and sudden, intense drags on cigarettes; and quick shifts in mood and register. These connote assertiveness, intelligence, internal emotional conflict and strength. Her performances are 'bravura' – they call attention to their own skill and display pleasure in it. It is a 'powerful' performance style and adds an extra dimension of transgressive excess to the Independent Woman film roles.

As forceful in constructing a star image as film roles and performance style is the publicity material written *about* the star: commentary, biography and gossip. Since it appears not to be deliberate image-making, it appears '... more authentic. It is thus privileged or rather taken to give privileged access to the "real person" of the star' (Dyer, p. 69). This drama of the star's personal life is a central feature of the workings of the star-system, serving as a kind of anchor to identification, drawing the spectator 'close' to this 'person' and encouraging empathy, which can be brought into play in the reading of a film.

In looking at a variety of articles on Davis, written from 1934–42, I am struck by how similar they are to the themes and forms of women's fiction (see below, pp. 151–154), especially the fan magazine features, and how much they differ from what Dyer describes as the major motifs of the discourse of stardom – an elaborate lifestyle featuring large homes, swimming pools and limousines; leisure activities such as sports, hobbies and parties and, especially for female stars, notions of charm, sex appeal and glamour.

By contrast, the Davis 'story' is of a plucky, resourceful, 'self-made' woman, whose success is due not to beauty, but to personal qualities of talent, determination, and down-to-earth self-awareness. The product of a fatherless, mother-supported, lower-middle-class family, Davis, like the heroines of women's fiction, meets and surmounts adversity because she knows who she is and what she wants:

> She's not your ordinary blue-eyed blonde, this Davis girl. She's ambitious, courageous, un-complaining with a distinct mind of her own ... willing to work for what she gets out of life; the world is too full of women – and men – who think it owes them a living. ('Bette from Boston', *Silver Screen*, in Martin Levin (ed.), *Hollywood and the Great Fan Magazines*.)

Thus, the image is strongly marked by attributes of strength and independence, constructed in another way through the depiction of Davis as anti-glamour and anti-consumerism, eschewing all the trappings of stardom:

> Davis dislikes equally the stuffed shirts and glamour girls of Hollywood and makes no effort to please them ... Her social circle is made up of non-professionals, including her sister; her closest approach to a hobby is her interest in dogs. Informality is her keynote ... she no longer dyes her hair and she never diets. ('Bette Davis', *Life*, 8 January 1939.)

Work is the privileged aspect of the Davis image; she is portrayed as completely dedicated to her career. The qualities of strength, independence and devotion to career find their most forceful representation in the widely reported stories of Davis's 1936 lawsuit against Warner Bros. The first actor to try to break the infamous seven-year contract, Davis stressed in her suit that she wanted control over her work, contending that the studio's choice of material jeopardised her career. The press reports are sympathetic to her position. *Life*'s cover story on Davis, written three years after the trial, begins with a lengthy account of the suit – an index of its centrality to her image – and states that she was a better judge of material than her employers and that, though she lost her case in court, she won the battle for better parts. They add, 'if Davis had won her case, other stars would have rebelled also and she would have become the Joan of Arc of a cinema revolution.'[7] Davis, then, came to signify rebellion against authority and a willingness to fight for herself and her autonomy as an artist.

Attempts are made to contain this relatively unconventional 'femininity'. One method is to explain her 'eccentricities' in terms of the regional stereotype of Davis's native New England, the Yankee. Yankees are thought to be particularly strong-minded, self-reliant, self-disciplined and ascetic, devoted to the Puritan value of hard work. (Interestingly, two other similarly unconventional Independent Woman stars, Katherine Hepburn and Rosalind Russell, are also New Englanders.)

Another is to claim that she is a great artist and not just a mere movie star: hence she is justified in deviating from feminine norms. It is acceptable that finding time to spend with her husband is difficult 'with Bette working pretty consistently most of the time'[8] and that she says 'I'm not very domestic',[9] because she is 'the ablest US-born movie star',[10] 'Dramatic Actress No. 1',[11] and 'the screen's finest actress and Hollywood's most regular person'.[12] A different approach calls Davis's sexuality into question and this strategy has a double edge. On the one hand, questions are raised about Davis's desirability to and desire for men (and the Yankee stereotype is recruited here, with references to Davis's 'New England conscience'). On the other hand, her image's transgressiveness is reinforced in more positive ways for women. Thus, while doubt is cast on whether she is sexually passionate in her marriages – Davis divorced and remarried during this period – a more companionate and egalitarian idea of marriage (much like that of nineteenth-century women's fiction) emerges, and passion is shifted to the realm of work and creativity. Two quotes are exemplary here:

> Another indication of how satisfactory she finds her professional life was an opinion of marriage, 'Domesticity is all right if it's not carried too far.' ... Characteristic was the reason Harmon Nelson divorced the screen's most celebrated impersonator of vixens ... she studied her parts in bed. ('Bette Davis', *Life*, 8 January 1939)

> Bette said she wasn't going to miss all the fun of a partnership marriage because she was a movie star. They had a plan of living which would prevent either of them from feeling dominated or cheated of independence. Ham paid his way, Bette paid hers. They had separate expense accounts and shared household expenses. ('That Marital Vacation', *Modern Screen*, 1938, in Martin Levin (ed.), *Hollywood and the Great Fan Magazines*.

The emphasis on economic independence and mutuality and the idea that a woman popularly thought to be neither beautiful nor sexy could become a major film star on the basis of her talent, persistence and appeal to female spectators, contradict the dominant patriarchal discourses on the achievement of female stardom – the myths of (passive) 'discovery' due to beauty and of 'sleeping one's way to the top'.

Thus, Davis's image in 1942 could offer a certain kind of ego ideal for women: a woman who is intelligent, articulate, self-possessed, dedicated to her profession and an artist, willing to fight for herself; a woman whose satisfaction and success are not based on passivity, romance or male approval; a woman with (a relative amount of) power. As an historical construction of 'woman', it enters into the circuit of female discourses and discursive struggle.

In the first part of *Now, Voyager*, and particularly in its promotion, consumerist discourse attempts to use the Davis image as a commodity. The film was sold as a Davis vehicle, exploiting spectator knowledge of her previous roles and personal life as major marketing tools. Thus, exhibitors are exhorted to 'remind your fans that Bette Davis has given them some of their most dramatic film entertainments' and the Press Book lists them at length. However, the roles stressed are the 'bitch' roles, with *Now, Voyager* presented, inaccurately, as a completely new departure: 'Recent releases seemed to indicate she was reaching new heights of insolence and selfishness ... the change in character in *Now, Voyager* is sudden, complete and probably healthy'. The Press Book differentiates between these roles and the 'real' Bette Davis. She is not 'a neurotic, hyperthyroid young woman with a tragic outlook on life' but rather 'a lady whose chief enthusiasms are her New England farm, her horses and practical jokes'. The 'real' Bette 'is from New England and therefore knows what an inhibition is'.

The Press Book attempts to link the representation of the 'real' Davis with her character in *Now, Voyager*, Charlotte Vale. Like certain elements of the Davis image, Charlotte is a New Englander from Boston, inhibited and unglamorous; during the course of the film she is physically transformed and her sexuality is freed. The Press Book's strategy is to use the name of the actress and the character interchangeably, implying that it is Davis who is being glamorised: 'Bette is unattractive to begin with but beautiful before the film is well underway.' This blurring of actress and role reinforces the recruitment of the Davis image to promote a consumerist discourse on female beauty and grooming. By enlisting the strong, sensible and poised elements of the Davis image in the form of her supposed beauty advice to women, with a covert playing on her reputation as unglamorous and uninterested in fashion, the impression is given that Davis, as well as Charlotte Vale, has changed in appearance and has learned to value these skills.

However, as the film progresses the contradictoriness (for female audiences) of consumerism and the Davis image are activated as they intersect with the major structuring discourse of women's fiction and are thereby pulled into the circuit of women's culture, underscoring the contradictions of the woman's film as a genre.

Women's Fiction and the Woman's Film: Literary Sources and Conventions
Discussion of melodrama and the woman's film has consistently attempted
to trace back the sources of the conventions and ideologies which shape these
film genres. French melodrama (Elsaesser, 1972), Greek drama (Mulvey,
1977) and pulp women's romantic fiction (Cook, 1983 and Harper, 1983)
have been advanced as major antecedents. Each has contributed to the fund
of forms and values which structure these genres but there is, in this listing, a
major lacuna: the American corpus of the literary genre which feminist scholars have approached under the rubric 'women's fiction'. An examination of
this largely neglected literary corpus dismissed previously on much the same
grounds as the woman's film, amplifies the meanings produced by the films.
An important aspect of this endeavour is the *national* specificity it brings to
the existing analysis. Hollywood cinema is, after all, a national cinema with
roots in the pre-existing forms of American culture and with a specific set of
national preoccupations and representations. Thus, American women's fiction is important since it has provided not only many popular representations
of women but also was often the source of the films themselves – for example
novels by Fannie Hurst, Olive Higgins Prouty and Edna Ferber.[13]

The object of recent feminist literary scholarship,[14] women's fiction as a
genre originated in the 19th century, peaked at mid-century and then evolved into a variety of literary off-shoots in the 20th century. It was a quite different form from the current mass female audience fiction, the Harlequin or
Gothic pulp romance with its purple prose and purposely unrealistic (fantastic) narratives, settings and characters. This latter strand of fiction derives
from the Gothic tradition exemplified by the Brontë novels, *Jane Eyre* and
Wuthering Heights, and has existed side by side with the realism of the
women's fiction I wish to discuss. Nineteenth-century women's fiction was
based in the formal, ideological realm of bourgeois realism. Great attention
to realistic detail, regional difference and class manners and mores were
prominent features of the genre's conventions. In narrative and setting,
the novels and stories were committed to a 'realistic' rendering of women's
social and subjective experiences, with clearly moralistic and didactic
intentions.

The basic narrative pattern of women's fiction is a 'heroine's text', a story
of a woman's personal triumph over adversity. The dominant variation features a young woman who is forced, because of circumstances beyond her
control, to endure a series of hardships completely on her own. As she
struggles to survive and build a satisfactory life for herself she finds the inner
resources – will, courage and intelligence – that permit her to succeed.
(Perhaps the best known example today is *Little Women* by Louisa May
Alcott.)

The form, then, on one level espouses a quintessential American bourgeois
ideology, but with an important twist: the notion of the self-made *woman*.

Nina Baym (*Woman's Fiction*, 1980, p. 3) claims for the particular phase of the genre she discusses a 'limited, pragmatic feminism'. That is, while the texts focus on the individual, they locate the source of her suffering in the disadvantaged status of her gender and advocate female literacy and education as the route to the power and knowledge necessary to remedy the situation.

But the emphasis of the novels is on the personal and relational, not the institutional and economic. Women can change their lot in life by changing their personalities, cultivating a new sense of self-worth and acquiring knowledge. America offers the opportunities to the women who have the 'will' to take advantage of them. The key is 'finding oneself', one's 'true identity'. This is a classic message of American ego psychology and, as Baym says, these novels are about 'the formation of the feminine ego'. (Baym, p. 4). Today this might be criticised as a reactionary ideology but it is important to take into account that in a nineteenth-century context the assertion that women *have* a self, that is, are subjects and fully human rather than unknowably Other or elements of nature, is, to some extent, subversive.

This narrative trajectory is an aspect of women's fiction that continues into the 20th century. Many novels and stories centre on the heroine's process of self-discovery, on her progression from ignorance about herself (and about the world in general) to knowledge and some kind of strength. *Now, Voyager* both as film and novel (the film closely follows the book, written in 1941 by Olive Higgins Prouty) is an almost literal dramatisation of this theme. The heroine, Charlotte Vale, begins in a state of self-loathing and lack of individual identity, and with the help of psychoanalysis, succeeds in building a firm 'ego-identity': she both 'finds' and remakes herself.

The ideology of women's fiction is not limited, however, to this level of individualism/identity. The corpus also subscribes to the Victorian 'cult of domesticity'. More than just a term to describe settings and plot concerns, it refers to a strain of nineteenth-century feminism which valorised the domestic – defined by the values of love, support and shared responsibility – over the brutal, masculinist values of early industrial capitalism.

The ideal and ultimate project of the cult of domesticity was the eradication of the patriarchal capitalist distinction between the social and the domestic. The latter would subsume the former and society would become one large 'home'. The family was seen as the central agent in this social transformation: its highest values – love, caring for the weak, and mutual responsibility – would prevail and women would gain social power and value accordingly. In women's fiction, it is the heroine's project to *create* the happy home, to transform the original unhappy and abusive biological family – a symbolic microcosm of the contemporary society – into a domestic community composed of relatives, friends and the homeless and needy. The ending of *Now, Voyager* offers a vision of exactly this kind of utopian, female-created and governed domesticity, substituting for the earlier destructive biological family.

The issue of the representation of female sexuality and its connection to a thematic of female sacrifice, much debated by feminist critics of the woman's film, can be contextualised and historicised by an analysis of their treatment in women's fiction. Baym argues that the form is structured by a Victorian world-view: 'an oppressive sense of reality and its habit of disappointing expectations' and the belief that 'duty, discipline, self-control and sacrifice (within limits) were not only moral but also useful strategies in getting through a hard world' (p. 7). This belief-system continued to inform many twentieth-century examples of the form, such as *Stella Dallas, Back Street* and *Imitation of Life* which were to serve as the paradigmatic texts for many of the woman's films of the 30s. One explanation for the popularity of this type of film is the resonance this world view must have had during the Depression. The belief in progress, upward mobility and a future of unlimited opportunity that characterised much of the discourse of the 20s was profoundly shaken. In lieu of that decade's cult of hedonism and personal fulfilment, there was a turn back to the more nineteenth-century notion of the necessity for sacrifice and its potentially ennobling effect.

In American film, the Depression coincided with the imposition of the Hays Code of censorship which restricted certain forms of representation, particularly of sexuality and political or individual rebellion through violence, enforced especially in stories of contemporary life. Thus, the general cultural search for a philosophy of life adequate to the hard times of the Depression and the film industry's search for acceptable material within the strictures of the Code was partially satisfied by turning to the vast fund of nineteenth-century literature and its twentieth-century descendents, a great deal of it expressing a moral philosophy that resonated with the conditions of the 30s.

But the articulation of sacrifice with the repression of female sexuality in nineteenth-century women's fiction needs to be further contextualised. On one level, women's fiction was reacting to an earlier popular mass fiction, the 'novel of sensibility' in which the heroine is seduced, abandoned and destroyed. The notion of women's innate carnal weakness in the face of male sexual power was countered with a depiction of women as innately good, pure and rational. As 'proof' women's fiction offered heroines who resisted sexual temptation and showed strength in adversity. In the Victorian form of the genre, sexuality was a force that must be transcended (partly on account of traditional Christian ideology and also, presumably, because of the lack of contraception and the dire social consequences of unwed motherhood).

As the form moved into the 20th century this became complicated by the rise of 'vulgar' Freudianism – by the 20s there was an ambivalent acknowledgment of the existence and even legitimacy of female sexuality, subject however to regulation by patriarchal institutions: marriage, monogamy and, in the case of deviance, psychiatry. Women's fiction began to represent female desire and even to embrace the (vulgar Freudian) notion that sexual repression leads to neurosis.

The difficulty, however, of negotiating ideas of female desire in the context of an immediately post-Victorian society gave rise to certain narrative patterns – and convolutions. Motifs of adulterous relationships, impossible true love, noble illegitimate motherhood, can be seen as strategies in the attempt somehow to sanction female desire and escape regulation while at the same time remaining somewhere within the law of society.

Perhaps the purest form of representation of female desire is in the type of ideal heterosexual relationship and ideal romantic hero featured in women's fiction, ideals which remain remarkably constant from the Victorian period onward. This construction of heterosexuality, predominant in female-created fictions, is noticeably absent in much of male-authored fiction.

The enduring appeal for women of this fantasy has been addressed by feminist theorists such as Chodorow.[15] While men feel an intense ambivalence towards the experiences of merging and fusion, and towards 'feminine' maternal emotions and behaviours, an ambivalence produced by their position in the traditional patriarchal nuclear family, women, because they are differently placed, feel this much less. Since girls are never forced to reject identification with their mothers, they continue to attempt to re-experience and recreate the bliss of mother–child fusion and nurturance.

The themes and conventions of women's fiction, upon which the woman's film drew, proved remarkably durable in attracting female spectators to the cinema and promotion of *Now, Voyager* used women's fiction as part of its selling strategy, testifying to its power as a female discursive circuit. Davis is linked with bestselling books, primarily written by women, in a featurette entitled 'Bette the Bestseller Girl' which lists the title and author of every Davis film adapted from a well-known novel. The actual advertisements to be used in newspapers and magazines, and as posters for the theatre also stress the link with women's fiction. There, *Now, Voyager* is described as 'from the bestseller by the author of *Stella Dallas*', 'the bestselling novel that shocked Boston speechless'. The ads dwell on the transgressiveness and high emotionality of the film: 'Don't pity me ... in our moment together, I found the joy that most women can only dream of. Bette Davis as a woman who refused to accept society's code ... meets Paul Henreid, the lover, at last to match her every emotion!' These references to the structures of romance that mark women's fiction attest to the studio's attempt to bring in female audiences by any means necessary, even to the extent of endorsing women who 'break society's code' to find 'joy'. Thus women's fiction provided not only a rich source of raw materials for films, but in addition an important, long-standing and well established context of reception.

"don't blame me for what happened..."

It happens in the best of families!"

BETTE DAVIS
more radiant, more exciting than ever — in love with

PAUL HENREID
the man, at last, to match her every emotion

WARNER BROS'. TRIUMPH

Another best-seller from the author of 'Stella Dallas' — another great role for Bette!

"Now, Voyager"

| A HAL B. WALLIS PRODUCTION | with CLAUDE RAINS |

GLADYS COOPER • BONITA GRANVILLE • ILKA CHASE • Directed by IRVING RAPPER
Screen Play by Casey Robinson • From the Novel by Olive Higgins Prouty • Music by Max Steiner

THEATRE & DATE BUY WAR BONDS AT THIS THEATRE AS A SALUTE TO YOUR HEROES!

155

Consumerism, Bette Davis and Women's Fiction in 'Now, Voyager'

We can now look at *Now, Voyager* as structured around two problematics: the representation of female sexuality and questions of female independence and autonomy. These are linked along the axis of female desire which indeed is the central structuration of the woman's film.

Now, Voyager is on a manifest level the story of a woman's discovery of her identity and recovery of her sexuality. The film links the two through the use of a psychoanalytic discourse on repression and individuation which in part structures the narrative and finds its overt expression in the words of Dr Jacquith. Like other instances of twentieth-century women's fiction, the narrative is an amalgam of aspects of popularised Freudianism – repression of sexuality leads to hysterical neuroses and dominating mothers keep children dependent, preventing them from developing a mature sexual identity – and themes of female self-discovery, triumph over adversity and heroic sacrifice common to the 19th century.

Now, Voyager grapples with these themes and ideas in the terms of women's fiction and the woman's film: it focuses on the family, the mother–daughter relationship and romantic love as the arenas for the drama of women's lives. The emphasis is on the personal life, yet it opens out into questions of mastery, independence, achievement and work. Particularly important in this process is the Bette Davis discourse; her image provides a link to the struggles of women in the social world of economic and cultural power.[16]

Female desire then is figured in two ways: sexuality/romance and independence/mastery, and female subjectivity is constructed by a female point of view on these.

The film begins with Charlotte in a state of lack. Her sexuality is repressed, she is dependent on her mother, she does not know herself. Very much in line with the conventions of women's fiction/woman's film, Charlotte's family is incomplete – her father is dead – and unhappy. Within the family, Charlotte is used and abused (Charlotte: 'I am my mother's companion; I am my mother's servant.'). As in the classic narrative trajectory of nineteenth-century women's fiction, she is forced out of the family and into the world: first to Cascade and the cruise, and then again, after her return home, to Cascade and the camping trip with Tina. Charlotte's struggle is the same as the heroines of women's fiction: she struggles to know herself and to become strong so that she can create, on her own, a better family, and a satisfactory life for herself.

Female sexuality is a key term throughout the film. The beginning posits repression of female sexuality as a major cause of Charlotte's neurotic misery and ties this repression to her lack of independence from her mother. As long as Charlotte allows her mother to dictate the terms of her life, her sexuality as an adult female cannot be expressed for this means separation from her

156

mother. Following a classically Freudian female oedipal scenario, it is Dr Jacquith, the paternal masculine figure, who intervenes between the two women to push Charlotte out of the family.

A major project of the first sequence of the film is to establish that Charlotte *is* sexual, that she is merely 'inhibited' rather than frigid or asexual. When Jacquith asks Charlotte to show him around the Vale home in an attempt to gain her confidence, she allows him to enter her room where the signs of her sexuality, hidden from her mother, manifest themselves.

JACQUITH (noticing the concealed cigarette ashes): You don't happen to have a cigarette hidden away someplace?
CHARLOTTE (with increasing hysteria): Do you think I hide cigarettes, Doctor? Where do I hide them? Behind the books? Cigarettes and medicated sherry and books my mother won't allow me to read. A whole secret life hidden up here behind a locked door.

The cigarettes, liquor and 'adult' books are all signs of Charlotte's sexual desire 'hidden behind a locked door'.

Charlotte continues: 'How very perceiving you are . . . I was just about to hide this album. You really should read it . . . The intimate journal of Miss Charlotte Vale, spinster.' This even more titillating reference to her secreted sexuality leads us into the flashback, where we will be allowed to enter into the subjectivity of the most despised of women, she who is rejected by men.

I want to look at the flashback closely for it is a condensation of all the discourses that structure the film. It is preceded by a medium close-up of the album with the camera taking up a position behind Charlotte and Jacquith as they look at it. Charlotte's hand turns the pages and her voice starts to tell her story, 'You wouldn't have known me then; I was twenty then.' There is a dissolve from the pages of the album turning from left to right to a close-up of the printed pages of a book turning the other way – a chapter heading is clearly discernable. Dissolve to a close-up of Charlotte and Leslie, the young ship's officer, kissing passionately, romantic music up.

Here Charlotte's book, her journal, becomes a printed book and refers, I think to the novel, *Now, Voyager*: books by women, a woman's novel, a woman's story: authenticating the film – and the flashback – by tying it to the circuit of popular women's fiction.[17]

The first shot of the flashback, the first image of Charlotte's subjectivity (Charlotte by Charlotte) is one of passion. That its content is her sexuality is made clear not only by the visuals but also by the dialogue and Charlotte's voice-over. After Leslie compliments her on the fieriness of her kiss – 'I say, that was a scorcher!' – she moves to kiss him again and he pulls back in surprise. Charlotte: 'Leslie you look so funny . . . I thought men didn't like girls who were prudes.' Leslie: 'Oh you're gorgeous, Charlotte! Give us

157

another.' And they kiss again. Charlotte's voice-over then comments: 'I had read that in books about men not liking girls to be prudes.' This is followed by an extremely dynamic tracking shot of Charlotte walking energetically across the deck, her face glowing, her hair blowing in the breeze while her voice-over continues: 'Leslie said he preferred me to all other girls because I was so responsive. He said the others were like silly schoolgirls compared to my lovemaking.'

The emphasis is on the strength of Charlotte's sexuality: she is desirable and *desiring*. In terms of the film's narrative, this sets the precedent for Charlotte's future sexual liberation; it indicates that she is a spinster not because she is afraid of sex, not because she hates men — all-pervasive explanations in the 30s for female neurosis and 'spinsterhood'. The reference to books is interesting in that it seems to suggest that knowledge about female sexuality can be found there.

The flashback continues with Charlotte's voice-over recounting how she deceives her mother by telling her she will be in the library when, in fact, she has gone to join Leslie in one of their favourite 'trysting places', a limousine on the freight deck. They are discovered there in the midst of a passionate embrace by Mrs Vale and the Ship's captain. Charlotte (defiantly): 'I don't care. I'm glad.' Leslie: 'I want to marry your daughter. We're engaged to be married.' Mrs Vale orders Charlotte to her room and the camera tracks with her as she strides proudly down the shadowy deck. Charlotte (voice over): 'I had said I was glad and I *was* glad. He had defied my mother and placed me on a throne and before witnesses too. It was the proudest moment of my life.' Dissolve once again to the printed pages turning and then to Charlotte in the present.

Although Charlotte displaces the rebellion onto Leslie, it is clearly hers; her assertion of her sexuality against her mother's attempts to control it. This calls up the Bette Davis image: the sharp way she delivers her lines, the striding walk, the defiant eyes, are all her characteristic Independent Woman performance style (as opposed to the sweet, naïve Charlotte of the rest of the flashback and the cowering, hysterical Charlotte of the 'present'). The flaunting of sexual transgressiveness refers back to her 'evil woman' roles and the assertion of independence in the face of authority is a strong part of the discourse of the 'real' Bette Davis. Although, as Charlotte says to Jacquith, 'my moment didn't last', this vision of Charlotte, which connects her with the Bette Davis discourse — her subjective 'description' of herself — resonates over the repressed and oppressed Charlotte of the rest of the sequence.

Charlotte's struggles with her mother are, on one level, over the expression of her sexual desire. The family is the repressive agent which clamps down on female sexuality; marriage is not a matter of passion but of economics and class. Mrs Vale did not permit Charlotte to marry Leslie because he was not good enough for a 'Vale of Boston'. She thoroughly approves when, much later in the film, Charlotte is wooed by Elliot Livingstone: 'I'm only surprised that you, of all people, should bring such a feather to the family cap.' And Charlotte's decision to end the engagement and 'remain in single blessedness' brings about the quarrel that causes Mrs Vale's fatal heart attack. Thus, while at first it seems that Mrs Vale wants only to keep Charlotte attached to her and asexual, she does resign herself to Charlotte's leaving with the promise of an alliance to a more powerful family.

When Charlotte leaves the family space to go on the cruise (with Cascade as interim 'good family' where she is 're-educated', as Jacquith says), the film turns to a more thorough representation of romantic passion than the flashback can offer.

Romance

The notion of 'romance' is a very significant one for the woman's film and for women's fiction. Having discussed representations of female sexuality and desire in a general way, I want to turn now to a more specific consideration of romance as a way in which female desire is figured in female fictions. In the novels of women's fiction, the ideal heterosexual relationship is always represented in terms of perfect understanding, a mutual transparency between the lovers, a relation of 'soulmates'. Caring and mutuality are part of this relation, as is admiration and respect on the part of the man for the woman. The romantic hero is a 'maternal man' capable of nurturing the heroine; tender, expressive about his feelings, he does not hesitate to express his love and admiration, passionately and often poetically. The woman's film follows these conventions. To these are added a particular *mise en scène* of female desire that focuses on the lovers' faces and, in particular, the eyes and mouth. The gaze, the kiss, the voice become the locus of eroticism. Charlotte and Jerry's romance is visually constructed around a series of gazes at each other, and around rituals of lighting and smoking cigarettes.

The progress of their romance, and of the activation of Charlotte's desire is marked by the intensity and duration of their looking into each other's eyes. At the beginning of the cruise sequence, Charlotte's eyes are shaded by the wide brim of her hat and her eyes are often downcast. Jerry, by contrast, maintains a warm and intense gaze at Charlotte that culminates in a medium close-up the first time he lights her cigarette. Charlotte resists this look, only able to give him quick glances. What enables Charlotte to look actively at Jerry is his growing admission of his vulnerability. As he confesses to her the details of his unhappy family life, it is Jerry who has difficulty looking at Charlotte and Charlotte who activates her own intense looks at Jerry. These 'looks at' finally culminate in 'looking into' each others' eyes as they grow to know each other; it is this intimate gaze that marks the erotic.

Both visually and narratively, Charlotte and Jerry are figured as alike, as male and female twins, mirrors. Formally, they alternate in taking up enunciatory positions, first one, then the other holding the point of view. This is marked in the narrative by alternating confessions of personal unhappiness and by alternating positions of strength and weakness.

After Charlotte first hears the full story of Jerry's marriage from his friend, Deb, Jerry approaches her on the deck and is unable to meet her eyes. It is then that Charlotte touches him for the first time, putting her hand on his arm; and only when she takes control of the situation by distracting his attention to the sights of Rio Harbour and admonishing him to 'listen to your tour guide', can he raise his eyes to hers and whisper, 'Thank you.' This is an exact parallel of a previous scene where Charlotte finally confesses her illness to him and he shows tender concern for her well-being. She looks into his eyes and whispers, 'Thank you. Oh, many, many thanks.'

Similarly, in the scene in which they have an accident with their rented car, it is Jerry who is anxious and confused in his dealings with the Brazilian driver and Charlotte who is calm and rational. This is the necessary prelude to the night they spend together waiting to be rescued in which Charlotte is finally able to 'lose her inhibitions'.

What this indicates is that in female fictions, the romantic hero must be 'feminised'; that is, he must abandon his position of masculine control, aggressiveness and dominance and take up a position of equality to the woman. Female desire here is based on identification with the other through knowledge of the personal – the sharing of emotions and life stories. It makes sense in this context that the face and the voice should be the centre of eroticism for these are the most individualised parts of the body.

Thus, this is an eroticism very different from the voyeurism and fetishism of male genres which are dependent on distance from and disavowal of knowledge about the object of desire.

However, another kind of distance is structured into the eroticism of romance. There is always an obstacle to complete merging and mutual possession. Romance is often figured in terms of the forbidden. In the case of *Now, Voyager* the first romance, between Charlotte and Leslie, is transgressive on both sides: Charlotte is lying to her mother and Leslie is not allowed to consort with passengers.

Charlotte and Jerry's romance is clearly illicit because he is married to someone else. The one relationship that is socially acceptable, that promises to lead to marriage and children, is between Charlotte and Elliot Livingstone and it is dull and passionless. Any reference to sex, no matter how indirect, shocks him; Charlotte feels 'depraved' at her own sexuality in his presence. The depiction of the one married couple seen in the film, Jerry's friends on the cruise, Deb and Mack, is similar; they hardly relate to each other and are older, parental figures. Jerry's marriage, which is only referred to, is nightmarish; it is the result, according to Deb, of 'propinquity and propriety' and of Jerry's 'ruling passion not to hurt Isabelle'. Isabelle is a weak, clinging martyr who tyrannises and rejects both her daughter Tina and Jerry himself: 'My wife calls my lighter moments *"trying to be funny"*.'

Thus, the depiction of marriage does not offer fulfilment of desire, but rather its end. The impossibility of the heroine's marriage to the hero in the woman's film is not necessarily a renunciation of sexuality on the woman's part; rather it is the prolongation of passion and desire. Emotional intensity is substituted for genital sexuality. The woman is neither fully possessed by the man nor taken for granted; she must continually be wooed and courted; romantic love is kept outside the mundanity of the everyday. Furthermore, the hegemonic placement of woman in the family is subverted. Romance is always structured outside and against the family. In *Now, Voyager* the family is the site of repression and frustration.

This is figured at the end of *Now, Voyager* by the repetition of the cigarette-smoking ritual at the moment when Jerry finally accepts a relationship with Charlotte that is outside marriage and sexual union. Jerry places both his and Charlotte's cigarette in his mouth, lights them, hands one to Charlotte, both inhale deeply and exhale smoke at the other. The 'excess' of this gesture with its allusion to genital sexuality suggests that their relationship will remain intense and erotic if not sexual.

In *Now, Voyager* there is a second discourse of female desire that is fully as strong as the discourse of female sexuality: the desire for autonomy, independence and mastery, which is strongly linked to the Bette Davis image. This is structured in much the same way it is in women's fiction, by a specifically female narrative trajectory: the separation from the mother and the achievement of an independent identity as a 'healthy' mature woman. Thus, although on one level Charlotte's cure comes through beauty and the help of men, on another level it is through moments of female self-creation, when she is the agent of her own desire, moments when she asserts herself against authority and exhibits her strength and independence.

Charlotte's hysteria is caused as much by her inability to separate from her mother as by sexual repression. Her first attempt to move away from her mother's dominion, as represented in the flashback, fails. It is only the intervention of Dr Jacquith, as the paternal substitute, and Lisa as the 'good mother' that allows her to begin her journey to self-discovery. This is the 'voyage' of the film's title and the several actual voyages in the film – the two cruises, the two stays at Cascade, the camping trip with Tina – constitute the narrativisation of this theme. Charlotte must leave the family home to find herself as an autonomous individual.

Significantly, the two cruises and the two romances are not enough; there is a further journey beyond them that Charlotte must make before she is fully 'cured', fully mature.

The second half of the film, which begins with Charlotte's arrival in Boston after her affair with Jerry, takes up this theme, which becomes the dominant one. As it gains force, Charlotte is progressively less and less glamorous: she remains attractive, but her clothing and makeup are simpler, less central to the *mise en scène*.

In formal terms, now that Charlotte is alone again and must confront her mother, she assumes the enunciatory position which she maintains until the end of the film. Her point of view and her subjective states are elaborately constructed through internal monologues, asides to herself, aural flashbacks, shots of her alone in her rooms, on a train, writing a letter and by dwelling on her reactions when others are present. In terms of her character, she is suddenly much more consistently confident and poised than she was at any time during the cruise. There, in her relationship with Jerry (and, importantly, in terms of the discourse of consumerism, at the height of her representation as glamorous and fashionable) she is often unsure of herself and self-deprecating. The unsteadiness of her identity is marked by the fact that she has borrowed someone else's identity for the voyage: the name and clothing of Renée Beauchamp. The moment she returns, at the Boston docks, she is self-knowing and self-possessed, witty, warm and dignified – a manner that forcefully calls up the discourse of the 'real' Bette Davis.

Once back in the family home, she must engage in a struggle to stay separate and self-determining in the face of her mother's renewed attempts to force her into 'a daughter's duty to her mother'. This is carried out on one level in Charlotte's insistence on defining her own space, and in dressing as she pleases, that is, as a sexually mature woman. The debate over who will pay for Charlotte's clothes if she does not dress as her mother wishes becomes a central moment in her inner emancipation. At this point the consumerist equation of freedom with the right to buy is pushed into another dimension when Charlotte's mother makes her last stand for control over Charlotte. She has thrown herself down the stairs after Charlotte refuses to accede to her demands. Now Charlotte enters her mother's room after successfully negotiating her first encounter with the extended family and Mrs Vale, although bedridden, tries once more to assert her authority by quizzing Charlotte about the cost of her 'outrageous' black evening gown and threatening to discontinue her monthly allowance if she continues to 'buy what you choose, wear what you choose, sleep where you choose.' This leads Charlotte to ask, 'When Father set up the trust for the two boys, why didn't he make one for me, too?' For the first time, Charlotte is questioning the economic basis of her dependency. Although the answer to her question would seem to be her sex, this is sidestepped in Mrs Vale's answer, 'Because you were a mere child ... I'm sure you've had everything in the world you want,' to which Charlotte replies, 'I haven't had independence.' Charlotte then says, 'I could earn my own living; I've often thought about it. I'd make a very good head waitress in a restaurant,' a comment that acknowledges her lack of formal education and training and the kinds of positions that were open to women of her class in the pre-War years. It also calls up the Bette Davis discourse of determination and the value of work, which is reinforced in the series of shots that follow:

> A medium shot of Charlotte, highly lit, both hands gripping the back of the chair she kneels on, as she responds to her mother's suggestion that she will change her mind: 'I don't think so. I'm not afraid, Mother.'
> Reaction shot of Mrs Vale, very startled.
> Close up of Charlotte, radiantly lit. Music comes up on the sound track as she turns her head away and says to herself in discovery: 'I'm not afraid.' The music swells; she turns her head back to look at Mrs Vale and says again, in joyous wonder: 'I'm not afraid, Mother.'

It is a very intense moment – the highly emotional *mise en scène* and Davis's delivery of the lines mark it as a turning point in the narrative. Charlotte loses her fear, not because of her romance with Jerry, but because she realises herself as a separate, autonomous individual who is able to survive in the world of her own. The consumerist discourse of fashion and the right to 'buy what one chooses' is transformed, pulled away from its patriarchal moorings into the circuit of female discourses.

The centrality of Charlotte's struggle to separate as a factor in her 'cure' is marked by her breakdown on her mother's death. While she not only survived, but was stronger after her separation from Jerry, now she must return to Cascade. It is there that the final movement of her journey begins when she finds Jerry's daughter Tina, the exact mirror of her child self, as neurotically miserable and unattractive as she herself was at the film's beginning. By becoming the good mother to Tina – thus by identification, to herself – Charlotte achieves mastery both of herself and in the world. While biological mothers in the film are distinctly lacking in mothering skills (with the exception of Lisa, who has not been terribly successful with her own daughter, June), Charlotte turns motherhood into a profession – part psychotherapist, part nurse, part charming companion.

In order to do so, she must defy the patriarchal authority of Dr Jacquith:

JACQUITH: I hear you're running Cascade now. You give orders to my doctors, you give orders to Miss Trask.
CHARLOTTE: I didn't give orders, I requested.
JACQUITH: I thought you came up here to have a nervous breakdown.
CHARLOTTE: Well I decided not to have one. If it's all the same to you.
JACQUITH: Well, since you're no longer my patient, since you're now a member of my staff, doctor ...
CHARLOTTE: I know I've been impertinent.
JACQUITH: Oh go ahead, maybe I like it.

CHARLOTTE: It's just that the child is so unhappy here. I don't think she's being treated wisely. I used to be proud of you; this time I'm ashamed.

JACQUITH: Then isn't it wonderful you know so much better.

He then sets the condition that she must not continue her affair with Jerry. However, she has already made that decision in a previous scene when she and Jerry meet again at a party and must part once more. As they stand on the station platform, waiting for the train that will take Jerry away, he explains his situation: 'There isn't a thing I can do about it. Isabelle depends on me more and more. She's ill and getting worse. There's Tina ... And if I could chuck everything, Charlotte.' 'I wouldn't let you,' she replies.

Therefore, in a sense, it is not really Jacquith's doing, but that Charlotte wants Tina more than she wants Jerry. Or rather that the arrangement allows her to be in control of their relationship and master of her own household. Jerry must ask if he can visit and 'sit with you and Tina in peace and contentment' so that Charlotte can say, magnanimously, 'It's your home, too; there are people who love you here.'

In the last scene of the film the miserable matriarchy of the film's beginning has been substituted by an ideal one. The space has been transformed into one of laughter, light, music and gaiety. June is there (and not Lisa) and she is kinder and more human than before. Tina is happy, as is everyone in the house. Thus, Charlotte has created the equivalent of the domestic utopia of women's fiction. She has assumed a position of equality with Dr Jacquith because of her competence and the financial independence which allows her to endow a wing of Cascade and sit on the Board of Directors. Their new relationship as adult equals is figured in the way they sit on the floor together, informally discussing the plans for the new wing, with Dr Jacquith the recipient of Charlotte's hospitality.

This is not to imply, however, that *Now, Voyager* ends with any kind of closure. There is no real resolution of the discourse of female sexuality; the film begins with a strong stand against the repression of female sexuality, and although romance and eroticism are permitted, a complete expression of sexuality is not. Similarly, although female independence is stressed, Charlotte must exercise it from within her home. And even though glamour and female attractiveness are no longer the central concern for Charlotte, Tina must mirror her transformation by appearing for Jerry at the head of the stairs in a long frilly party dress, with curls and ribbons and without glasses or braces.

Nevertheless, spectators with knowledge of the Bette Davis discourse can interpret the ending such that it can be made to speak for women: knowing that Davis values work, mastery and creativity, Charlotte's 'motherhood', as much as her new activities with Cascade, takes on the connotations of the

Davis image. Charlotte can be a mother without having to be placed in the family and defined by it. The Davis valorisation of independence over marriage finds an echo in Charlotte's refusal to follow Jerry's advice to 'find some man who'll make you happy'. And even the passion that Charlotte exhibits in her relationship with Tina can refer to the passion that Davis has for her work.

Thus, in *Now, Voyager* the fictional processes of the woman's film, drawing on a wider woman's culture, have pulled commodity consumption and the commodity aspect of the star system into a different orbit – a symbolic system in which women can try to make sense of their lives and even create imaginative spaces for resistance, a system which the film, seeking to address women, drawing on a woman's popular novel and a popular woman's star, enters despite itself.

Notes

1. Warner Bros., 1942, produced by Hal Wallis, directed by Irving Rapper from the Casey Robinson screenplay which closely follows the 1941 best-selling novel by Olive Higgins Prouty, lifting entire 'literate passages of dialogue' from it. (*Hollywood Reporter*, 17 August 1942).
2. Stuart Ewen, *Captains of Consciousness* (New York: McGraw Hill, 1976).
3. Charles Eckert, 'The Carole Lombard in Macy's Window', *Quarterly Review of Film Studies*, Winter 1976.
4. For the screenplay see Jeanne Allen (ed.), *Now, Voyager* (Madison, Wisconsin: The University of Wisconsin Press, 1984).
5. Press Book for *Now, Voyager*, held by the library of the Academy of Motion Picture Arts and Sciences, Los Angeles.
6. Richard de Cordova, 'The Emergence of the Star System and the Bourgeoisification of the American Cinema', *Star Signs* (British Film Institute Education, 1982); Richard Dyer, *Stars* (British Film Institute, 1979).
7. 'Bette Davis', *Life*, 8 January 1939.
8. 'Bette from Boston', *Silver Screen*, 1935, in Martin Levin (ed.), *Hollywood and the Great Fan Magazines* (New York: Arbor House, 1970).
9. Ibid.
10. 'Bette Davis', *Life*, 8 January 1939.
11. 'That Marital Vacation', *Modern Screen*, 1939, in *Hollywood and the Great Fan Magazines*, op. cit.
12. 'The Man Bette Davis Married', *Photoplay-Movie Mirror*, 1941, in *Hollywood and the Great Fan Magazines*, op. cit.
13. Fannie Hurst: *Lummox* (Herbert Brenon, 1930), *Backstreet* (John Stahl, 1932), *Imitation of Life* (John Stahl, 1934); Olive Higgins Prouty: *Stella Dallas* (King Vidor, 1937); Edna Furber: *Cimarron* (Wesley Ruggles, 1931), *So Big* (William Wellman, 1932), *Come and Get It* (Howard Hawks/William Wellman, 1936),

Saratoga Trunk (Sam Wood, 1946), *Giant* (George Stevens, 1956), *Ice Palace* (Vincent Sherman, 1960).

14. Nina Baym, *Woman's Fiction: A Guide to Novels By and About Women in America, 1820–70* (Ithaca: Cornell University Press, 1978).

15. Nancy Chodorow, *The Reproduction of Mothering: Psychoanalysis and the Sociology of Gender* (Berkeley: University of California Press, 1978); Dorothy Dinnerstein, *The Mermaid and the Minotaur: Sexual Arrangements and Human Malaise* (New York: Harper and Row, 1977).

16. In Davis's autobiography, *The Lonely Life*, she expresses her sense of identification with the character of Charlotte Vale: 'the part was perfect for me.' (p. 259). Although the role was originally offered to other actresses, Davis fought to get it, so intent was she on playing Charlotte Vale. She went to Hal Wallis, the film's producer, and told him that as a New Englander, she understood Charlotte better than anyone else could. (Whitney Stein and Bette Davis, *Mother Goddam*, 1983, p. 163); *Bette*, Charles Higham, 1981, p. 160). Davis greatly admired the novel, *Now, Voyager*: 'it was a constant vigil to preserve the quality of the book by Olive Higgins Prouty.' (*The Lonely Life*, p. 259). Davis claims that she personally worked on the screenplay, keeping in Prouty's original situations and dialogue (Stein and Davis, p. 165). In Higham's biography it is claimed that Davis carefully constructed an image of the 'real' or 'private life' Davis for the press; the character she chose for her public self resembles the cheerful, sturdy heroines of women's fiction and in particular resembles Jo of *Little Women*, a Yankee, ambitious, eccentric, unfeminine and a creative artist.

17. This same superimposition of printed pages turning occurs later in the film when Charlotte is on the second cruise. She has just been introduced to Jerry and is about to refuse his request that she accompany him sightseeing. There is a close-up of Charlotte's eyes looking to the side, a lap dissolve of the pages turning, followed by a brief flashback of Charlotte being counselled by Jacquith on the gangplank of the departing cruise ship. Jacquith: 'Now pull your own weight. I've taught you the technique, now use it. Forget you're a hidebound New Englander' – camera tracks in closer to the two of them facing each other – 'Unbend, take part, contribute, be interested in everything and everybody.' The pages are superimposed again as Charlotte returns to the present and answers Jerry in the affirmative. Here the pages seem almost to contain Jacquith within them. His authority, which serves to give Charlotte permission to explore her sexuality and autonomy, is encompassed by theirs: he is the creation of a female author, and his words are authorised by the extra-filmic text of the novel.

Historical Pleasures
Gainsborough Costume Melodrama

SUE HARPER

MELODRAMA, like all *genres*, is historically specific. Stylistic flamboyance and emotional 'excess' may be its recurring features, but these will be structured in relation to the class of the target audience, production conditions, and the precise historical period. Melodrama will thus exhibit a variety of relationships between narrative codes, and a range of 'permitted' gratifications will be distributed throughout a text in different ways.

I hope to show that a highly popular series of 'costume' melodramas produced in England at Gainsborough Studios during and just after World War Two achieved that popularity partially because J. Arthur Rank then operated his monopoly in a relatively permissive way, thus allowing a space to be opened up at that studio where ideas about history and sexuality could be expressed which were impossible in existing, more 'respectable' signifying systems.

This costume cycle was made with the same production, star, and technical teams.[1] The weekend premier dates for these films are *The Man in Grey* (July 1943), *Fanny by Gaslight* (May 1944), *Madonna of the Seven Moons* (December 1944), *The Wicked Lady* (December 1945), *Caravan* (April 1946), and *Jassy* (August 1947). The films have a rich visual texture and evince a preoccupation with the sexual mores and life-style of the upper reaches of the landed classes; they all contain female protagonists (usually visually or diegetically coloured by 'gypsyness') who actively seek sexual pleasure and whom the plot ritually excises by the end. There are contradictions between the verbal level of plot and scripts, and the non-verbal discourses of décor and costume; the massive popularity of these films attests that the audience *could* decode their complex and sometimes inconsistent messages. The costume *genre* at this period thus required a high degree of audience creativity. Gainsborough provided a site for the development of a carefully costed 'expressionism', whose practitioners had been manoeuvred out of the theatre or other studios by the dominance of a realist orthodoxy; it was precisely in this expressionism that the audience's fears or desires could be pleasurably rehearsed. As I shall indicate, this audience was specifically female, and the films received unparalleled critical approbrium since they did not conform to the criterion of 'good taste'. Predictably, their lack of quality is related by critics to their low-status audience:

a carefully compounded bromide, the lines aiming no higher than *Mabel's Weekly*.[2]

if Lady E. F. Smith's novel found a large public, this will certainly find a larger. It will certainly make lots of money.[3]

to enjoy it, you need to have a mind that throbs to every sob of the novelette and a heart that throbs to every exposure of Stewart Granger's torso.[4]

This, and related attempts to cleanse popular forms of their supposed prurience was successful insofar as such films became 'invisible' in cinema history until relatively recently. However, they are crucial in any mapping of the field of popular taste in the 1940s and should be given major currency in any debates about the cultural resources or the construction of 'femininity' in that period.

The Production Context
J. Arthur Rank's acquisition of Gainsborough in 1941 at first left the existing team unhampered. His philistinism – 'Who is Thomas Hardy?'[5] – permitted literati such as producer R. J. Minney to gain intellectual control at the studio until mid-1946, and enabled entrepreneurs such as Ted Black (an Associate Producer) to exploit their instinct for popular taste. Although financial control rested with Rank, the range and complexity of whose empire rendered him all but invincible, the Ostrer brothers (Executive Producers) were permitted to run the studio in as tight a way as they wished. It is clear that the Ostrers and Minney parted company, intellectually speaking, with Rank over the question of the latter's definition of culture as basically educational. Minney suggested that a Shakespeare film which could only appeal to a minority audience should only cost £70,000:

the commodity must be what the public wants, and what the public is at present educated enough to like.[6]

Rank was increasingly drawn into 'quality' films such as *Caesar and Cleopatra*, which as projects had critical kudos but which were financial disasters and necessitated a consolidation of his disparate interests.

All our films except *Jassy* were made under studio conditions dominated by Black, the Ostrers and Minney; the appointment of Sydney Box as producer in August 1946 led to a huge percentage increase in the cost of sets and locations, and probably to the demise of the studio at Shepherd's Bush in March 1949.[7] Management philosophy expressed itself in the area of careful pre-shooting costs and tight commodity control. Very stringent analysis of the shooting diary was in evidence on *The Wicked Lady*:

it had to be kept up to the minute ... everything had to be kept absolutely ... we had to be able to explain what the delay was and whose fault it was. Inquests all the time.[8]

Gainsborough producers attempted considerable control over the stars' behaviour, but did not interfere with artistic matters unless the budget was exceeded.[9] There was very little location work, and the rigorous six-week schedule necessitated building sets at night.[10] Such conditions were deemed necessary by studio producers in order to ensure a certain excess profit. Ostrer noted:

I want the whole amount budgeted for the film to appear on the screen in the production, and not to have a large percentage frittered away behind the scenes in extravagant and needless waste.[11]

Black even forbade personal phone calls and kept writing paper at a premium.[12] Also emphasised was the need for careful assessment of market size, advance breakdown of costs, and predictability of the product's visual style and profit.[13] The profitability of the costume cycle was considerably greater than the Gainsborough films in modern dress, since, besides being more popular, the former were cheaper to make due to tighter control. The producers explicitly placed no credence in bad reviews by critics, since high costs could only be justified by mass appeal.[14] Hence the studio's 'low-brow' orientation. Star appearances, elaborate advertising and negotiation of longer bookings, were the means of capturing a large audience.[15]

Further economies were exacted in the area of equipment. The only modern machinery at Gainsborough was the meteorological equipment designed to predict weather conditions, to avoid needless expenditure of time.[16] Wind-machines and back-projection equipment were obsolete, there was no illuminated footage in sound-mixing, and the Sound Department were unwillingly obliged to use British Acoustic equipment because it was an Ostrer subsidiary company.[17]

The workforce of the studio displayed a classic 'Taylorism' in its structure; all the sections had separate union meetings, and studio union consciousness was difficult to establish. Interestingly, the union structure was precisely analogous to the management's. None of the units were kept informed of the others' filming activities:

it all came from high up, and we were the last in the line.[18]

Everyone I interviewed on the technical side attested to the separateness of management and labour:

they were all so far removed from us;[19]

you'd get the occasional morning visit from Black or Ostrer, but then they'd disappear;[20]

all the heads stuck together. They used to eat together at lunchtime.[21]

The scriptwriters, however, were separated from the rest of the workforce and were in a privileged relationship with the studio management. As I hope to show, they were engaged in making a bid for intellectual power, and their interests were allied with the management's. Only they, the director, and the Heads of Departments saw the rushes with the producers; comments and criticism were filtered down privately to the technical workers.[22] The intellectual chain of command meant that new script pages were constantly replacing old ones at very short notice.[23] This made an intellectual or critical engagement by the technical workforce impossible, and it deprived them of a sense of corporate responsibility. That was 'carried' by the scriptwriters. They attempted to circumvent production control by defining themselves as 'special' intellectual workers. One expression of their struggle was the alteration in class-orientation of the popular novels on which the films were based.

Gainsborough's management philosophy produced the conditions for a strong generic cycle. Tight economic control, a strongly hierarchised organisation, a privileged intellectual elite, an insistence that production values appear in visual terms – all these were combined with an uncompromising slanting of the films towards a female audience. Although many 40s audience researchers had problems in defining melodrama,[24] Gainsborough publicists were assailed by no such difficulties. They recognised melodrama's gender bias and suggested that *Madonna* be marketed so as to redefine schizophrenia as a specifically female ailment, with the headline 'Split-mind Disorder Gives Idea for Year's Finest Romance!' Cinema managers were advised to appeal 'to that great feminine characteristic, curiosity. Trade on this!'[25] Female fascination with dominant males is stressed as a selling point, and H. Ostrer defined the films as the female equivalent to horse racing, the dogs, or boxing – low status anodynes which defused aggression.[26] The poster for *Caravan* displayed Granger, earringed, curled and lipsticked, and bearing a startling likeness to Valentino. While the selling power of his befrilled torso was castigated by such papers as *Sunday Graphic*,[27] the Gainsborough publicists confidently implied that the films would usher the female audience in to an 'unspeakable' realm of sexual pleasure. R. J. Minney was largely instrumental in choosing those historical novels for dramatisation which were low-status,[28] since they were by and for women. He defined melodrama as popular fiction *par excellence*, 'with blood and thunder', and believed that such films and novels should exemplify a structurally conservative *Ur-text*, 'a full-blooded story such as may be found in the pages of the Bible.'[29] Against all advice he selected on his own instinct the novel of *Madonna of the Seven Moons*:

170

The experts all said there wasn't a film in it. The subject had been rejected so often that it was regarded as voodoo. Minney went quietly to work, wrote his own script, planned the production, costed it ...[30]

Minney insisted that documentary realism would not fulfil the emotional needs of a mass audience,[31] and ensured instead that the Gainsborough costume cycle was deeply and profitably embedded in popular forms which other studios like Ealing and Cineguild were unable to emulate.[32]

Verbal Languages
I have described in more detail elsewhere the cycle of 'new' costume fiction from which the films were made.[33] If we turn to some Mass-Observation material, it is evident that the audience which these profitable 'costume' novels attracted was predominantly female. Male readers were uniformly hostile to this type of fiction, demanding realism without sentiment. In a range of replies to an October 1943 directive about reading habits, men asserted that historical romances:

fairly turn me up;

I hate the mud, blood and midden school;

real history is more interesting than fiction about it;

a novel dealing with the aristocracy bores me.[34]

A predilection for Hemingway and detective fiction (a genre whose plot structure is more labyrinthine than the historical romance) is clearly, from Mass-Observation material, a male one. Women preferred historical novels as a *genre*, but many, usually the more educated ones, appeared shamefaced about deriving pleasure from such low-status books. Women make the following comments about historical romance:

I am sometimes rather snobbishly ashamed of being seen with my current bromide, and would prefer to be reading Meredith.

I take it as I do cigarettes – nothing so potent as a drug, merely a harmless bromide.

When a novel has an historical interest, or deals with an economic or social problem, there is a reason for its existence, apart from its literary value.

They help you to be patient; I found them particularly helpful earlier on in the war, when we were still adjusting our ideas to it.

It's nice to be able to read about that sort of love and better class people, because you don't notice things as much then.[35]

A sense of proportion, escapism, access to a historically vivid past – these are the alibis most frequently provided by women for historical novels. It was the most heavily subscribed type of light reading among those classified as 'serious' readers (that is, the middle class)[36] and high praises for it as a *genre* came from female students and the occasional female lecturer. Even after the war, middle-class women *in jobs* were those with the most avid interest in historical stories of this type.[37]

These texts present history as unfamiliar, and they also emphasise strongly such non-verbal elements as costume and movement. The novels share a complex series of 'framing' devices. *Caravan* and *Fanny* are told through intermediary newspaper reporters; *The Life and Death of the Wicked Lady Skelton* has three initial flashbacks, and *Jassy* is fragmented into four different personas' interpretation of the heroine. This distanciation puts the reader at one remove from history, and the effect is not neutralised by the extreme opulence of the language, which is dense, metaphorical, and 'writerly', without exception. Unlike subsequent 'bodice-rippers', these novels do not evince a nostalgia for the past. Rather, they express a material change in the composition and style of the aristocracy, and a sense of historical inevitability. The novels select ambiguous groups 'on the boundary' – the upper reaches of the aristocracy, gypsies, and sexually aggressive women – and examine them for signs of social pollution. Such groups exhibit exotic energy when poised thus ambiguously, and the audience is encouraged to take *initial* pleasure in their excesses in costume, sexual behaviour, or class power. The novels impel the reader ultimately to *judge* such excess and to co-operate, so to speak, in its excision. Creativity and complicity are thus inextricably mixed in the readership response demanded by the texts.

All the novels carefully stress the source of aristocratic wealth as rent – a different category from capital and labour – and those who evade the responsibility of office are cast beyond the pale. Hester, in *The Man in Grey*, marrying into the gentry class, abuses the luxuries that the rents produce:

I never knew that such unobtrusive comfort could exist. I never knew flowers could bloom so sweetly in winter, or fires burn so recklessly for people who never came in at all.[38]

For a wartime audience, this preoccupation with aristocratic 'surplus' would be translated into more immediate concerns about the equitable allocation of limited resources. It is the female protagonist who consumes uncontrollably. Aristocratic energy is linked with that produced by gypsies, who symbolise exotic, eccentric, predominantly sexual energy of a group notoriously de-classed. Gypsy blood in the novels can be inclined to 'danger' and sexual excess, but these may be counterbalanced by second sight and 'special' knowledge. A third component of this ambiguous 'boundary' group in the novels is the sexually agressive female. If female sexuality is indissolubly linked with aristocratic excess, it is always categorised as 'danger'; otherwise it may be recuperated by marriage and 'true love'. Oriana's behaviour in the following passage from *Caravan* is later exonerated by her fidelity and death:

> Without a word, he got into bed beside her. And they made love with a fury, a violence, that left him exhausted ... He knew her then, at last, for what she was, a sensual woman, who had always wanted him. And as he embraced her, he remembered the sailors' talk of witch-women, of *sorcières* from whom no man could escape ... he lay there, indulging her wanton ways.[39]

Rosal in the same novel is removed after a series of bold sexual initiatives on her part, and Barbara in *The Life and Death of the Wicked Lady Skelton* sallies forth in search of love and profit by donning male clothes:

> How she had smiled at her own unfamiliar reflection as she dressed herself behind locked doors for the night's adventure, telling herself that she made a very pretty young man ... beneath the large, flat-brimmed beaver hat her face was provocatively feminine. But a mask would soon remedy that. The high, spurred boots, the leather belt and pistol holder – what a piquant change from muffs, lace cap and painted fans! She drew the loaded pistol from the holster and examined it carefully.[40]

This results in her death at her lover's hands; she is shot as a male highwayman. The novels implicitly correct such *hubris*; the females who survive are domesticated, prolific, and free from desire. 'Femininity' (always an ideologically-determined construct) is not equally weighted in these novels with the 'gentry' and 'gypsy' strands, but none the less the readership is offered the spectacle of a female sexuality poised between self-gratification and predatoriness.

The novels on which the Gainsborough cycle is based suggest via their structure that there is no one secret to unravel, and no single cathartic release. Instead, pleasures are scattered throughout, by a series of intense sensual moments which constitute 'the past'. It is the historical dimension which is responsible for the novels' popularity; treatment of the aristocracy with a *modern* setting did not capture a mass market in the same way, nor did they permit the fruitful elision of different 'strange', marginal groups.[41]

The women novelists insisted on their own similarity to the gypsies, who were outsiders to polite society. Lady E. F. Smith insisted on her own supposed gypsy blood,[42] and Norah Lofts suggested:

173

If we revert to barbarism, I hope to be allowed to carry my mat from place to place and tell stories for copper coins ... one would thus always be one step ahead of the critics.[43]

Their novels produce pleasure by the ambiguous placing of such groups on the purity/danger axis; the complex negotiations they required of their readers in terms of moral value and 'literariness' indicate that they provided a particularly compelling version of history, sexuality, and reading practices. History becomes a country where female refugees from common sense may temporarily reside, but it is a place of banishment none the less; and there, gypsy, gentry and female excess are safely placed. These novels by implication put the readership in a position to envisage (and perhaps regret) a post-war world in which such extravagance would be absent.

The 'structures of feeling' contained within the scripts prepared by Gainsborough scriptwriters differ from the novels in important ways. As I have already suggested, the scriptwriters at Gainsborough had a privileged rôle in the studio. They were a highly specialised group, who had sufficient initiative to found, in March 1937, the Screenwriters Association.[44] Kennedy, Pertwee, Gilliatt, Minney, Launder and Arliss were founding members, and continuity existed through until the mid-1940s, with Minney taking a major rôle.[45] They had a highly developed degree of awareness of their own institutional, material and industrial constraints; I hope to show how they fought to place themselves in a different market relationship from the popular novelists.

The only extant authorship theory advanced by a Gainsborough scriptwriter, Margaret Kennedy, shows a marked advance on earlier professional definitions such as Ursula Bloom's 1938 ABC of Authorship. The latter is obsessed with the necessity of reducing artistic discourses to the lowest common denominator; whereas Kennedy, in her The Mechanical Muse (1942) expresses as her ideal project a film of 'The Eve of St. Agnes'.[46] Her whole aesthetic is coloured by contempt for the film audience – 'a community which never reads' – and she discourages the novelist from adapting his own text, as he will 'break his heart' on realising 'how anomalous his position is, and how small the chance that any fragment of ideas will find its way to the screen.'[47]

The 'illiteracy' of the screen audience produces only three alternatives; to 'adapt a second-rate book towards which one has no conscience', to become an 'author-cutter' with 'directional power', or to develop the 'vacant and pensive' writing mood of the director.[48]

It is a familiar argument; that mass culture has lamentably replaced a high one of literary value, and that the employed artist either totally concedes, hack-like, or fights for total control. Either way the original novelist is excluded from the act of mediation. It is of interest that Kennedy's strictures were followed by the studio. There is only one mention of a novelist being on set, as recounted in the publicity material for *Caravan*; otherwise the script-writers attempted to augment their power by becoming directors. Minney explicitly suggested this, and it was upheld by the director Crabtree,[49] and more crucially by Arliss who both scripted and directed two of the films.[50] Rank is reported to have been sympathetic to such claims.[51] Although Maurice Ostrer had demanded a 'cast-iron script' before shooting,[52] studio practice was to implement last-minute alterations according to screenwriters' interpretations of the rushes. Gainsborough screenwriters had remarkably advantageous notice arrangements.[53] The studio staff were in agreement with the notion of scriptwriter-as-author, and deliberately avoided reading the novels:

> we thought that it didn't do to get too involved like that, because you put all sorts of emotions into it, and the script would change a relationship, or chop things, and then you'd be upset.[54]

The exclusion of the novelists meant that the scripts were more directly tailored for a different class of consumption. The scriptwriters separated themselves off as a kind of 'aristocracy of labour' from the rest of the work-force, and the Screenwriters Association, which they helped to found and in which they were very active, fought for higher basic payments, for the crea-tion of a jointly-owned 'story fund',[55] for the freedom of radio film-critics,[56] and for the free collective bargaining for a loose affiliation of individuals. Two events suggest that its institutional definitions had become widely acceptable; its being contracted as a 'voluntary' workforce for the M O I,[57] and the acceptance by the Inland Revenue of its terms of reference:

> From what Mr Williams and Mr Minney have said, I understand that nearly all screenwriters can be said to exercise a profession, and if they take contracts from time to time, they do so incidentally in the cause of that profession, and not in the intention of obtaining a post and staying in it.[58]

Two disputes further clarify the S W A's definition of authorship as non-industrial and 'free'. As early as 1943 the A C T had claimed to be the negotiat-ing body;[59] the S W A membership firmly rejected its claims, and Launder noted 'screenwriters are neither reactionary conservatives nor reactionary unionists, but just simple, progressive, benevolent anarchists.'[60] By 1947 the S W A felt empowered to act as a trade union, and Cripps reprimanded the A C T for its intransigence.[61] G. D. H. Cole added his support to the S W A's claims for autonomy:

> I think the screenwriters must act with authors and other creative artists and must not let themselves be swallowed up.[62]

So notions of writerly creativity and craftsmanship were indubitably linked to a loose guild structure and the institutional power of the SWA was able to defeat the powerful, Rank-backed 'Scenario Institute Limited' of del Giudice, Del Giudice suggested that Minney underestimated the audience,[63] and attempted to establish a rival institution more concerned with 'culture' and 'quality'; his and Rank's Institute would be a quasi-university, with 'an intellectual and artistic atmosphere'[64] to raise cultural standards. The SWA took particular offence at the notion that the Institute was 'a private commercial venture although not really a speculative one'; del Giudice's proposal to buy up film rights from books before publication[65] was rejected on the grounds of the power this would place in the hands of monopoly capital. The campaign launched by the SWA routed the Institute; even Balcon saw it would produce a 'corner' of story wealth.[66] Thus the SWA rejected monopolism and 'trade' arrangements; it wished screen authors to be 'free' to negotiate a percentage rate for resale of their own work.[67]

The Gainsborough scriptwriters, three of whom were women, produced scripts which endorsed their own class position, clarified lines of class power, and imposed 'normative' morality upon deviant females. The novels had spoken to a middle-class audience, conceived as the equals of their authors; the scripts, addressing a working-class and largely female audience, shifted and reinterpreted the 'marginal' groups from the novels, profoundly affecting the texts' ideological function.

The novels had all used an extremely complex series of 'framing' devices; but the scripts all begin without narrators *in medias res*. Although the film of *The Man in Grey* is structured as a meditation on a portrait, the flashback effect is concealed; *Caravan*'s script begins with a reprise, but from half-way through the narrative. The first *Wicked Lady* script has two modern tramps interrupting Barbara's ghost, but this is removed from the final version of the film;[68] all that remains of 'ghostliness' is the camera movement and changed sound quality of her death. Gainsborough screenwriters plunge the audience, with few delayed gratifications, into 'unmediated' history; they implicitly suggest that access to it is unproblematical by employing verbal language stripped of literary or historical resonance. They accord more utterance to lower-class characters. Belinda in the novel *Jassy* is a mute, to whom the film grants speech, and the Toby rôle in *The Man in Grey* is similarly transformed. The audience is encouraged by the scripts to identify with, rather than distance themselves from, historical characters, but this is done by reducing the amount of dialogue in the novels. Information instead is carried by music, a language with easier access to the emotions. Attention to the last fifteen minutes of *Madonna* will show five minutes of dialogue to ten of highly atmospheric music.

The foregrounding of class has a different emphasis in the scripts. Sir Ralph is accused by his fellows of 'betraying his own class', and the hero of

Fanny suggests that 'a hundred years from now such class distinctions won't exist.' The novels balance the aristocracy against an undefined residuum, whereas the films compare aristocratic excess with 'professional' middle-class restraint, to the latter's advantage. Sir Francis in the novel is an amiable invalid – his wife, Oriana, says:

> I never had any particular reason for hating him...[69]

whereas the script converts him into a libertine of whom even whores remark:

> he's a beast – he's the worst of the lot!

The film *Oriana* remarks that:

> He changed the moment we became married – he became evil.

Sir Francis' comeuppance is signalled by the swamp to which he succumbs, and which the bourgeois hero successfully negotiates, after appropriating his whip. Much more positive rôles are accorded to the middle-class male by the scripts; the architect in *The Wicked Lady*, the librarian in *The Man in Grey*, the dispossessed farmer in *Jassy* do not appear as such in the novels. The aristocratic class is by contrast consistently denigrated: Lord Rohan in *The Man in Grey* is converted from an honourable man declaring emotional severance from Hester[70] into a Byronic figure – I've yet to meet a woman I don't despise.' He beats Hester to death – 'you'll die for it – in my own time and in my way'. The script notes that the brutality of a dog fight 'appeals to his sadistic sense'. The aristocratic quartet in the film of *The Wicked Lady* propose a double divorce and 'swap', but the script does not permit them to flout convention in the end.

On the whole, then, the scripts explicitly add to the novels such remarks as Rokesby's:

> I wonder what they [the gentry] ever did to deserve all this.

The scripts present the aristocracy as an unambiguous site of fascination, fear, and 'unspeakable' dark sexuality. Gypsies no longer present, as in the novels, an exotic eccentric wisdom, but a social threat. The *Caravan* script has them murder and rifle the body, whereas the book insists on their cultural purity; Pertwee converts the gypsy energy in *Madonna* into dirt and violence,[71] and has the virgin heroine raped by a gypsy instead of her husband.[72] Excessive female sexuality is similarly moved from the ambiguous margins into the 'danger' category by the scripts. They foreground the problems of female friendship, and bitchy vituperation: 'you two have shared so much', 'I'd rather look worn than dull'; 'wear *that*? I wouldn't be buried in it.' Thus the scripts structurally endorse Mason's gallows recommendation, 'Never trust a woman.' Hester is ritually excised because, as the script suggests, 'in her black dress ... she *does* look very like a witch.' The cinematic Barbara wants 'a house – children – all the things I never thought would matter', as a restitution for wanting 'a hundred mouths' to kiss with. The most significant alteration Arliss makes to *The Wicked Lady* is the revenge, by rape, of the returned Jackson. He is first glimpsed, mouthless, in a mirror and the sado-masochistic nature of his and Barbara's exchanges is absent from the book: the film contains the exchanges: 'I hate you;' 'But I am thrilled by you', and 'I like to drive a hard bargain;' 'So do I.' All the scripts suggest that females are an unfathomable, almost pathological, puzzle: 'the woman [in *Madonna*] is a mystery; she always was', and 'I can't think what can have happened to her [the Wicked Lady herself]; she used to be so sweet.'

Gainsborough scriptwriters, then, strove to place themselves in a different market relationship from the popular novelists. The latter had arrived, either by private research or individual instinct, at market dominance; Gainsborough screenwriters desired instead a loosely-strung, quasi-guild authorship. Petty-bourgeois in origin and outlook, they paid more explicit attention to questions of mass audience and artistic control than the novelists did. Because of their rejection of the mass-culture manufactory within which they worked, Gainsborough screenwriters were unable to reproduce the structures of social feeling of the novels. In the latter, ramshackle though they were in cultural mediation, women, gypsies, the aristocracy are dynamically poised in a sophisticated balance, and offer a pleasingly 'ambiguous' choice to the audience, whose class anxieties they may then defuse. In the scripts, on the other hand, these groups are impelled head-long into a dark chasm where only fear and excess reside. The audience is granted little creativity by the scripts, which is impelled, on the verbal level of the text, towards perceiving females as greedy and strange, and the working class as culturally inferior. The institutional struggles faced by the scriptwriters were clearly instrumental in causing them to draw the boundaries of class and gender more sharply in their texts. The novelists had had an identity of interest with their readers, since they also were middle-class and female; whereas the scriptwriters, forced to define their market position with some rigour, finally took refuge in a rhetoric of dismissal and disdain towards their working-class female audience.

Visual Languages

The lines of morality, and class and gender power, are very strictly drawn by the scripts. However, different concepts of knowledge, history and pleasure are contained within the language of the décor and costumes. The Art Direction of these films viewed history as a source of sensual pleasures, as the original novels had done. The Department worked under conditions of extreme pressure and difficulty, but managed to gather together a small number of expert 'period' artists; strict control of overspending and overbuilding was tempered by laxity in the area of historical interpretation. Maurice Carter told me that:

> ... provided you could perform money-wise, and get the sets there on time, they were reasonably happy. [Executive producers] didn't have much to say on the artistic side.[73]

The art director of 'costume' melodrama has to indicate a past which is both familiar and stimulating; the audience of a successful film must recognise familiar signs and confidently fill in the 'gaps' in the discourse. The 'costume' genre as a whole tends to underplay historical authenticity as such, and the Gainsborough films of this period avoid 'documentation'. If it does appear, it is intensely personalised by a voice-over (as in Clarissa's diary pages in *The Man in Grey*) or it is so brief as to make only a ripple in the narrative flow (as in the newspaper cutting in *The Wicked Lady*). The affective, spectacular aspects of *mise en scène* are foregrounded, to produce a vision of 'history' as a country where only feelings reside, not socio-political conflicts. The potency of this for a war-time audience requires little elaboration.

We should make distinctions at the outset between the various art directors who constituted the Gainsborough period team, since their origins affect their respective styles. Maurice Carter, with architectural and furnishing experience, was a supervising art director, and personally art-directed *Jassy*, *The Bad Lord Byron*, and half of *The Man in Grey*. He and Vetchinsky, who was an architect by training, were permanent staff with long-term contracts. Andrew Mazzei, formerly a commercial artist, did *Madonna*, and John Bryan, with a theatrical background, did *The Wicked Lady*, *Fanny By Gaslight*, and *Caravan*. The sets of the latter are far more stylised and less concerned with detail than those of the others.

Gainsborough provided a space for those art directors who came from a commercial or applied arts background, and gave the opportunity for those who were opposed to the décor realism of other art directors like Morahan, Relph, and Sutherland, to practise in a non-realist way. The latter-day careers of Carter and Bryan show a clear continuity with the style they developed at Gainsborough; Carter's *Anne of a Thousand Days*, or Bryan's *Blanche Fury*, or *The Spanish Gardener* on which they collaborated, all display an avoidance of naturalist technique.

The influence of continental art directors such as Andre Andrejev, Ferdie Bellan, Vincent Korda and Alfred Junge can be seen far more clearly at Gainsborough than elsewhere. They, along with a number of other art directors from Berlin, had emigrated to Britain, where Junge initially went to Lime Grove and Korda to Shepperton; they had a formative influence on the early attitudes of Bryan and Carter. The art directors from Germany are widely recognised as anti-realist.[74] Their expressionism was filtered through to Gainsborough art directors and tempered their concern with craftsmanship. If we analyse some of John Bryan's work, we see an interesting selectivity. In the *Wicked Lady*, for example, the interiors are highly eclectic in their construction. Each object is reproduced in an historically accurate way, but it relates to the other objects in an unpredictable way spatially. Generally, the surfaces on which they are placed – bland, unmarked and plain – throw them into heightened relief. The avoidance of tapestry, carpets and serried paintings is not historically accurate and cannot be accounted for by war-time shortages or lack of expertise, and it must therefore be 'read' as a deliberate aesthetic strategy. A Jacobean door, a Baroque candleholder, an Elizabethan canopied bed, a Puritan bible, a medieval fire-basket are combined to form an unpredictable and dense visual texture. The past is signified not as a casual, linear structure, but as a chaotic amalgam – an opened cache of objects with uncertain meaning but available 'beauty'. The undoubted scholarship available at Gainsborough – through period advisers and so on – is always discreetly used so as not to alienate an uninformed audience. *Semper Fidelis* is the only Latin to appear in the film, and it appears inscribed on a plaque which is centrally placed between Roc and Griffiths as they finally affirm their love. The three-cornered gallows in the execution scene had its accuracy carefully proved by Minney,[75] but the first shot of the scene shows miniaturised toy versions of it on display, and this 'lightens' any heaviness of tone which the accurate but unfamiliar object might produce. Bryan's décor shows great wit; when Lockwood lowers her eyes on her wedding night, a short dissolve proceeds to compare her expression and posture ironically with the Botticelli madonna on her petit-point tapestry in the next scene.

It is important to note that the only visually explicit sexual scene in *The Wicked Lady* is totally stripped of any historicising *mise en scène*. When Lockwood and Mason make love by the river, only mist, water and trees are seen; no houses, horses or accoutrements. Bryan conceals history here; sexuality is presented as 'naturally' without codes, practices or historical determinants. Carter remarks that:

> your instinctive reaction was to make the thing as rich as possible, because that sort of thing was already set by the script.[76]

Precisely; the script permits an (idiosyncratic) historicised décor, but not an historicised sexuality. Contemporary analogies are clearly being drawn in the area of sexual pleasure, and 'richness' of décor is, by implication, supernumary when compared with the 'richness' of desire.

The complex sets which Bryan designed for *Caravan* were erected and struck with remarkable speed, although they were extremely labour-intensive, especially for the property department.[77] An instructive comparison may be drawn with the representation of the historical past in *The Wicked Lady*. *Caravan*'s 'Spanish' scenery is an uncivilised wilderness, while the sets indicate a more cultivated disorder. The interiors are crammed with random exotica, spasmodically concealed by darkness. The film presents to its audience a visual cornucopia in which images of Victorian aristocratic décor, Spanish landscape gardening, and gypsy caves are of equal weight. The audience is put in the position of being able to perceive these components as of equal cultural *value*; it is put at the same distance from all these selected, 'privileged' locales.

The other art directors in this cycle display a similar avoidance of historical 'value', whether expressed tonally, compositionally, or via focus. For example, the ruined Gothic garden and the Florentine 'gypsy' interiors in *Madonna* share the same compositional techniques and a picturesque wildness; Mazzei's work as art director here is clearly influenced by his collaboration with Crabtree, whose early training as a cameraman and interest in lighting technique are important signifying features.

Visual style at Gainsborough until the advent of Box in late 1946, then, presented the historical past as a site of sensual pleasure; it was neither regular and linear, nor 'closed'. Under the different set of managerial constraints instituted by Box, such expressionist (and cheap) set work and design ceased. Extensive and expensive location work was undertaken for *The Bad Lord Byron*, and Box insisted on extreme verisimilitude in using the poet's own furniture.[78] The location work abroad for *Christopher Columbus* was so costly as to nullify any profitability. As the 40s progressed, location work came to have a strong 'prestige' aroma; Ealing's *Saraband for Dead Lovers* had even been made at Blenheim.[79] Box attempted to follow the practice of the 'quality' film by increasing the set allocations for *Jassy* to an unprecedented degree.[80] With the advent of Technicolor, quite different skills came to be demanded of the Art Department. In many ways, *Jassy* marked a turning point; made at Denham, unlike all the others, and with a different set of technicians, it also displays a markedly different aesthetic and management philosophy.

A set of managerial circumstances permitted a group of like-minded art directors to produce a *visual* aesthetic which at the same time undercut the class positions inscribed in the scripts. Their visual strategies produced contradictions between the verbal level of the scripts and the non-verbal discourses of décor and costume; a carefully costed visual expressionism permitted and encouraged fantasies which combined history and sexuality, in a way which is (paradoxically) not unlike the mode of procedure of the original novels.

If we turn now to the area of costume design in the Gainsborough cycle, we can examine the ways in which different historical determinants affect the 'narrative' of dress. Research indicates that the audience preferring costume melodrama was predominantly female and working-class,[81] whilst records of contemporary responses to these films suggest that the style of costume was a very important factor in audience enjoyment.[82] The cycle's costumes foreground sexual difference. For example, breasts are unambiguously displayed as a site of female erotic power – they are not teasingly evoked. The swaying skirts in *Caravan*, *The Wicked Lady*, *Jassy*, and *Madonna of the Seven Moons*, and the tinkling ear-rings of the latter, signal the heroines' combination of pleasure and control through the broad range of movement permitted by these clothes. Jean Kent's dance in *Caravan* is no authentic flamenco; her extreme postural shifts are there to cause the bells on the bodice to ring and the skirts to rustle, and these sounds signify her desire towards Granger. The immobile aristocratic wife in *Madonna* alters her kinesic behaviour once she glimpses the flowing hair and clothes of her 'libidinal' gypsy self in the mirror. It is only after she dons exotic costume that she protests 'I belong to no one but myself.' At her death the supine, desexualised mother again 'belongs' in her civilised nightgown, to society. Such 'expressionist' costume practice is markedly imprecise historically. *The Man in Grey*, for example, is inaccurate on the hairstyles and the sartorial tastes of the 'Young Corinthians', and it is thirty years out in its presentation of a dominant, 'mesmeric' relationship.[83]

Turning to the costume narrative which is embedded in *The Wicked Lady* and which contradicts the verbal level of the rather moralistic script, we can examine the possibility that the audience was competent to decode complex visual messages. The phenomenal success of the film, and the marked preference by the female audience for its 'costume' aspect, indicate that the audience could read the narrative inscribed into the non-verbal, 'unconscious' parts of the discourse.

The costumes of *The Wicked Lady* present Lockwood in an unambiguously positive way while we are prepared for the initial failure of the Patricia Roc/Griffith Jones relationship by their early lack of sartorial 'match'. He has scrolls and curlicues, flamboyant lace and full cuffs; Roc has military frogging, no cuffs and a straight-cut jacket which makes her appear narrow-hipped. Lockwood's first appearance in the film – androgynously with leather gloves and fur muff – links her with the gorgeous voluptuousness of the Griffith Jones aristocratic male. Her velvet fur-trimmed coat is pulled back to reveal its silken interior and swept round to form giant peplums which emphasise an hour-glass figure. Of even greater importance is the back view which we are afforded of this ensemble immediately after her arrival. The satin interior is held in place by a concealed fastening, and from this centre issues a plethora of folds and pleats. This 'secret' view is hidden from the male – he is seen approaching from the other side – but it is displayed to Roc and to the audience. This 'female' pattern is echoed in Lockwood's

Lockwood's 'vortex' hairstyle in *The Wicked Lady*

hairstyles here and elsewhere, which radiate, either in plaits or curls, from a hidden centre or vortex. Three of the four hairstyles she sports in the film are like this; the remaining ringlet style is seen only from the front. Such stylised back views of Lockwood's hair and dress ensemble are repeatedly displayed; indeed they might tentatively be called 'vulval plaits' and 'labial pleats'. The genital symbolism of her hair and clothes is not lost upon Mason – 'so it's a skirt we have in the saddle.' Hence the extended play with the idea of the private room with its 'secret passage' to the freedom of the park, and the lost key to that passage which is held by the Puritan servant. The film signals two sorts of female sexuality by carefully differentiating between the two wedding veils. Roc's has cuddlesome, kittenish 'ears', whereas Lockwood's is a mantilla, redolent of passion. When Roc's sexual fortunes improve, she changes from austere stripes to frills, curlicues, pearls, and a 'vortex' hairstyle, which the newly besotted Griffiths kisses from behind ('I couldn't help it').

Lockwood is presented throughout as a figure likely to give pleasure to a female viewer. She is identified with the mother – rather than the father – principle; her mother's brooch is cradled in her hands in a remarkably long insert, whereas Roc's hands, in a shot near the end of the film, *display* the jewel in quite a different gesture on the flat of her palm. Lockwood combines this with the active pursuit of sexual pleasure, which is facilitated by the donning of male attire; her riverside love-making with Mason is conducted in a shoulder-padded, tailored blouse, redolent of maleness *and* of severe 1940s female fashion. Clearly, Elizabeth Haffenden, the designer of the costumes in this and all others in the cycle, uses them to challenge and redefine sexual stereotypes and often to cut across the narrative of the script.

We should turn here to the theatrical origins and aesthetic of Haffenden's early work. None of her early designs in theatrical costume or décor were naturalistic. She worked extensively with masks, notably in Dean's 1939 production of *Johnson over Jordan*, in which Carrick's décor displayed clear continuities with the spectacular, expressionist tradition of *mise en scène* originated by his father Gordon Craig, and by Reinhardt and Appia. Much critical hostility was directed in the late 30s towards these theatrical styles. 'Expressionist' was equated with 'pro-German', and Haffenden's designs were dismissed as 'travesties of well-known types' in an article which insisted that 'the alien methods, rather loosely called expressionist, are not interesting or impressive.'[84] Comparable defences of a national 'addiction to realism' occur throughout the hostile reviews in the late 1930s of Haffenden's theatrical work; the *Bystander* critic notes that the costume and *mise en scène* of one of her plays is 'nothing more interesting than our old friend Expressionism repeating its well-worn tricks'[85] and *The Sphere* satirised the 'Reinhardian methods of mingling actors and audience' in a play using Haffenden's costumes and Goffin's décor.[86] Clearly, 'Englishness' and 'realism' had

Lockwood's male attire in *The Wicked Lady*

become interchangeable and compelling critical terms in the theatre by mid-1939, and debates about costume drama were confined to moralising or superficialities. In a review of a Haffenden-designed play, the *Telegraph* critic suggests that 'we may do worse than look up our histories and re-read some of the great novels of the past, particularly those that have played a part in our social developments.'[87]

Haffenden's interest in 'expressionist' costume could not, therefore, be accommodated within war-time theatre. After staging the 1939 costume pageants for de Gaulle's London visit, she worked almost exclusively from 1942 to 1949 on period films at Gainsborough.[88] Her theatre work in 1945, 1946 and 1949 indicates a continuing concern with costume as a symbolic index; but now the critics praised her 'heraldic magnificence'.[89] All her postwar theatre designs were period work – either set in, written in, or dressed in, the past – and were non-naturalistic.[90]

From 1942, then, Gainsborough constituted a space for expressionist costume work, and a site from which to develop. Minney encouraged such stylisation – 'one must not copy, one must adapt and evolve'[91] – and he wanted historical models to be creatively and suggestively altered. Such flexibility was banished by Box, who insisted on cumbersome historical 'reality' and sent original nineteenth-century fashion plates to Haffenden for faithful 'copying'.[92] Hitherto, her designs had always been cost-effective, but when Box insisted on verisimilitude of embroidery for the clothes in *The Bad Lord Byron*, the costume department could not complete on schedule; the studio had to compete with Ministry of Labour embroiderers, and as the latter were working on Princess Elizabeth's wedding dress, the struggle was an unequal one.[93] Box even spent time studying the design of Byron's *real shoes*, to ensure that Dennis Price got the limp right.

Management style, therefore, minimised Haffenden's expressionism after *Caravan*; *Jassy* was also the first Technicolor film that she had done, and it affected the design range, necessitating the learning of a different colour 'language'.

Hedda Hopper, in 'Clothes and the British Film Industry'[94] suggested that the box-office appeal of clothes should be increased by fostering a more intimate relationship between the cinema and fashion industries; but there were important differences between the studios. Male couturiers such as Hartnell, Strebel, Messel and Molyneux were used by other British studios such as Ealing and British Lion to lend status.[95] Maurice Carter recalled that such designer clothes would be kept by the stars, and their clothing coupon difficulties could thus be circumvented. However, no such arrangements existed at Gainsborough. 'Period' clothes could not be appropriated for everyday wear; moreover, period dresses designed by *women* (Haffenden and Joan Ellacott) lacked the trend-setting prestige of Beaton's period work.[96] The modern-dress films at Gainsborough, designed by Yvonne Caffin and Julie Harris, had no stylish couturier pretensions. Our films' relationship to contemporary fashion, then, was not a straightforward one. Even Len England of Mass Observation worried away at the lack of direct correlation between costume fiction and the dress of its consumers:

> Is there a trend in fashion towards bustles and brimmed hats? And yet surely such books as *Fanny by Gaslight* have been very popular this season.[97]

Although Gainsborough carefully supervised Margaret Lockwood's wardrobe on her promotion tours,[98] it never encouraged direct audience imitation. Mark Ostrer insisted that costume's role was to provide a visual 'feast', 'pageantry' and 'romantic gaiety' for civilians,[99] and the publicity material and press releases stressed the 'substitution' aspect of costume. The tie-ups suggested for *Caravan* were restricted to Spanish-style window-dressing and usherettes in gypsy uniform.[100] The *Madonna* material suggested that cinema managers 'stir up the feminine interest in the significance of the sign' (*seven moons*) by persuading a hat shop to exhibit a gypsyish hat (hats were coupon-free). *Madonna*'s 'wide fashion appeal' was to be taken up through a 'dress designing competition' which reproduced its markedly medieval dresses while asking for modern sketches by members of the audience. These, called 'elastic' imitations, were to be judged by Haffenden. The only direct area of 'fit' suggested was in hairstyles; the film's coiffeurs are pictured and instructions given 'which any girl can do herself'. The only encouragement to audience imitation of specifically period film dress was in *The Wicked Lady* material especially tailored for American audience and release; the management suggested giving free handkerchieves to the critics:

> Have some woman embroider 'The Wicked Lady' on each. The embroidery need not be of the best.[101]

The publicity material for *Blanche Fury* campaigned for a new lipstick 'Fury Red', and for specially-made blouses – 'yesterday's creation is today's fashion'; but this was not a Gainsborough film.

The *Madonna* publicity, rather, suggested that the costume's function is not to inculcate audience imitation, but to signal 'passion in the grand manner'. This, in the 'five terrific love scenes' in the gypsy part, was 'located in the heyday of Valentino and Navarro'. Romance, silent film, and exotic dress were synonymous because 'modern screen love is anaemic'. Respectable underpinning for the whole project was offered by references to the practicality of Haffenden's economies – glamour 'with the minimum amount of coupons'.[102] Her accurate prediction of the New Look is mentioned in 1946: she 'is recognized in the fashion world as an excellent prophet of women's fashions, and in 1944 she forecast in an article the swing over to glamour and to what men would call outrageous fashion. That she was correct is seen in the recent fashion displays of export garments of the big export houses.'[103]

The appeal of the garments in the costume melodramas is predicated upon what was *not* available under contemporary clothing conditions. Clothes rationing had been introduced in 1941 primarily to release 450,000 workers from the clothing industry into munitions.[104] It forced a redefinition and restriction of the female wardrobe, the disappearance of pretty underwear and, post-1942, the banning of the manufacture of heels over two inches high.[105] 'Utility' clothes were by law unembroidered, narrow-skirted and single-breasted, and fashion houses restricted the quality of fabrics and the variety of range.[106] Spurning the enthusiasm of the fashion writers for simplicity and economy of means, the female population clearly felt unhappy about its sartorial conditions. A 1941 Mass-Observation survey showed that more than half of women were buying fewer clothes, and that they much regretted the decline in 'dressy' evening wear and the equally marked increase in practical trousers.[107] Consolatory hairdressing visits boomed, and the heavy use of cosmetics increased in spite of chronic market fluctuations.[108]

The popularity of the Gainsborough costumes – 'tasteless', flared, exotic, excessive – should be seen in the context of the Paris shows of Spring 1946 with their tight bodices, huge layers of material, heavy embroidery and di-amanté studs. Dior's 'New Look', launched in February 1947, also empha-sised the waist, breasts and a swirling largesse of skirt. This quickly became *de rigueur* in England, and not just among the moneyed classes. Clearly the mass aficionados of the Gainsborough costume films shared a definition of 'femininity' with those who welcomed the New Look. Both 'read' the female body as a flowing mystery – a mobile flower lacking male muscular strength. Such a view would be compelling to a female workforce resenting its dun-garees, and in such circumstances frills might have a talismanic significance. Such a notion of femininity might have been a reflection of anxieties about the post-war roles of women, and might have made a retreat into fertility a more attractive prospect.[109]

We may conclude, then, that one reason for the cycle's popularity was its representation, through 'costume narrative', of a female sexuality denied expression through conventional signifying systems. The aesthetics and the preoccupations of its designer and studio management techniques combined to form a costume practice which may be termed *anti-fashion*.[110] Like haute couture, this is a rule-based activity with a syntax and semantics;[111] in anti-fashion, however, the components of the costume ensemble are less strictly related to each other. Pieces from separate garment systems are frequently combined, producing an overall effect which is often inconsistent. Moreover, when garments from different historical periods are worn together, any sense of authenticity is much reduced.

After 1946, a more direct relationship between Gainsborough costume practice and the fashion world became feasible; but by then such clothes may, as I suggested above, have symbolised not female pleasure but a plea-sure in retreat.

The Female Audience

The 'packaging' of Lockwood was clearly extremely successful. There is evidence to suggest that female adolescents sympathised with her to such an extent as to affect their memory of a film's characters.[112] Black's view that 'Lockwood had something with which every girl in the suburbs could ident-ify herself'[113] was extremely astute. However, the female audience was *selective* about the aspects of the Gainsborough films it took on board. Lockwood's energy and self-will produced pleasure for the audience; their accounts of the films suggest that it is the visual, not plot, elements which structure that pleasure.

If we turn to female cinematic taste in the period, we can see that while there was little gender difference in humour,[114] there was an appreciable one in the area of war films[115] and 'costume' melodramas. One of the Mass-Observation directives for November 1943 was 'what films have you liked best during the past year? Please list in order of liking.' The question was not a 'priority' one, and it was the last of six, and this must be taken into account. The sample is 104 men, and, unaccountably, 18 women.[116]

The Life and Death of Colonel Blimp figured very largely in the mens' favourites, and *The Man in Grey* was only mentioned by 4 men. A clerk, 33, liked it because 'the restraint and good taste of English films are superior to most of the Americans'; another likes it as 'a piece of history', and a technical researcher, 20, praises it thus:

> it is 'escapist', and we forget the present in order to dwell on the past when young ladies were taught what to say to men who asked for their hand in marriage, even though the latter were scoundrels.

'Good taste', 'real history', nostalgia for sexual inequality; such are the male alibis for enjoying the films. In Mayer's survey, the males desexualise their response (loving Calvert for her *diction*)[117] or they berate the films' salaciousness.[118] Granger is defensively rejected by a student because: 'I sincerely dislike *showing off* in films.'[119] Even schoolboys noted the bawdiness of *The Wicked Lady*, while ignoring the costumes and settings which so preoccupied the girls.[120]

Female film response differs interestingly. In the 1943 directives, *Random Harvest* is comparable to the men's *Blimp*, and *The Man in Grey* is a favourite of 4 of the 18 respondents; 2 like it for its 'good acting', its dramatic qualities impressed another, and a teacher likes its escapism, particularly noting the costumes, setting, and 'Becky Sharpe' theme.[121] The film in this survey is favoured by six times as many women as men, and for reasons of star identification and visual pleasure. Mayer's extracts here are useful. A hairdresser, 16½, reconstructs herself after viewing as 'the lovely heroine in a beautiful blue crinoline with a feather in her hair.'[122] Respondents are quite selective when it comes to *making* the dresses for themselves.[123] Female masochism clearly found ample material in these films: a typist, 17, notes Mason's similarity to Rhett Butler, remarking: 'I simply revel in seeing bold bad men.'[124] The female audience frequently attests to the films' emotional 'sincerity': this gives a respectability to their own cathartic release.[125] This extends into a demand for 'realism' by two schoolgirls, but it is clearly a realism of a different *type*, to do with emotional expressivity.[126] The costumes are a major source of pleasure, as are the sets, especially of *Madonna*.[127]

Of paramount importance is the 'dream' section in Mayer's 1946 book. The women select as dream-material resonant images from the films which are potent cultural symbols: the mirror and the whip. A typist draws the *seven moons* sign on the mirror *without knowing what it means*, but 'nothing further from the narrative';[128] a clerk saw 'the terrifying look on James

Mason's face as he beat Hester to death'.[129] Their dream-work selects out symbols of self-identification and male dominance. What is seen in the mirror is not understood. What is unlike the self is predatory. Clearly the films aid a kind of ritual expression and excision of deep-seated female fears.

It is predictable, therefore, that schoolgirls modelled their body language on such films,[130] and were 'speechless with longing'.[131] Ideological pressures inevitably directed their taste towards drama and 'human relationships'.[132]

Of course, caution needs to be exercised with Audience findings for the period. Bernstein and the 1943 *Kinematograph Weekly* survey on taste do not distinguish between classes, and Box has a naive belief in the reality of statistics *as such*.[133] Fear of the mass effects of film motivates many academic studies,[134] and Mayer held élitist views on popular culture, evoking Petronius in his distaste for the 'decadence' of *The Wicked Lady* and *Madonna*.[135] Mass-Observation work on film favours middle-class respondents, and often shows a peevishness in the face of historical contingency.[136] Nevertheless, it appears clear that the female audience of the period, subjected to the most extreme pressures and anxieties about the future, chose to 'read' these texts as an index of pleasure and optimism.

The 'gentry' theme in popular texts is a vital and enduring strand in British culture, and the mass audience clearly responded favourably to the Gainsborough style of aristocratic 'disguise'. Costume melodrama of this sort, I suggest, permits the expression of anxieties about the boundaries of political power and moral value. The function of such films is to articulate the audience's fears on issues of class and gender and (possibly) ritually to excise them. Ideology – that set of relations preferred by a hegemonic class – may be straightforwardly represented, or complicated, or *disguised* by art. The latter is clearly the case with the Gainsborough films. The ideological constitution of culture is such that a confident class will permit (indeed, will *require*) artistic representations of the classes over which it holds sway.

In conclusion, it would appear that the standard and generalised definitions of melodrama do not apply to this case. These melodramas do *not* foreground the family as an issue, and the *mise en scène* functions quite differently from American 40s historical films of the genre, such as *Forever Amber* or *Frenchman's Creek*. Moreover, what is often referred to as the cardinal sin of male scopophilia does not obtain here. The female stars, as I have shown, function as the source of the *female* gaze both on screen and in the audience; and males, gorgeously arrayed, are the unabashed objects of female desire. Class is an indisputable part of the films' structure of feeling, and is in no way representational of 'real events'.

It is instructive to compare Ealing historical films of this period. These display the usual realist consonance between different codes: dress, music, script, décor all *reinforce* each other with a quality 'gloss' and attention to historical verisimilitude. But the films are monolithic; they do not contain creative spaces or interstices for the audiences, and do not present the past as a place where answers to present predicaments might be found. Rather, the past only contains disappointment and sexual repression, and female attractiveness is predicated on extreme youth and chastity, a combination unlikely to please or comfort all its audience. We may conclude that, in our period, British costume melodrama (as opposed to historical film) manifests a positive interpretation of the past, and grants a freedom to the audience to manoeuvre its own way through narrative codes.

Notes

1. See *Kinematograph Weekly*, 20 December 1945, 19 December 1946, and *Daily Film Renter*, 29 April 1946 and 9 May 1946, for accounts of the cycle's profitability.
2. *News Chronicle*, 19 November 1945.
3. *Tribune*, 12 April 1946.
4. *Sunday Graphic*, 14 April 1946.
5. A. Wood, *Mr Rank* (London: Hodder and Stoughton, 1952), p. 123.
6. R. J. Minney, *Talking of Films* (London: Home and Van Thal, 1947), p. 19.
7. *The Times*, 3 March 1949. See *Kinematograph Weekly*, 19 April 1945, for a cost breakdown of *The Man in Grey*, which should be compared with that of Box's *The Bad Lord Byron*, in *The Daily Herald*, 2 March 1948.
8. Interviews conducted by me with Mrs Paddy Porter, continuity girl at Gainsborough, in unpublished M A thesis in Film Studies for the Polytechnic of Central London, 1982.
9. Interview conducted by me with Maurice Carter, Art Director at Gainsborough, in S. Aspinall and R. Murphy (eds.), *Gainsborough Melodrama* (London: British Film Institute, 1983), p. 58.
10. Ibid., p. 56.
11. *Today's Cinema*, 4 January 1945. See also *Kinematograph Weekly*, 21 March 1945. Minney, *Talking of Films*, p. 77, concurs with Ostrer's ideas about costing.
12. A. Wood, *Mr Rank*, p. 147.
13. *Kinematograph Weekly*, 19 April 1945.
14. Ibid.: 'rapturous notices from the critics will be the delight of the highbrows.' See Minney, *Talking of Films*, p. 16.
15. *Kinematograph Weekly*, 20 December 1945.
16. B. Woodhouse, *From Script to Screen* (London: Winchester Publications, 1947), pp. 63–4.
17. Interviews conducted by me with Mr Bill Salter and Mr Dennis Mason, sound recordists, in Aspinall and Murphy, *Gainsborough Melodrama*. Lengthier versions of these are in my unpublished M A thesis, 1982.
18. Interview with Mrs Porter, in M A thesis, 1982, p. (ix).
19. Ibid. p. (viii).
20. Interview with Maurice Carter in *Gainsborough Melodrama*, p. 58.

21. Ibid.
22. My interview with Mr Salter in *Gainsborough Melodrama*, p. 53.
23. Interview with Mr Mason, ibid., p. 55.
24. For example, W. D. Wall and E. M. Smith, 'The Film Choices of Adolescents', *British Journal of Educational Psychology*, June 1949, pp. 135–6.
25. *Madonna of the Seven Moons* press-book in BFI library.
26. *Today's Cinema*, 5 January 1944.
27. *Sunday Graphic*, 14 April 1946.
28. Magdalen King-Hall, *The Life and Death of the Wicked Lady Skelton* (London: Peter Davies, 1944); Marjorie Lawrence, *Madonna of the Seven Moons* (London: Hurst and Blackett, 1931; reprinted 1945); Lady E. F. Smith, *Caravan* and *The Man in Grey* (London: Hutchinson, 1943 and 1941 respectively); Norah Lofts, *Jassy* (London: Michael Joseph, 1944). The only exception to female authorship here is Michael Sadleir, *Fanny by Gaslight* (London: Constable, 1940).
29. R. J. Minney, *Talking of Films*, p. 4. See also p. 35.
30. N. Lee, *Log of a Film Director* (London: Quality Press, 1949), pp. 34–5.
31. R. J. Minney, *Talking of Films*, p. 43.
32. See E. Britton, *Blanche Fury: The Book of the Film* (London: World Film Publications, 1948) and Vera Caspary, *Bedelia*, (ed.) William R. T. Rodger (London: Eyre and Spottiswoode/John Corfield Productions, 1946).
33. In 'History with Frills: the "Costume" Novel in World War II', *Red Letters* 14, 1983.
34. These are male replies to the October 1943 directive in the Mass-Observation Archive at Sussex University, from a commissionaire (aged 19), a schoolboy, a commercial traveller (35), and Education Inspector (36), in that order.
35. The first reply is from a female press agent (34) in the Mass-Observation October directive. The second is from Mass-Observation File 2018, p. 85, 'C' class female aged 35. The third is ibid., p. 92, housewife (28). The fourth, ibid., p. 93, clerk (35). The last is in Mass-Observation file 2537, p. 34 (unascribed, but female).
36. Mass-Observation file 2018, p. (ix).
37. *Reading in Tottenham*, Mass-Observation file 2537, p. 37.
38. Lady E. F. Smith, *The Man in Grey*, p. 139.
39. Lady E. F. Smith, *Caravan*, p. 97.
40. Magdalen King-Hall, *The Life and Death of the Wicked Lady Skelton*, p. 97.
41. See my account of John Drummond's 1942 novel, *The Bride Wore Black*, in *Red Letters* 14.
42. See her *Life's a Circus* (London: Longmans, 1939).
43. S. Kunitz and H. Haycroft, *20th Century Authors* (New York: H. W. Wilson, 1942), p. 842.
44. Lee, *Log of a Film Director*, p. 133.
45. The Executive Committee of July 1944 of the Screenwriters Association contained Launder, Gilliatt, Minney and Arliss, and Minney went on the Association's behalf to conferences in Paris and Madrid. Material on the SWA was formerly in the archives of the Society of Authors, and is now the property of the British Library.

46. M. Kennedy, *The Mechanical Muse* (London: Allen and Unwin, 1942), p. 39.
47. Ibid., p. 29.
48. Ibid., p. 53.
49. Crabtree directed both *Caravan* and *Madonna*; in the B F I press book of the former, he suggests that 'it is imperative for a director to be vitally interested in the story.'
50. Memo from Launder in S O A files, 15 May 1944. Arliss was co-opted to the Executive Committee to discuss credits in 1946, and he and Kennedy were on council of the S W A until 1954.
51. N. Lee, *Log of a Film Director*, p. 133.
52. *Kinematograph Weekly*, 19 April 1945.
53. Letter from Launder to Society of Authors, 11 November 1946, in S O A files. A very highly paid screenwriter could be hired by the week.
54. Interview with Mr Salter in *Gainsborough Melodrama*, p. 53.
55. Draft constitution of S W A, 11 March 1937, in S O A files. Resolution 14 is to 'provide facilities to encourage the register of stories and scenarios which members might consider to their advantage'.
56. Report of the Annual General Meeting of the S W A, 18 July 1944.
57. Letter in S O A files from Launder to the Secretary of S O A, 5 January 1942: 'It is our business to suggest or consider stories and ideas with the object of recommending to the Ministry suitable subjects for propaganda films. We believe the majority of writers will not look upon payment.' Note that they produce ideas, not actual treatments.
58. Letter from Inland Revenue to Launder, 12 October 1943.
59. See Letter from Launder to the Secretary of S O A, 20 May 1943, and account of a mass S W A meeting, 25 September 1946, in S O A files.
60. Letter from Launder to Screenwriters Guild, June 1947.
61. Letter from Morgan to the Secretary of S O A, 12 October 1947: 'I hear that the A C T have been rapped over the knuckles by Cripps, and told to interest themselves a little more in production, and a little less in power politics.'
62. Letter from G. D. H. Cole to Morgan, 8 November 1947.
63. *Kinematograph Weekly*, 1 January 1943. See also Wood, *Mr Rank*, pp. 134–7.
64. Letter from Del Giudice to the Secretary of S O A, 10 December 1942.
65. Letter from Del Giudice to the Secretary of S O A, 14 December 1942.
66. Rough notes for the private information of Kilham Roberts in S O A files, in what looks very like Balcon's handwriting and bearing his initials. These are undated, but clearly relate to the Scenario Institute.
67. Letter from Launder to Kilham Roberts, 15 April 1943.
68. The end of the script in the B F I library has 'thundering hooves' as her spirit makes its exit. These are absent from the actual film.
69. Lady E. F. Smith, *Caravan*, p. 202.
70. Lady E. F. Smith, *The Man in Grey*, p. 245.
71. M. Lawrence, *Madonna of the Seven Moons*, pp. 14, 155.
72. Ibid., p. 131: 'at last his long-held patience gave way, and he took by force what should only be given in love.'
73. Interview with Maurice Carter in *Gainsborough Melodrama*, p. 58.
74. See E. Carrick (ed.), *Art and Design in the British Film* (London: Dennis Dobson,

1948), pp. 16, 64, 92, and L. Barsacq, *Le Décor du Film* (Paris: Seghers, 1970), p. 77.

75. R. J. Minney, *The Film-Maker and His World: a Young Person's Guide* (London: Gollancz, 1964), p. 86.
76. Interview with Maurice Carter in *Gainsborough Melodrama*, p. 59.
77. *Kinematograph Weekly*, 16 August 1945. See also *The Cinetechnician*, November/December 1948, for an interesting account of the replica work on Christopher Columbus.
78. S. Box and V. Cox, *The Bad Lord Byron* (London: Convoy Publications, 1949).
79. See the press book for *Saraband* in the BFI library.
80. Maurice Carter commented to me that it was 'the biggest budget I'd ever had for sets. It was *all-out*; it was meant to be another *Wicked Lady*.'
81. See J. P. Mayer, *British Cinemas and their Audiences* (London: Dennis Dobson, 1948), pp. 144, 252, 257. See also B. Kesterton, 'The Social and Emotional Effects of the Recreational Film on Adolescents of 13 and 14 years of age in the West Bromwich Area', University of Birmingham PhD thesis, 1948; and W. D. Wall and E. M. Smith, 'The Film Choices of Adolescents'.
82. See Mayer, *British Cinemas*, pp. 22, 81, 184; and J. P. Mayer, *Sociology of Film* (London: Faber and Faber, 1946), pp. 183, 216.
83. See J. C. Reid, *Bucks and Bruisers: Pierce Egan and Regency England* (London: Routledge & Kegan Paul, 1971), and F. Kaplan, *Dickens and Mesmerism* (Princeton: Princeton University Press, 1975).
84. *Illustrated London News*, 11 March 1939.
85. *The Bystander*, 8 March 1939.
86. *The Sphere*, 9 April 1938.
87. *Daily Telegraph*. See also *The Sphere*, 17 September 1938.
88. Information available in the publicity file for *Madonna* in the BFI library. For full credit lists, see E. Leese, *Costume Design in the Movies* (Isle of Wight: BCW Publishing, 1977), p. 47.
89. See *The Tatler*, 26 June 1946, and Picture Post, 26 March 1945.
90. A complete theatrical list from 1939 is: March 1945, *Three Waltzes*; May 1946, *The Kingmakers*; July 1946, *Marriage à la Mode*; May 1949, *The Beaux Stratagem*; February 1951, *Man and Superman*; June 1951, *Dido and Aeneas*; September 1951, *The Tempest*; November 1953, *Pygmalion*.
91. R. J. Minney, *The Film-Maker and His World*, pp. 91, 116.
92. S. Box and V. Cox, *The Bad Lord Byron*, pp. 88–9.
93. Ibid., pp. 93–4.
94. *Kinematograph Weekly*, 27 June 1946.
95. See E. Leese, *Costume Design in the Movies*, p. 17.
96. Credit lists in E. Leese, *Costume Design*, p. 47. See also C. Spencer, *Cecil Beaton, Stage and Film Design* (London: Academy Editions, 1975), p. 81.
97. In Mass-Observation file no. 485 (7 November 1940).
98. M. Lockwood, *Lucky Star* (London: Odhams Press, 1955), pp. 112, 135.
99. *Kinematograph Weekly*, 11 January 1945.
100. *Caravan* publicity in BFI library.
101. American publicity material for *The Wicked Lady* in BFI library. *Blanche Fury* material is in BFI library. See also an article by Orrom on tie-ups in general in

Screen and Audience, 1947, and B. Woodhouse, *From Script to Screen*, pp. 142–7.

102. In the *Madonna* publicity material in BFI library.

103. In *Caravan* material in BFI library.

104. N. Longmate, *How We Lived Then: History of Everyday Life During the Second World War* (London: Arrow Books, 1973), p. 246.

105. Ibid., pp. 250, 252. See also J. Robinson, *Fashion in the Forties* (London: Academy Editions, 1976), p. 25 of 1980 edition.

106. Robinson, *Fashion in the Forties*, pp. 16, 25.

107. Mass-Observation file no. 728, *Changes in Clothing Habits* (9 June 1941).

108. Longmate, *How We Lived Then*, pp. 273, 276.

109. Of particular interest here is Mass-Observation report 2059 (8 March 1944), *Will the Factory Girls Want to Stay Put or Go Home?* The Report blandly concludes that 'both men and women agree ... that men should be the bread-winners', but this is not borne out *at all* by the general restlessness expressed by the younger women. Only those older women who had been at home as house-wives before the war unambiguously wished to return there.

110. See T. Polhemus and L. Procter, *Fashion and Anti-Fashion: Anthropology of Clothing and Adornment* (London: Thames and Hudson, 1978), p. 16.

111. As described by Roland Barthes in *Elements of Semiology* (London: Jonathan Cape, 1967), p. 27, and in his *Système de la mode* (Paris: Du Seuil, 1967).

112. Wall and Smith, 'Film Choices of Adolescents', p. 130. Here they note from a retelling of *The Wicked Lady*, adolescent girls called the heroines 'Margaret' and 'Patricia'.

113. A. Wood, *Mr Rank*, p. 146.

114. As indicated by the Mass-Observation survey on *Let George Do It*.

115. Mass-Observation report on Film Themes (17 March 1940), Appendix I. This was a reply to a 1939 question, 'do you like a different sort of picture now to what you did before the war?' Mass-Observation concluded that women over 30 were the main objectors to war films.

116. The present Mass-Observation archivists are unable to account for this im-balance.

117. J. P. Mayer, *British Cinemas and their Audiences*, p. 41.

118. Ibid., p. 49.

119. Ibid., p. 129.

120. See Kesterton, PhD thesis, p. 72: '*The Wicked Lady* was classified as a film whose main appeal is to sex-instinct. Yet it has a lively quick-moving story, and picturesque gowns. It is probably these qualities that give the film considerable appeal for the girls. They, unlike the few boys who mentioned this production, concentrated on the costumes and the settings, rather than the bawdy parts of the plot.'

121. A holiday-home manageress (26) likes its 'unusual plot and good acting'. Two servicewomen praise the female acting style. [It is against Mass-Observation's policy to publish the names of respondents, many of whom must still be alive].

122. Mayer, *British Cinemas and their Audiences*, p. 22.

123. Ibid., p. 81, where chemist's assistant (female, 21) talks about clothes. See also

Mayer's *Sociology of Film*, p. 215, where a female clerk (17) realises that you have to 'select'; she proposes to copy a coat from the 'civilized' part of *Madonna*, not from the 'gypsy' part.

124. Mayer, *British Cinemas and their Audiences*, p. 73.
125. Ibid., p. 92, female clerk (20): 'it is very seldom that we find faked scenes.'
126. Ibid., p. 161. See also schoolgirl (15), p. 166; female clerk (16), p. 169; female student (17), p. 179; female clerk (16), p. 174.
127. Ibid., textile worker (18), p. 184. See also Mayer, *Sociology of Film*, p. 183. Female clerk (16): 'I also wish we could go back a few centuries and the ladies wear beautiful crinolines.' See also *British Cinemas and their Audiences*, female typist (19), p. 189. *Madonna* and *The Man in Grey* feature most strongly. On the latter, see ibid., p. 227, female telephonist (25), and p. 234, female housekeeper (46) and female typist (24), p. 214. See also Mayer, *Sociology of Film*, p. 92 (female, 14½) on *The Man in Grey*.
128. Mayer, *Sociology of Film*, pp. 201–2. Respondents were asked to describe any dreams influenced by films.
129. Ibid., p. 213. See also p. 217, firewoman's dream.
130. See also W. D. Wall and W. A. Simpson, 'The Effects of Cinema Attendance on the Behaviour of Adolescents as seen by their Contemporaries', *British Journal of Educational Psychology*, February 1949.
131. Kesterton, PhD thesis, p. 99.
132. Ibid., p. 84: 34% of girls like love stories, and only 9% of the boys; p. 79 suggests that 54% of girls and 18% of boys attach importance to 'sentiment and pathos'. See also pp. 257–8 where 67% of the girls admitted imitating star's make-up (especially Lockwood). This 67% was largely composed of 'lower' educational sector.
133. See K. Box, *The Cinema and the Public* (London: Central Office of Information, 1946) in Mass-Observation 2429, and L. Moss and K. Box, *Wartime Survey: The Cinema Audience* (London: Ministry of Information, 1943) in Mass-Observation 1871.
134. Such as Kesterton, PhD thesis; or Wall and Smith, 'Film Choices of Adolescents'.
135. J. P. Mayer, *British Cinemas and their Audiences*, p. 8.
136. Hapless Mass-Observation film-observers were unable to categorise such *données* as 'I can't talk to you now, ducks, I've got no teeth look!' (in Mass-Observation box 15, with loose papers). The Bernstein film questionnaire is unable to decode working-class respondents' jokes and irony.

Hollywood, Freud and the Representation of Women

Regulation and Contradiction, 1945–early 60s

JANET WALKER

> My chief objection is still that I do not believe that satisfactory plastic representation of our abstractions is at all possible. We do not want to give our consent to anything insipid. Mr Goldwyn was at any rate clever enough to stick to the aspect of our subject that can be plastically represented very well, that is to say, love.
>
> Sigmund Freud in a letter to Karl Abraham
> regarding Pabst's *Secrets of a Soul*, 1925

BETWEEN the end of World War Two and the early 60s the historical conjuncture of social problems, the difficulty of gender roles, and the institutions of American psychoanalysis and psychiatry became an obsession of the media. During this era a number of films were produced which took women and psychotherapy as their explicit subject matter.[1] The films in question are not all technically women's films (as defined either by feminist theory or as a studio production category), nor are they all melodramas (as defined by genre theory). But they do share with these categories a concern with romance and feminine psycho-sexuality, and/or domesticity versus the world of work outside the home. Because of their overt adoption of what seem to be ill-used, jargon-ridden psychoanalytic scenarios, these films have often been derogated critically. I do not deny that the versions of psychoanalysis and other therapeutic techniques employed in the films are extremely crude. However, these films should not be read as providing a legitimate account of the psychological theories they recruit. Instead, I would argue that as examples from the realm of cultural production they form an interesting and rich part of the larger social sphere. The examination of the specific systems of regulation and contradiction figured in these films can provide a fruitful approach for the study of gender relations against a wider field of cultural and social institutions and problems.

The economically and rhetorically enforced allocation and division of productive and reproductive roles according to gender[2] reached the peak of its social installation in the United States between the end of World War Two and the beginning of the American Women's Movement. As retainers of the domestic sphere, women were crucial to the upkeep of the system as a whole. World War Two occasioned the only decrease in the average age of first marriage since the start of the century. By 1960 the average marriage age for women had fallen to 20.3 years.[3]

The baby and consumer booms and the expansion of wealth and leisure time added to the era's optimistic sheen. Commentators defined domesticity, respectability, security, TV, advertising, affluence, suburbia, and superhighways as the order of the day. As Fenton Turck wrote in *Reader's Digest* in 1952, 'A fresh and exciting age emerges, alive with expanding opportunities. Today's Americans are living in one of these extraordinary periods.'

But recent social historians point to an undertow of sexism, poverty, racism, economic imperialism, and fear:

> The bomb, communists, spies, and Sputnik all scared Americans. And fear bred repression both of the blatant McCarthyite type and the more subtle, pervasive, and personal daily pressures to conform.[4]

The concept of conformity at the centre of the 50s mindset seemed, on the one hand, to describe the positive, organic, homogeneity of the collective realisation of a dream of affluence and security. But it gaped open to reveal the pressures subtending the unproblematic surface. Positive valuation of conformity necessitated the exclusion of groups not even in the running. Blacks and poor people in general were invisible to the celebrants of suburban consumer culture.[5]

Large scale social and political problems did not go unnoticed at the time. Problems such as McCarthyism and above-ground nuclear testing were being reported in newspapers and mass circulation magazines such as *Life* and *Look* during the period under discussion, and some social commentators were criticising social arrangements. For example, *The Lonely Crowd* (1950, 1953) pointed out what was wrong with popularly advocated conformity.[6] Authors Reisman, Glazer, and Denney wrote that in seeking to be like others, men (sic) lose the social freedom and individual autonomy essential to real social and personal actualisation.

However, these troubling issues in foreign and domestic politics and policy tended to be eliminated from the *Reader's Digest* condensed version of the world, a sanitised version particularly strong in major women's magazines. Betty Friedan pointed out that mass circulation magazines such as *Ladies Home Journal* and *McCalls* did carry hundreds of articles on political topics in the 30s and 40s (for example, 'Can the US Have Peace After This War?' by Walter Lippmann), but that by the 50s they 'printed virtually no articles except those that serviced women as housewives, or described women as housewives, or permitted a purely female identification.'[7] What is missing is the *joint* consideration of social problems and 'women's issues'. Women and social problems seemed to designate separate spheres and received separate treatment in much popular and academic literature of the postwar period of economic growth.

Complications multiply under the joint consideration of 'general' history and 'gender' history. For example, the debate raged in magazines, anthropological works, government studies – it seemed that everyone was obliged to take a stance: *should* women work outside the home? And, was it paid labour or housewifery which could fulfil the essential identity of the woman? Researching the era for which the descriptive shorthand image could be the sunny apron-clad housewife, I found another image, thanks especially to recent social histories written from a feminist perspective: the woman at work outside of the home. Contrary to would-be common knowledge about the 50s, working women did exist even after World War Two, though there were significant changes in the demography and job function of the female workforce. In *The American Woman* (1972), William Chafe argues that there may have been widespread firing of women *immediately* after the war, but that by 1946 there were one million *more* women in factories than there had been in 1940.[8] The debate over whether women should work outside the home covered over the fact that they already did in great numbers. Posing the issue as purely one of gender led to the elision of one reading of history.

Chafe points to what he calls a 'paradox' and what other recent historians have called the 'work myth'. While unprecedented numbers of women were joining the work force, only minimal progress was made in areas of greatest concern to women's rights advocates – employment in the professions, child-care centres and a uniform wage scale. According to Chafe:

> A job for a wife over thirty-five became normal – at least by a statistical standard – but most Americans continued to subscribe to the belief that women were (and should remain) primarily homemakers.[9]

The fact that women at work for pay outside their homes were overlooked allowed the perpetuation of economic and social disadvantage. It also indicates the way in which an ideology defining the optimal female role as exclusively that of wife and mother might be called on to justify an economic need, in this case for a casual workforce.

Many women, both those at work outside the home and those who devoted all their time to housewifery, seemed to see their lives as less fulfilled than the utopian vision of the 50s would have it. Working women were often desperate with self-doubt and their 'double days' as housewives and paid workers. Reporting from the home front, Betty Friedan names what had previously been 'the problem with no name': the 'vision of the happy modern housewife as she is described by magazines and television, by the functional sociologists, the sex-directed educators', was, precisely, a vision, and one that didn't correspond to any women Friedan was able to find and interview.[10] Instead she found unhappy women in analytical psychotherapy, on tranquillisers, alcohol, hospitalised, or otherwise depressed and ill.[11] Women were seeking help from the psychological professions in great numbers.[12]

Psychotherapy was recruited into service both to help women failing under the feminine mystique *and* to advertise the benefits of domestic life. While the economic imperatives of post-World War Two affluence designed a new market of professional housewives, women were drawn into what Betty Friedan called 'The Sexual Sell'.[13] A pop version of Freudian psychoanalysis was utilised by Viennese psychologist Ernest Dichter and his colleagues of the Motivational Research Institute to find out how to sell detergents, vacuum cleaners, creams, powders, cake mixes, etc. The approach was complex. The trick was to convince women that they were scientific experts battling 'hidden dirt and germs', without succeeding to such an extent that women 'freed from the drudgery of housework for more creative pursuits' would actually gain the confidence to discover a fulfilling career outside the home.

The histories which reveal the elision of social problems by commentators of the period are crucial but not sufficient to the examination of the *operation* of the elision itself. What is revealed in the joint study of gender roles and social problems is precisely that there was a popular and professional discursive condensation of social problems onto the 'problem' of the nature of woman. To the real socio-economic difficulties faced by women was added a discourse of blame.

The widely-read manifesto, *Modern Woman: The Lost Sex* (1947) by sociologist Ferdinand Lundberg and psychoanalyst Marynia Farnham[14], is a good example of a text which locates woman as the source of social ills. Discussed in popular magazines, and cited by period and recent critics as the pre-eminent representative of its point of view, the book acknowledged that women were more than homemakers, but viewed that fact as a violent and unfortunate breach of nature brought down on society by progress and the Industrial Revolution. Women's lack of a secure home base was seen as responsible for widespread social malaise (the hidden underside of wealth and conformity):

> unhappiness not directly traceable to poverty, disease, physical malformation or bereavement is increasing in our time. The most precise expression of [this] unhappiness is neurosis. The bases for most of this unhappiness, as we have shown, are laid in the childhood home. The principal instrument[s] of their creation are women.[15]

Lundberg and Farnham advocated a return to eighteenth-century social and productive constellations as a system under which women were happy.

According to this rhetoric, feminine maladjustment presented problems which took on primary social importance because of the role of women/ mothers in the reproduction of culture. The rehabilitation of individual women, therefore, would seem to provide the solution to social problems.

Widespread popular familiarity with psychoanalytic ideas and psycho-therapeutic practice had been growing at least since Freud's visit to Clark University in 1909, but wartime uses consolidated this diffusion. The psychiatric evaluation of draftees was the evidence which brought home to the public the sense that all was not well. Reuben Fine, author of a well-known history of psychoanalysis, mentions that the high rejection rate of draftees and the high rate of neuropsychiatric disabilities were traced to poor mothering.[16] The discovery that America's young men were failing to shoot to kill in battle, so-called GI cowardice, inspired a new look at family structure. It was 'discovered' that 'Momism', or maternal overprotection, was at the root of the trouble. Philip Wylie coined the term 'Momism', and Wylie and Farnham and Lundberg enumerated the various ways in which mothers could fail.[17] 'Overprotection' was the most ironic because women were simultaneously exhorted to place all their energies into home and children and yet to allow their children to grow away from them to independence. The only way to overcome this double bind was total self-effacement – not a feasible option.[18]

Books, magazines, plays, movies, newspapers and their syndicated help columns, TV, radio, and advertising all profited from the public's fascination with psychoanalysis and psychology in general. The specialised terminology of psychoanalysis entered into colloquial speech, and sociologists claimed that the spread of psychoanalysis was indicative of and/or influenced the changing shape of American thought, society and culture. Henry R. Luce, editor-in-chief of *Life* magazine contracted for a series on psychology, psychiatry, and psychoanalysis which ran in the issues of 7 January through 4 February 1957, and which was then published in book form as *The Age of Psychology* by Ernest Havemann.[19] The blurb on the back cover of this book (quoted here in part) is typical of the kind of arguments being made about psychology in the period:

> We live in the Age of Psychology.
> Most of us are fully aware that a new science of human behaviour has, within a few decades, completely changed the nature of modern life. Few of us are completely aware of how deeply its findings (often misinterpreted, often virtually turned upside down by untrained 'middle men') have pervaded our lives, subtly changed our thinking, our actions, our very language...

Within the book, which is itself indicative of the popular craze for psychology, Havemann cites examples to support the readily apparent truth of its pervasiveness. He claims that nine out of ten of the major US daily papers were carrying at least one column dependent on psychology. 'The Worry Clinic', a syndicated column claimed a circulation of 19 million, 'Mirror of Your Mind', 20 million, and 'Let's Explore Your Mind', 21 million. Books of psychology, psychiatry, and psychoanalysis written for the layman often reached best-seller status: Lucy Freeman's *Fight Against Fears*[20] sold 385,000 copies by 1957; Robert Linder's *The Fifty-Minute Hour*[21] was an extremely popular collection of case histories. On Broadway the psychiatrist had become a stock character, and Havemann mentions a study by a psychiatrist that claimed that in 1955 one movie in ten contained a psychiatrist or a psychiatric problem. Even professional literature achieved high sales on the general market. *The Basic Writings of Sigmund Freud*, a Modern Library Giant, had sold over a quarter of a million copies by 1957.

Others, writing from within the psychological professions (writers more serious than Havemann), emphasised the social import and pervasiveness of psychoanalysis. Hendrik M. Ruitenbeek for example, in *Freud and America* (1966), explained the diffusion of Freud's ideas in the us, while *The Freudian Ethic* (1959) by Richard LaPiere took the view that the Protestant ethic, the source of American initiative and greatness, was being replaced by the Freudian ethic, a debilitating and socially corrosive social movement.[22] Regardless of whether Freudianism was decried or optimistically embraced, the number and widespread popularity of such writings attests to the fact that it was *the* phenomenon of the day for laymen and professionals both.

Sociologies of the period typically included a chapter on Freudianism in America, one on the modern woman, and chapters on leisure time and suburbanisation, technology and corporate capitalism, associating discourses on femininity, psychiatry, and social function.[23] From the perspective of the 80s, the fact that these particular realms were repeatedly juxtaposed is significant. That both separately and together they were seen as indicative of an era, underscores the profound centrality of the discourses as condensed ciphers for historical inquiry.

I have argued that the representational media of the post-World War Two period through the early 60s publicised the psychological professions as institutions whose function it was to respond to individual and social malaise. Psychoanalysis, clinical psychology, psychiatry, social work, and related disciplines were turned to as *curative* and *regulatory* agencies. But both psychoanalytic theory and its institutional history reveal profound inconsistencies with an approach stressing regulation, adaptation, or adjustment. Basic to psychoanalysis is its emphasis on the *inevitability* of repression and unconscious processes. This disparity is relevant to an historical description of the period foregrounding the contradictory nature of other pervasive institutional discourses suggested above, for example, conformity, essential femininity, and the 'work myth'. Furthermore, the dual function of the psychoanalytic institution is crucial to the understanding of its place and operation in Hollywood narrative.

It is tempting to see the disparity between adjustment/adaptation and analysis as an institutional division where clinical psychology, psychiatry, and social work are viewed as favouring adjustment, and psychoanalysis as favouring analytic investigation. If an adaptive strain *within* psychoanalysis is acknowledged, there is a tendency to see it as confined to practical American innovations or to therapeutic practice rather than Freudian psychoanalytic theory or methodology. But I believe there are problems with such divisions.

Firstly, in the United States psychoanalysis and psychiatry, a medical specialty, were and still are integrally connected on theoretical and institutional levels. In the postwar years psychoanalysis constituted the psychological theory taught in medical training and one had to hold an M D to be a member of the American Psychoanalytic Association. In the 1950s 82 per cent of the members of the American Psychoanalytic Association were also members of the American Psychiatric Association.[24]

Secondly, the field of post-World War Two American psychoanalysis was itself torn by the tensions between classical analysis and adjustment therapy. The institutional interpenetration of psychiatry and psychoanalysis provoked some members of the American Psychoanalytic Association to attempt to distinguish the two by defining 'classical analysis' as oriented against adjustment.[25] However, the impetus to define American psychoanalysis, and to align it with its European theoretical underpinnings, brought notoriously stormy debate and much confusion. A committee of the A P A launched a four-year project (from 1947 to 1951) to come up with a definition of psychoanalysis. The project ended with the publication of a report stating that it is 'impossible to find a definition of psychoanalysis that is acceptable to even a large group of members of the A P A'.[26]

Robert P. Knight's outgoing presidential address reveals the dual tendencies characteristic of the central bastion of classical American psychoanalysis: the desire to remain faithful to classical Freudianism, and the urge to bring a notoriously American utilitarianism to psychoanalytic practice.

> It is my impression from talking with many analytic colleagues that the 'pure' psychoanalyst, one who does only classical psychoanalysis, is a much scarcer individual at present, and that many analysts would privately admit that they are treating a number of patients with modified analytic techniques, or even with psychotherapy, and have relatively few patients with whom they employ a strictly classical technique.[27]

Remaining faithful to classical Freudian theory meant shoring up the profession's prestige and power, and distinguishing it from related disciplines. But it was precisely the American utilitarianism, the boldness about experimentation and the adoption of any technique which had demonstrated its usefulness, which caused psychoanalysis to catch hold so strongly and to sustain its presence in the U S.[28]

It is this constellation of issues focusing on social problems, women, and psychoanalysis which gets further circulated but also refigured in the films of the period which treat psychoanalysis and femininity. The subject matter of psychoanalysis and femininity promised a pleasurable spectacle which could both bring up fascinating aberrant sexuality and unconscious processes, and also diffuse and regulate issues threatening to get out of hand.

The 'literalisation' of psychoanalysis in these Hollywood narratives follows the same path in filmic representation as the shifts undergone by psychoanalysis in its popularisation in America of the 40s and 50s. Where the discourse of adaptation focused on the role of the woman in the social sphere, the enactment of narrative resolution by psychoanalysis in these films required the complicit representation of women.[29] For example, *Whirlpool*, *The Seventh Veil*, *The Dark Mirror*, *The Snake Pit*, *The Locket*, *The Three Faces of Eve*, and *Lady in the Dark*, are some of those films in which psychoanalysis and love collude to provide the happy ending.

Nevertheless, this process of resolution accounts only partially for the work of the texts here in question. In various ways these texts also present systematic resistances to the symbolic representation of patriarchal capitalist hegemony. These resistances may be theorised through psychoanalytically informed textual analysis if one retains an awareness of the limitations of this theory. The films refigure a troubled form of American postwar psychoanalysis, clinging to its classical analytic roots against the rising trend towards adjustment, and they draw on female social roles which feminist analysis reveals to be fraught with contradiction.

In the following section I will use the film *Whirlpool* (1949) to show how one film figures the difficulty of regulation and the conflicts characteristic of both psychoanalysis and cinema. *Whirlpool* may best be generalised with regard to other 40s psychoanalytic films, although some significant stylistic traits are specific to this film. In the 50s and 60s the issues of regulation and contradiction remain, but the film's negotiation of these issues changes.

Whirlpool opens as Ann Sutton (Gene Tierney) is caught for shoplifting at the Wilshire Department Store in Los Angeles. In the store offices a stranger comes to her aid, revealing that she is the non-working and independently wealthy wife of a distinguished psychoanalyst, Dr William Sutton (Richard Conte). Ann feels compelled to hide her kleptomania from her husband for fear he will no longer love her. The stranger turns out to be David Korvo (Jose Ferrer), a hypnotist. He convinces Ann that he can cure her problems. Ann begins to receive treatment by hypnosis from Dr Korvo although she is warned away from him by a former patient and lover of his, Theresa Randolph, who is now in analysis with Dr William Sutton. One night when Dr Sutton is away at a conference, Ann, following a post-hypnotic suggestion, takes a recording from her husband's office and goes to Terry Randolph's home. There she finds Randolph dead. She is discovered at the home and arrested. She remembers nothing of these events. Dr Sutton comes to her aid until he becomes convinced that Ann was the lover of Korvo and is covering for him. But Korvo has a good alibi. He was post-operative at the time of the murder. Ann finally 'confesses' her kleptomania and its origin to the police. Dr Sutton realises that Ann's basically good character couldn't have altered in a flash. He figures out that Korvo could have killed Randolph if he used self-hypnosis to gather the strength to leave his hospital bed. Sutton persuades a kindly detective to let them take Ann back to the scene of the crime, saying, 'The solution's hidden in her brain and I can bring it out.' Dr Sutton shows Ann that his insistence that she start marriage with him as a poor doctor's wife, instead of spending money left her by her father, brought back her illness. Her renewed trust in her husband removes the power of Korvo from her mind and she remembers where she hid the evidence of the recording in which Randolph accused Korvo of swindling her. Korvo has been hiding in the house. He accosts the Suttons and detective Colton. But he is bleeding from his surgery and he falls down dead. Ann and her husband embrace.

Whirlpool overtly asks not so much 'who killed Terry Randolph?' – the traditional enigma of a film noir-melodrama like *Mildred Pierce* – but 'what is wrong with Ann Sutton?' The 'confession' Ann makes to Lt Colton, the police psychiatrist, and her lawyer, is not a confession at all in that it doesn't pertain directly to the murder being investigated but to her adolescent relationship with her father. Here again the film bears a resemblance to the prototypical *Mildred Pierce* in which a police detective oversees Mildred's tale of her past. But *Whirlpool* furthers the presentation of the search for 'the' truth as a retrospective, troubled, psychoanalytic process.

The shift to psychological terms and the contingent therapeutic resolution involve a displacement of materialist explanations of conflict and trauma which are present but downplayed. The rejected explanations are of two related types: references to 'the war' and references to economic deprivation.

The main outcome of the first scene between husband and wife is a re-affirmation that their marriage is a happy one:

> DR SUTTON: I'm a busy doctor and a happy husband – an enviable combination. I wouldn't trade it for a dozen books.
> ANN SUTTON: You've always been so very wonderful to me. I just wish that . . . I could help you. If I were only brighter and you could talk to me about your scientific problems.
> DR SUTTON: Just stay as you are. As you've always been. Healthy and adorable.

But there has been another allusion in the conversation – to the war – which is here glossed over and displaced. Ann has expressed worry over having been the cause of an interruption in her husband's analytic session with a 'veteran who won't talk', but he assures her that no harm will be done. Dr Sutton goes on to describe his projection of the patient's future progress:

> DR SUTTON: He will [let me help him] eventually. It's just that it's difficult to begin unloading fears and secrets and guilts. Poor fellow. *The war was an easier conflict than the one he's in now.*

The unspecified war is referred to as an 'easier conflict' than the unspecified psychological trauma of the film's present. In this scene a relay is set up between the war, general emotional trauma, and marital happiness. As we will learn, Ann is not 'healthy and adorable'. She is merely adorable. It is only when she is taught to admit and respect the psychological illness that she ridicules in this scene ('Oh Bill, struggling all day with those wretched people and their wretched complexes. How you must hate them.') that she will be open to the cure.

What seems to be at stake here is the transformation of the psychoanalytic problem from soldier to wife. This is accomplished by way of the veteran character (never actually seen in the film) who stands as an indicator that the war is over and who is 'replaced' by Dr Sutton's wife when his analytic session is interrupted and later when Dr Sutton's work becomes more and more involved with his wife's acquittal and cure.

Like the war, economic disadvantage is figured but then displaced. Ann's confession, the centre of the narrative, links the control of her parsimonious father to money as well as love. The issue of economic control is here quite significant, especially when control is passed into the hands of the husband.

> ANN SUTTON: I did it before. I stole in school. When my father wouldn't let me spend money. And even after he died he tied it all up in a trust fund. Thousands and thousands of dollars but I could never have a new dress or have anything I wanted. That's how I fooled my father . . . by stealing. *He didn't love me. He thought he did but he didn't.* Nobody ever caught me. I thought it was over when I left school and met Bill. I wanted to tell him but I was afraid he couldn't love anybody who'd done that. I didn't tell him. It came back because he was like my father. He treated me like my father did and I had to do it again. I tried not to. I couldn't sleep and got a pain and had to do it again. I stole a pin from a store.

A woman prohibited from spending her own money. A woman who 'couldn't have anything (she) wanted', for whom desire takes the form of 'a new dress'. In this scenario the new dress becomes a profound cipher for female economic powerlessness and emotional powerlessness. It represents both purchase power and the desire to please, continuing the iconographic theme of fashion and appearance introduced in the credits (written out over silhouettes of fashion-plate women) and extended when the background of the credit roll becomes a roll of department store wrapping paper.

However, the narrative trajectory of the film performs a shift from a woman's need for economic independence from men (fathers and husbands) to the need for male love and protection. This obviates altogether the necessity of economic independence, since security lies in the love of a man. The imbrication of romance and psychoanalysis is *Whirlpool's* formula for proposing a cinematic solution to social, economic, and political issues.

In the plot of *Whirlpool* the link between love and psychoanalysis is literal. The psychoanalyst and the husband are one and the same, so that the story of the romance between husband and wife becomes a pop version of Freudian transference. This narrative refiguration of transference has more in common with a postwar American model of transference than with the Freudian model. In the classical Freudian sense, transference means the reemergence of the patient's infantile conflicts so that they may be reexperienced in the patient's relationship to his or her analyst.[30] Alternatively, in another characteristic American model, transference was seen as a therapeutic mechanism for advice-giving and efficacious adjusting of behaviour patterns. Transference was a way of 'working out' (rather than 'working through') problems, and a system whereby 'counteracting, neutralizing or freshly coating experiences are relied upon to coerce emotion into new patterns without paying too much specific attention to old.'[31]

Nevertheless, *Whirlpool* may be read alternatively as undercutting its own tendency toward resolution. This subversive process consists in a complication of the issues of transference and control, for, as I argued earlier, American Freudianism was not *only* adjustment oriented. The issue of transference, for Freud, is bound up with the notion of resistance. While the transference is crucial to a successful analysis, it also functions as an obstacle to treatment. The transference onto the psychoanalyst is triggered precisely at the moment when the most important repressed material is in danger of being revealed. When the acknowledgment of the repressed wish must be made to the very person who, because of the transference, the wish concerns, the admission is made more difficult. If transference is narrativised as the doctor-patient marriage, transference-resistance may be read in the woman's resistance to the marriage, a form of resistance which connects up with social conflicts explored above.

The woman's resistance to the dominance of her psychoanalyst-husband is played out through her relationship to Korvo. While he uses Ann unscrupulously and against her will, there is a sense in which his function is to help her *express* her deep wishes, bringing forward the idea of resistance to marital oppression.

KORVO (TO ANN): You've locked yourself away in a characterisation – the serene and devoted wife. That playacting is destroying you...

KORVO: You musn't be afraid of what you want. It's better than stealing. Better than exploding with neuroses...
KORVO: I can release you from a torture chamber called Mrs William Sutton.

Korvo controls Ann but on the other hand he *is* Ann. Thus when he says he knows her, when he gives her soul leave to 'undress' before him, this is not only evocative of sexuality, but of an emotional affinity. In hypnosis the hypnotist is introjected into the subject's ego boundaries where his volition functions like the super-ego.[32] The narrativisation of this process leads to a king of double character – the good and bad wives within Ann Sutton.

So far I have emphasised examples from *Whirlpool*'s plot and dialogue to argue the film's subversive system of resistance to the controlling institutions of psychoanalysis and marriage. But in fact, it is at the stylistic level that the film's articulation of female resistance is the most thoroughgoing and sophisticated. It is here that the male oedipal trajectory, described by Bellour and Laura Mulvey[33] as contingent upon the man's look at the woman, is challenged.

In *Whirlpool*, the classical structure of the gaze is resisted by a marked absence of point-of-view shots or shots approximating character points of view,[34] despite the presence of hypnosis with its characteristic 'look into my eyes' imperative. When present, such shots articulate a scenario *explicitly about* the control of feminine sexuality, thereby calling it into question. The cumulative effect of such instances of a non-normative use of point of view is to resist the male objectifying gaze at the female – to throw the look back in the face of he who would look.

At the two interrogation locales, the department store and the police station, Ann Sutton is surrounded by men who seek to understand her actions and motives and perhaps to punish her. Many of the individual shots are crowded with men gazing down at Sutton in the centre of the shot, demanding to know what she knows so that they may pass judgment, futilely trying to pierce her mask-like exterior. But there is, with the exception of one shot of Korvo looking at the group, no individual inquisitor, no individual male point of view to provoke spectator identification and further the narrative. Instead, the collective gaze constitutes an institutionally supported attempt to get and record her history.

This is a very common compositional device in psychoanalytic films of this period. In *The Seventh Veil* a psychiatrist demonstrates his technique on the Ann Todd character before a group of colleagues who crowd the frame to gaze at her. Near the start of *Possessed* there are several shots from Joan Crawford's point of view as she stares up (from a 'non-traumatic stupor') at two doctors attempting to diagnose her case who conclude: 'take her up to "psycho".' The reverse shot of her face against the white of the examining table (see also the famous shot of Barbara Bel Geddes' head framed against her hospital room pillow in *Caught*[35] becomes the object of the joint gazes of the doctors leaning in to shine a light into her eyes.

The point of spectator identification in all of these scenes is not the male protagonist as in *Morocco*,[36] *Marnie*,[37] or *Gilda*.[38] Instead the enunciator of the point of view is the woman. But her look is not an objectifying look at a male, the possible alternative to the patriarchal structure of the gaze for which some have tried to argue (for example, close-ups of Gary Cooper in *Morocco*). Instead her look is a look *back* at a collective inquiring gaze. Her view, whether marked by an actual point-of-view shot or by a glance around the room, point up the controlling presence of the medical, corporate or legal collective gaze at the woman.

Even more important to the subversion of classical point-of-view structure (argued to be the seat of patriarchal control) is the nuancing of the usual shot-reverse shot structure of romantic points of view found in *Whirlpool*. What might be *coup de foudre* romance is presented as a threat. The introduction of Dr William Sutton is a moment when the romantic exchange of points of view is undercut by being imbued with threatening connotations. After returning from her interrogation at the department store, Ann Sutton goes to her bedroom. Agitatedly, she sits down at her desk and picks up a photo of her husband and herself, barely visible in the film but described in the script as a girl sitting on a rock flanked by an adoring young man gazing down at her. As she stares at this symbol of the expectation of marital bliss, she hears her husband approach the closed bedroom door. Panicky at being caught with anxiety in her eyes, she leaps up and runs to her vanity area – the proper place to assure her wifely appearance. But before she runs for cover, there is a significant shot: the camera executes a slight dolly-in to a close-up of Gene Tierney as she leans forward, wide-eyed and frightened. As she leaps for her dressing room, there is a cut to Dr Sutton in medium close-up as he enters the bedroom calling her name. What would be a classical exchange of romantic looks is interrupted by a woman's fear of discovery and by the ultimate failure of the glances to meet.

The spatial and narrative relationship between Ann Sutton and hypnotist David Korvo is paradigmatic of the connection between the gaze and the issue of cine-psychoanalytic control in this film. Though on one hand, Korvo and Ann are two facets of a unified self, they are simultaneously investigator and object of research, hypnotist and passive medium. This oscillation of subject and object and the film's excessive play with point of view aid the denaturalisation of the cinematic rhetoric of power. In the first demonstration of hypnosis, there is a short dolly-in to a close-up of Korvo's face as he begins the procedure. This is followed by a close-up of Ann as she begins to feel the effects. This exchange is repeated with successively tighter close-ups. In the second close-up of Tierney her face is shadowed and the non-diegetic music fades as she closes her eyes and her head droops. Throughout the procedure Korvo intones the familiar words:

> I can make you sleep. Trust me. Don't think of anything. Forget. There is nothing to remember.

Once Ann is under, the film cuts to a two-shot as Korvo says, 'You can hear only my voice. All of the other sounds have faded away. You must do what I say. Do you know that?' Korvo then gives Ann a series of commands ranging from 'close the door', to 'put your hand in mine'. Ann hesitantly carries out all of the commands except the repeated 'hold my hand'. The personal relationship which Korvo tries to initiate while Ann is under his power is resisted to the tune of the popular tenet that one never does anything under hypnosis which one wouldn't do while awake. The exchange of point-of-view close-ups, both between Dr Sutton and Ann and between Korvo and Ann, signals not only sexuality and control as in *Gilda*, but rebellion as well.

I have argued that the doubling of Ann and Korvo allows the expression of anti-marriage sentiment. This doubling is articulated stylistically as well as narratively. Both Ann and Korvo are concerned with their exterior appearance and are seen primping in front of mirrors, and both cast aspersions on Dr Sutton's 'twisted' patients, initially sharing a negative view of illness and cure. But the crucial connection is made in a sequence where Korvo hypnotises himself – a scene which repeats, with a difference, the scene in which he hypnotises Ann. The camera dollies-in on Korvo's face which is illuminated by a light he shines into his own eyes as he tells himself, 'I'm getting stronger, stronger, there's no pain.' The film then cuts to his own reflection in huge close-up in a round hand mirror he holds. Korvo's lighted eyes alone fill the whole surface of the mirror which in turn fills most of the screen. He intones, 'I'm able to do what I want.' The commands he gave Ann, to sleep and forget, are replaced by the auto-commands to get stronger and feel no pain.

But the shot-reverse shot which accomplishes Korvo's self-hypnosis also inaugurates his downfall. He overestimates his physical strength and undergoes a fatal collapse. The throwing back of his own hypnotic gaze initiates both the demise of the evil controller *and* the deflation of Ann's resistance to another controlling agency – psychoanalysis – because the demise of Korvo is also the demise of Ann's resistance. At the end of the film Ann has taken her place as the true (no longer only superficially true, no longer resistant) realisation of her husband's scenario of desire, his 'greatest kick':

> You know the greatest kick I get when we go to a party together is when people stare at you and say, who is that lovely girl? Why, that's Dr Sutton's wife. She's very devoted to him.

The film becomes neither an unqualified feminist nor anti-feminist tract through the utilisation of psychoanalytic material. Rather, the refiguration of psychoanalysis along particularly American lines allows the expression of contradictory ideological positions available in the society of the day – the dual discourses of regulation and resistance.

The integration of psychoanalytic concepts into plot across the issue of gender takes different forms. To conclude this article I would like to make some suggestions for a possible strategy of periodisation.

Like *Whirlpool*, the psychoanalytic films of the late 40s are frequently structured aronnd a trauma from a character's past, the unconscious and sexual roots of which must be revealed for both the psychological cure of the character and the narrative resolution of the film (*The Locket*, 1946; *The Snake Pit*, 1948; and *Possessed*, 1947). While these films are able to exploit the heady *pleasure* of dark traumas from the past stirred up by the discourse of psychoanalysis, anxieties and doubts are sometimes *regulated* by the authoritative discourse of psychoanalysis. Often, however, as in *Whirlpool*, that regulation is incomplete.

The psychoanalytic films of the 50s engage more markedly the absolutely contradictory self-descriptive discourses of the period discussed earlier in the context of feminine psycho-sexuality. The case study became prominent in the 50s (for example, *The Three Faces of Eve* (1957) with Joanne Woodward and *Lizzie* (1957) with Eleanor Parker). To the psychoanalytically derived idea of the past event is added the notion of the multiple personality. Although it is difficult to theorise the link between the split personality film and the multiplicity of contradictory social positions available to women in the 50s, I would argue that the confusing array of socially acceptable and unacceptable roles for women got represented as multiple personality for an audience of women whose material conditions were quite diverse.

The Cobweb (1955) presents a much less obvious exploration of feminine psycho-sexuality than the multiple personality film. The narrative is divided into two interconnected plots: Dr McIver's (Richard Widmark's) work at the luxuriously endowed and appointed psychiatric clinic, and his relationship with his wife Karen (Gloria Grahame) and their children. Near the opening of the film, a title which reads 'The Trouble Began' is written out across Karen's face. 'The Trouble' is in part Karen's sexual desire which her husband cannot (refuses to) fulfil. The creation of a therapeutic 'family' at the clinic (comprised of Dr McIver; his patient, young Stevie; and a clinic staff member (played by Lauren Bacall) becomes the transitional phase through which the proper functioning of McIver's personal family is restored. But while his wife Karen is eventually put into place as undemanding and maternal rather than sexual, and a superimposed title indicates 'The Trouble is Over', the only difficulties which the film shows being dealt with are those involving the clinic family. The film elides the crucial scene of a reconciliation between actual husband and wife so that one has no idea what issues were raised and resolved. Only the tail end of the scene is shown, and it is photographed in extreme long shot so that it is difficult to determine at first whether it is the Lauren Bacall character or the Gloria Grahame character with whom Dr McIver speaks. The authoritative or regulatory nature of the psychoanalytic discourse so strong, though not thoroughly victorious, in the late 40s is here confined to the institutionally based portion of the narrative. *The Cobweb* bings up more problems than it can resolve in the problem of feminine sexuality.

In the early 60s the growth of the American psychoanalytic organizations started to taper off from their postwar spurt. Group therapies and crisis hotlines joined behaviourism and humanistic psychology, aiming at the sociologisation of the field which psychiatry and psychoanalysis had dominated.

In *The Slender Thread* (1965) Sidney Poitier tries to save potential suicide Anne Bancroft over the telephone after she reaches him at a crisis prevention centre. In *The Chapman Report* (1962) a doctor modelled after Dr Kinsey questions several women about their sexuality and their marriages. Psychiatric institutions still appear as in *Lilith* (1964) and *Shock Corridor* (1963), and psychoanalysis still is found in melodrama – *Tender is the Night* (1962). But neither neurosis and psychosis on one hand nor the psychological professions on the other are defined as neatly circumscribed or regulated by their Hollywood representation. Madness spreads from patients to doctors and orderlies, and often it is society itself which is viewed as sick or racist or responsible for the creation of illness. Rejection of the benevolent, omniscient expert coincides with questioning of authority – response of movements in social consciousness such as the women's movement, the free speech movement, the anti-Vietnam War movement, and the civil rights movement which interrogated 50s ideology to reveal its contradictions and oppressiveness. Political action was called into service, for the therapeutic discourse was ultimately deemed insufficient, even in the representational sphere, to confront huge problems, the roots of which were economic and political.

Notes

I would like to thank Janet Bergstrom and Diane Waldman for their encouragement and suggestions, and for the inspiration provided by their work. I would also like to thank Christine Gledhill for her invaluable editorial support.

1. These films are actually part of a larger body of psychological movies which don't prioritize women's issues.
2. See the discussion in Marxist terms of the separation of public and private spheres by Chuck Kleinhans in 'Notes on Melodrama and the Family Under Capitalism', *Film Reader* 3, 1978, pp. 40–47.
3. Lois Banner, *Women in Modern America: A Brief History* (New York: Harcourt Brace Jovanovich, 1974), p. 217.

4. Douglas T. Miller and Marion Nowak, *The Fifties: The Way We Really Were* (New York: Doubleday, 1977), p. 6.

5. Miller and Nowak, ibid., p. 11.

6. David Riesman, Nathan Glazer and Reuel Denny, *The Lonely Crowd* (New Haven, New York: Yale University Press, 1950).

7. Betty Friedan, *The Feminine Mystique* (1963) (New York: Dell Publishing, 1974), p. 45.

8. William H. Chafe, *The American Woman: Her Changing Social, Economic, and Political Roles, 1920–1970* (New York and London: Oxford University Press, 1972).

9. Chafe, ibid., p. 181. Also see Alice Kessler-Harris, *Women Have Always Worked: A Historical Overview* (Old Westbury, New York: The Feminist Press, 1981).

10. Friedan, *Feminine Mystique*, p. 224.

11. Friedan, *Feminine Mystique*, p. 225.

12. Joseph Veroff, Richard A. Kulka, and Elizabeth Douvan, *Mental Health in America: Patterns of Help-Seeking from 1957–1976* (New York: Basic Books, 1981).

13.. Friedan, *Feminine Mystique*, Chapter Nine, 'The Sexual Sell', pp. 197–223. Also see the account by Marty Jezer, *The Dark Ages: Life in the U.S. 1960* (Boston: South End Press, 1982), Chapter Five, pp. 124–9.

14. Ferdinand Lundberg and Marynia Farnham, *Modern Woman: The Lost Sex* (New York: Harper & Brothers, 1947).

15. Lundberg and Farnham, ibid., p. 71.

16. Reuben Fine, *A History of Psychoanalysis* (New York: Columbia University Press, 1979).

17. Philip Wylie, *Generation of Vipers* (New York: Farrar and Rinehart, 1942).

18. Michael Zuckerman ('Dr Spock: The Confidence Man' in *The Family in History*, Charles E. Rosenberg (ed.), The University of Pensylvania Press, 1975) argues that Dr Spock's *The Common Sense Book of Baby and Child Care* embodies yet another contradiction by simultaneously assuming that women are 'natural' mothers and that they need step by step advice on child-rearing.

19. Ernest Havemann, *The Age of Psychology* (New York: Simon & Schuster, 1957).

20. Lucy Freeman, *Fight Against Fears* (1953) (New York: Pocket Books, 1953).

21. Robert Lindner, *The Fifty-Minute Hour: A Collection of True Psychoanalytic Tales* (New York: Rinehart and Co., 1954).

22. Hendrik M. Ruitenbeek, *Freud and America* (New York: The Macmillan Company, 1966) and *Psychoanalysis and Social Sciences* (New York: E. P. Dutton & Co., 1962). Richard LaPiere, *The Freudian Ethic: An Analysis of the Subversion of American Character* (New York: Duell, Sloan, and Pearce, 1959).

23. A. W. Zelomak, *A Changing America: At Work and Play* (New York: John Wiley and Sons, Inc., 1959).

24. Fine, *A History of Psychoanalysis*; Robert P. Knight, MD, 'The Present Status of Organized Psychoanalysis in the United States', *Journal of the American Psychoanalytic Association*, vol. 1, no. 2, April 1953, pp. 197–221; Clarence Oberndorf, *A History of Psychoanalysis in America* (New York: Harper & Row, 1964).

25. This definition followed Freud's counsel against advice-giving, where Freud argued that the analyst 'does not seek to remould [the patient] in accordance with his own – that is, according to the physician's – personal ideals; he is glad to

avoid giving advice and instead to arouse the patient's power of initiative'. Sigmund Freud (1922), 'Psycho-Analysis', *Collected Papers*, vol. 5 (London: Hogarth Press, 1950), pp. 107–30

26. Oberndorf, *History of Psychoanalysis in America*, p. 234.
27. Knight, 'The Present Status of Organised Psychoanalysis', p. 217.
28. Oberndorf, 'A History of Psychoanalysis in America', p. 247.
29. Marc Vernet ('Freud: effets spéciaux – Mise en scène: U S A', *Communications*, vol. 23, 1975, pp. 223–34) and Diane Waldman (*Horror and Domesticity: The Modern Gothic Romance Film of the 1940s*, doctoral dissertation, University of Wisconsin – Madison, 1981, Chapter 5) explain that this use of psychoanalysis for narrative resolution has led Hollywood films of the 40s to incorporate the early Freudian notion of catharsis which Freud himself later criticised. Waldman also argues that it supports the institution of marriage against more radical Freudian models of 'civilised' sexual morality. See also Mary Ann Doane, 'The Clinical Eye: Medical Discourses in the "Woman's Film" of the 1940s', *Poetics Today*, vol. 6, no. 1–2, 1985, pp. 205–28, and Janet Bergstrom, *The Logic of Fascination: Fritz Lang and Cinematic Conventions*, doctoral dissertation, University of California, Los Angeles, 1980. This work includes a chapter on *Secret Beyond the Door* and other 'noir psycho-melodramas'.
30. J. Laplanche and J.-B. Pontalis, in *The Language of Psychoanalysis*, trans. Donald Nicholson-Smith (New York and London: W. W. Norton & Co., 1973), pp. 455–64.
31. Phyllis Greenacre, 'The Role of Transference: Practical Considerations in Relation to Psychoanalytic Therapy', *Journal of the American Psychoanalytic Association*, vol. 2, no. 4, October 1954.
32. Lawrence S. Kubie, M D and Sydney Margolin, M D, 'The Process of Hypnotism and the Nature of the Hypnotic State', *The American Journal of Psychiatry*, vol. 100, no. 5, March 1944.
33. Laura Mulvey, 'Visual Pleasure and Narrative Cinema', originally published in *Screen*, vol. 16, no. 3, Autumn 1975. For an excellent English introduction to Raymond Bellour's work see his articles translated in *Camera Obscura* 2 and 3/4. Also see the interview with Janet Bergstrom, 'Alternation, Segmentation, Hypnosis: Interview with Raymond Bellour', *Camera Obscura* 3/4, Summer 1979, pp. 71–103.
34. Andrew Sarris points out that all of Preminger's films resist point-of-view shots in favour of presenting their issues and problems 'as [the] single-take two-shot, the stylistic expression of the eternal conflict' (*The American Cinema*, New York, E. P. Dutton Co., 1968), p. 106.
35. Mary Ann Doane, '*Caught* and *Rebecca*: The Inscription of Femininity as Absence', *Enclitic*, vol. 5, no. 2/vol. 6, no. 1, Fall 1981/Spring 1982, pp. 75–89.
36. Mulvey, 'Visual Pleasure and Narrative Cinema'.
37. Raymond Bellour, 'Hitchcock and Enunciator', *Camera Obscura* 2, Fall 1977, pp. 69–92.
38. Mary Ann Doane, '*Gilda*: Epistemology as Striptease', *Camera Obscura* 11, 1983.
39. Thierry Kuntzel, 'The Film-Work, 2', *Camera Obscura* 5, Spring 1980, pp. 7–69.

PART THREE

Hollywood's Family Romances

Questions of Fantasy, Desire and Ideology

Vincente Minnelli

THOMAS ELSAESSER

From *Brighton Film Review* no. 15, December 1969, pp. 11–13.

MINNELLI'S critical reputation has known a certain amount of fluctuation. Admired (or dismissed) in America as a 'pure stylist' who, in Andrew Sarris' phrase 'believes more in beauty than in art', his work reached a zenith of critical devotion during the late 50s and early 60s in France, with extensive studies in *Cahiers du Cinéma*, especially in the articles by Douchet and Domarchi, who saw in him a cinematic visionary obsessed with beauty and harmony, and an artist who could give substance to the world of dreams.

In England *Movie* took up his defence, from their first number onwards. But strangely enough, they concentrated almost exclusively on Minnelli's dramatic films of the early 60s (a memorable article by Paul Mayersberg on *Two Weeks in Another Town* comes to mind), and gave rather cursory treatment to the musicals, while the later films, such as *Goodbye Charlie* (1964) and *The Sandpiper* (1965) were passed over with visible embarrassment. With this, Minnelli joined the vast legion of American directors whose work was supposed to have suffered decline, if not total eclipse, in the Hollywood of the middle and late 60s.

The following remarks are merely a preliminary attempt to disentangle a few essential characteristics from a singularly rich and varied body of work, and to trace some of the dominating lines of force in his style. Above all, I am concerned with the fundamental *unity* of Minnelli's vision.

At the risk of displeasing the genre-critics and antagonising those who share the view that thematic analysis generally exhausts itself in what has (rather summarily) been referred to as 'schoolboy profundities', I would like to look at some of Minnelli's constant themes and furthermore, conduct some kind of special pleading for Minnelli as a *moralist*, even though this will mean flying in the face of the 'stylist' school – both of the Sarris variety and *Movie*, who claim for Minnelli as for Cukor that he never writes his own scripts, and therefore never uses other people's material for the propagation of his own views, that he confines himself to the interpretation, the *mise en scène* of the ideas of others, and that, consequently, his work is best regarded as lacking in consistent themes, and rather excels on a supreme level of visual competence.

I think this is a fundamental misunderstanding. True, there are superficially two 'Minnellis' – one the virtual father of the modern musical, and the other the director of dramatic comedies and domestic dramas. Other critics – even sympathetic ones – would probably claim a different Minnelli for almost every film – the loving 'pointillist' of American period pieces or of 'Gay Paree' (*Meet Me in St. Louis, Gigi, An American in Paris*), the catalyst for Gene Kelly and Fred Astaire musicals (*Ziegfeld Follies, Yolanda and the Thief, The Pirate, The Band Wagon, Brigadoon*), the ingenious vulgariser of painters' lives (*Lust for Life*) and best-selling novels (*The Four Horsemen of the Apocalypse*), the handiman who puts together a star vehicle for an ambitious producer (*The Reluctant Debutante*), and lastly, perhaps the 'difficult' director of such problem pieces as *Some Came Running, Home from the Hill*, and of Hollywood self-portraits – *The Bad and the Beautiful* and *Two Weeks in Another Town*.

Altogether, Minnelli has directed some thirty-two films, not counting the episodes and sketches contributed to other people's films. It might seem difficult to find a personal vision in as vast an oeuvre as his, not to mention the fact that all films (except one) have been made in the MGM studios, under the supervision of a few, themselves very gifted and articulate, producers like John Houseman (4 films) and Arthur Freed (12). But surely anyone who is reasonably familiar with his films will see in Minnelli more than the glorification of the *metteur en scène*, the stylish craftsman of the cinema, the dandy of sophistication. I for one am convinced that Minnelli is one of the purest 'hedgehogs' working in the cinema – an artist who knows one big thing, and never tires to explore its implications.

In Walter Pater's famous phrase, all romantic art aspires to the status of music. My contention is that all Minnelli's films aspire to the condition of the musical. In this resides their fundamental unity. However, in order to substantiate this point, I shall insert a few remarks to explain what I mean by 'musical'.

The classic Hollywood cinema is, as everybody knows, *the* commercial cinema par excellence – out merely to entertain. Usually this is taken to be a fundamental drawback, at worst utterly precluding its products from the realms of serious art, at best, presenting the film-maker with formidable odds against which he has to test his worth, an artist *and* entrepreneur. (I shall try to show how deeply Minnelli's conception of his art, indeed his 'philosophy' of life, are formed by the conflict between the necessity of circumstance and the vital need to assert – not so much one's self, but rather one's conception of meaning, one's vision of things. It furnishes his great theme: the artist's struggle to appropriate external reality as the elements of his own world, in a bid for absolute creative freedom. When I say artist, I hasten to add that this includes almost all of Minnelli's protagonists. (Insofar as they all feel within them a world, an idea, a dream that seeks articulation and material embodiment.)

Yet there is another side to the 'commercial cinema' syndrome, which is rarely ever given its full due. (At least in England: in France, the *Positif* and *Midi-Minuit* équipes have always paid tribute to the commercial cinema *qua* commercial cinema.) I am referring to the fact that perhaps the enormous appeal of the best Hollywood cinema, the fundamental reason why audience-identification and immediate emotional participation are at all possible, lies in Hollywood's rigorous application of the *pleasure principle* – understood almost in its Freudian sense, as the structure that governs the articulation of psychic and emotional energy. It seems to me that a vast number of films 'work' *because* they are built around a psychic law and not an intellectual one, and thus achieve a measure of coherence which is very difficult to analyse (as it must be extremely difficult for a film-maker to control and adhere to), and yet constitutes nevertheless an absolutely essential part of the way the cinema functions – being indeed close to music in this respect.

For a superficial confirmation of this fact, namely that there is a central energy at the heart of the Hollywood film which seeks to live itself out as completely as possible, one could point to the way in which – superimposed on an infinite variety of subject matters – the prevalent plot-mechanisms of two major genres of the American cinema (the Western and the Gangster film) invariably conform to the same basic pattern. There is always a central dynamic drive – the pursuit, the quest, the trek, the boundless desire to arrive, to get to the top, to get rich, to make it – always the same graph of maximum energetic investment.

For the spectator, this means maximum emotional involvement, which depends upon, and is enhanced by, his maximum aesthetic satisfaction – or rather, by the skilful manipulation of his desire for as total a sense of satisfaction as possible. Intellectual insight and emotional awareness are transmitted in the best American cinema exclusively as a drive for *gratification* which the audience shares with the characters. The more a film director is aware of this interrelation of morality and aesthetics in the cinema, the more his *mise en scène* will be concerned with the purposeful ordering of *visual* elements, to achieve a kind of plenitude and density, which inevitably, and rightly, goes at the expense of ideas. In other words, there seems to exist, particularly in the American cinema, an intimate relationship between the *psychological* drives of the characters (i.e. the motives *beneath* the motives that make them act), the *moral* progression which they accomplish, and the *aesthetic* gratification afforded to the audience by the spectacle; and these are held together by some profound mechanism, identical in both audience and characters – be they criminals, detectives, gunfighters, shop-assistants, song-writers or millionaires.

Perhaps one of the most interesting consequences of this fact is that this, if true, would entail a thoroughly different concept of cinematic realism, which would have nothing to do with either literary realism or the realism of pictorial art. In a very definite sense, the Eisenstein–Rossellini–Bazin–Metz–Wollen controversy has seriously underrated the question of a psychic dynamism as part of our aesthetic experience. Even the most rudimentary awareness of its existence would dispose of such arrant nonsense as Metz's claim that 'in the last analysis, it is only by the richness of its connotations that a film by Visconti differs from a documentary on the methods of surgery' (*Communications*, no. 4, pp. 81–2). If semiology is not to degenerate, I think it must find, above all, a more positive validation of a film's sense of physical *continuity*, and that, it would seem, necessitates a novel idea of cinematic realism – not just as continuity of space and time, but both dimensions seen as elements of a perhaps predominantly *psychic* continuity. (To forestall certain obvious objections, this evidently applies to the American cinema more than it does to the modern European cinema. There is no such 'psychic continuity' to be found in the later films of either Godard, Bergman, or Pasolini – and whatever continuity there is, situates itself on a more complex level whch is often an uneasy mixture of intellectual, symbolic and 'old-fashioned' emotional appeal – with varying degrees of success.

After this rather devious excursion, I am back to Minnelli and the assertion about the 'musical' nature of his films. For what seems to me essential to all of Minnelli's films is the fact that his characters are only superficially concerned with a quest, a desire to get somewhere in life, that is, with any of the forms by which this dynamism rationalises or sublimates itself. What we have instead, just beneath the surface of the plots, is the working of energy itself, as the ever-changing, fascinating movement of a basic impulse in its encounter with, or victory over, a given reality. The characters' existence is justified by the incessant struggle in which they engage for total fulfilment, for total gratification of their aesthetic needs, their desire for beauty and harmony, their demand for an identity of their lives with the reality of their dreams. Minnelli's films are structured so as to give the greatest possible scope to the expansive nature of a certain vitality (call it 'will', or libido) – in short, to the confrontation of an inner, dynamic, reality and an outward, static one. Minnelli's typical protagonists are all, in a manner of speaking, highly sophisticated and cunning day-dreamers, and the *mise en scène* follows them, as they go through life, confusing – for good or ill – what is part of their imagination and what is real, and trying to obliterate the difference between what is freedom and what is necessity. (This is not the place to analyse whether there is, philosophically or ethically, something suspect about such a conception of the self and the world – suffice it to say that these ideas have a long, intellectual tradition, which is relevant, even if Minnelli has neither heard nor even read about it.)

What, in this context, characterises the Minnelli musical is the total and magic victory of the impulse, the vision, over any reality whatsoever. The characters in his musicals transform the world into a reflection of their selves, into a pure expression of their joys and sorrows, of their inner harmony or conflicting states of mind. When Gene Kelly begins to dance, or plays with the first words of a song, say in *Brigadoon*, the world melts away and reality becomes a stage, in which he and Cyd Charisse live out their very dream. Or when Louis Jourdan, in utter confusion about his feelings, rushes to the Jardin du Luxembourg to sing the title number of *Gigi*, Minnelli leads him into a wholly mysterious, wholly subjective landscape of the imagination, pregnant with the symbols of his newly discovered love for the one-time schoolgirl. Such a confrontation with their innermost words always gives the characters a kind of spontaneous certainty from which, ultimately, they derive their energy.

The Minnelli musical thus transforms the movements of what one is tempted to call, for lack of a better word, the 'soul' of the characters into shape, colour, gesture and rhythm. It is precisely when joy or sorrow, bewilderment or enthusiasm, that is, when emotional intensity, become too strong to bear that a Gene Kelly or a Judy Garland has to dance and sing in order to give free play to the emotions that possess them. And it is hardly exaggerated to compare what Minnelli did for the musical with Mozart's transformation of the comic opera. One only needs to hold a Busby Berkeley musical – with its formally brilliant but dramatically empty song-and-dance routines and elaborate visual compositions – against even an early and comparatively minor Minnelli effort, say, the 'Limehouse Blues' sequence from *Ziegfeld Follies*, to see how the musical with Minnelli has been given an authentic spiritual dimension, created by a combination of movement, lighting, colour, décor, gesture and music which is unique to the cinema.

Thus defined, the world of the musical becomes a kind of ideal image of the medium itself, the infinitely variable material substance on which the very structure of desire and the imagination can imprint itself, freed from all physical necessity. The quickly changing décor, the transitions in the lighting and the colours of a scene, the freedom of composition, the shift from psychological realism to pure fantasy, from drama to surreal farce, the culmination of an action in a song, the change of movement into rhythmic dance – all this constitutes the very essence of the musical. In other words, it is the exaltation of the artifice as the vehicle of an authentic psychic, and emotional reality. Minnelli's musicals introduce us into a liberated universe, where the total freedom of expression (of the character's creative impulse) serves to give body and meaning to the artistic vitality in the director, both being united by their roles as *metteurs en scène* of the self.

The paradox of the musical, namely that a highly artificial, technically and artistically controlled décor and machinery can be the manifestation of wholly spontaneous, intimate movements, or the visualisation of submerged, hardly conscious aspirations, becomes not only Minnelli's metaphor for the cinema as a whole, but more specifically, it makes up his central moral concern: how does the individual come to realise himself, reach his identity, create his personal universe, fulfil his life in a world of chaos and confusion, riddled with social conventions, bogus with self-importance, claustrophobic and constricting, trivial and above all artificial, full of treacherous appearance, and yet impenetrable in its false solidity, its obstacles, its sheer physical inertia and weight? – epitomised in the sticky, rubbery substance Spencer Tracy has to wade through, as he is trying to reach the altar, in the nightmare sequence of *Father of the Bride*. Minnelli's answer, surprisingly enough for this supposedly obedient servant of other people's ideas, is a plea for chaos, where his characters embrace flux and movement, because it is closest to the imagination itself. Minnelli's motto might well be that 'rather no order at all than a false order'.

And here we have the crux of the matter: for the Minnelli musical celebrates the fulfilment of desire and identity, whose tragic absence so many of his dramatic films portray. Looked at like this, the dramas and dramatic comedies are *musicals turned inside out*, for the latter affirm all those values and urges which the former visualise as being in conflict with a radically different order of reality. In his non-musical films – from *The Clock* to *Home from the Hill*, from *Meet Me in St. Louis* to *Two Weeks in Another Town* – tragedy is present as a particular kind of unfreedom, as the constraint of an emotional or artistic temperament in a world that becomes claustrophobic, where reality suddenly reveals itself as mere décor, unbearably false and oppressive. That is when the dream changes into nightmare, when desire becomes obsession, and the creative will turns into mad frenzy.

It is in this absence of that freedom which the musical realises and expresses through dance and song, through rhythm and movement, by indicating that peculiar fluidity of reality and dream which alone seems to offer the possibility of human relationships and of a harmonious existence – it is in the absence of this that Kirk Douglas or Judy Garland, Robert Mitchum or Glenn Ford and Ronnie Howard (*The Courtship of Eddie's Father*) suffer anguish and despair, neurosis and isolation, spiritual and physical enclosure, if not death. And it is precisely the possibility, the promise of a return to chaos, to movement, which saves Spencer Tracy or Judy Holliday (*Bells are Ringing*), Gregory Peck and Lauren Bacall (*Designing Woman*), Rex Harrison and Kay Kendall (*The Reluctant Debutante*) in the dramatic comedies from becoming hopelessly trapped in their own worlds.

The above is Part One of a two-part article; Part Two appeared in *Brighton Film Review* no. 18, March 1970, pp. 20–22. Reprinted in full in *Genre: The Musical*, (ed.) Rick Altman (London: RKP/BFI, 1981).

Griffith's Family Discourse: Griffith and Freud

NICK BROWNE

From *Quarterly Review of Film Studies* vol. 6, no. 1, Winter 1981. 'Special Issue: Essays on D. W. Griffith'.

THE PROBLEM of Griffith and of *Broken Blossoms* is not explained nor even adequately posed, I submit, by reference to the stylistics of realism. Ordinarily the explanation of the phenomenon of cinema, and of Griffith in particular, is treated as an extension of the realist tendency in the nineteenth-century novel and its conjunction with melodramatic theatre. Within film theory proper, explanation of the problem of the origin of cinema and its attending 'impression of reality' has often been formulated in psychological terms. The cinema in this account (Bazin is exemplary) corresponds to the fulfilment of a prehistoric or archaic wish for a realistic moving image. The other related psychological explanation for the appearance of cinema takes the form, from Benjamin to Comolli, of a social *demand* or appetite expressing itself, and answered by cinema, at a certain historical moment in Western culture. Such explanations, challenging as they are, have their field of pertinence: namely, of the *ontology* of the film image produced by the apparatus.

From another vantage point we can see cinema as a specifically *social* fact. *If* we can regard the *origin* of a phenomenon as what enables it to live and to be conserved as such, the origin of cinema as a social form is in its institutional affiliation with narrative. It was because of narrative that cinema escaped from the side show. From this social perspective, the cinema is less a matter of the apparatus and of the 'impression of the real' it guarantees, than of a language and a form. Explanation of the form early cinema took is more crucially related to the forces and personalities shaping narrative form than to a general continuity in the stylistics of pictorial realism.

As Christian Metz claimed in 1964, in his first essays on the cinema, the elaboration of this narrative film language is a specifically semiotic problem. Whatever its continuities with nineteenth-century art forms, cinema as a means of signification is the product of an original transformation. The articulation of this new language had to arbitrate between the mode of presentation of theatrical spectacle and novelistic forms of narrative signification. As even a very brief examination of key works will show, development of the cinematic language was, from the very start, linked to a particular subject matter.

This subject was the family – typically the threat of its dismemberment either by loss of a child or by the death, separation, or violation of a parent. Porter's script, for example, for the first extended American narrative film, *The Life of an American Fireman* (1903), begins with the heading: 'The fireman's vision of an imperiled woman and child.' We claim, on the basis of a preliminary study, that starting with Griffith's first film, *The Adventures of Dolly* (1909, in which a child is stolen by gypsies), either the formal and technical advances in cinema as a medium are introduced, or their meaning is normalised, by reference to some family drama. In *Enoch Arden*, for example, Griffith's first use of the close-up is tied to a scene in which a wife is imagining her castaway husband. In *The Lonely Villa*, cross-cutting, a strategy that later becomes Griffith's personal signature, is employed to dramatise the peril of a mother and her children at the hands of some thieves, and the strenuous efforts of the husband to effect a rescue. He arrives, of course, just at the last moment.

The effect and force of many early Biograph films is not to render the action spectacular as in the stage machinery of late Victorian melodrama, but rather, to render the subjectivity of a response within and toward the general situation of a character in a family. The transformation of theatrical space by film language in accord with the desire to shape spectator perception of structure and significance of the action within the visual field is at the service of a narrative vision. It is from this project – telling a story – that the simple structures and conventions of scale, screen direction, and pictorial rhetoric emerge. Moreover, the elaboration and normalisation of certain formal cinematic strategies and the emergence of a certain narrative form are tied, in the first years of the institution 'cinema', to a precise subject matter.

This narrative function of film, the rendering of drama through novelistic forms, precipitates the appearance of a new figure: the composite figure of the director-narrator. This new narratological function is characterised by what it owes to novelistic strategies for the stabilisation of meaning, namely to the structure and operation of 'point of view', the means by which narrative authority in the new medium is formally exercised.

In Griffith, we can perhaps discern, if not yet completely delineate, an archaeology of this new narrative function, and discover the forces and conjunctions by means of which cinema assumes its specific historical and semiotic forms. What is the object of this archaeology? Within a certain American social setting at the beginning of the twentieth century, it is the way by which narrative function institutes the structure and determines the value of what I shall call Griffith's family discourse.

Broken Blossoms (1919) continues the intimate non-epic style of the Biograph films and is, I submit, the site of a summarising re-enactment of an obsession with a certain image of the family and its precarious social situation that so often characterises Griffith's work.

The prologue of the film is divided into two parts, separating the story of the lovers, the 'tale', as it is called, from the level of presentation, what the second intertitle calls 'belief' and the 'message' (see figures 1 and 2). This level we might call the narration. By use of the pronoun 'we', reflecting presumably Griffith and his audience, the second text connects the spectator and his position, not with the Buddha or the lovers, but with sadistic Battling Burrows, the one with the brutal whip. The function of this rhetorical identification is to identify the figure from whom we are to learn, by negative example, the intended lesson. The spectator, so far as his moral position is adequately defined at the outset, is the one who is already, perhaps unknowingly, inflicting pain. To this spectator, already inclined to violence, the film addresses, somewhat tentatively to be sure, a warning.

Following Griffith's division of tale and narration, let us first consider the story.

The narrative traces the actualisation of, and defeat of, a dream – the Yellow Man's visionary religious project to bring the message of the Buddha to the West. However, much of the film dramatises the role of fate and fortune in the order of events. The formal shape of the film – the recurrence of the painted panels, like the rocking cradle, and replaying the beginning prayer at the end – brings the story under the aspect not of accident or history, but of the fatality of the eternal return. Through a secular declension of the story of the Yellow Man, the film transforms his religious vision of a love devoted to the Buddha into a Religion of Love whose object of worship is Woman. This transformation of dream vision into literal perception is dramatised in the scene in which the Yellow Man rubs his eyes in disbelief upon seeing the woman lying on the floor of his shop. It is within the context of the correspondence and dissolution of the dream vision with perception that the film's thematics of seeing are situated.

The central trope through which the narrative takes on thematic significance is this religious one. It is this trope which founds the complex metaphoric system of the film. Its composition is condensed in the contrast between two versions of a common place: this central symbolic site is the bed, the one in the Yellow Man's upstairs room which serves as an altar, and the one in her father's house on which she is attacked and dies. The central terms of symbolic expression in the film, high and low, priest and animal, ecstatic worship and incestuous violation, constitute the diacritical coordinates of the space and action of the film. It is from this context that the central place of Woman and the flower imagery of the title derive.

Within this system of symbolic topography, the inversion of worship is the *perverse*. The perverse in *Broken Blossoms* is the blasphemous. The central

225

dramatic and metaphoric structure links worship and incestuous rape by comparison and inversion, and thus introduces a religious idiom into the family discourse. In Griffith the pervasiveness of a Christian ethic tending towards religious idealisation leads to an evaluation of family positions in accord with, if not always on, the model of the Holy Family.

The family discourse of the film is composed of the relations between positions in two nuclear families. Lucy, remember, is the illegitimate daughter of Battling Burrows and an unnamed prostitute who is absent throughout the film. The mother, though, in anticipation of Lucy's future marriage, which Lucy sometimes also contemplates, has left a small dowry. Within this first family, Lucy plays the double role of a daughter who carries out the wife's domestic duties. A second family structure, more or less hypothetical and symbolic, but nevertheless of equal significance in the film, is compared and superimposed on the first. It is composed of Lucy, the Yellow Man, and, as it were, the substitution for the child, the Doll which she has noticed in his shop window, which the Yellow Man presents to her on the bed, and which she clings to her breast as she dies.

The film, in accord with its general symbolic plan, relates the two families and the methods of conception as profane and holy. The family stands in an intermediary position between idealisation (as immaculate conception) and perversion (incestuous rape). This ambiguous and even enigmatic structure of personal relations constitutes for Griffith the problem of the family – torn in two generations, between romance and sexuality. It is this that founds what we have come to recognise as the subtext of the typical Griffith story, and which evokes as a formal solution the last-minute rescue, or, as in *Broken Blossoms*, its frustration.

Typically, as in the earlier *The Lonely Villa*, the family, or often just the woman, is barricaded in the house which is invaded, step by tortuous step, from the outside. The threat against the body of the woman – her recognition of imminent danger is hysteria – is integrated as the female half of a narrative structure of suspense based on cross-cutting. The father or male suitor is the rescuer in this scenario. This psycho-narrative paradigm of threat, hysteria, penetration (in *Broken Blossoms* penetration with the axe through the closet door and then the beating with the whip) is the fatal result of a perversion, if not of the natural, then of the holy. The Yellow Man's religious vision is at the end inverted and negated by murder.

For Eisenstein, cross-cutting and the narrative form it summarised represented an ideological analogue of American class relations. We can perhaps see this form today as a discourse on the family. In its own way, *Broken Blossoms* is a story of a courtship that is opposed by the girl's father, a plot recognisable enough as a form of comedy, a genre in which a wish is represented as fulfilled. Here, however, this wish is seen as impossible, is reformulated, and presented in a perverse mode.

226

This form, what we have called the Griffith plot, is not the drama of a single figure. But insofar as the central figure is an orphan or a lost child, the films underline the theme of homelessness. The family is more than just the setting of this story, for the true subject of these films, I suggest, is the intrapersonal drama of the family within its social and historical setting. From within or from without, the family is under attack. This attack is always represented, however, by a generalised moral weakness or aggressivity and not by a sociological or institutional condition. But nevertheless, the structure of the drama is usually an attack on and defence of the integrity, should I say the virtue, of the woman, and on the social codes and prohibitions which enable her to maintain her place.

This general configuration of the family, the medium through which the paradigmatic narrative takes form – that is, the complex of incestuous, repressed wish, the prohibitions nearly breached, the girl-child, the strong demanding paternal figure, the idealisations – in a word the Law, and its effects of sublimation and hysteria, constitute what I have been calling Griffith's discourse on the family. As a discourse it mirrors the story psychoanalysis gives of the dynamics of desire, law, and identity within the structure of the family, which Freud was in the process of formulating, first clinically, then theoretically in the very years the cinema was taking form.

Following Peter Brooks's suggestion about melodrama in his *Melodramatic Imagination*, we propose that psychoanalysis, considered as a discourse on the structure and dramaturgy of the family, is the most searching theoretical statement of the narrative form of *Broken Blossoms*, and the basic drama of its characters, insofar as the film summarises a history of Griffith's obsessive re-enactment of the family problem. So far as Griffith's family discourse is not simply personal, but reflects (sociologically, through the audience he attracted) a certain state of American social relations contemporaneous with the films, we may have delineated a common source – the integrated structure of the family and fantasy, and not pictorial 'realism' that might link that appearance of the phenomenon of film with the institutionalisation of psychoanalysis, two narrative and institutional forms matched, almost uncannily, in their schedules of development at the beginning of the twentieth century.

But the way toward an account of the archaeology of the narrational function in early cinema, as it is related to a family discourse, can not be the same as (though it can not ignore either) psychoanalytic approaches to Griffith as a personality. Certainly there are unexpected revelations in his writings. His elder sister Mattie, whom he calls a 'brillantly cultured woman' and who gave the children of the family their education, never married. She would say, as Griffith relates it, '(she) never found a man equal to her father and that none of less quality would ever satisfy her as a husband.'[1] But I am thinking here particularly of what he describes as his first, and extraordinarily persistent, memory – of his father's sword. In a strikingly direct juxtaposition he links the memory of this sword with his vocation as a writer. 'My first and last ambition, until Fate turned me into a picture man, was to be a writer. I determined on that when I was six years old. My father's sword and its early effect on my mind, his noble career, his wounds, for he was all shot to pieces, did impart a martial trend to my character, but there was no war, and the scholarly atmosphere of my home, I suppose, was responsible for my inclination to become a great literary man.'[2] There is too the statement of the great attraction, even obsession, which *Broken Blossoms* had on him. 'It made an impression on me that I could not overcome and my dramatic sense was so touched that I kept repeating over to myself that here was a story demanding production.'

An archaeology of the narrational function of course does not rest on such a slim profile, but it does suggest some central themes. The object here is not a psychoanalytic picture of Griffith, but the structure and genealogy of a function. *Broken Blossoms* offers us a concrete instance to examine the structure of this function in its symbolic action. As our reading of the prologue suggested, the moral content of the film is linked to the level of the presentation, to the narration, and hence to point of view. The effort to join spectacle with the concentration and focus of novelistic discourse takes the shape of a search for a language, a form of cinematic *écriture* capable of rendering the interiority of character with didactic means of exposition and judgment. The result is a certain form of the relation between image and text (of the intertitle) in Griffith's silent films. It is not that image and text are aligned in any simple way with spectacle and the narrative. On the contrary, the two together perform the narrative function. They are at the service of the realisation of the Yellow Man's dream story, his love and loss of the woman.

The syntactical organisation of the images conforms, more or less, to the basic forms of découpage that sustained Griffith's other work. Certain features of the organisation of space in relation to the *mise en scène*, namely, the perpendicularity of the camera to the action and the corresponding sense of frontality, create something of an allusion to the persistence of the theatrical tradition. But as a manner of framing, it is fully appropriate to broad physical action.

In the scene of the Yellow Man before the Chief Priest, this kind of framing makes it difficult, symptomatically in Griffith's style, I think, to distinguish at every point on screen literal images from representations of the scene invoked or read from the priest's book as he points upwards, and from the scene of prayer behind them. The ringing gong, first literal, serves then as a symbolic icon. At certain points, ambiguities persist between views, vision, memory, and references to off-screen space. These points of narrative and spatial disarticulation appear at the point narrative syntax seeks to place and register these different orders of subjective experience.

Certainly this disarticulation of spatial and narrative elements is in the context of a story having to do with vision as dream and as perception. The relative weakness of motivation in the link between image and narrative corresponds, perhaps, to the freedom of figurative and spatial order permitted in medieval painting before perspective, by the uniformity and centrality of its vantage point, rationalises and stabilises the disparate elements in the fictional scene. The unity of the theatrical space guaranteed by the fixed place of the spectator seems fragmented by the wish to find, through the disarticulating of a single perspective through different camera views, a narrative form capable of articulating a complex image of subjective experience.

The organisation of space in a subjective model takes the form in some versions of the shot/counter-shot. By generally avoiding a camera position that can be read as the literal view of a character, that is, by insuring sufficient obliquity of angle and distance between camera and character, Griffith can better control the description of action and at the same time render it subjectively.

In one of the crucial scenes, the 'Shopping Trip', the one in which Lucy and the Yellow Man first see each other through the window, there is a revealing exception to the general form of the relatively impersonal découpage that suggests what is at stake in the deployment of seeing and of shots in Griffith. Recall that Lucy has taken a small bundle of tin foil from its secret hiding pace. A title – 'Enough tin foil might get something extra' – informs us of the theme of economy (see figures 3 and 4). Recall too that the general framework of the scene is set by showing the Yellow Man looking out through his window, a privileged viewer, when Lucy enters (see figures 5– 14). We are opposite him and equidistant from her. Lucy's attention is instantly drawn to the window with the dolls. The change in scale focusing finally on a single doll indicates her inner concentration. The episode that follows makes the crucial point. Framed on one side by 'Evil Eye' and the Yellow Man on the other, each looking furtively at her, she discovers she doesn't have 'quite enough' foil even for a flower (see figures 15–20). On the level of Yellow Man's seeing of her and Griffith's seeing them, the level at which the framing of views and shots are organised, vision is structured by dramaturgy of lack and desire. The Yellow Man too lacks the desired object, the woman, who in turn is defined by the story as a figure of lack ('not enough'), by an inability to represent herself, by a sign like the flower (cf. the name, 'Broken Blossoms') by which she might be recognised or even recognise herself. She is embedded in and defined by an economy of desire and of (non)possession.

Griffith's composite perspective, male and female, locates the female's drama of self-identity under the aspect of the male vision. He will later give her the flower, and she will come to see herself in the mirror for what she is. Within the symbolic economy of the film, money provides significance: the

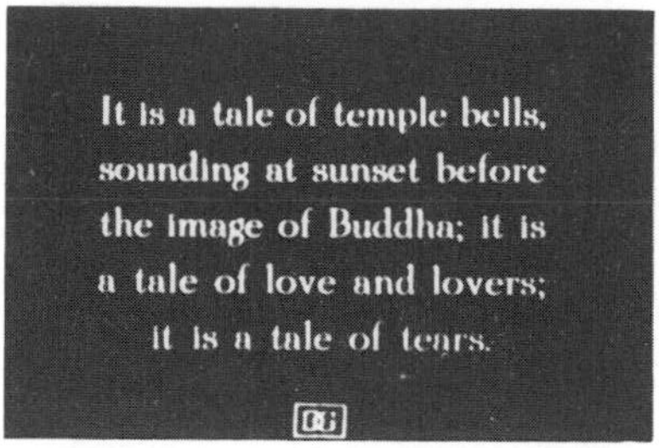

It is a tale of temple bells,
sounding at sunset before
the image of Buddha; it is
a tale of love and lovers;
it is a tale of tears.

Figure 1

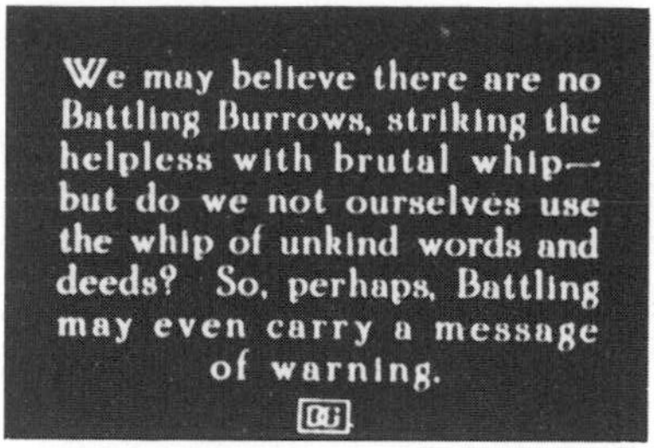

We may believe there are no
Battling Burrows, striking the
helpless with brutal whip—
but do we not ourselves use
the whip of unkind words and
deeds? So, perhaps, Battling
may even carry a message
of warning.

Figure 2

Figure 3

Enough tin foil might
get something extra.

Figure 4

Figure 5

Figure 6

Figure 7

Figure 8

Figure 9

This child with
tear-aged face—

Figure 10

Figure 11

Figure 12

Figure 13

Figure 14

Evil Eye also watches.

Figure 15

Figure 16

Figure 17

Figure 18

Figure 19

Figure 20

woman is the valued lack whose honour, the film's central focus, is to be both defended and then attacked by the father.

The written inter-titles of the film, extraordinarily various as to form and effect, are related to the reading of these images. Indeed, seldom are they given over to the quotation of dialogue, or a report of 'inner speech' arising from the level of the story. Rather, they usually are characterised by a kind of language and by a kind of commentative perspective associated with the level of narration. In fact, they carry Griffith's signature: DG. At the crucial point, when, from a singularly unusual first-person vantage point, the Yellow Man sees and is seen by her (figures 8–14), an inter-title (figure 10) intervenes between him and the object of his view. Within this sequence of images, it literally intervenes, breaks the continuity, and acts as a kind of announcement. The sentence 'This child with tear-aged face –' is clearly neither quotation nor indirect discourse. The form of indication '*this*' and the dash, which sets up the image to follow, mark it not as character speech, but as an inscription of the narrator – more precisely, his designation, *to us*, of his presentation of the woman. Griffith thus defines himself as a figure outside the story proper but inscribed in his function through sight on the analogy to the Yellow Man, and through a voice very close to his own. He intervenes as if against the natural prerogative of the depicted character in his desire to see and possess, in order himself to present the Girl – Lillian Gish, as his symbolic possession within the order of discourse.

The solution to this problem of narrative discourse in film, of cinema writing, of text and image, has an analogy that we recognise from literary study: namely, indirect discourse. Images are organised in a discursive unity by which character discourse – which takes the form not of speech, but of direct action and the discourse of seen objects – and authorial comment, shaped through a syntax that makes such views intelligible as representations of a character's mental world, are mixed. With the addition of a written text we have a further level of complexity in the mixed discourse of character and narrator. It is the discourse of the image – that of action, object, vantage point, and the literal text that are coordinated under the auspices of the narrative agency. The film's inheritance from the novel is of course certain forms of the organisation of the level of narrative proper, melodrama for example. This is obvious enough. But what is original and creative in Griffith's achievement is a system of narration that brings together the syntax of the dialogue system of drama without the dialogue – through the silent discourse of the seen object – in the shot/counter shot figure, with the power of the novelist's point of view, not necessarily localized in the position of the camera.

If there is a fantasy animating Griffith's narrative project, which cross-cutting and the threat of rape come to symbolise, it has to do, I think, with the seduction and at the same time the defence of the woman by his symbolic possession of her through his art. This scenario of rescue is essentially a chivalrous project couched in a kind of medieval and allegorical idiom, that has as its end the stabilisation of the place and integrity of the bourgeois family against the threat of abandonment, dismemberment, homelessness or worse, that constitute the clear and present danger in his films. It is in this role that the moralism of Griffith's vision as a director lies. The Griffith fantasy – and he stands in a line of other American directors with the same general concern (Ford and Capra come to mind) is the protection or restoration of the holiness of the American family. It is a prerequisite of this vision that it be achieved in the mode of nostalgia.

To perform this function and institute this powerful project could only mean Griffith's constructing a place for himself in a system of public speech. The form of indirect discourse which he ultimately adapted enabled him to both enact a fantasy and to discipline it through morality. His originality as a constructor of narrative form is exactly the inverse of Freud's: he lives the scenario, but doesn't want to know its secrets. The archaeology of the narrative function and early film form is embedded in the family discourse by disavowal. The public role which 'D. W. Griffith' finally created could be none other than the mask he has left behind for history, as the 'father' of 'narrative film form'.

That the archaeology of this language of specifically cinematic authority should take us to the family and that as a form it should coincide historically and more or less theoretically with the reception of psychoanalysis in America sets out a body of critical problems rather different from those posed by the problem of realism. It invites us to contemplate, for example, from the vantage point of Foucault's most recent work on the history of sexuality, the place of Griffith and the industry that followed in his trail, within the social history of the authority on which fictional, legal, and economic discourses in relation to their audiences are sustained, and which they in turn institute.

Notes

1. D. W. Griffith, 'My Early Life', quoted in *Focus on D. W. Griffith*, (ed.) Harry Geduld (New York: Prentice-Hall, 1971), p. 14.
2. 'My Early Life', p. 15.

Artful Racism, Artful Rape

Griffith's *Broken Blossoms*

JULIA LESAGE

From *Jump Cut* no. 26, 1981. Reprinted in *Jump Cut: Hollywood, Politics and Counter Cinema* (ed.) Peter Steven (Toronto: Between the Lines, 1985).

SEXIST and racist films and television programmes continue to engage women as viewers, women of all classes and races. The mass media catch us up in their violence and sensuality. As a woman I must ask how the media can so seduce me that I enjoy, either as entertainment or as art, works that take as one of their essential ingredients the victimisation of women. The immediate answer is that historically, from the silent film era to the present, bourgeois film has developed various mechanisms for structuring in ambiguity and for keeping us emotionally involved; one of film's hallmarks as a 'democratic' art form is its ability to allow for and co-opt an oppressed group's response. Feminist film criticism takes as its task the exposure of these ideological mechanisms and the analysis of how they function in ways both internal to a film and in a broader cultural and political context.

Specifically, if we look closely at narrative films, with the intent of decolonising our minds, we will find a similar 'story' about sexual relations running below the surface of film after film. Over and over again, male and female film characters are assigned certain familiar, recognisable sexual traits, which provide a ready way of expressing the culture's commonly-held sexual fantasies.[1] The way these fantasies are expressed varies, of course, from film to film, where they are manipulated and often displaced or condensed according to the exigencies of the plot and/or the social acceptability of directly expressing a given fantasy.[2]

Strikingly, the same kind of sexual-political 'story', or assignation of sexual traits, is repeated from film to film, no matter how much the manifest content differs. This repetition is not ideologically neutral. Persistent configurations of assigned sexual traits, deriving perhaps most directly from nineteenth- and twentieth-century literature, have a vitality in contemporary film because these patterns emerge from and serve to reinforce patriarchal social relations in the world outside the film.[3] Fictional sexuality parallels the real options that hegemonic male culture would like to continue offering men and women today, and real power differentials exist between the sexes. The emotional options for both men and women – the patterns of characterisation – are, in fact, usually oppressively perverse.

'Broken Blossoms': Characters, Plot and Sexual Traits

The sexual-political structures in film are not only perverse, but exceedingly durable. D. W. Griffith's *Broken Blossoms* was one of the first films in the United States received as high art and as a progressive and emotionally moving statement against both masculine brutality and racial prejudice. The film was released in 1919, one of a number of poetic and intimate depictions of domestic life that followed Griffith's monumental epics of 1915–16, *The Birth of a Nation* and *Intolerance*. *Birth of a Nation*, originally entitled *The Clansman*, had valorised the founding of the Ku Klux Klan, depicting it as a paternalistic, semi-feudal organisation bringing order to a south suffering under the 'chaos' of reconstruction. Consequently, the film provoked a national scandal because of its racist content. *Broken Blossoms* was Griffith's cinematic rejoinder to the charges against him.

Broken Blossoms deliberately tried to counter the then dominant racist ways of depicting Asians in popular literature, magazines and film. In reaction to the importation of masses of Asian labourers and congruent with U S imperial ambitions in the Pacific, the United States had seen waves of anti-Asian prejudice in the late nineteenth and early twentieth centuries. Newspapers sensationally editorialised on and presented stories about the 'yellow peril'. Fictional narratives often used 'inscrutable orientals' as villains, or located vices such as drug addiction or white slavery in a U S Chinatown. In the decade before *Broken Blossoms*, films treated what seemed the most dangerous threat of all: 'miscegenation'.[4]

Within this context, *Broken Blossoms* was perceived as a sensitive and humanitarian film. It daringly presented a chaste and ideally beautiful love between an immigrant Chinese man and a young white girl. The plot of the film was derived from Thomas Burke's short story. 'The Chink and the Girl', from his *Limehouse Nights*, tales of lumpen criminal life. Griffith changed Burke's Chinese protagonist from a schemer and 'worthless drifter of an Oriental' to a poetic, peaceful Buddhist lover of beauty.[5] Ostensibly, *Broken Blossoms* has a moral message: Asian Buddhist peacefulness is superior to Anglo-Saxon ignorance, brutality and strife.

Griffith embodies his moral message in his two male protagonists, who both live in London's Limehouse slum district: a gentle Chinese storekeeper, played by Richard Barthelmess; and a working-class brute, Battling Burrows, played by the large-framed, muscular actor Donald Crisp. Burrows prides himself on masculine prowess. He is master both in the boxing ring and at home, where he bullies his housekeeper and daughter, the 15-year-old Lucy. Lucy, played by Lillian Gish, is a poverty-stricken, beaten child who awakens for one brief moment to emotional life before she is killed.

The plot of the film is simple. The film opens in a Chinese port city with Barthelmess in his ornate robes saying goodbye to his Buddhist mentor and trying unsuccessfully to break up a fight between brawling US sailors. The Chinese man is going out to the West to bring a message of peace. The setting shifts to a London Limehouse slum, where we find out that the young Chinese man has become a disillusioned shopkeeper and opium addict. Elsewhere in the slum, Battling Burrows sits in his shack reminiscing about a fight he has just won and is reprimanded by his manager for drinking and womanizing before his next fight.

The film introduces Burrows's daughter Lucy sitting huddled on a coil of rope on the wharf outside their house. Here the set plays its part as well. As Charles Affron points out in *Star Acting*, all the sets in this film are claustrophobic, even the outdoor ones. Departing from the epic scope of *Birth of a Nation*, *Broken Blossoms* formally accepts and uses the edge of the frame as limiting the scope of the action and incorporates within the frame many other boundaries such as walls, arches and corners to enhance a claustrophobic effect.[6]

Two sequences, showing either Lucy's reverie or perhaps moments recently experienced, present Lucy's 'education' about women's lives. First, a woman in a crowded one-room apartment is cooking a meal for her huge family and fighting with her husband. The woman advises Lucy never to get married. Then Lucy is seen on the street retrieving a compact dropped by one of two prostitutes, who also warn her about men. Lucy gets up and enters the shack.

Still smarting from his manager's rebuke, Burrows bullies Lucy. Before he goes out on the town again, he demands that she have tea ready when he gets back and also that she put a smile on her face. Lucy makes a pathetic gesture, using her fingers to turn up the corners of her mouth – it is a gesture she will repeat four times in the film.

In Burrows's absence, Lucy takes a few treasures out from under a brick on the floor, puts a new ribbon in her dirty hair, and goes out to shop. She looks longingly at the dolls in the Chinese man's shop window, buys a few essentials from a street stand, and wants to trade in some tinfoil to buy a flower but does not have enough foil. She is harassed on the street by another Chinese man, Evil Eye, but is protected by Barthelmess. When she goes home, her father, irritated by his manager's restrictions on his social life, bullies her again. In nervousness, she drops hot food on his hand. Burrows angrily takes a whip out from under the bed and beats her into unconsciousness. He then goes to work out in the gym, preparing for his big fight.

Lucy staggers to her feet, leaves the house and weaves down the Limehouse streets. She falls unconsciously through the door of the Chinese man's store.

He has prepared himself an opium pipe and sits and gazes at her as if she were a vision from his drugged dream. She stirs and startles him into full awareness. He bathes her wounds, takes her upstairs to his living quarters, gives her his robe to wear, and puts her on his bed as on an altar. He surrounds her with all his beautiful things, gives her a doll, and it becomes clear that he is sexually attracted to her. As he moves to kiss her, he sees her fear and kisses the sleeve of her robe instead. The sequence is intercut with shots of Burrows slugging it out and winning his big fight amidst the wild cheers of a working-class male audience.

One of Burrows's friends, while shopping at the Chinese man's store, discovers Lucy asleep alone upstairs and runs to tell Burrows of the daughter's 'sin'. The boxer and his friends agree to wait till after the fights to settle the affair. When they get to the store, the Chinese man is away on an errand. Burrows hits his daughter, forces her to change back into her rags and come with him, and destroys everything in the upstairs room. His friends downstairs keep Lucy from escaping. Once back at home, Burrows chases Lucy, who takes refuge in the closet. When she refuses to come out, Burrows smashes in the closet door with an axe; the sequence is shot from inside the closet, showing Lucy's hysterical reaction and absolute fear. The claustrophobic visual composition and Gish's acting indicate that we are intended to be 'inside' Lucy's experience in this cinematic equivalent of rape. When Burrows chops through the door, he pulls Lucy through it and throws her on the bed, where he beats her to death.

When he discovers the destruction in his room and Lucy's abduction, the Chinese man throws himself on the floor and sobs hysterically. He takes a gun, goes to Burrows's shack, finds Lucy dead, acknowledges the challenge Burrows gives him to fight, and shoots and kills the brute. Taking Lucy's body with him, the Chinese man goes back to his room and lays her body once again on his bed as on an altar.

Burrows's friends discover the boxer's body and get the police to round up the Asian killer. Before they can do so, however, in a last act of tranquil and sorrowful love, even ecstasy, the 'yellow man' prays before his Buddha and stabs himself, joining his child-woman in death. This is the 'plot' of *Broken Blossoms*.

The Abuses of Masculinity
When we analyse the story line closely, looking particularly at the visual elements and cinematic tactics, it becomes clear that the film is *about* sex roles as much as *about* race. In particular, it is about masculinity. In the figure of Battling Burrows, the film presents the potential *evil* of masculinity, here safely attributed to a grotesque Other from the lower classes. Projected onto the Chinese man's character are all the traits of the nineteenth-century sensitive outsider, the romantic hero – a self-destructive dreamer who never

lives out the fulfilment of his dreams. I wish to examine how and why such traits have been divided and assigned to the two major male characters in the film, and also what it means that the narrative places both men in relation to a 'virgin'. Finally, I wish to look at the kind of role assigned to Lillian Gish and Gish's impact on/attraction for me as a woman viewer both drawn to and distressed by this film.

In *Broken Blossoms*, if we look closely at the gestures, clothing and course of events in any given sequence, we see that our interpretation of the character's behaviour relies on and indeed underscores many popular notions about masculinity and the abuses of masculinity. Donald Crisp as Battling Burrows uses exaggeration to delineate the attributes of a working-class bully and macho brute, carrying the traditional attributes of masculinity to an abusive extreme. In contrast, Barthelmess plays the Chinese man as being in many ways not fully a man, as woman-like. Compare, for example, our judgments on the costumes and gestures of the two men as we first see them. We notice the ornateness of Barthelmess's robe, his facial gestures, especially his acts of looking upward with half-closed eyes or of carrying a fan, his small movements, and his semi-static poses and stance.

The opening titles and the choice of content in the film's early shots – the initial contrast between a port in the Far East and a Limehouse slum – emphasise a social and moral point, namely that Asian civilisation and altruism outshine European and American immorality and grossness. Yet another set of reflections is simultaneously elicited from the audience – an evaluation and comparison of effeminacy and brutal manliness. In his scripted role and in his physical movements and appearance, Barthelmess as the young Chinese man elicits from the audience a common social accusation: effeminacy. Time and time again the viewer seems led to conclude, 'That's an effeminate man – or effeminate gesture, or article of clothing, etc.' His robe is excessively ornate; in the exterior shots, its shirts conspicuously blow in the wind. It is shapeless, making the shape beneath androgynous in form. When he is in the Buddhist temple with his mentor, the temple itself filled with flowers, exotica and ornate design, Barthelmess acts 'girl-like': holding a fan, moving only with slight restrained gestures, and standing with eyes cast down.

In contrast with the Chinese man's demeanour, these sequences also present other men self-consciously proud of their masculinity. These are the US sailors whom Griffith calls in one intertitle, 'barbarous Anglo-Saxon sons of turmoil and strife'. They swizzle down liquor, stuff food grotesquely into their mouths, make large gestures and swagger around as ugly Americans totally insensitive to their milieu. They seem incapable of being together without violent physical discord, and foreshadow Griffith's critique of Battling Burrows.

In the Limehouse environment, we first see the Chinese man huddled against a wall, one foot up against it, arms wrapped around himself, eyes cast sadly down. The soft curve of Barthelmess's body seems to 'catch' the contrasting, harsh linear angles of the architecture. For a man to have his arms wrapped around himself is to assume a typical 'woman's' gesture of depression, insecurity and even sad self-hatred. The Chinese man takes a stance which is as far from that of masculine doer, a self-determining agent of one's own life, as it is possible to present. In his store we see him semistatically posed, smoking his opium against a background of meagre beauty. The life he creates for himself is one of melancholy, contemplation and escape.

The opium den that the Chinese man frequents suggests not only moral but sexual derangement. As a matter of fact, fictional films usually 'signal' moral derangement by showing women in sexually transgressive roles. Here, we see mannishly dressed women in sexually active poses or in compositions of sexual self-sufficiency or dominance, often with a man of another race. In one composition, an Anglo woman is sitting above a totally self-absorbed, opium-smoking Turk and looking down on him. Another shot shows a blonde woman interacting with a black worker; another, an Anglo woman flirting with a Chinese man we later know as Evil Eye. We see a woman lying on a couch, filmed either as if she wishes to seduce someone or as if the opium is giving her an orgasmic experience on her own. She is panting slightly, wetting her lips, and looking towards the camera with an expression that suggests illicit ecstasy. This shot parallels a later one of Barthelmess stretched out full length on a couch, with the opium seller tending this completely passive figure. The equation of the protagonist's vice with sexual derangement and a suspiciously feminine passivity could not be more explicit.

In contrast, the figure of Battling Burrows is a study in established norms of masculine dress, gesture, attitudes and behaviour. Every aspect of Burrows's character is heightened to make us reflect on the falsity or brutal consequences of those norms. What do we see Burrows doing? In the ring he fights strictly by heavy slugging. After winning, he is proud and struts about. Before the fight he makes faces at his off-screen opponent, juts his chin out, and pounds his gloves up and down on his legs – indicating that he thinks a fight will clearly prove to the whole world who is the 'better man'.

Back home, he drinks and entertains the advances of a Loose Woman. The signs of her looseness are many: her activity, her smiling, her friendliness, and her initiative to visit a man in his house. She walks in, hands in her pockets, looks Burrows in the eye, immediately moves over to where he is standing, receives a quick embrace from him, and then goes back out, still looking at him with a flirting glint in her eye, presumably having made a date to meet him later.

Burrows's typical posture asserts macho self-confidence in a socially coded way, particularly in the use of cinematic gestures normally assigned to figures supposedly from the working class. He stands with feet spread apart, lets his eyes sweep around the room possessively, pulls his vest down, puts his hands in his pockets to pull his pants tight across his crotch, and sways back and forth from one foot to another. Such a stance is a way of declaring himself master of a given space, and especially master over the woman in his domestic space.

When angry, Burrows knocks one fist against the palm of the other hand, and when proclaiming his opinion he gestures with his hand open and palm down. Although he is characterised as stupid, he is also shown as having the prerogative of having his emotions and opinions respected as law in his house – a witty cinematic comment on the nuclear family – the place where all of us can observe patriarchy as insane.[7] To portray this man's physical excess, which culminates in beating his daughter, Griffith has Burrows pick up a chair and swing it around, eat like a pig, throw a spoon at Lucy's rear-end and then oblige her to smile, upon which pathetic act he passes judgment. There are many such gestures of dominance towards Lucy before Burrows beats her. Indeed, all of Burrows's gestures in the film form part of a brutal whole.

Burrows's male friends reinforce for him the rightness of his behaviour and attitudes. They form a Boys' Club, the kind of thing all socially successful men use to protect their men's rights in a man's world. When the men go to the police station to report Burrows's death, the police's co-operative interaction with them reveals an unusual degree of male cohesiveness, for in another context we might expect more of a conflict to be presented between the police and the fight-loving element of a portside slum. The conflicts among Burrows's associates function well within the confines of the boys' club, for the manager only wants the fighter to fight better; and the associates band together to get the woman back for their friend once the joke of telling him about it has been sprung.

In fact, the tale is told to Burrows just as if it were a spicy story of local adultery. The man who had spied on Lucy paces his account to arouse Burrows's sexual curiosity, to bring forth laughter and contempt for any cuckolded man who would lose a woman to a weakling and a 'Chink'. In a competitive fashion, his friends found it great fun to see the boxer's chagrin at 'losing' both to a girl, his own daughter whom he was supposed firmly to possess, and to a man who seemed Burrows's inferior because that man would not fight and because he was of another race. There is no love between Burrows and his associates but a lot of mutual self-protection. When they 'recover' Lucy, they all assume that Burrows will – and should – beat her, both to assuage his wounded masculine pride and to put her firmly in her place.

241

Possessing a Virgin and a Child

Certain perversities in the film are labelled as such by the intertitles and the story line: namely, racism, opium addiction and physical violence. Yet equally important to the development of the film are other perversities: rape, incest and the seduction of a child. It is testimony to the force of the intertitles and the declared narrative line – the overt story of racism and child abuse – that few critics have looked closely at the specifically sexual perversity of this film.[8] In fact, if we look at the *mise en scène* and composition, in visual terms it is clear that both the brutish father and the gentle, dope-smoking Chinese man 'get' the girl. Visually we see both men symbolically consummating sexual contact with Gish. The film allows both men to possess a virgin, a child.

It is clear that Burrows's breaking into the closet with an axe and dragging the cowering Lucy out through the broken boards visually symbolises rape. Indeed, this is one of the most emotionally powerful sequences of sexual assault on film. Yet there are many other indications in the film that Burrows's relation to his daughter is a sexual one. He abuses her for the same reasons and in the same way that a working-class man is supposed to abuse his wife. That is, when the world is down on you, if you are a married man you can always take it out on the wife and kids at home. Aside from one intertitle introducing Lucy, there is no other indication of a father–daughter relation, and all of Burrows's actions towards Lucy would appropriately be those of a man towards a wife.

More explicit in visual composition and *mise en scène* is the role of the bed in the Burrows household. Sometimes, especially when Burrows is alone drinking or with his manager, the composition is cast towards the room's centre, with the bed predominantly visible behind Burrows. When Lucy is alone in the house doing her domestic chores, looking at her treasures or looking in the mirror, the composition is cast towards the right side of the room, the domestic corner that includes the hearth. On the opposite side, the bed and closet form an angle, which compositionally becomes a trap.

The first time Burrows beats Lucy, he grabs a whip from under the mattress and stands in the centre of the room, holding the whip at penis height. The lighted areas in the composition form a triangle, with the pillow and Lucy's and Burrows's faces forming the triangle's corners, and the whip-phallus aligned midway between the pillow and Lucy's face. Lucy cries, cowers by the door, and clings to the far right wall away from the bed. Burrows is filmed in a symmetrically-composed medium-shot, whip prominently in the centre, and he points for her to move away from the right wall, that is, towards the direction of the bed.

Lucy tries to create a diversion by telling him there is dust on his shoes. She bends down to wipe off his shoes with her dress. Here, the change in composition from one shot to another connotes the act of fellatio. In the long shot before Lucy wipes the shoes, the whip hangs almost to the floor. But in the close-up of her wiping the shoes, the whip's tail is at the height of Burrows's penis, and as Lucy raises her face the whip swings past her lips. As Burrows grabs Lucy's arms and throws her towards the bed near the closet, the whip is again between his legs at penis height. We see blurred, orgiastic shots of him beating her senseless.

In the film's final beating sequence, the same connotative devices are repeated, but in a more exaggerated way. Burrows beats Lucy's face with the whip handle, and the bed becomes the site of her death.

Finally, the way Burrows dies emphasises that his relation to the Chinese man was one of sexual competition after all. When the Chinese man discovers the dead Lucy on the bed and is about to shoot Burrows, both men face off and tacitly acknowledge the other's 'manly' challenge to fight to the death over the 'cause' of this woman. Posed next to a fight poster on the wall and standing with his back to the angle formed by the bed and closet (the trap-like locus of Lucy's rape and death), the Chinese man shoots Burrows, discharging the gun held at penis-height.

In paradigmatic contrast to sexual violence is the sensual completeness of Lucy's one night at the Chinese man's home. And yet that relation is not only tender and beautiful, but also explicitly perverse. We see this most clearly in the sequence where the Chinese man overcomes his lust just after the girl Lucy has received her first doll. Lucy, wrapped in her new protector's ornate, 'womanly' robe, cuddles the doll with delight. However, her friend with the gentle eyes now wears a look of acquisitive passion, and he is seen moving in on Lucy, his eyes in shadow. Shots of Burrows at his big fight are intercut with this sequence: we see Burrows slugging heavily and an all-male audience, primarily working-class, on their feet wildly cheering. When we see the Chinese man and Lucy again, there is fear in her eyes as she clings to the doll. He picks up the hem of her sleeve and kisses that instead, his face moving to the light where we see his illuminated, gentle, ecstatic smile as he goes away.

Significantly over-apologising for the man's sexual intent, the intertitle announces: 'His love remains a pure and holy thing – even his worst foe says this.' In fact, the title makes no sense, because no one at the time knew that Lucy was there, and later her father and his friends just assumed that a sexual relation had taken place. Griffith seems to use the title to deny the sequence's visual explicitness, yet this very denial creates suspicion about and thus confirms the reality of that sexual passion which the sequence has both presented and repressed.

After the Chinese man withdraws, we see Gish examining the sleeve that had been kissed and then stirring in bed. Both gestures indicate the child's emotional, indeed sexual, involvement with this gentle yet seductive man. The visual lushness of this sequence, the child's gestures of preening and of loving the doll, the advances of the Chinese man, and the child's awakening to both maternal and sexual emotion: all these visual details offer a clear erotic message, a message that is then ambiguously denied.

Male Options Under Capitalism

Two men, a brute and an effeminate beauty-lover, 'get a virgin'. This is the sexual plot of *Broken Blossoms*. What does that mean? What is the power of such a plot? Why did Griffith construct his story that way?

First of all, their slum environment, brutality and opium-smoking cast the male protagonists as Others. Griffith safely assigns perversity to other races and to the poor. Onto the working class are displaced Griffith's unconscious, artistic insights about the problems of the nuclear family under capitalism, an understanding he never could have admitted to since he was very much the patriarch, a man who fondly recalled the paternalistic and militaristic values of the Old South and who always had a love for pretty young women.[9]

In fact, the film presents two key aspects of male life under capitalism. A man can be socially successful and conventionally masculine, or he can cultivate his sensitivity and imaginative capacity and live as an outsider. Since the last century, middle-class men have had as a model of emotional success either the role of 'breadwinner' and thus possessor of a home, wife and family; or the role of 'free-spirited' (in fact petit-bourgeois) rebel, usually an artist or intellectual. *Broken Blossoms* utilises and heightens the contrast between these two emotional options. It reduces the outlines of these male roles to a schematised emblematic form, and it displaces the whole 'problem' of masculinity onto a story about the lives of the very poor. The film is thus particularly useful to feminist critics, to show how popular art transmits patriarchal assumptions. The roles of the two major male characters not only set out two contrasting sides of a single sexual-political configuration, but the film also makes the emotional implications of each kind of role totally explicit.

The figure of Burrows represents conventional notions of masculinity as enacted by a socially successful man. Within that formula, the corollary to a 'real man's' aggression in taking what he can in the social and economic world is his 'wearing the pants' at home. That is, he is the boss or the possessor of a wife and family, and his woman must always know her place. In *Broken Blossoms*, Battling Burrows seemingly has no wife, only a daughter. Yet multiple notions of women's servitude, dependency and helplessness – and reception of sexual abuse – are condensed in the figure of Lucy.

Women's role in the nuclear family under capitalism was classically described by Friedrich Engels using the metaphor of prostitution.[10] Across class lines and cultures and across historical periods, we have sold our bodies for sustenance. Furthermore, the ideological compensations given to 'good' women in western culture – the romantic love myth and the courtly 'woman-on-a-pedestal' or Victorian 'wife-as-moral-focus' myth – are, as Kate Millett wrote,

> grants that the male concedes out of his total power. Both forms of compensation have the effect of obscuring the patriarchal character of western culture and, in their general tendency to attribute impossible virtues to women, have ended by confining them to a narrow and often remarkably conscribing sphere of behavior.[11]

Symbolically, in *Broken Blossoms* Lucy functions as the Good Wife. But what is most daring about this film is that it pushes Engels's metaphor of prostitution, used to describe the way women are possessed in the nuclear family, one step further. *Broken Blossoms*'s metaphor equates the possession of women in the family with incest. Many works of literature, especially from the nineteenth century on, deal with the relation of father-figures and sons as the sons come into their patrimony or struggle to become self-made men. This has also been a favourite theme in contemporary film (*The Apprenticeship of Duddy Kravitz*, 1974, *Star Wars*, 1977, and *The Godfather*, 1971, immediately come to mind). But *Broken Blossoms* is unusual in the way it faces the opposite question, not the coming into patrimony but the servitude of women, a servitude enforced by threats of deprivation, emotional bullying and the potential or actual use of physical force.

In *Broken Blossoms* the father rapes his daughter: what does that mean? In Burrows's case, murdering Lucy is clearly the ultimate abuse of his prideful masculinity. In real life, we know that on the individual level rape is not an act of sexual desire but one of possession.[12] On the social level, as Susan Brownmiller points out, rape is analogous to lynching. It is an act supposedly committed by lumpen proletarian men or a crazy few, but in fact rape performs a more general social function as a reminder and brutal enforcer of women's 'place'.[13]

When we take the second half of the term, 'the father rapes his *daughter*', and ask what *incest* means to the sexual-political structure underlying the film, we arrive at the same answer: possession. The challenge to patriarchy that this film poses (or can pose through a feminist reading) is the following: if a man's social world consists primarily of a boys' club, of a nexus of economic and power relations conducted principally among men, how can a man ever set his daughters free or even conceive of what their freedom might mean? For the emotional implication *Broken Blossoms* dares to draw out is that for a man to be the possessor at home means to be incestuous towards his girl children as well as towards his wife.[14]

Griffith is perfectly clear about Burrows's excesses and is morally righteous in disliking abusive masculinity, here safely assigned to the working class. We all see what Burrows is like and know why the brute is wrong.

More interesting to me, and more ambiguous, is Burrows's complement, the Chinese man. On the superficial level, the film is an anti-racist text, but the film says nothing from an Asian person's point of view, just as it says nothing from a woman's point of view. The images of the East, of Buddhism, of racial traits and of an oppressed person's reaction to oppression are all drawn from hegemonic, white stereotypes. In fact, not only is Griffith working with received opinions and prejudices about Asians, women and the working class, but when he sets up his basic opposition of brute vs. sensitive man, he is also working with a set of oppositions that has nothing to do with race.

The Man of Action Vs. the Sensitive Observer
What are these oppositions set up by the use of two contrasting male figures – the boxer and the opium smoker?

The one character is a violent, selfish, insensitive man of action. Burrows moves with large gestures and commands a large space wherever he is. He is self-assured and demanding, even to the point of being physically and emotionally destructive to others around him. The other male figure in the film is a gentle, altruistic lover of beauty. He is a soft person, often emotionally paralysed into inaction. He burns his days up in reverie and opium. But even though he would waste himself with drugs, he is basically fatherly and tender. He is totally self-sacrificing for a child-woman that he would wish to, but cannot, possess. Furthermore, he understands the hypocrisy of most social values in the capitalist West; his solution is to surround his own life with beauty and otherwise to withdraw. In his love life, the yearning is all.

The character whom Griffith can demean by calling 'Chinky' has all the traits of a male cultural persona which has been valorised in western literature for several centuries now – a persona Griffith himself surely must have identified with. 'Chinky' is no less than our old friend, the romantic hero. He is the sensitive lover of beauty and the pursuer of unattainable women. The Chinese man could have stepped right out of Thomas DeQuincey's *The Opium Eater*, and it is indeed likely that the author of *Limehouse Nights* was influenced by DeQuincey's depiction of London poverty and a young man's opium addiction and friendship with a girl waif. That Griffith, the artist who always thought of himself and his role in idealised terms, identified with the Chinese man can be seen in the way that *Broken Blossoms*'s plot and *mise en scène* constantly valorise the young man's tenderness, aesthetic sensibility and moral superiority. Indeed, all the Chinese man's virtues are conflated in a romantic way: to recognise beauty and to surround oneself with beautiful things are indices of moral superiority that people enmeshed in the workaday world do not recognise. Only artists, fellow outsiders and women can recognise such a virtue for its worth.

To carry my analysis of sexual politics in *Broken Blossoms* one step further, I think we should ask why this figure is characteristically male and

246

what his social role is. In fact, the romantic hero and the sensitive outsider (or, to use a more familiar equivalent, the film-maker and the professors of literature and film) have a specific class position under capitalism; their chance to *choose* that position is the escape valve that capitalism allows for dissatisfied male members of its petite bourgeoisie.

To put it schematically, there are three roles available to men in capitalist society: outsider, worker, or boss. If you pursue profit and power, you also exploit others. To avoid facing that, you have to dull your emotional sensibility as you move up in social position. That is what *Duddy Kravitz*, *Godfather II* (1974), and *Room at the Top* (1959) were all about. The capitalist has to believe that the profit motive serves society the best and cannot look with regret either at how he is exploiting others or at how his emotional and social forms of interacting with others might be better. Possession and dominance become embedded in a way of life. Or a man may be a worker, putting in time at a stultifying job for a weekly pay cheque, suffering humiliation both from superiors at work and from the threat of unemployment and/or illness – the threat of not being able to take care of one's own. Both for male workers and for bosses, most of whom are male, there are many reasons why men continue to suffer from rigid notions of sex roles, emotional paralysis, moral compromise and a crippling of the imagination – and also why they oppress women.

The one 'out' that has traditionally been offered to men since the last century has been to the artist, the outsider, the rebel. This person has the insight and the inner drive to reject social respectability and emotional sterility. He can turn to creating art, living alone in nature, or taking drugs – often doing all these at once. Instead of pursuing money, success and power in bourgeois terms, the romantic hero idealistically lives by virtues that seem to be precluded if one searches for social success: these virtues include creativity, passion, love, authenticity, honesty, sincerity, beauty, innocence, spontaneity and contemplation of nature. At the same time, the romantic hero in his self-gazing is also like Hamlet, often paralysed into inaction, usually ineffective, yearning for the unattainable woman, and inevitably self-destructive. That this is a *male* role can be seen from the fact that the rebel goes off to the woods or into dope, but not back into the domestic sphere to raise a bunch of kids. That has just not been one of the options that men have imagined for themselves.[15]

Displacement

Furthermore, Griffith's 'ruse' of using the Asian man as the romantic hero hides the social reality of racism. The romantic hero is more like Griffith's image of himself; Griffith wrote that he sought to live by the pen as a way of identifying with his earlier and most beloved image of his father, that is, of a man brandishing a sword (and in fact, it was brandishing a sword against a black servant to teach the man his place).[16] When Griffith came of age in the South, the illustrious days of the Civil War and family prosperity were for him sadly a part of the legendary past. To be a writer was for Griffith to find a more modern, petit-bourgeois way of being a real man in a culture not instinctively his own, of being socially functional yet still maintaining his felt identity as an Outsider, and of devoting himself to Creativity and Art.[17]

Perhaps reacting against the charges of racism that *Birth of a Nation* had provoked, Griffith clearly wanted *Broken Blossoms* to be considered anti-racist, but the film represses all understanding of the real mechanisms of racism. Griffith did not embed his depiction of doomed interracial love within an artistic structure that would clarify understanding of race and racial oppression. Instead, he assigned to the Asian man the traits of his own class, that element of the petite bourgeoisie who feel themselves as individuals to be above economic and social constraints − sensitive outsiders morally superior to the bosses and brutes.

If the artistic structure of *Broken Blossoms* deals only superficially with race, it deals profoundly with sexual politics, especially masculinity. In particular, it implies that all three 'types' of men under capitalism desire the same type of woman: the unattainable or non-sexually active woman.[18] Battling Burrows represents the 'family man'. Because he is an entrepreneur, an aggressive boxer, he represents the self-made man, and because of his economic level, he also represents the working class. Thus Griffith has condensed onto the figure of Burrows traits of both the capitalist and the worker. In this context, Burrows possesses his blonde virgin and good wife and child within the context of a man's possession of his family.

As I mentioned before, Griffith condensed and displaced all his notions of the potential evil of family life onto the figure of a lower-class man both for his own protection and that of his audience. Similarly, projected onto the figure of the Chinese man are all the traits of the romantic hero, living only for the pursuit and never living out the fulfilment. The woman that both men need, each for different reasons, is played by Gish in a way that collapses virgin, child and wife all into the same role. For the father, she is the traditional good woman and also the virgin child. For the Chinese romantic hero, she is like Faust's Gretchen and DeQuincey's waif or even Werther's Lotte: a figure desirable from afar.

When I first saw *Broken Blossoms* I asked myself, what does it mean that both men have to get a virgin? Griffith's emblematic schema of the sexual possibilities for men in the West, that is, under capitalism, makes the answer clear. The men in the film live in a world of men, and Burrows embraces that world while the Chinese rejects it. None of the men in the film can enter into or even imagine a world where women are sexually active, initiators and agents of actions and decisions, and bearers of social power.

Coming to the same conclusion, but in a contrasting way, G. W. Pabst's silent film *Pandora's Box* (1928) also took up the theme of the capitalist's and the romantic hero's sexual decisions, but that film traced the fate of two men who aligned themselves with the seductress, the dark woman. Lulu, played by the dark-haired Louise Brooks, is the mirror opposite of Gish. Lulu is a destroyer of men and the bearer of chaos. In *Broken Blossoms*, the function of the good woman, the virginal woman, is to be put on a pedestal and yearned for, and after marriage or within the family, she is to be possessed. It is not Lucy's own vision, for Griffith early included scenes which showed Lucy losing all illusions about her future as a woman, either in marriage or as a prostitute.

That all the main characters must die at the end of *Broken Blossoms* and that the sexual-political situation as Griffith presents it is so static and despairing is no accident. Griffith presents a sparse yet emotionally charged outline of what happens when men cling to established norms of masculinity or rebel against those norms as a romantic hero would. *Broken Blossoms* has the vision to present both kinds of emotional possibilities that men in capitalist culture can allow themselves as, at worst, murderous in their consequences, and, at best, as crippling to men and oppressive to women.

A Woman Viewer's Response

To conclude, I would like to try to analyse why I liked the film. First, as I pointed out, Griffith's films have many ways to pacify our superego while promulgating a racist and sexist ideology. *Broken Blossoms*'s intent seems to be to combat racism. The fact that the Chinese man has the outlook of the romantic hero more than the point of view of someone from a non-white race does not at first seem racist, since the romantic hero has long been a figure women have found sympathetic. Sheila Rowbotham in *Woman's Consciousness, Man's World* spoke for my whole generation when she exposed the basic infantile selfishness of that figure as encountered by women in real life. But even so the sensitive, often androgynous man in fiction still has his appeal. Male authors give him 'womanly' virtues and also a man's right to be agent of his own destiny. *Broken Blossoms* takes a clear stand against violence and male brutality and, in the figure of the Chinese man, it valorises male tenderness, gentleness, and appreciation of beauty and innocence. No matter how many times I see the film, its simple praise for virtues I too prize in men comes through with an emotional power.

For most viewers, the other side of that message, that Brutality is Wrong, is conveyed not through the caricature of masculinity as enacted by Donald Crisp as Battling Burrows, but through the pathos elicited by Lillian Gish. *Broken Blossoms* established Gish's critical reputation and was part of a series of films Griffith made in this period which looked lovingly at the small detail and at women in the domestic sphere. Griffith's films were famous for their female roles, and Griffith was admired for the performances he drew from actresses and the way he filmed them. *Broken Blossoms*, for example, featured Griffith's first use of the irregular 'Sartov' lens, which resulted from then on in his dramatically exploiting softly-blurred close-ups of Gish.[19] It was also one of the first commercial films in the United States to be promoted successfully as high art.[20]

Although our attention is constantly being drawn to Gish, she is not playing a woman seen on women's terms or from a woman's point of view. Her role is reduced to the depiction of a virgin, a 'vision' of women often manipulated in male or, rather, patriarchal art. Within the narrative structure, the figure of Lucy is a term or a marker in a male story about male concerns.

The critical question that remains unresolved for me as a feminist viewer is this: where does Lucy's pathos, which affects me so strongly, derive from? Are my eyes constantly on Lucy in the way that a male viewer's would be, insofar as traditional feature films constantly have us look *at* women as objects in stories told through men's eyes?[21] Do I or can I stay on the film's surface and admire it as anti-racist and/or as art? Do I respond to the figure of Lucy primarily because I appreciate this virtuoso film role for an actress, one which demands a range from childlike ingenuousness to complete hysteria? By extension, do I admire other of Griffith's films for such roles and for women's acting in them?

Most students I have taught remember specific Griffith films through 'what happens' to the female lead and the actresses' performances. *Broken Blossoms* is seemingly 'about' Lucy's plight, her moment of love, and her murder. The surface emphasis on Lucy's story is enhanced both by Gish's acting and the close-ups of her face and glowing hair. Such an emphasis on the waif, Lucy, gives the film an appeal to both men and women. Although, for me, the device of Lucy's making a smile with her fingers is repulsively saccharine, the way Gish captures Lucy's limited emotional experience and the way her figure is filmed seem so 'right' for this sad tale. For example, Griffith brilliantly assigns Gish the prop of a doll to represent Lucy's awakening to her childhood, sexuality and maternal emotion all at once, and he maintains a visual emphasis on the child clinging to that doll while she is attacked in the closet. While seemingly fixed in a rigid stance, Gish can let her eyes, posture or fluttering hands express a whole range of emotions, and when she is attacked in the closet, she can let her body totally respond to the hysteria of impending death.[22]

Gish draws us in and holds us, and our sympathy for the child's plight both pacifies our superego and assures us that such things happen only to poor waifs and not to us. The other drama, that of masculinity and of men's need to get a virgin, is enacted on a level of the film which I think many people can observe but which goes by relatively uncommented on either by the overt story line or by the intertitles. And on this level, the film leads us all to participate in Lucy's rape by her father and her seduction by the Chinese man, the seduction in fact of a child who has just been given her first doll.

The film depicts intterracial love yet hides the ways it makes that love 'safe'. It protests male brutality yet draws us into male violence and child-abuse. I cannot speak for a Third World person's reaction to the film's ambiguous combination of anti-racism and racism. I do know that, as a feminist, the fact that I am drawn into cinematic depictions of this kind of sexual perversion disturbs me the most. It seems a gauge of my own colonised mind.

Lucy's pathos draws me into identifying with a cinematic depiction of woman as victim.[23] On the one hand, as a viewer, I want to protect this girl as a motherless child. Her helplessness calls out to me. As a girl and also as a woman, I have both felt helplessness (even been addicted to it) and nurtured others from helplessness to independence (the teacher's role, the lover's role, the mothering role that I have learned in my female socialisation).

On the other hand, *Broken Blossoms*' patriarchal, extreme depiction of father–daughter relations also reflects my own internalised and eroticised fears of male authority, dominance and control: fears that also derive from my girlhood in this culture. I have to ask myself: in what ways as a viewer do I 'participate' in Lucy's brutalisation and rape? I know how many levels of culture (from the structure of language to the structures of fiction to the structures of the economy) operate in a way that would encourage me to turn female submission into something erotic.[24]

In her key work on the presentation of women in male pornography, Angela Carter compares *Broken Blossoms* to de Sade's *Justine*:

Sometimes this waif, as in Griffith's *Broken Blossoms*, is as innocently erotic and as hideously martyrised as Justine herself, and, as a sexual icon, the abused waif allows the customer to have his cake and glut himself upon it, too. She could be as enticing in her vulnerability and ringletted prettiness as she was able but the audience knew all the time that the lovely child before them was a mature woman whom the fiction of her childishness made taboo. The taboo against acknowledging her sexuality created the convention that the child could not arouse desire; if she did so, it was denied. A sentimental transformation turned the denial of lust into a kitsch admiration of the 'cute'.[25]

Carter discussed the mechanism of denial by showing the response of male spectators to Gish's roles. I would also apply that mechanism to my own response. My response may include a denial of 'lust', that is, my own erotic reaction to my preferred female stars. But more clearly, Gish's role as waif-woman both elicits my own Oedipal fears and fantasies and allows me to deny them. The extremity of Lucy's condition allows me to deny that there is an internalised, 'masochistic' drama of the brutalised girl child that I, the mature woman, still carry around with me emotionally. Furthermore, Gish, acting the desired and abused girl, represents the vision I as a 'good girl' had to have of my sexuality: it was there but denied, and I long thought that its destiny was to be possessed.[26]

Broken Blossoms openly teaches that its configuration of male dominance/ female submission is destructively perverse. Do woman viewers who identify strongly with Gish's role sense that *Broken Blossoms* has artistically presented their own problems in such a way that it has brought sexual-political problems to the surface for conscious consideration? I suspect not. As a viewer, pathos has overwhelmed me. When I identify with women on the screen as victims, it is difficult to move away from 'feeling' to a more active, self-aware response.

Even with this caveat, my response to *Broken Blossoms* is ambiguous. I cannot help but admire it. In a visual style fully adequate to expressing the complex interrelationships between romantic striving and male brutishness, the film offers a symbolically complete, although schematised and condensed, representation of masculine options under capitalism. Like most bourgeois, patriarchal narrative art, it provides a social and superego 'cover' for its viewers so that they can immerse themselves in its flow.

Yet here the 'cover' is honourable and exhaustive: high art, anti-racism, anti-child abuse, male idealism and tenderness pitted against brutishness, female pathos and admirable women's screen roles. Below this manifest content, *Broken Blossoms* demystifies the romantic hero as a semi-paralysed pursuer of unattainable ideals. And it creates a daring metaphor – based on incest – to describe the patriarch's possessive role in the nuclear family.

Notes

1. How films assign characters recognisable traits and how connotations are 'readable' in film because they are reinforced in the action and in the narrative development are two topics I deal with extensively in the following articles, where I apply the methodology of Roland Barthes's *S/Z* to film: '*S/Z* and *Rules of the Game*', *Jump Cut* 12–13, Winter 1976–77; 'Teaching the Comparative Analysis of Novels and Films', *Style* 9, Fall 1975.
2. For a discussion of the mechanisms of *condensation* and *displacement* in Hollywood film, see Charles Eckert, 'The Anatomy of a Proletarian Film: Warner's *Marked Woman*', *Film Quarterly* 17, no. 2, Winter 1973–74.
3. Kate Millett's *Sexual Politics* (New York: Avon, 1970) deals precisely with this topic and remains a model of feminist criticism which moves fluidly back and forth from historical to literary analysis.
4. The historical background here comes from Vance Kepley, Jr., 'Griffith's *Broken Blossoms* and the Problem of Historical Specificity', *Quarterly Review of Film Studies* 3, Winter 1978.

5. Ibid, p. 41.
6. Charles Affron, 'The Actress as Metaphor: Gish in *Broken Blossoms*', in *Star Acting* (New York: E. P. Dutton, 1977), p. 12.
7. I use the term 'insane' in the sense of a *system of oppression*. R. D. Laing in *The Politics of the Family* (New York: Random House, 1969) views this systematic oppression from a psychological perspective. Rayna Rapp offers an analysis of the family from a multi-class, social and economic perspective in 'Family and Class in Contemporary America: Notes towards an Understanding of Ideology', *University of Michigan Papers in Women's Studies*, Special Issue, May 1978; and Lillian Breslow Rubin in *Worlds of Pain: Life in the Working-Class Family* (New York: Basic Books, 1976) presents through interviews a poignant and telling analysis of the systematic deformation of emotional life in white working-class families in the United States.
8. The major exception is Marjorie Rosen, whose discussion of 'Griffith's Girls' in *Popcorn Venus* (New York: Avon Books, 1973) inspired me to go back and take another look at Griffith from a feminist point of view.
9. Marjorie Rosen, Gary Gordon, 'The Story of David Wark Griffith' (a biography of Griffith based on interviews), *Photoplay*, June and July 1916, excerpted in Harry Geduld (ed.), *Focus on D. W. Griffith* (New York: Prentice Hall, 1971).
10. Friedrich Engels, *The Origin of the Family, Private Property and the State* (New York: International Publishers, 1967).
11. Kate Millett, *Sexual Politics*, pp. 60–61, citing the work of Hugo Beigel.
12. For a discussion of feminist cinematic treatment of rape, see Lesage, 'Disarming Rape: JoAnn Elam's *Rape*', *Jump Cut* 19, Winter 1978.
13. Susan Brownmiller, *Against Our Will: Men, Women and Rape* (New York: Simon and Schuster, 1975).
14. Some readers may find this conclusion outrageous, so I shall add a few examples from daily life. We have all observed fathers' discomfiture at the thought of their daughters' sexual activity; at the same time male adolescents are excused for 'sowing wild oats'. And with girls of a younger age, when a father yells, 'Wipe that lipstick off your face!' or challenges, 'Where were you so late?' his reaction is a sexually as well as paternally possessive one. It is the sexual connotation of the girl's action that is disturbing to him, and his excuse for his reaction is often that he knows 'how men are'.
15. For a psychoanalytic explanation of the cross-cultural and trans-historical division of male and female roles into the 'public' and the 'domestic' sphere, see Nancy Chodorow, *The Reproduction of Mothering: Psychoanalysis and the Sociology of Gender* (Berkeley: University of California Press, 1978).
16. D. W. Griffith, 'My Early Life', in Geduld, *Focus*, p. 33. That such an act was a lesson in masculinity as well as racism is implied in Griffith's comment that his father winked at the terrified child to assure him all was a joke. What was the black servant feeling? Griffith's inability to ask that question in relating this, his most sacred memory, parallels his inability to depict the real mechanisms of racism in *Broken Blossoms* or *Birth of a Nation*.
17. D. W. Griffith, 'My Early Life', in Geduld, *Focus*, p. 35.
18. Kate Millett traces the close relation between an esteem for virginity and the fear and desire that women provoke as the 'dark force', seen as part of uncontrolled

nature and destructive to male-defined culture. (*Sexual Politics*, pp. 72–82). Thus, a paradigmatic variation to *Broken Blossoms* in the treatment of the nuclear family in fictional film is to depict a dark-haired siren destroying families and individual men and social cohesion.

19. Lillian Gish and Billy Bitzer, in their respective autobiographies, describe the introduction of the Sartov lens; Gish discovered this flattering way of being photographed and promoted it after she first had her passport picture done by Sartov. Lillian Gish (with Ann Pinchot), *The Movies, Mr Griffith, and Me* (New York: Prentice Hall, 1969); G. W. Bitzer, *G. W. Billy Bitzer, His Life* (New York: Farrar, Straus and Giroux, 1973).

20. For a discussion of how *Broken Blossoms* was exploited commercially as high art, see Arthur Lenning, 'D. W. Griffith and the Making of an Unconventional Masterpiece', *Film Journal* 1.

21. Key essays on this subject are Laura Mulvey, 'Visual Pleasure and Narrative Cinema', *Screen* 16 (Fall 1975), and Pam Cook and Claire Johnston, 'The Place of Women in the Cinema of Raoul Walsh', in Phil Hardy (ed.), *Raoul Walsh* (Edinburgh Film Festival, 1974). A discussion among feminist critics that deals extensively with the subject of how women are presented in dominant male cinema and how this affects us as women viewers can be found in 'Women and Film: A Discussion of Feminist Aesthetics', *New German Critique*, 13, Winter 1978.

22. Charles Affron's *Star Acting* provides a good formal analysis of this sequence.

23. For discussions of the adverse effects of presenting woman as victim in a portrait intended to elicit audience sympathy, see my article, 'Disarming Rape' and Charles Kleinhans, 'Seeing through Cinéma-Vérité: *Wanda* and *Marilyn Times Five*', *Jump Cut* 1, May–June 1974.

24. Ellen E. Morgan, 'The Eroticization of Male Dominance/Female Submission', *University of Michigan Papers in Women's Studies* 2, September 1975.

25. Angela Carter, *The Sadeian Woman and the Ideology of Pornography* (New York: Harper and Row, 1978), p. 60.

26. See my extended discussion of *Céline and Julie Go Boating* and that film's relation to female fantasies in 'Subversive Fantasies', *Jump Cut* 23/24, Spring 1981.

A Case of Mistaken Legitimacy

Class and Generational Difference in Three Family Melodramas

RICHARD DE CORDOVA

ALLUSIONS to Freud's work on the family romance have been central to much recent work on film melodrama. Yet, as Griselda Pollock noted in *Screen*'s 'Dossier on Melodrama', there has been both an imprecision in the use of the term and an uncertainty over the sense in which it is applicable to film.[1] In this essay I want to present a brief re-reading of Freud's description of the family romance. My aim is to demonstrate the way the fantasies grouped under this term are taken up – and transformed – by three family melodramas: *Home from the Hill* (Minnelli, 1960), *Splendor in the Grass* (Kazan, 1961) and *Written on the Wind* (Sirk, 1956).

In his 1909 paper, Freud described two distinct stages of the family romance: one asexual and one sexual.[2] In the asexual stage the child imagines itself to be a foundling and by doing so replaces both of its parents with imaginary ones from a higher class. The fantasies of the sexual stage repeat this general ambition, but must be adjusted in accordance with the child's newfound knowledge of sexual diffeence and the details of sexual reproduction. The child no longer attempts to replace *both* of its parents. It learns that its maternity is certain, and must then reinvest the whole of its ambitious fantasies in the question of its paternity, by imagining that it is a bastard and that its true father is a nobleman of some sort. The mother, in this stage, is made into an adultress so that the child, who secretly desires her, can bring her into fantastic 'situations of secret infidelity and into secret love affairs'.[3] In fact, for Freud, this erotic aim of the family romance overrides the ambitious one in importance.

Freud is careful to stress the plurality of these fantasies, their 'many sidedness' and their 'great range of applicability';[4] their specific content may vary according to the needs, experience and ingenuity of the child. There are, however, at least two general features which unite these various fantasies and which therefore underlie and circumscribe the course of the child's imaginative activity. First, all of these fantasies are motivated by a common goal, one of which is stated quite clearly in the opening of Freud's paper:

> The liberation of an individual, as he grows up, from the authority of his
> parents is one of the most necessary though one of the most painful results

brought about by the course of his development. It is quite essential that that liberation should occur, and it may be presumed that it has been to some extent achieved by everyone who has reached a normal state.[5]

For Freud, the family romance, in all of its various manifestations, is to be seen in this context. The fantasies are a means through which the child, in its own mind, may oppose its parents and challenge their position of authority. Activity of this sort is motivated by the child's perception that it has been slighted by its parents and supported by the perception that other parents would be preferable to its own. The child's retaliation through family romance fantasies is part of a more general psychical struggle which will finally, and ideally, result in the successful resolution of the Oedipus complex.

Second, all of these fantasies make use of the same conceit in order to achieve this imaginary liberation. In one way or another, they all turn upon the question of parentage and biological legitimacy. By denying that its parents are in fact its parents the child ingeniously finds a way to disassociate itself from them.

To these two general features we might add a third which is to some extent ignored by Freud. As noted earlier, Freud privileges the erotic implications of the family romance over the ambitious. It is important to note that in doing so, he marshals the class material – which is so prominent in the fantasies he describes – into a schema that gives it virtually no importance. Two different formations can be located in the paper: the first, the Oedipus complex, concerns the articulation of sexual difference and generational difference; the second, an 'other scene' (other to Freud's method itself) articulates class difference and generational difference. It is the former, of course, that ultimately commands Freud's attention. Although he seems, at points, to acknowledge that the concerns of the family romance extend beyond a hermetic familial dynamic, the course of his argument elides this fact.

The opposition between generations in the family romance proceeds quite explicitly through class, however. The child first opposes its parents and disidentifies with them through the knowledge that there is a disjunction between its real parents and the ideal. The ideal, recognised elsewhere, is shifted away from the actual parents to those of a higher class:

> The child's imagination becomes engaged in the task of getting free from the parents of whom he now has a low opinion and of replacing them by others who, as a rule are of a higher social standing. He will make use in this connection of any opportune coincidences from his actual experience, such as his becoming acquainted with the Lord of the Manor or some landed proprietor if he lives in the country or with some member of the aristocracy if he lives in the town.[6]

In Freud class appears simply as a prop for the child's Oedipal desires in these fantasies. But arguably it has its own importance and its own effectivity in determining the psychic interests of the child. What Freud fails to examine sufficiently is the possibility that patterns of idealisation are conditioned to some degree by forces outside of the family. The child's desire to replace its parents with those of a higher class might indeed have something to do with the historical reality of class. But Freud finally disavows the historical implication of this disjunction between the real parents and the ideal and its articulation with factors outside of the family. In the last paragraph of his paper he states, 'the whole effort at replacing the real father with a superior one is only an expression of the child's longing for the happy, vanished days when his father seemed to him the noblest and strongest of men and his mother the dearest and loveliest of women'.[7] In effect, he collapses the 'other scene' of class difference into the machinations of a purely familial drama.

It can be argued that these fantasies were in part a response to two contradictory features of the late nineteenth century. There was increasingly the formal possibility of distinguishing oneself from one's family through upward mobility in the class system. And, at the same time, there were powerful remainders of a feudal caste system in which social position was determined solely by birth. The latter provided the position which functioned as ideal in the fantasies described by Freud. To pursue this as an ideal was, in an odd way, to deny the legitimacy of one's birth.

The family melodrama repeats many of the motifs of the family romance: the problem of legitimacy, the feudal lord, the child reaching puberty, etc. However, it is the articulation of class difference and generational difference that most clearly connects the structure of these fantasies with the films I will discuss. Each of these films works to inscribe an opposition between classes within the dynamics of a familial drama. And each specifically uses the child's desire for liberation from its parents as a way of critiquing the parents' class and positing another order of things as ideal.

In pointing to the similarities between the family romance and the family melodrama I am not arguing that the two are in any way synonymous. Although the articulation of class and generational difference is central to both, the family melodrama mobilises this problematic toward somewhat different ends. As I have noted, the family romance draws upon material that exceeds and contradicts the terms of a purely private drama. The fantasies in fact depend on an uncritical acceptance of an ideal external to the family. Of course, Freud's concern is with the internal workings of the privatised family, and so his analysis finally regards this external class material as a displaced expression of a familial problem. This drastically reduces the significance of the feudal ideal for Freud, but it does not directly question or criticise it. The family melodrama by contrast actively works to disclaim the ideality of the

257

feudal order. It therefore takes a tack quite different from the fantasies themselves. And, although the melodrama, like Freud's analysis, promotes the privatised family it does not do so by retreating from the question of class and restricting itself to the internal dynamics of the family. It confronts class in order to challenge it as a legitimate basis for idealisation. The family melodrama therefore concerns itself more explicitly (though no less deviously) with the placement of the family in broader patterns of social organisation.

Home from the Hill is a particularly good example of the way in which the structure and motifs of the family romance are incorporated into the family melodrama.

The Captain owns 40,000 acres and nearly everything in a nearby town. His authority clearly stems from his position in a feudal order. This order is critiqued by the film largely through the presentation of the Captain as a figure of unyielding excess. He is excessive in part because of his financial exploitation of the townspeople, yet the main term of his conflict with them is symbolised through his sexual excess. The film opens with a man's attempt to kill the Captain for making love to his wife, and throughout the film the discourse on property is articulated with and represented through the realm of the sexual. The Captain owns the men's land. But he also wants 'their' wives. His avariciousness cannot be contained.

The Captain's wife is actually the only viable site of resistance to this exploitation early in the film. She, more than anyone else, is outside of his law, having refused to sleep with him for seventeen years. She tries to keep the son, Theron, away from the Captain's influence, but after some struggle he wrests the boy away from her in order to 'make a man out of him'. The stakes become those of lineage and generational continuity: the father sets out to make the son just like himself.

Theron's trajectory toward manhood is accomplished through the initiatory rite of hunting, an activity which perhaps best crystallises the Captain's exploitative prowess in the film. The trophies he shows Theron are not only possessions but conquests as well, testaments to his domination of all life in the region. Hunting is linked both to his ability to defend his land against all intruders (the wild boar) and, in a more complicated way, to the predatory nature of his sexual desire.

The conflation of sexuality and hunting is most clearly orchestrated through Theron's initiation. After shooting the wild boar Theron collapses breathless, as if his initiation were a sexual one. It is at this point that Theron's identification with his father is consummated. He repeats the Captain's claim to glory (linked with the Captain's claim to the land) by killing the wild boar.

Just after this, Theron becomes interested in Libby, and his more literal sexual trajectory begins. Rafe, the illegitimate son, mediates between the

258

Captain and Theron in educating the latter – both in hunting and women. His mediatory position between father and son is shifted at a certain point in the film, however, and he becomes the term of a conflict between the two. This is effected through motifs of the family romance.

Theron comes home late one night and tells his mother that Libby's father hates him for no apparent reason. The mother says the family name is all Libby's father sees and tells him that Rafe is the Captain's illegitimate son. This knowledge radically alters Theron's position in the narrative in the same way that the child's position is altered through knowledge in Freud's paper on the family romance:

> For a small child his parents are at first the only authority and the source of all belief. The child's most intense and most momentous wish during these early years is to be like his parents (that is, the parent of his own sex) and to be big like his father and mother. But as intellectual growth increases the child cannot help discovering by degrees the category to which his parents belong. He gets to know other parents and compares them to his own.[8]

In this scene Theron finds out precisely the category to which his father belongs. This category explicitly concerns the Captain's sexual exploitativeness but Theron's rebellion against his father is on other grounds as well. Not only does Theron deny the validity of the family and refuse to further the family name; he also quits hunting (until in the end he hunts his father's killer), and gets a working-class job in a cotton mill. Theron's disidentification with his father is a disidentification with him as exploiter.

It is clear that the articulation of class difference and generational difference distinguishes this film from the family romance as Freud described it. In the family romance the real parents cannot live up to the ideal that is situated in the feudal order. In *Home from the Hill* the real parents actually represent the feudal order and the ideal is elsewhere – in the values of the privatised bourgeois family.

The narrative does not allow Theron to reach this ideal, though. Although he attempts to change classes and disintricate himself from his family name, his legitimacy, oddly enough, renders illegitimate his claim to a normal family life. He ends up repeating another of his father's actions – fathering a child without taking responsibility for it.

Home from the Hill is typical of family melodrama in that it opposes an old order and a new order through successive generations. Theron is too closely linked to the old order to constitute a real break with it. Rafe is the figure around which this new order is founded. He is constituted more than any other character as the victim of the Captain's exploitation, both financial and sexual. It is knowledge of his victimisation in fact that causes Theron to oppose his father.

The question this film poses seems to concern the legitimacy of social power. It certainly wrests legitimacy away from any notion of social power based on biology or inheritance, that is, the power of a caste system. The question we must ask here is, 'what does it replace it with?' Rafe's ascendancy has very little to do with power. He just starts a family and everyone else dies or runs away. Everyone of course except Theron's mother. It stands to reason that she would inherit her husband's wealth and power. However, she contents herself with moving into the private world of Rafe's family, literally moving from the family mansion to Rafe's cottage. No mention is made of the fact that she owns 40,000 acres. What we see in this movement from an old order to a new order is in fact an effacement of the problem of social power.

A point should be made here which concerns the significance of references to a feudal order in a film made in America in 1959. One must wonder exactly what was at stake in these references. They do not seem to point explicitly to any aspect of contemporary society of the 1950s and are in fact made only in relation to the two eras of American history in which the vestiges of a feudal order are most apparent. The first is the pre-civil war era of slavery in the South (the Captain owns a colonial style mansion and is involved in the cotton industry) and the second is that of the late nineteenth and early twentieth centuries when robber barons (named in reference to a feudal order) exploited thousands through an unchecked industrial capitalism in order to amass enormous fortunes. The great families of American finance arose from this era: Rockefeller, Morgan, etc.

Why are these two eras mobilised in the 1950s and for what ideological ends? This appeal to history can be seen as a displacement of sorts. Symbolising social power in an archaic form (instead of in a contemporary form) allows the film to efface it more convincingly.

The feudal order is not a mere straw man the narrative posits, however. It should be seen in terms of its function in symbolising what is perhaps the central opposition in these films – that between the public sphere and the private. It is indeed in this context that we can best understand the significance of the references to feudalism.

The privatised bourgeois family is only presented as ideal in these films over and against a more public one, one symbolised through the feudal order. All of the Captain's excesses can be attributed to his intrusion into the public sphere. His family's power (all power in these films in fact) is by definition public. We have seen that in the family romance the distinction between public and private guides the child's recognition of class difference. She must be outside of the private confines of the family to recognise it. In the Oedipal scenario, which is explicitly a description of the dynamics of the privatised family, the phallus articulates sexual difference and generational difference (the latter through the prohibition of incest). The 'other scene' implicit in

Freud's paper, however, is precisely what is *exhibited* in the Captain's family. The Captain, as phallus, articulates not only sexual and generational difference but class difference as well. Theron can oppose his father only through this articulation; so in protesting his father's exploitation he only becomes exploited – a member of the working class. This is why Rafe's position in the narrative is so crucial. He can be extricated from the binary articulated by the Captain and come to represent a third position exterior to it through the opposition public/private. The privatised family Rafe sets up has nothing to do with class difference, which, like social power, is a matter of the public sphere. Thus, we can see in this film an attempt to constitute an ideal family which, in its privatised self-containment, is mythically outside of all social determination.

Splendor in the Grass is very similar to *Home from the Hill* both in its articulation of generational difference and class difference and in its constitution of a privatised family. Bud's father is associated with a feudal order in much the same way the Captain is. He is an oil tycoon in Kansas in the 1920s, and the whole town is clearly dependent upon him for its livelihood. The activity of his stock seems to be the major concern throughout the community.

The father's major concern, however, is that his son, Bud, develop into a man fit to continue the family name. In short, he wants Bud to identify with his position. This would normally be accomplished through the successful resolution of the Oedipus complex; but the public nature of Bud's family makes this highly problematic since any resolution offered by the film would be across class lines. There are, after all, no women of Bud's class in the film except for his sister and mother. Bud just wants to marry Deanie, move outside of town and start a bourgeois family. His father has more ambitious goals for him.

Here we see a clear case of class conflict articulated through generational difference. However, Bud, unlike Theron, never takes an oppositional stance toward his father. Instead he internalises the conflict through the problem of teenage sexuality. Sexuality is in fact the means through which class boundaries can be crossed. Bud's sister, Jeanie, has opposed her father precisely on these grounds, making love to an array of lower-class men. Her position in the film is extreme in that she is concerned neither about her father's approval nor the bourgeois norm.

Jeanie's sexuality is excessive because of her activity: Bud's is excessive because it is frustrated. He is in a double bind of sorts – between his father's authority which calls for marriage within one's class and the bourgeois order which forbids sex before marriage. The father prevents Bud from marrying Deanie through his plans to send him off to college for four years. Since Bud cannot marry Deanie, he cannot have sex with her. His ever intensifying sexual frustration prompts him to quit seeing her. As his frustration grows he becomes ill, and, after collapsing on the basketball court, he is hospitalised. The hyperbolic nature of Bud's desire (and his attempts to control it) points to a certain problem the film has in splitting apart the ideal couple and, moreover, in representing Bud's internalisation of his father's law. A certain logic would have ended the film halfway with Bud defying his father and marrying Deanie. The father, however, is somehow successful in turning Bud completely away from his (Bud's) desire.

In both *Splendor in the Grass* and *Home from the Hill* the father indirectly interferes with the successful resolution of the Oedipus complex, and the son begins to ignore his 'natural' mate. In the latter film Theron, after realising his father's 'category', shuns the very idea of the family and thus quits seeing Libby. In *Splendor in the Grass* Bud turns away from Deanie, and, following his father's suggestion, takes up with 'another kind of girl' (Juanita) who, except for her parentage, is a near double of his sister Jeanie. Then he goes off to college and starts drinking heavily. As if protesting his own helplessness in the face of his father's authority, he succumbs to the decadence and excess that distinguish his family from the bourgeois norm.

To this point there has been little discussion of Deanie's position in the narrative. It can be said that the first part of the film focuses primarily on Bud's subjectivity and the problems he has with the double bind described above. The film divides around one scene. Deanie is at school the day after Bud and Juanita have been out parking. The kids in her class are snickering behind her back (very loudly) about Bud and Juanita's 'romance'. The teacher makes Deanie read the poem 'Splendor in the Grass' out loud. After reading it she becomes hysterical and must be taken to the nurse's office. Two points suggest the way this scene appears as a break in the film. First, it is clear that the public nature of Bud and Juanita's sexual relationship (everybody knows about it) appears in contrast to and as a renunciation of the trajectory of Bud and Deanie's relationship, which was toward the ideal, private realm of the bourgeois family. Secondly, in this scene we see a veritable explosion of Deanie's subjectivity into the forefront of the film. Her psychology becomes the object of the film through a medical discourse.

Deanie, who has been a model daughter, becomes a problem within her own family and begins to act in excess of the bourgeois norm. She tries to become like Juanita and Jeanie, offering herself to Bud, but he refuses, calling her a 'nice girl'. Her problems with him seem irresolvable; she becomes hysterical and runs onto the waterfalls, apparently in an attempt to commit suicide.

The rest of the film is about Deanie's cure except for a couple of scenes depicting Bud's degenerate life at Yale and – important for this analysis – one other scene in which Bud's father commits suicide after the stock market Crash of 1929. What is significant about this is the way that history must erupt in order for the narrative to be resolved. In all of these films it takes something of a *deus ex machina* to eliminate the feudal father, but *Splendor in the Grass* is an extreme case of this. Nothing within the fiction previously presented could plausibly kill him since his power has been unopposed throughout the film. There does not seem to be anything wrong with his health, but his death is necessary if Bud is going to extricate himself from the stifling law imposed upon him. The reference to the Crash is perfect since it resolves in a single blow the central project of the film – the articulation of class difference and generational difference. Bud is not only rid of his father; he is also automatically of a different class since his father loses practically everything in the Crash.

The prostitute arranged for Bud by his father before committing suicide very economically reiterates and recirculates the terms of Bud's conflict. The father publicly procures the woman with money as a substitute for Deanie. When Bud walks out of the cabaret he actively resists his father for the first time in the film. It is important to note, however, how little emphasis is placed on Bud's subjectivity in the later scenes. When his father dies we get no clue to Bud's feelings. His subjectivity is in fact pushed into the background in the latter half of the film. It is not until the final scene, the couple's 'reunion', that we once again get a strong sense of Bud's point of view, which at this point appears in a symmetrical relation with that of Deanie – primarily through a series of shot/reverse shots. The film actually achieves its closure through Deanie's voice-over, but the lines she quotes (from 'Splendor in the Grass') appear to represent not only her feelings but Bud's as well:

No, nothing will bring back the hour of splendor in the grass,
glory in the flower; we will grieve not
Rather, find strength in what remains behind.

Both Bud and Deanie have succeeded in entering into privatised families, though it is clear that the ideal the film posits is the couple in the past that was never formed – Bud and Deanie. Although the end of the film may suggest that chance or fate was responsible, it is clear that Bud's father, with his associations with a feudal order, prevented the realisation of this ideal. The last half of the film traces the tragedy caused by this interference.

Bud and Deanie complete a movement from public to private in quite different ways. For Bud, the feudal order in which he was born constituted the public sphere. For Deanie, it was a public institution, a mental hospital. The respective value placed on these two spheres is worth noting. The feudal order is definitely presented as destructive; the mental hospital, however, is associated with much more positive values, providing Deanie help when she could no longer find solace in her family. Finally, she is cured and can be reintegrated into a normal family situation. We noted that in *Home from the*

Hill everything public that hinted at a social power outside the family was effaced in favour of a completely self-contained privatised family. In *Splendor in the Grass* a public power is represented and valorised in the mental hospital. The goal of these institutions of course is to cure people and thus re-establish them in the privatised family. *The Cobweb* might be mentioned in this regard since its resolution consists precisely of the establishment of the family outside of the public institution. The father, the mother and the wayward son (a patient) end up huddled around the family sofa.

Written on the Wind emphasises the problem of legitimacy in articulating class and generational difference and works to problematise any notion of legitimacy based upon biology. Legitimacy is no longer linked with biology but rather with a specific ideology or value system. Here we see two forms for the reproduction of the conditions of production in conflict. The first, the caste system, reproduces the structure of social power through an appeal to birthright. Inheritance is the means through which power (and property) is passed on and therefore perpetuated. The film is about the deterioration of this form and its potential supplantation by another form – that of the bourgeois family. This is the form the film legitimises.

It is clear from very early in the film that this feudal order is not in fact in order. The father presides without opposition, but his legitimate children, Kyle and Mary Lee, hardly seem capable of ever assuming his position. They point to the decay and dissolution of their father's class. Kyle refers to himself and his sister as two of the three black sheep of the family.

Mitch and Lucy are model children but unfortunately for the father they are not his children. Mitch helps run the family oil business and is the only person (says Kyle) who can fill the father's shoes. The father tries to get Mitch to marry Mary Lee to make him a 'legitimate' member of the family, but Mitch replies that she is too much like a sister to him. The five characters make up a family of sorts, but the film makes distinctions between the children in terms of legitimacy. Biologically these distinctions can be charted like this:

LEGITIMATE	ILLEGITIMATE
Kyle	Mitch
Mary Lee	Lucy

And 'ideologically' like this:

LEGITIMATE	ILLEGITIMATE
Mitch	Kyle
Lucy	Mary Lee

264

There is a conflict between these two versions of legitimacy throughout the film. The first represents what could be called the law of the feudal order; the second is the 'natural' law of bourgeois value. This 'flip-flop' structure, in which a character is both legitimate and illegitimate according to the different systems operative in the film, is further complicated by two factors: the articulation of class difference and patterns of coupling.

Kyle and Mary Lee's biological legitimacy is given in the film, but the boundaries of their class identity are constantly giving way as they 'step out' of their class and associate with the milieu of the workers. Both frequent a working-class bar. Kyle goes there to buy liquor, and Mary Lee goes there (and elsewhere) to satisfy her sexual desire. Her position in the film is very much like that of Jeanie in *Splendor in the Grass*. Both films represent the decadence of the feudal order by linking it in some way with the working class. It is as if class is figured on a continuum which goes full circle, allowing lower and upper class to meet as two extremes and thus casting the bourgeois order as the ideal middle ground.

Mitch's class status is left completely ambiguous in the film. Perhaps his origins are in the lower classes, but the only real clue we get (the scene with *his* father) seems to indicate that he does not have a class origin but rather comes from nature itself. If Mitch is from the lower class it is certain that he has no class consciousness. When Mary Lee chases lower-class men, Mitch follows to uphold the father's law and separate these ill-formed couples. In this respect, he fulfils the same function as the police, who enforce a law that keeps Mary Lee away from a gas station attendant.

Although Mitch enforces the father's law, he does not fall under it. He belongs neither to the working class nor, for that matter, to the feudal order. Mitch's class status is completely effaced in the film, which is to say (in the logic the film offers) that he is bourgeois – a third position the film offers that is outside of the public sphere that articulates class difference.

Almost from the beginning of the film it is clear which couples are the most ideologically compatible: Mitch and Lucy on the side of biological illegitimacy, and Kyle and Mary Lee on the side of biological legitimacy. However, the coupling in the film crosses the sides, as it were (necessarily if it is to honour the prohibition of incest). The following chart makes the terms of this coupling clear.

There is a narrative because the 'wrong' couple is formed early in the film. Kyle marries Lucy, leaving Mary Lee for Mitch. Mitch holds out, however, saying Mary Lee is just like a sister to him. (This is an odd twist on the family romance. Freud says the male child can make one of his sisters illegitimate if he finds himself sexually attracted to her. Here we see Mitch making Mary Lee his legitimate sister in order to avoid sexual relations with her.) Mitch finally declares his love for Lucy, and this indirectly leads to Kyle's death. Although coupling mixes the two sides of the previous charts, the film's resolution straightens them back out, allowing the ideologically legitimate couple, Lucy and Mitch, to leave the feudal world that had trapped them.

The events which lead to this resolution are heavily overdetermined by questions of legitimacy and generational continuity. First, Kyle finds out from the doctor that he has a 'weak' sperm count. Kyle and Lucy had been living a happy, normal life before this. This knowledge makes Kyle crazy; he goes out and gets drunk (after a long period of abstinence), tortured by his assumed inability to continue the family name by having a child.

The father's death, which immediately follows this, is predicated upon two occurrences. Kyle is brought home drunk, and Mary Lee is caught by the police with a gas station attendant. The father declares himself a failure and dies. His failure is that he failed to produce a child who could unproblematically assume his position in the feudal order. Apparently Kyle has inherited the same failing. The feudal order is becoming more and more impotent in its ability to reproduce the basis of its rule.

It is ironic but perhaps appropriate that Kyle accidentally kills his baby, thinking it is illegitimate. It *is* illegitimate in terms of the ideological position of the film in that it is not Mitch and Lucy's baby. It is the baby's class identity that is at issue here. Will the next generation spring from a feudal order or a bourgeois family? Kyle's paranoia leads him to assume the latter and his actions practically assure its inevitability.

In the opening of his paper on the family romance Freud asserts that 'the whole progress of society rests upon the opposition between successive generations.'[9] The fantasies that he goes on to describe are thus placed in a rather grandiose context – as a preliminary means for the child to conceive this opposition. The question of the *kind* of progress that might one day proceed from this opposition in fantasy is not addressed by Freud. But in the fantasies he describes the opposition (and, for that matter, the progress imagined) is clearly one of class.

Each of the films I have discussed takes up the structure and motifs of the family romance. And each represents a progress, one effected across class lines in the transition from one generation to the next. An old order, with its links to a feudal past, is replaced by a new order, the bourgeois family. These two orders are not placed in direct conflict in such a way that the transition between them could be considered a revolution, however. The conflict is instead located in the old order itself, in a familial drama which must, because of its feudal underpinnings, display the tensions and contradictions of class difference. The bourgeois family is finally separated from this conflict and presented as a private alternative to the more public spectacle of class difference. This work of privatisation as a form of resolution is astonishingly clear in the last shots of all of these films. In all, the heroes walk or drive away from the public scenes of the spectacle and disappear from the fiction into their own little worlds, as if escaping from the worst of dreams.

Notes

1. Griselda Pollock, 'Report on the Weekend School', *Screen*, vol. 18, no. 2, Summer 1977, pp. 105–13.
2. Sigmund Freud, 'Family Romances', *Standard Edition*, vol. 9, pp. 235–41.
3. Ibid., p. 239.
4. Ibid., p. 240.
5. Ibid., p. 237.
6. Ibid., pp. 238–9.
7. Ibid., p. 241.
8. Ibid., p. 237.
9. Ibid., p. 237.

Madness, Authority and Ideology

The Domestic Melodrama of the 1950s

DAVID N. RODOWICK

From *The Velvet Light Trap*, no. 19, 1982, pp. 40–45.

THE DIFFICULTY with submitting the term melodrama to a conclusive, critical definition is that it is such a historically complex phenomenon. Moreover, this problem is complicated by the apparent ease with which it is possible to point out melodramatic situations and conventions in a wide variety of dramatic and literary media of different historical and cultural situations.

The development of a melodramatic tradition would seem to coincide, in fact, with the evolution of many popular narrative forms, including that of the cinema. Without doubt, the early development of the American narrative film was determined in part by its internalisation of a melodramatic tradition, inherited from the nineteenth-century novel and theatre, which was already characterised by considerable formal and stylistic diversity. The problem of melodramatic 'specificity' was then further complicated through its incorporation by a new narrative form which, in its turn, blossomed into a variety of styles and genres; Warner's social melodramas, Capra's 'populist' melodramas, the domestic or family melodrama, and so on were themselves engaged in patterns of cross-fertilisation. Thus, even well-defined genres like the western and gangster film[1] were heavily determined by their melodramatic content.

In this manner, Thomas Elsaesser discusses melodrama not as a distinct genre, but 'as a form which carried its own significant content: it served as the literary equivalent of a particular, historically and socially conditioned *mode of experience*,'[2] which, as he points out, was endemic to the history of the bourgeoisie as a social class. He then continues by saying that 'even if the situations and sentiments defied all categories of verisimilitude and were totally unlike anything in real life, the structure had a truth and a life of its own ...' In this respect, melodrama might best be understood as an aesthetic ideology which, in accordance with a historically specific complex of social, cultural and economic determinations, 'enables a series of possible forms and disables others.'[3] As such, it is a structure of signification which may reproduce itself within a variety of narrative forms (or indeed, create new forms) by organising the historically available series of discourses, representations, concepts, values, etc., which constitute the dominant ideology, into a system of conflict, which, in its turn, produces the fictive logic of particular texts.

Perhaps this can be clarified by addressing a historically specific form of melodrama – the domestic or family melodrama of the 1950s. According to Geoffrey Nowell-Smith[4] the domestic melodrama may be understood as the conjunction of three sets of determinations, which I would like to revise and expand in the course of this article. They are: 1) a set of social determinations (which restricts the representation of the social relations of production to the sphere of influence of the bourgeois family); 2) a set of psychic determinations (which concerns the problem of individual identity within the represented set of social relations), and 3) a formal history. It is necessary to understand that these determinations are themselves the products of more general ideological formulations whose internalisation by the melodramatic text may promote varying degrees of difficulty in its narrative structure. In this manner, a particular aesthetic ideology (in this case the domestic melodrama) is produced which confronts the organisation and enunciation of its principal sets of determinations as a problematic to which it must find an aesthetic 'solution'. As Terry Eagleton notes:

> It is important to grasp here the closeness of relation between the 'ideological' and the 'aesthetic'. The text does not merely 'take' ideological conflicts in order to resolve them aesthetically, for the character of those conflicts is itself overdetermined by the textual modes in which they are produced. The text's mode of resolving a particular ideological conflict may then produce textual conflicts elsewhere – at other levels of the text for example – which need in turn to be 'processed' (*Criticism and Ideology*, p. 88).

Thus, it is also essential to recognise that the relationships formed among the sets of determinations are not necessarily symmetrical. They may develop unevenly with respect to one another in their particular advancement of the narrative through the statement and (partial) resolution of dramatic conflict. And rather than mutually reinforcing one another, the narrative relations accruing between the social, psychic, and formal determinations are equally predisposed towards developing internal incoherencies within the system of the melodramatic text. In a given film, these determinants will therefore have their own internal complexity and 'a series of internally and mutually conflictual relations may exist between them' (Eagleton, p. 61). As critic Pierre Macherey has noted,[5] such relations may introduce elements of structural dissonance within the text which are visible in its failures of signification.

These dissonances are not, however, the reflection of ideology (which, in any case, will admit no contradictions to itself), but they can be read in the structure of its effects in the text: its discontinuities, abjurations, equivocations; in sum, its 'eloquent silences'. Thus there is a lack of fit between ideology and the textual modes in which it is worked, a distance between the 'aesthetic' solution and the determinate condition which ideology has placed on the articulation of the problem.

Therefore, what ideology cannot admit appears as contradiction within the work of the text, and what the text cannot resolve it must displace and attempt to work out at another level or within another problematic. It is precisely the structure of these displacements within the melodramatic text, and the system of textual silences in which they are dispatched, which interest this analysis.

1.1 Social Determinations

In the domestic melodrama this set of determinations concerns itself with a representation of the social relations of production in which the institutions of family and marriage, as well as the iconography of the middle-class home, are privileged 'contents'. This does not mean that other institutions (for example, the law, medicine, education, etc.) are excluded from representation; however, it is significant that institutional authority, and its function in the represented social formation, is depicted only to the degree that it reproduces familial politics.

But notice the curious paradox which takes form here: although the family tries to substitute itself, *pars pro toto*, for the global network of authority in which it is implicated, it also imagines itself as a world divested of significant social power addressing itself to an audience which does not believe itself to be possessed of social power.[6] The domestic melodrama is attentive only to problems which concern the family's internal security and economy, and therefore considers its authority to be restricted to issues of private power and patriarchal right. The power it reserves for itself is limited to rights of inheritance and the legitimation of the social and sexual identities in which it reproduces its own network of authority. The right of inheritance, then, may be enlarged to describe the social values and norms valorised by an ideology which produces the family as 'a microcosm containing within itself all of the patterns of dominance and submission that are characteristic of the larger society ...' or 'a legitimising metaphor for a hierarchical and authoritarian society'.[7]

1.2 Psychic Determinations

'In all institutions, something of the individual gets lost.' This line of dialogue from *The Cobweb* perfectly expresses the central crisis of the domestic melodrama where individual identity is defined as a problem to the extent that it is out of sync with the relations of authority which are required to legitimate it. As Geoffrey Nowell-Smith explains:

> What is at stake (also for social-ideological reasons) is the survival of the family unit and the possibility of individuals acquiring an identity which is also a place within the system, a place in which they can both be 'themselves' and 'at home', in which they can simultaneously enter, without contradiction, the symbolic order and bourgeois society. It is a condition of the drama that the attainment of such a place is not easy and does not happen without sacrifice, but it is very rare for it to be seen as radically impossible. ('Minnelli and Melodrama', p. 73 of this anthology.)

It is in this process that the sets of social and psychic determinations are crucially linked.

In this intersection of the two sets of determinations, the social and the psychic, the figuration of patriarchal authority plays a central role. The figuration of patriarchal authority need not be characterised by a single character (although this is often the case); rather it defines the centre of a complex network of social relations. Thus, in a film like *Magnificent Obsession*, the symbolisation of patriarchal authority can be played out across a purely imaginary figure (the saintly Dr Phillips, whose death causes a deep structural wound in the social–ideological fabric of the text which can only be repaired by gradually moulding the character of Bob Merrick to fill his place in the social economy of the narrative), or indeed this function can be split, distributed across a number of characters as in *The Cobweb*.

It is in this manner that institutional and familial authority are condensed in the figuration of patriarchal power as an overdetermined instance in the representation of social power *per se*. As the lynch-pin on which narrative conflict must turn, the problem of familial authority and stability therefore establishes a frame of reference against which the logic and the order of the representations of social relations are measured. Thus, the figuration of patriarchal authority in a given text will formulate the terms of conflict through the perpetuation of a series of symbolic divisions and oppositions which organise the narrative around the problem of individual identity, both social and sexual. Moreover, it is interesting to note that the domestic melodrama demands that, in the last instance, sexual identity be determined by social identity. In this manner, the family both legitimises and conceals sexuality by restricting it to a social economy defined by marriage – men assume the place of their fathers in the network of authority, and women are mirrored in this network by their relationship to men as wives, mothers, daughters, etc.

The form which the problem of identity takes is one of the crucial, defining characteristics of the domestic melodrama. The forward thrust of narrative is not accomplished through external conflict and the accumulation of significant actions, but rather through the internalisation of conflict in a crisis of identification: the difficulty which individual characters find in their attempts to accept or conform to the set of symbolic positions around which the network of social relations adhere and where they can both 'be "themselves" and "at home" '. And here I must emphasise the word 'difficulty', for although the domestic melodrama rarely acknowledges the *impossibility* of this identification (as Nowell-Smith points out), it may readily concede its *failure*. The signs of this failure are given form in the dissatisfaction and sexual *angst* so common in the melodramatic protagonist as well as the unpredictable outbreaks of violence which are given an expressly psychological tone: from impotence to hysteria and from alcoholic depression to full-blown psychoses, the domestic melodrama runs the full gamut of psychological disorders.

The conditions of this failure are already apparent in an ideology which considers desire to be a fundamental danger to successful socialisation and thus requires the division of sexuality from sociality. This problem is especially crucial in the representation of women who, split between the passive, suffering heroine and the turbulent sexual rebels are identified in the relations of patriarchal authority only by their systematic exclusion. The terms of this exclusion refer of course to the assumed right of patriarchal authority to confer social and sexual identity. As opposed to the male characters, whose conflicts devolve from the difficulty of attaining an active sexual identity in which patriarchal power can be confirmed and reproduced, the conflict of the women stems from the difficulty of subjugating and channeling feminine sexuality according to the passive functions which patriarchy has defined for it; that is, heterosexual monogamy and maternity. In this manner, feminine sexuality is always in excess of the social system which seeks to contain it. One need only think of the scene in *Written on the Wind* where Dorothy Malone's wild dance is cross-cut with her father's death, to comprehend that the domestic melodrama can only understand sexuality as a kind of violence and a threat to narrative stability.

It is significant here that the melodramatic text forces the equation of sexuality with violence, for the greater the repression of desire in the narrative the greater the energy of its displacement as violence against the textual system. Unlike more action-oriented, outward-directed genres, whose narrative structures may contain and evenly distribute excesses of violence and sexuality across a closely regulated system of conflict, the melodrama is better characterised as a centripetal form which directs these forces inward. Or more precisely, the expression of violence would seem to be regulated only by an economy of masochism which often gives the narratives a suicidal thrust, channeling the expression of sexuality as a violence against the text in a manner which maximises the potential for disruption and incoherency. In this manner, the melodramatic text is balanced on the edge of two extremes, one of which is inertial (the paralysis of the system, its resistance to change or any form of external development) and the other of which is entropic (where action is expressed only as an irrational and undirected surplus energy).

The inability to resolve these two extremes — that is, to find a way to compromise the inertia of the law (the social system defined by patriarchal authority) and the restlessness of desire within the individual characters — constituted a real crisis of representation for the domestic melodrama. In other words, the domestic melodrama was required to build concrete, cinematic narrative structures out of a highly internalised and introverted system of conflict which would also rationally account for the *failing* of this system. The solution of the genre was the incorporation of the discourse of popular Freudianism[8] and the tendency to organise its patterns of conflict in rather self-conscious Oedipal terms. Thus, even melodramas which did not explicitly refer to psychological subjects seemed to demand this interpretation by several criteria: 1) the refusal to understand the economy of the social formation in anything but familial, personal, and sexual terms; 2) the definition of conflict as a struggle with patriarchal authority; 3) the tendency to describe in psychological terms the difficulty of identifying oneself in the social network founded in patriarchal authority. This solution had two distinct advantages. First, it provided a means for naturalising the often irrational and unpredictable behaviours of the melodramatic protagonists. But secondly, and most importantly, it produced a frame of reference which could satisfy, but only in an ambiguous way, the domestic melodrama's contradictory formulations of the problem of sexual identity.

Thus, on one hand, the adoption of a self-conscious Oedipal structure established a predetermined symbolic path in which the resolution of the conflict was measured against a successful identification with authority. In this scenario, patriarchal authority could automatically represent itself in the network of social relations as a self-producing, and thus ahistorical category. That this path was mined with contradictions, I have already explained. However, even in those moments when the narrative systems produced by this scenario of identification were on the point of collapse, the Oedipal structure was ready to consider itself reflexively as a hermeneutic system which could produce a rational explanation for the objective signs of its own failure.

In summary, even though the incorporation of the Oedipal scenario enabled the domestic melodrama to establish a concrete form of narrative organisation, this scenario still reproduced, within its own structural relations, the central contradiction of the genre — the impossibility of an individual reconciliation of the law and desire. This structure could thus resolve itself either on the symbolic level (acceptance of authority) or on the hermeneutic level (which accepted madness and usually self-destruction), but not both. In a moment, I will attempt to explain the historical conditions which led to this stalemate.

1.3 Formal Determinations

It is necessary to understand that structurally and stylistically the domestic melodrama is a product of a history of forms – a confluence of narrative codes and conventions – some of which are cinematically specific, some non-specific. As I have already pointed out, the narrative structure of the domestic melodrama was at least partially determined by a number of non-specific conventions (with which, one might add, it was also historically non-synchronous) through its internalisation of a nineteenth-century narrative tradition.[9] At the same time, of course, the development of the domestic melodrama was determined more directly by a history of cinematically specific forms and styles in which the film melodrama had already concretised a network of influences drawn from diverse styles of composition, lighting, and editing, etc., as well as conventionalised forms of cinematic narrative structure.

Briefly, I would like to examine some points of form which characterised (more or less specifically) the domestic melodrama of the 1950s. As Thomas Elsaesser explains, the domestic melodrama was

> ... perhaps the most highly elaborated, complex mode of cinematic signification that the American cinema has ever produced, because of the restricted scope for external action determined by the subject, and because everything, as Sirk said, happens 'inside'. To the 'sublimation' of the action picture and the ... musical into domestic and family melodrama corresponded a sublimation of dramatic conflict into decor, colour, gesture and composition of frame, which in the best melodramas is perfectly thematised in terms of the characters' emotional and psychological predicaments. ('Tales of Sound and Fury', p. 52 of this anthology.)

It should be understood here that the highly expressive *mise en scène* of the domestic melodrama did not so much *reproduce* as *produce* the inner turmoil of the characters; or in other words, the dynamic relations of the *mise en scène* took over the objective signification of the social network which entrapped the characters and strictly determined their range of physical and emotional mobility. This is emphasised, Elsaesser continues,

> by the function of the decor and the symbolisation of objects: the setting of the family melodrama almost by definition is the middle-class home, filled with objects, which ... surround the heroine [or hero] in a hierarchy of apparent order that becomes increasingly suffocating ... [it] also

274

brings out the characteristic attempt of the bourgeois household to make time stand still, immobilise life and fix forever domestic property relations as the model of social life and a bulwark against the more disturbing sides of human nature. (pp. 61–2.)

Here, one might also point out the extreme compartmentalisation of the frame common to the domestic melodrama in which the decor of the home (via window and door frames, mirrors, partitions, grille-work, etc.) is used to isolate the characters architecturally and emphasise the lack of human contact in their home environment.

The isolation of the characters is also expressed in the organisation of point of view and in the more global orchestrations of narrative structure. It is in this manner that the domestic melodrama thrives on the multiplication of silences, alibis, and misunderstandings generated in the characters' incomplete comprehension of the melodramatic situations in which they are implicated, or the degrees to which their actions (or lack of action) tend to further complicate those situations. Thus, narrative devices such as alternating montage (as in *The Cobweb*) or flashback structures (as in *Written on the Wind*) tended to introduce an ironic distance between character point of view and the narrative voice of the film which underlined not only the power and complexity of the represented social network, but also the absence of any possibility of self-determination within that network.

It should be clear, then, that the domestic melodrama tended to reproduce in its formal economy the drama of inertia and entropy in which the social and psychic determinations collided. Thus, on one hand the reification of the bourgeois universe was reproduced in the compositional space through the compartmentalised frame and the proliferation of a world of objects which defined the characters only in their isolation. On the other hand, the mobility of the syntagmatic relations, and the ironic point of view they provided, were able to cumulatively give form to the progressive disorder which individual characters could unknowingly introduce into the narrative system.

2 History and Ideology: The Ambiguity of Domestic Melodrama

In 'Tales of Sound and Fury', Thomas Elsaesser points out that the popularity of melodrama often coincides with periods of intense social or ideological crises, and that relative to the given historical context, melodrama could function either subversively or as escapist entertainment according to ideological necessity. Thus, in the period where the bourgeoisie was still a revolutionary class, the melodrama served a subversive function, but later,

with the bourgeoisie triumphant, this form of drama lost its subversive charge and functioned more as a means of consolidating an as yet weak and incoherent ideological position. Whereas the pre-revolutionary

275

melodramas had often ended tragically, those of the Restoration had happy endings, they reconciled the suffering individual to his social position by affirming an 'open' society where everything was possible. (p. 46)

In either case, an extreme polarisation of values remained constant (e.g., good vs. evil, virtue vs. corruption, heroism vs. villainy, etc.), and despite a variety of situations and predicaments, the structure of conflict was essentially the same, preserving the moral order from a largely external threat. Both cases were also concerned with the representation of the bourgeois family as the means through which the structure of patriarchal authority could be reproduced and reconfirmed. In this manner, the nature of the conflict and the conditions of its resolution relied on either the enforced separation of families or the resistance to their formation as prompted by an immoral force; but in either instance, the natural 'right' of bourgeois authority and values ultimately went unchallenged. Thus, when the melodrama functioned 'subversively' it was because its class interests were being challenged by an enemy (the aristocracy) which resisted its historical destiny.[10]

What isolates the domestic melodrama of the 1950s from this historical tradition is its inability to fully internalise either of these two functions. In other words, it contained within itself two contradictory demands – one determined by a history of conventions which required an 'affirmative' resolution, the other the product of an anxiety that post-war promises of economic expansion, social mobility, and political stability were incapable of being fulfilled. On the one hand, the affirmative tendency seems to have been restricted to the conventional 'happy end', though as Douglas Sirk described, it could often be only an ironic appurtenance included at the demands of the studio heads.[11] On the other hand, the structure of conflict common to the domestic melodrama was produced *internally* by contradictory forces which challenged the bourgeois family and patriarchal authority from within. Therefore, the domestic melodrama could only lapse into an ironic form because it lacked several traditional criteria for arriving at the narrative 'solution' demanded of it: faith in the power of self-determination and the ability to transform society through individual action, a structure of conflict built on a system of black and white values, and a transcendental faith that identification with the law (patriarchal authority) pre-determined the outcome of conflict through a moral destiny.

Here I can only suggest a highly schematic outline of the historical conditions which produced this phenomenon: though risking oversimplification, I would tend to characterise it as the failure of the general ideology (in Eagleton's terms) of the post-war period to insure social normalisation and the orderly transition to a peace-time economy. In this context, the necessity of redefining and re-establishing the place of the individual in the social formation became crucial.[12] This was initially confined to the reintegration of men into the labour force, and thus the restoration of women to the home. This re-establishment of social identities was effected in the promise that, through the sacrifice of the war effort, the restoration of 'democratic capitalism' and a free enterprise system would reinstate the possibilities of economic and social mobility. However, the ideals that one's future could be self-determined and that prosperity was assured through individual labour and adherence to the system, were largely contradicted by the aggressive expansion of corporate capitalism along with a burgeoning system of bureaucracy. It soon became clear that social identity was not determined through individual effort, but by one's place in a monolithic and hierarchic network of authority in which the range and power of individual action were highly restricted.

A second area involved a changing perception of the nature of potential threats to a political and ideological stability. The threat of nuclear annihilation had tempered somewhat the possibility of direct, armed confrontation, and therefore the Cold War was conceived mostly as a conflict of ideologies with 'domestic' stability at stake. Moreover, there was an increasing paranoid fear that the next threat to society would come from within through the internal subversion of democratic ideologies (witness, for example, the power of the Red Scare and the scale of its effects on the entertainment industry). In addition, the relative affluence of the Eisenhower era, and the steady growth of a commodity culture, paradoxically contradicted this vision of internal instability – one began to wonder if economic stability really did guarantee social stability.

Thus, what characterises the aesthetic ideology (that is, the domestic melodrama) is the absence of any reflection on the terms of the general ideology which has placed a determinate condition on its production. Of course, this is perfectly consistent with the demands of the melodramatic imagination which, as Althusser points out, can only be dialectical as long as it ignores the real conditions which subtend it by barricading itself within its own myth.[13]

Similarly, in order to understand the historical specificity of the domestic melodrama, it is necessary to avoid the position of a vulgar empiricism which would posit a direct and spontaneous relation between aesthetic texts and the historical/ideological situations in which they are produced. Rather, as Fredric Jameson explains, history finds form in the text as an 'absent cause'.[14] It is the 'political unconscious' of the text, and similar to the irruption of the unconscious in parapraxes and other 'mistakes' in language, it is only legible in the structure of its effects: the detours, abjurations, and gaps of narrative logic. Therefore, it is precisely by virtue of the distance between the historical demands of the general ideology of post-war American society and the impossibility of their fulfilment according to the logic of melodramatic conventions that we can trace the specificity of the domestic melodrama by mapping out the network of resistances in which its narratives fail. At the very centre of this network is the figuration of patriarchal authority which serves paradoxically to give form to the contradictions and anxieties of the prevailing general ideology of the 1950s precisely by ignoring their historically given forms and sources. It is in this manner that the domestic melodrama, as a specific aesthetic ideology, barricades itself within an already eroding myth of a society founded on the centrality of the family and patriarchal power.

Thus, where the melodramatic Father formerly functioned to legitimate the system of conflict and guarantee its resolution by successfully identifying its heroes on the side of the law, morality, and authority, in the 1950s he functioned solely to throw the system into turmoil by his absences through death or desertion, his weaknesses, his neglects, etc. In this manner, the failures of identification so characteristic of the domestic melodrama, and the self-conscious 'Oedipal' solutions they demanded, can be directly linked to the figure of the Father as representing either the very sign of madness (the transgression of the law he represents) or as an empty centre where the authority of the law fails. As a film like *Bigger Than Life* demonstrates so well, the relationship between madness and authority was in a sense, two expressions of the same term. Either pathetically castrated, or monstrously castrating, the figurations of patriarchal authority completely failed the social and sexual economies of the melodramatic narrative and the structure of conflict in which they found form.

The failure of the domestic melodrama, then, would seem to take place in the form of a historical displacement in which the contemporary demands of ideology had become partially disjunct with the set of formal conventions which were required to articulate them. Unable to achieve a successful integration of the social, psychic, and formal relations in which it was generically forged, and incapable of formulating a convincing happy end which could 'reconcile the suffering individual to his social position', the domestic melodrama could only

> produce ideological discourses as to display variable degrees of internal conflict and disorder – a disorder produced by those displacements and mutations of ideology forced upon the text by the necessity to arrive, in accordance with the laws of its aesthetic production, at a 'solution' to its problems. In such a text, the relative coherence of ideological categories is revealed under the form of a concealment – revealed by the very *incoherence* of the text, by the significant disarray into which it is thrown in its efforts to operate its materials in the interest of a solution (Eagleton, p. 86).

3 Conclusion
The domestic melodrama of the 1950s might best be understood as an aesthetic ideology whose means of expression were organised by three sets of

determinations – social, psychic, and formal. In this matter, the kinds of narratives produced by this aesthetic ideology were characterised by three factors: a) the systematic refusal to understand the social economy of the text, and the historical conditions which gave it form, in anything but familial and personal terms; b) a highly internalised narrative structure taking form in a drama of identification which often understood itself in self-consciously oedipal terms, and c) a system of conflict determined by the figuration of patriarchal authority which in turn mediated the relationship between the social and psychic determinations in the text.

However, the internal economy of the aesthetic ideology was disrupted by the contradictory demands of the general ideology which promised, through an acceptance of its authority, a world of economic mobility, self-determination, and social stability, but delivered in its stead a hierarchic and authoritarian society plagued by fears of the internal subversion of its ideologies. This contradiction was structurally reproduced in the inability of the melodramatic text to evolve as either a fully affirmative or fully subversive form. Split between madness and authority, it could either adopt an arbitrary and purely formal resolution (in which case its social and psychological dilemmas would remain unresolved), or else it could let its crises of identification follow their self-destructive course (in which case the power of authority came into question). In reality, the domestic melodrama usually opted for a partial solution – articulated through one or two of the sets of determinations – which fell between these two extremes. In this manner, the melodramatic Father, failing the symbolic order of which he was the centre, still functioned as a sort of 'destiny' in the narratives, but one which introduced a structural disorder in the organisation of the three sets of determinations into a system of conflict.

Notes

1. See, for example, Charles Eckert's 'The Anatomy of a Proletarian Film: Warner's *Marked Woman*', *Film Quarterly*, 27, no. 2 (Winter 1973–74), pp. 10–24.
2. 'Tales of Sound and Fury: Observations on the Family Melodrama' (reprinted in this anthology, pp. 43–69).
3. Terry Eagleton, *Criticism and Ideology* (London: Verso Editions, 1978), p. 4. Throughout this essay I will be following the terminology which Eagleton develops in this book. Perhaps a moment of clarification will be useful, then, especially with respect to the important distinction between 'general ideology' and 'aesthetic ideology'. For example, Eagleton writes that every mode of production

   also always produces a dominant ideological formation – a formation I provisionally term 'general' to distinguish it from that specific region within it known as the aesthetic region, or, more summarily, as 'aesthetic ideology'. A dominant ideological formation is constituted by a relatively coherent set of 'discourses' of values, representations and beliefs which, realised in certain material apparatuses and related to the structures of material production, so reflected the experiential relations of individual subjects to their social conditions as to guarantee those misperceptions of the 'real' which contribute to the reproduction of the dominant social relations.

> ... In speaking of the 'relations' or conjunctures between GI and aesthetic ... ideologies, then, one is speaking not of certain extrinsically related 'sets', but of the mode of insertion of ... aesthetic formations into the hegemonic ideology as a whole (p. 54).

Also, see his chapter entitled 'Towards a Science of the Text', pp. 64–101.

4. See his 'Minnelli and Melodrama' (reprinted in this anthology, pp. 70–74).
5. See his 'Lenin, Critic of Tolstoy' in *A Theory of Literary Production*, Tr. Geoffrey Wall (London: Routledge and Kegan Paul, 1978), pp. 105–35.
6. See, for example, Nowell-Smith, pp. 70–74 of this anthology.
7. Sylvia Harvey, 'Woman's Place: The Absent Family of Film Noir' in *Women in Film Noir*, (ed.) E. Ann Kaplan (London: British Film Institute, 1978), p. 24.
8. See, for example, Elsaesser, pp. 43–69 of this anthology.
9. For an interesting discussion of the relationship between nineteenth-century narrative and film, see Janet Bergstrom, 'Alternation, Segmentation, Hypnosis: Interview with Raymond Bellour', *Camera Obscura*, no. 3/4, Summer 1979, especially pp. 87–103.
10. Elsaesser notes, 'The same pattern is to be found in the bourgeois tragedies of Lessing (*Emilia Galotti*, 1768) and the early Schiller (*Kabale and Liebe*, 1776), both deriving their dramatic force from the conflict between an extreme and highly individualised form of moral idealism in the heroes and a thoroughly corrupt yet seemingly omnipotent social class (made up of feudal princes and petty state functionaries)' (p. 11).
11. See Jon Halliday, *Sirk on Sirk* (New York: Viking Press, 1972), especially pp. 82–135.
12. While writing this section, I was fortunate to see, for the first time, *The Best Years of Our Lives* (1946), a film which not only addresses this problematic with surprising directness, but which in the end also adopts a purely melodramatic solution for its series of conflicts.
13. See his 'Le "Piccolo" Bertolazzi et Brecht (*Notes sur un théâtre matérialiste*)' in *Pour Marx* (Paris: François Maspero, 1977), pp. 130–52.
14. *The Political Unconscious: Narrative as a Socially Symbolic Act* (London: Methuen, 1981). See especially Chapter one, pp. 17–102.

PART FOUR

What do Women Want?

Problems in Representation and Reading

The 'Woman's Film'

Possession and Address

MARY ANN DOANE

From *Re-Vision: Essays in Feminist Film Criticism*, (eds.) Mary Ann Doane, Patricia
Mellencamp and Linda Williams (Frederick MD: University Publications of America,
1984).

MUCH of the effort of already classical feminist studies has been that of a
certain recapture of the past, defined not as a rewriting of history but as its
'filling out' or completion. The aim of such a project is the demonstration
that, although women have been censored from the texts of history, they
populate its reality and must be saved from obscurity. The underlying themes
of such an approach are that women were 'really there' or 'did really do
things', and that we can know in some direct and unmediated way what these
things were. Feminist film theory and criticism have shown themselves to be
particularly resistant to the empiricism of this methodology. Claire Johnston
clearly delineates the difficulties in an attempt to situate the work of Dorothy
Arzner:

> ... do feminist critics simply want to introduce women into film history?
> To answer this question, it is necessary to examine the ideology which has
> dominated film history up to now. Film historians ... have until very
> recently confined themselves to an accumulation of 'facts' and the con-
> struction of chronologies. From these, they have attempted by a process of
> induction to derive an interpretation of historical events closely linked to
> liberal notions of 'progress' and 'development'. The historicism and
> pseudo-objectivism of this approach leaves little room for theory of any
> kind. Indeed, it is commonly believed that the pursuit of theory must
> inevitably be at the expense of 'facts'. Merely to introduce women into the
> dominant notion of film history, as yet another series of 'facts' to be
> assimilated into the existing notions of chronology, would quite clearly be
> sterile and regressive. 'History' is not some abstract 'thing' which bestows
> significance on past events in retrospect. Only an attempt to situate
> Arzner's work in a theoretical way would allow us to comprehend her real
> contribution to film history. Women and film can only become meaning-
> ful in terms of a theory, in the attempt to create a structure in which films
> such as Arzner's can be examined in retrospect.[1]

The pseudo-objectivism Johnston refers to is especially apparent in the notions of the individual and agency which ground the 'discoveries' of this woman's history. To retrieve and re-establish women as agents of history is to construct one's discourse upon a denial of the more problematic and complex aspects of subjectivity and sexuality.

On the other hand, the reaction against this crude historicism has often resulted in the virtual exclusion of the term 'history' in its relations to the sexed subject which has become the focus of film theory's formulations. This is especially true of theories of spectatorship, of the consumption of the film object, its terms of address. What has been elided in the conceptualisation of the spectator is not only historical but sexual specificity. The spectator purportedly anticipated and positioned by the text, defined by the psychical mechanisms of scopophilia or voyeurism, fetishism and a primary mirror identification, is inevitably male. In this context, Hollywood narratives are analysed as compensatory structures designed to defend the male psyche against the threat offered by the image of the woman. Although this analysis has certainly been productive in understanding classical film narrative, it merely repeats the historical tendency of psychoanalysis to focus on the male psyche at the expense of that of the female. Furthermore, in a society which relies so heavily on a continual and pervasive inscription of sexual difference, it would seem problematic to assume that this sexual differentiation would not apply to spectatorship, to modes of looking and hearing, as well. The male spectator posited by film theory is a discursive construction; there is a female spectator who exists as a construction of the textual system and its discursive emplacement as well.[2] This is perhaps most apparent when one takes into account Hollywood's analysis of its own market, its own grouping of films along the lines of a sexual address. Thus, the nomenclature by means of which certain films of the 40s are situated as 'woman's pictures' – a label which stipulates that the films are in some sense the 'possession' of women and that their terms of address are dictated by the anticipated presence of the female spectator.[3]

The 'woman's film' is not a 'pure' genre – a fact which may partially determine the male critic's derogatory dismissal of such films. It is crossed and informed by a number of other genres or types – melodrama, film noir, the gothic or horror film – and finds its point of unification ultimately in the fact of its address. Because the woman's film of the 1940s was directed towards a female audience, a psychoanalytically informed analysis of the terms of its address is crucial in ascertaining the place the woman is assigned as spectator within patriarchies. The question then becomes: As a discourse addressed specifically to women, what kind of viewing process does the 'woman's film' attempt to activate? A crucial unresolved issue here is the very possibility of constructing a 'female spectator', given the cinema's dependence upon voyeurism and fetishism.

Given the apparent 'masculinisation' of the very process of looking in the cinema, these films often manifest a certain convolution and instability in their attempted construction of female fantasy. The narratives assume a compatibility between the idea of female fantasy and that of persecution – a persecution effected by husband, family, or lover. There is an almost obsessive association of the female protagonist with a deviation from some norm of mental stability or health, resulting in the recurrent investigation of psychical mechanisms frequently linked with the 'feminine condition' – masochism, hysteria, neurosis, paranoia. It is as though the insistent attempt at an inscription of female subjectivity and desire, within a phallocentrically organised discourse such as the classical Hollywood text, produced gaps and incoherences which the films can barely contain. Because female identity in the cinema is constructed in relation to object-hood rather than subject-hood, an investigation of the contradictions resulting from an attempt to engage female subjectivity in a textual process such as the 'woman's film' can be particularly productive. From this perspective, this essay has a quite limited aim – to trace certain obsessions which inhabit the texts across three different but related registers: the deployment of space and the activation of the uncanny; de-specularisation and the medical discourse; and the economics of female subjectivity. All three registers are characterised by a certain violence which is coincident with the attribution of the gaze to the female.

The deployment of space in the 'woman's film' is motivated rather directly by a fairly strict mapping of gender-differentiated societal spaces onto the films – the woman's place is in the home. Although this is quite clearly the case in the family melodrama (where the space of the house frequently dictates the weight of the *mise en scène*), I would like to shift attention to another subgroup of the genre in which the house is foregrounded in relation to mechanisms of suspense which organise the gaze. This cycle of films might be labelled the 'paranoid woman's films', the paranoia evinced in the formulaic repetition of a scenario in which the wife invariably fears that her husband is planning to kill her – the institution of marriage is haunted by murder. Frequently, the violence is rationalised as the effect of an overly hasty marriage; the husband is unknown or only incompletely known by the woman. A scene in *Secret Beyond the Door* (1948) exemplifies this tendency: a long flashback which details the meeting of Joan Bennett and the man she is to marry culminates with the image of her future husband, emerging from the deep shadows of the church on their wedding day, accompanied by her surprised voice-over, 'I'm marrying a stranger'. The conjunction of sexuality and murder, the conflation of the two verbs, 'to marry' and 'to kill', is even more explicit in *Suspicion* (1941), in a scene on a windy hill in which Joan Fontaine's resistance to Cary Grant's attempts to kiss her is met with his question, 'What do you think I was going to do – kill you?' As Thomas Elsaesser points out in reference to *Rebecca* (1940):

Hitchcock infused his film, and several others, with an oblique intimation of female frigidity producing strange fantasies of persecution, rape, and death – masochistic reveries and nightmares, which cast the husband into the role of the sadistic murderer. This projection of sexual anxiety and its mechanisms of displacement and transfer is translated into a whole string of movies often involving hypnosis and playing on the ambiguity and suspense of whether the wife is merely imagining it or whether her husband really does have murderous designs on her.[4]

This 'whole string of movies' includes, among others, *Suspicion, Rebecca, Secret Beyond the Door, Gaslight* (1944), *Undercurrent* (1946), *Dragonwyck* (1946), and *The Two Mrs Carrolls* (1947).

In this cycle, dramas of seeing become invested with horror within the context of the home. The paradigmatic woman's space – the home – is yoked to dread, and a crisis of vision. For violence is precisely what is hidden from sight. While the mainstream Hollywood cinema organises vision in relation to both spectacle and truth, and hence pleasure and fascination, the 'woman's film' evinces a certain impoverishment of this mechanism. Laura Mulvey's very important analysis of 'visual pleasure' focuses on films with a male protagonist.[5] Because the 'woman's film' obsessively centres and re-centres a female protagonist, placing her in a position of agency, it offers some resistance to an analysis which stresses the 'to-be-looked-at-ness' of the woman, her objectification as spectacle according to the masculine structure of the gaze. Thus, within the 'woman's film', the process of specularisation undergoes a number of vicissitudes which can be mapped. The textual assumption of a specifically female spectator also entails the assumption that she does not adopt a masculine position with respect to the cinematic image of the female body. In other words, because the female gaze is not associated with the psychical mechanisms of voyeurism and fetishism, it is no longer necessary to invest the look with desire in quite the same way. A certain de-specularisation takes place in these films, a deflection of scopophiliac energy in other directions, away from the female body. The very process of seeing is now invested with fear, anxiety, horror, precisely because it is object-less, free-floating. As Jacqueline Rose has demonstrated, to the extent that the cinema does involve an imaginary structuration of vision, it also activates the aggressive component of imaginary processes.[6] In these films, the aggressivity which is contained in the cinematic structuration of the look is released or, more accurately, transformed into a narrativised paranoia. This subclass of the 'woman's film' clearly activates the latent paranoia of the film system described by Rose. Its narrative structure produces an insistence upon situating the woman as agent of the gaze, as investigator in charge of the epistemological trajectory of the text, as the one for whom the 'secret beyond the door' is really at stake.

286

Hence, one could formulate a veritable topography of spaces within the home along the axis of this perverted specularisation. The home is not a homogeneous space – it asserts divisions, gaps and field within its very structure. There are places which elude the eye; paranoia demands a split between the known and the unknown, the seen and the unseen. Thus, many of these films are marked by the existence of a room to which the woman is barred access. In *Gaslight* it is the attic where the husband searches for the dead aunt's jewels, in *Dragonwyck* it is the upstairs tower room where the husband exercises his drug addiction, in *Rebecca* it is both the boathouse-cottage detached from the house and Rebecca's bedroom, ultimately approached by the female protagonist with a characteristically Hitchcockian insistence on the moving point-of-view shot towards the closed door. *Secret Beyond the Door* bases itself upon the hyperbolisation of this mechanism, a proliferation of rooms which the husband collects. In accordance with his architectural determinism (which, in a perverse reversal of German Expressionism, stipulates that a room does not reflect but determines what happens within it), the husband constructs exact replicas of rooms in which famous murders have taken place, concealing the final room – the wife's bedroom – from the eyes of both the public and his wife. The suspense generated by such strategies is no different in its dictation of subject positions from the more generalised cinematic suspense grounded by what Pascal Bonitzer refers to as the 'rule of the look and nothing else':

> In this system, each shot engages the spectators as subjects (as potential victims) of another shot, and the 'image of the worst' governs the progression; each shot, in its difference of intensity, portends and defers 'the screen of the worst' for the spectators, subjects of the fiction: this is the principle of suspense.... Suspense is not just a genre.... It is, from the point of view I have just expounded, essential to cinema.... But only insofar as this system is one for ordering the depth of field, which constitutes the take not only as a passive recording of the scene, but as a productive force in its own right expressing, producing the *fading* of a point of view (and of a point of view that is ... rather paranoiac).[7]

The cinematic generality of this system of suspense is specified by the 'woman's film' in only two ways: through the localisation of suspense in the familiarised female space of the home in relation to a close relative, almost always the husband; and in the violent attribution of the investigating gaze to the female protagonist (who is also its victim). This second specification effects a major disturbance in the cinematic relay of the look, resulting in so much narrative stress that the potential danger of a female look is often reduced or entirely avoided by means of the delegation of the detecting gaze to another male figure who is on the side of the law. (*Gaslight* is a particularly good example of this.) Nevertheless, in many of the films, and in the best tradition of the horror film, affect is condensed onto the fact of a woman investigating, penetrating space alone. And it is the staircase, a signifier which possesses a certain semantic privilege in relation to the woman as object of the gaze, which articulates the connection between the familiar and the unfamiliar, or neurosis and psychosis. An icon of crucial and repetitive insistence in the classical representations of the cinema, the staircase is traditionally the locus of specularisation of the woman. It is *on the stairway* that she is displayed as spectacle for the male gaze (and often the icon is repeated, as though it were nonproblematic, within these same films – think of Joan Fontaine descending the stairs in *Rebecca* in the costume she mistakenly believes will please Laurence Olivier, or the woman in *Dragonwyck*, dressed in her best clothes, who poses on the staircase when her future husband comes to call). But the staircase in the paranoid woman's films also (and sometimes simultaneously); becomes the passageway to the 'image of the worst' or 'screen of the worst', in Bonitzer's terms. In *Dragonwyck*, film noir lighting intensifies the sense of foreboding attached to Gene Tierney's slow climb up the stairs in the attempt to ascertain what her suspicious husband does in the tower room prohibited to her. What Barbara Stanwyck finally discovers in the room at the top of the stairs in *The Two Mrs Carrolls* is her own distorted and grotesque portrait, painted by her husband and evidence of his psychotic plan to kill her. The woman's exercise of an active investigating gaze can only be simultaneous with her own victimisation. The place of her specularisation is transformed into the locus of a process of seeing designed to unveil an aggression against itself.

The last site in this topography of spaces within the home with a pronounced semantic valence in relation to processes of specularisation is the window. Within the 'woman's films' as a whole, images of women looking through windows or waiting at windows abound. The window has special import in terms of the social and symbolic positioning of the woman – the window is the interface between inside and outside, the feminine space of the family and reproduction and the masculine space of production. It facilitates a communication by means of the look between the two sexually differentiated spaces. That interface becomes a potential point of violence, intrusion and aggression in the paranoid woman's films. In *The Two Mrs Carrolls* the traces of the poisoned milk which Barbara Stanwyck throws out the window are discovered on the sill by her psychotic artist-husband Humphrey Bogart, who later penetrates her locked bedroom in a vampire-like entrance through the window. In *Rebecca*, Mrs Danvers attempts to seduce Joan Fontaine into committing suicide at the window. In these films the house becomes the analogue of the human body, its parts fetishised by textual operations, its erotogenous zones metamorphosised by a morbid anxiety attached to sexuality. It is the male character who fetishises the house as a whole, attempting to unify and homogenise it through an insistent process of naming – Manderley, Dragonwyck, #9 Thornton Street.

Within the cinema, it is hardly surprising that the uncanny should be activated by means of dramas of seeing, of concealing and revealing. Freud himself in his article on 'The Uncanny', repetitively and obsessively returns to the relations of vision to the uncanny effect – the 'evil eye', the sight of himself in a mirror misrecognised, the fear of losing one's eyes embodied in 'The Sandman'. Even his etymological investigation of the word '*unheimlich*' (uncanny) revolves around the possibilities of seeing and hiding. Freud's rather long tracing of the linguistic deviations of the word serve finally to demonstrate that *heimlich* (belonging or pertaining to the home, familiar) is eventually equated with its opposite *unheimlich* (strange, unfamiliar, uncanny) – 'Thus *heimlich* is a word the meaning of which develops towards an ambivalence, until it finally coincides with its opposite, *unheimlich*.'[8] This sliding of signification is possible only because the word for 'home' is semantically overdetermined and can be situated in relation to the gaze. For the home or house connotes not only the familiar but also what is secret, concealed, hidden from sight. The paradigmatic process by means of which what is familiar becomes strange is situated as the male's relation to the female body:

> It often happens that male patients declare that they feel there is something uncanny about the female genital organs. This *unheimlich* place, however, is the entrance to the former *heim* (home) of all human beings, to the place where everyone dwelt once upon a time and in the beginning ... the prefix *un* is the token of repression.[9]

The female genitals are uncanny because they represent, for the male, the possibility of castration. In Samuel Weber's interpretation of Freud, the uncanny constitutes a defence against the negative perception of feminine castration, a vision which connotes nothing less than '*crisis* of perception and of phenomenality'.

> The uncanny is a defense which is ambivalent and which expresses itself in the compulsive curiosity ... the craving to penetrate the flimsy appearances to the essence beneath.... This desire to penetrate, discover and ultimately to conserve the integrity of perception: perceiver and perceived, the wholeness of the body, the power of vision – all this implies a *denial* of that almost-nothing which can hardly be seen, a denial that in turn involves a certain structure of narration, in which this denial repeats and articulates itself.[10]

Thus for both Freud and Weber, the uncanny is the return of the repressed, and what is repressed is a certain vision of the female body as the signifier of castration, and hence disunity. Suspense in the cinema – for Bonitzer the 'rule of the look and nothing else' – therefore involves a kind of fetishisation of vision itself, a reassertion of the integrity of perception along the lines of sexual difference.

But what does *this* have to do with the female spectator, for whom castration cannot pose a threat since she has nothing to lose? The different relation of the woman to the look must necessarily pose problems for a class of films which depends so heavily upon the mechanisms of suspense and the very possibility of attributing the gaze and subjectivity to the woman. In fact, the difficulty is not confined to the paranoid woman's films but pervades the genre, evinced in the continual inability to sustain a coherent representation of female subjectivity in the context of phallocentric discursive mechanisms. This is particularly explicit in the instability of certain privileged signifiers of enunciation – the voice-over and the point-of-view shot. The voice-over, introduced in the beginning of a film as the possession of the female protagonist who purportedly controls the narration of her own past, is rarely sustained (*Rebecca, Secret Beyond the Door*). Voice-overs are more frequently mobilised as moments of aggression or attack exercised against the female protagonist (*Gaslight, Undercurrent, Rebecca*). In *Suspicion*, the ending belies an inability to localise subjectivity in the point-of-view shot and the consequent collapse of the opposition between subjectivity and objectivity. In *Possessed* (1947), a scene in which Joan Crawford kills her stepdaughter is situated only retrospectively and traumatically as a subjectivised scenario – the image, in effect, lies.

Such an instability in the representation of female subjectivity, however, does not remain unrecognised by the texts, and is, instead, recuperated as the sign of illness or psychosis.[11] This is the operation of the second register – despecularisation and the medical discourse. In the 'woman's film', the erotic gaze becomes the medical gaze. The female body is located not so much as spectacle but as an element in the discourse of medicine, a manuscript to be read for the symptoms which betray her story, her identity.[12] Hence the need, in these films, for the figure of the doctor as reader or interpreter, as the site of a knowledge which dominates and controls female subjectivity – examples include *Now, Voyager* (1942), *A Woman's Face* (1941), *Dark Victory* (1939), *Possessed* (1947), *Caught* (1949), *The Dark Mirror* (1946), *Shock* (1946), *Johnny Belinda* (1948), and *The Snake Pit* (1948).

In *Possessed*, Joan Crawford's illness is indicated immediately by her fixed stare and the fact that she can only repeat compulsively one word – the name of the man with whom she is in love. This situation causes certain difficulties of narration since she is the only one in the hospital room who knows and can therefore tell her own story. The dilemma receives a rather remarkable narrative solution which is, in a sense, exemplary for the 'woman's film'. The mute Joan Crawford is given an injection by the doctor which induces cinematic narrative. The thrill of her story, the pleasure of the cinema, is encapsulated in the doctor's words, 'Every time I see the reaction to this treatment I get the same thrill I did the first time.' The woman's narrative, as a repetition of that first time, is nevertheless held in check by recurrent withdrawals from her flashback account to the present tense of the doctor's diagnosis. For instance, the first part of her story illustrates, according to one of the doctors, 'the beginning of a persecution complex', indicated by the fact that there is 'no attempt to see the man's point of view'. Within the encompassing masculine medical discourse, the woman's language is granted a limited validity – it is, precisely, *a* point of view, and often a distorted and unbalanced one.

In terms of both spatial configurations and language the female figure is trapped within the medical discourse of these narratives. In films like Ophuls' *Caught*, these framing procedures in the medical construction of the woman are quite apparent. Towards the end of the film there is a scene in which Barbara Bel Geddes' empty desk is used as a pivot as the camera pans back and forth between two doctors (James Mason and Frank Ferguson) discussing her fate. Obsessively moving across Bel Geddes' desk from doctor to doctor, the camera constructs a perfect symmetry by framing both of the men in their office doorways, ultimately returning to the woman's empty desk and closing the sequence with a kind of formal tautology. The sequence is a performance of one of the over-determined meanings of the film's title – Barbara Bel Geddes is 'caught' spatially, between an obstetrician and a pediatrician. Furthermore, the obstetrician's final diagnosis of Bel Geddes consists of a rejection of the object which at the beginning of the film epitomised the woman's desire – a mink coat ('If my diagnosis is correct, she won't want that anyway.'). Because the mink coat is associated with femininity as spectacle and image (its first inscription in the film is within the pages of a fashion magazine), the doctor's diagnosis has the effect of a certain de-specularisation of the female body.[13] That body is, instead, symptomatic, and demands a reading.

It is therefore important, within this group of films, to *know* the woman as thoroughly as possible. Unlike the film noir, the 'woman's film' does not situate its female protagonist as mysterious, unknowable, enigmatic. The site of potential knowledge about the woman is transferred from the Law to Medicine. This displacement is narrativised in *The Dark Mirror*, where the agent of the Law, the police detective, must appeal to a psychiatrist for a solution to the crime committed by one of two identical twins. Because the two women *look* exactly alike, a psychiatrist is needed to *see through* the surface exterior to the interior truths of the two sisters – in other words, to perform a symptomatic reading. And when the doctor falls in love with one

291

of the twins, the discourse of desire merges imperceptibly with the discourse of psychiatry: 'The more I know about you, the more I want to know, I want to know everything about you'.

Although the medical discourse is central to films like *Possessed*, *The Snake Pit*, and *Johnny Belinda*, it also informs and inflects the subgroup of 'paranoid woman's films' discussed earlier. In both *The Spiral Staircase* and *Dragonwyck* the heroic male figure, a site of wisdom and safety, is a doctor. Many of the films depend rather heavily upon the tableau of the sick woman in bed, effecting the transformation of a site of sexuality into a site of illness and pain. In *Rebecca*, it is the doctor's discourse which provides closure for the story of the absent Rebecca, an answer to the hermeneutic question concerning her disappearance. Of particular interest in this respect is *Shock*, which merges conventions of the medical discourse with those of the paranoid films. Like Jimmy Stewart in *Rear Window*, the female protagonist in *Shock* looks out the window when she shouldn't, and sees what she shouldn't have seen – a husband murdering his wife. But unlike *Rear Window*, the woman goes into shock as a result of this sight, of this image which suggests itself as a microcosm of the cinema–spectator relation. The murderer turns out to be a psychiatrist who is called in to treat the catatonic woman suffering from what she has seen. All of his efforts are directed towards making her forget the image and maintaining her in a state in which she is unable to articulate her story.

The attribution of muteness to the woman is by no means rare in these films. In *Shock*, *Possessed*, and *The Spiral Staircase* the female character loses the power of speech as the result of a psychical trauma, while in *Johnny Belinda* she is mute from birth. But in all cases language is the gift of the male character, a somewhat violent 'gift' in the case of *Shock* and *Possessed*, where the woman is induced to talk through an injection, and more benign, paternalistic in *Johnny Belinda*, where the doctor provides Belinda with sign language. This muteness is in some ways paradigmatic for the genre. For it is ultimately the symptoms of the female body which 'speak' while the woman as subject of discourse is inevitably absent. In his case history of Dora (another 'woman's narrative'), Freud posits a privileged relation between hysteria (often theorised as a specifically feminine illness, associated with the womb) and the somatic. 'Somatic compliance' is the concept Freud elaborated to designate the process whereby the body complies with the psychical demands of the illness by providing a space and a material for the inscription for its signs. The female body thus acts in this context as a vehicle for hysterical speech. The marked ease of the metonymic slippage in these films between the woman, illness, the bed, muteness, blindness, and a medical discourse indicates yet another contradiction in the construction of a discourse which purportedly represents a female subjectivity.[14] If the woman must be given a genre and hence a voice, the addition of a medical discourse makes it possible once again to confine female discourse to the body, to disperse her access to language across a body which now no longer finds its major function in spectacle. Yet, de-specularised in its illness, that body is nevertheless interpretable, knowable, subject to a control which is no longer entirely subsumed by the erotic gaze. What the body no longer supports, without the doctor's active reading, is an identity.

The medical gaze, de-eroticised, constitutes the woman in these films not only as the object of the trained gaze, but as the object of speech and of knowledge as well, much in the manner of Foucault's speaking eye.

> Over all these endeavors on the part of clinical thought to define its methods and scientific norms hovers the great myth of a pure Gaze that would be pure Language: a speaking eye. It would scan the entire hospital field taking in and gathering together each of the singular events that occurred within it; and as it saw, as it saw ever more and more clearly, it would be turned into speech that states and teaches.... A hearing gaze and a speaking gaze: clinical experience represents a moment of balance between speech and spectacle.[15]

As the field of the masculine medical gaze is expanded, the woman's vision is reduced. Although in the beginning of *Possessed*, point-of-view shots are attributed to Crawford as she is wheeled into the hospital, she is *represented* as having an empty gaze, seeing nothing, blinded by the huge lamps aimed at her by the doctors. The ending of *Dark Victory* is crucial in this respect. The first sign of Bette Davis' impending death from a brain tumour is blindness. But because her husband is planning to attend a conference to present his medical discoveries – a conference which meets only twice a year – she must pretend to be able to see so that he won't remain with her and retard medical science by six months. Davis' heroism, then, is delineated as her ability to mime sight, to represent herself as the subject of vision.

The third register of the texts – the economics of female subjectivity – must be defined in relation to this process of miming – miming a position which can only be described as masochistic, as the perpetual staging of suffering. Addressing itself to a female audience, the 'woman's film' raises the crucial question: How can the notion of female fantasy be compatible with that of persecution, illness, and death? In what way do these texts engage their spectator? Freud's explanation of paranoia and masochism relates them both to the assumption by the subject – whether male or female – of a feminine position. In Dr Schreber's paranoid delusions, his body is transformed, painfully, into the body of a woman. The masochism which Freud assigns to the classical sexual pervert (usually male) is labelled 'feminine' precisely because the fantasies associated with this type of masochism situate the subject in positions 'characteristic of womanhood, i.e., they mean that he is being castrated, is playing the passive part in coitus, or is giving birth.'[16] The economic problem of masochism, for Freud, lies in the apparent paradox of pleasure-in-pain. But this paradox is not unique to 'feminine' masochism in Freud's typology, for there is a sense in which masochism is primary for the subject, ultimately, for Freud, a manifestation of the fundamental and inexorable death drive.

Nevertheless, when confronted with concrete clinical cases where masochism is embodied in a particularly insistent fantasy – 'A Child is Being Beaten' – Freud is forced to make crucial distinctions along the lines of sexual difference. For it does, indeed, matter whether the subject of the fantasy is male or female. And it is not accidental that a certain ease of interpretation characterises the psychoanalysis of the female masochistic fantasy which takes the form of a three-part transformation of a basic sentence: (1) My father is beating the child whom I hate; (2) I am being beaten (loved) by my father; (3) A child is being beaten. In the construction of the male fantasy, Freud can isolate only two sentences: (1) I am being beaten (loved) by my father; (2) I am being beaten by my mother. Although both the female and the male instanciations stem from the same origin – an incestuous attachment to the father – their psychical meaning-effects are necessarily quite different. The woman's masochism can be located unproblematically within the terms of the 'normal' female Oedipal configuration, while the attribution of masochism to the man depends upon the possibility of an inverted Oedipal attitude in which the father is taken as the object of desire. The man can, however, avoid the homosexual implications by remodelling his fantasy so that the mother takes the place of the father as the agent of the beating.

For my purposes here, there are two aspects of this sexual differentiation of the masochistic fantasy which assume paramount importance; the relationship established between fantasy and sexuality, and the presence or absence of spectatorship as a possible role in the scenario. On the first point, Freud is quite explicit. The erotic implications of the fantasy are acknowledged no matter what the vicissitudes of its transformation in the case of the male – sexuality remains on the surface. Furthermore, he retains his own role and his own gratification in the context of the scenario. The 'I' of identity remains. On the other hand, the feminine masochistic fantasy, in the course of its vicissitudes, is desexualised: by means of the fantasy, 'the girl escapes from the demands of the erotic side of her life altogether'.[17] The fantasy, whose primary function in Freud's description is the facilitation of masturbation, becomes an end in itself. The women are prone to construct an 'artistic super-structure of daydreams', fantasies which in some instances approach the level of a 'great work of art' and eliminate entirely the need for masturbation. It is the fantasmatic gone awry, dissociated completely from the body as site of the erotic. But most crucially, the third sentence – 'A child is being beaten' – which is significantly absent in male masochism, necessitates the woman's assumption of the position of spectator, outside of the event. The 'I' of the fantasy is no longer operative within its diegesis and, instead, the child who is being beaten is transformed into an anonymous boy or even a group of boys who act as the representatives of the female in the scenario.[18] Confronted with Freud's insistent question, 'Where are *you* in this fantasy?', the female patients can only reply, 'I am probably looking on.'[19] Or, in Freud's eloquent summation of the sexual differentiation of the masochistic fantasy:

> ... the girl escapes from the demands of the erotic side of her life altogether. She turns herself in fantasy into a man, without herself becoming active in a masculine way, and is no longer anything but a spectator of the event which takes the place of a sexual act.[20]

Thus, simultaneous with her assumption of the position of spectator, the woman loses not only her sexual identity in the context of the scenario but her very access to sexuality.

Masochistic fantasy *instead* of sexuality. The phrase would seem to exactly describe the processes in the 'woman's film' whereby the look is de-eroticised. In the paranoid subgroup, the space which the woman is culturally assigned, the home, through its fragmentation into places that are seen and unseen, becomes the site of terror and victimisation – the look turned violently against itself. In the films which mobilise a medical discourse, where blindness and muteness are habitually attributed to the woman, she can only passively give witness as the signs of her own body are transformed by the purportedly desexualised medical gaze, the 'speaking eye', into elements of discourse. The dominance of the bed in the *mise en scène* of these films is the explicit mark of the displacement/replacement of sexuality by illness.

There is a sense, then, in which these films attempt to reverse the relation between the female body and sexuality which is established and re-established by the classical cinema's localisation of the woman as spectacle. As spectacle, the female body *is* sexuality, the erotic and the specular are welded. By de-eroticising the gaze, these films in effect disembody their spectator – the cinema, a mirror of control to the man, reflects nothing for the woman, or rather, it denies the imaginary identification which, uniting body and identity, supports discursive mastery. Confronted with the classical Hollywood text with a male address, the female spectator has basically two modes of entry: a narcissistic identification with the female figure as spectacle, and a 'transvestite' identification with the active male hero in his mastery.[21] This female spectator is thus imaged by its text as having a mixed sexual body – she is, ultimately, a hermaphrodite. It is precisely this oscillation which demonstrates the instability of the woman's position as spectator. Because the 'woman's film' purportedly directs itself to a female audience, because it pretends to offer the female spectator an identity other than that of the active male hero, it deflects energy away from the second 'transvestite' option described above and towards the more 'properly' female identification. But since the 'woman's film' reduces the specularisable nature of the female body, this first option of a narcissistic identification is problematised as well. In a patriarchal society, to desexualise the female body is ultimately to deny its very existence. The 'woman's film' thus functions in a rather complex way to deny the woman the space of a reading.

All of this is certainly not to say that the 'woman's film' is in any way radical or revolutionary. It functions quite precisely to immobilise – its obsession with the repetition of scenarios of masochism is a symptom of the ideological crisis provoked by the need to shift the sexual terms of address of a cinema which, as Laura Mulvey has shown, is so heavily dependent upon masculine structures of seeing. The very lack of epistemological validity ascribed to these films – manifested in the derogatory lable, the 'weepies' – is an active recuperation of the contradictions which necessarily arise in attributing the epistemological gaze to the woman. For a body-less woman cannot see. The impossibility of the contract which these films attempt to actualise is most succinctly articulated in a line from *Rebecca* – 'Most girls would give their eyes for a chance to see Monte.'

Notes

1. Claire Johnston, 'Dorothy Arzner, Critical Strategies', in *The Work of Dorothy Arzner*, (ed.) Claire Johnston (London: British Film Institute, 1975), p. 2.
2. The phrase 'discursive construction' is used here to indicate the operation whereby filmic texts anticipate a position for the spectator and outline the terms of their own understanding. This process pertains to both conscious and unconscious levels of understanding. Individual, empirical spectators may fail to assume such a position in relation to the text, but in this event a certain textual meaning-effect is lost. That meaning-effect may not be entirely dependent upon the filmic text's own mechanisms but may also be influenced by other discourses surrounding the film.
3. This article is a condensation of various motifs which are elaborated more systematically in my book *The Desire to Desire: The Woman's Film of the 1940s* (Bloomington: Indiana University Press, 1987). The notion of a 'woman's picture', or a genre of films addressed specifically to women, is clearly not limited to the 1940s. However, the ideological upheaval signalled by a redefinition of sexual roles and the reorganisation of the family makes the 1940s a particularly intense and interesting period for feminist analysis.
4. Thomas Elsaesser, 'Tales of Sound and Fury' (reprinted in this anthology, pp. 43–69).

5. Laura Mulvey, 'Visual Pleasure and Narrative Cinema', *Screen*, vol. 16, no. 3, Autumn 1975, pp. 6–18.

6. Jacqueline Rose, 'Paranoia and the Film System', *Screen*, vol. 17, no. 4, Winter 1976/77, pp. 85–104.

7. Pascal Bonitzer, 'Here: The Notion of the Shot and the Subject of the Cinema', *Film Reader*, no. 4, 1979, p. 113.

8. Sigmund Freud, 'The Uncanny', in *On Creativity and the Unconscious*, (ed.) Benjamin Nelson (New York: Harper and Row, 1958), p. 131.

9. Ibid., pp. 152–3.

10. Samuel Weber, 'The Sideshow, or: Remarks on a Canny Moment', *MLN*, vol. 88, no. 6, December 1973, p. 1133.

11. The obsessive association of women with madness is clearly not limited to the film medium and is a phenomenon which can already claim a tradition of feminist study. See, for instance, Phyllis Chesler, *Women and Madness* (New York: Avon Books, 1972) and Shoshana Felman, 'Women and Madness: The Critical Phallacy', *Diacritics*, vol. 5, no. 4, Winter 1975, pp. 2–10.

12. As Lea Jacobs has pointed out to me, this statement should be qualified. In films like *Now, Voyager* and *A Woman's Face*, the woman's 'cure' consists in a beautification of body/face. The doctor's work is the transformation of the woman into a specular object. (See Lea Jacobs, '*Now, Voyager*: Some Problems of Enunciation and Sexual Difference', *Camera Obscura*, no. 7, Spring 1981, pp. 89–109.) Nevertheless, in both films the woman's status as specular object of desire is synonymous with her 'health' – her illness is characterised as the very lack of that status. The narratives thus trace a movement from the medical gaze to the erotic gaze in relation to the central female figure. In *Possessed*, on the other hand, Joan Crawford is still the victim of a psychosis at the end of the film and never quite regains her 'looks'.

13. For a more complete analysis of the medical discourse in *Caught* see my '*Caught* and *Rebecca*: The Inscription of Femininity as Absence', *Enclitic*, vol. 5, no. 2/vol. 6, no. 1, Fall 1981/Spring 1982, pp. 75–89.

14. I make no distinction, in this section, between physical illness and mental illness because the films themselves elaborate strong connections between the two. They assume without question at the level of their manifest discourse a rather popularised Freudian notion of the psychosomatic.

15. Michel Foucault, *The Birth of the Clinic: An Archaeology of Medical Perception*, trans. A. M. Sheridan-Smith (New York: Vintage Books, 1975), pp. 114–15.

16. Sigmund Freud, 'The Economic Problem in Masochism', in *General Psychological Theory*, (ed.) Philip Rieff (New York: Collier Books, 1963), p. 193.

17. Sigmund Freud, 'A Child is Being Beaten', in *Sexuality and the Psychology of Love*, (ed.) Philip Rieff (New York: Collier Books, 1963), p. 128.

18. Freud's explanation for this sexual transformation is quite interesting and worth quoting in full: 'When they [girls] turn away from their incestuous love for their father, with its genital significance, they easily abandon their feminine role. They spur their "masculinity complex" (v. Ophuijsen) into activity, and from that time forward only want to be boys. For that reason, the whipping-boys who represent them are boys also. In both the cases of day-dreaming – one of which almost rose to the level of a work of art – the heroes were always young men; indeed women

used not to come into these creations at all, and only made their first appearance after many years, and then in minor parts.' (Ibid., pp. 119–20.) The positioning of the male as protagonist of the fantasy clearly makes a strict parallel between the 'Child is Being Beaten' fantasy and the 'woman's film' impossible. Nevertheless, the sexual transformation of female into male in the fantasy does parallel the de-eroticisation of the female body in the masochistic women's films and the consequent loss of the 'feminine' category of spectacle.

19. Ibid., p. 114.
20. Ibid., p. 128.
21. For a more thorough and detailed discussion of the female spectator's relation to the classical text see my 'Film and the Masquerade: Theorising the Female Spectator', *Screen*, vol. 23, no. 3/4, September/October 1982, pp. 74–88. For more on 'transvestite' identification, see Laura Mulvey, 'Afterthoughts on "Visual Pleasure and Narrative Cinema" inspired by *Duel in the Sun*', *Framework* 15/16/17, Summer 1981, pp. 12–15.

'Something Else Besides a Mother'

Stella Dallas and the Maternal Melodrama

LINDA WILLIAMS

From *Cinema Journal* 24, no. 1, Fall 1984, pp. 2–27.

Oh, God! I'll never forget that last scene, when her daughter is being married inside the big house with the high iron fence around it and she's standing out there – I can't even remember who it was, I saw it when I was still a girl, and I may not even be remembering it right. But I am remembering it – it made a tremendous impression on me – anyway, maybe it was Barbara Stanwyck. She's standing there and it's cold and raining and she's wearing a thin little coat and shivering, and the rain is coming down on her poor head and streaming down her face with the tears, and she stands there watching the lights and hearing the music and then she just drifts away. How they got us to consent to our own eradication! I didn't just feel pity for her; I felt that shock of recognition – you know, when you see what you sense is your own destiny up there on the screen or on the stage. You might say I've spent my whole life trying to arrange a different destiny![1]

THESE WORDS of warning, horror, and fascination are spoken by Val, a character who is a mother herself, in Marilyn French's 1977 novel *The Women's Room*. They are especially interesting for their insight into the response of a woman viewer to the image of her 'eradication'. The scene in question is from the end of *Stella Dallas*, King Vidor's 1937 remake of the 1925 film by Henry King. The scene depicts the resolution of the film: that moment when the good-hearted, ambitious, working-class floozy, Stella, sacrifices her only connection to her daughter in order to propel her into an upper-class world of surrogate family unity. Such are the mixed messages – of joy in pain, of pleasure in sacrifice – that typically resolve the melodramatic conflicts of 'the woman's film'.

It is not surprising, then, that Marilyn French's mother character, in attempting to resist such a sacrificial model of motherhood, should have so selective a memory of the conflict of emotions that conclude the film. Val only remembers the tears, the cold, the mother's pathetic alienation from her daughter's triumph inside the 'big house with the high iron fence', the abject loneliness of the woman who cannot belong to that place and so 'just drifts away'. Val's own history, her own choices, have caused her to forget the perverse triumph of the scene: Stella's lingering for a last look even when a policeman urges her to move on; her joy as the bride and groom kiss; the swelling music as Stella does not simply 'drift away' but marches triumphantly towards the camera and into a close-up that reveals a fiercely proud and happy mother clenching a handkerchief between her teeth.

It is as if the task of the narrative has been to find a 'happy' ending that will exalt an abstract ideal of motherhood even while stripping the actual mother of the human connection on which that ideal is based. Herein lies the 'shock of recognition' of which French's mother–spectator speaks.

The device of devaluing and debasing the actual figure of the mother while sanctifying the institution of motherhood is typical of 'the woman's film' in general and the sub-genre of the maternal melodrama in particular.[2] In these films it is quite remarkable how frequently the self-sacrificing mother must make her sacrifice that of the connection to her children – either for her or their own good.

With respect to the mother–daughter aspect of this relation, Simone de Beauvoir noted long ago that because of the patriarchal devaluation of women in general, a mother frequently attempts to use her daughter to compensate for her own supposed inferiority by making 'a superior creature out of one whom she regards as her double'.[3] Clearly, the unparalleled closeness and similarity of mother to daughter sets up a situation of significant mirroring that is most apparent in these films. One effect of this mirroring is that although the mother gains a kind of vicarious superiority by association with a superior daughter, she inevitably begins to feel inadequate to so superior a being and thus, in the end, to feel inferior. Embroiled in a relationship that is so close, mother and daughter nevertheless seem destined to lose one another through this very closeness.

Much recent writing on women's literature and psychology has focused on the problematic of the mother–daughter relationship as a paradigm of a woman's ambivalent relationship to herself.[4] In *Of Woman Born* Adrienne Rich writes, 'The loss of the daughter to the mother, mother to the daughter, is the essential female tragedy. We acknowledge Lear (father–daughter split), Hamlet (son and mother), and Oedipus (son and mother) as great embodiments of the human tragedy, but there is no presently enduring recognition of mother–daughter passion and rapture.' No tragic, high culture equivalent perhaps. But Rich is not entirely correct when she goes on to say that 'this cathexis between mother and daughter – essential, distorted, misused – is the great unwritten story.'[5]

If this *tragic* story remains unwritten, it is because tragedy has always been assumed to be universal; speaking for and to a supposedly universal 'man-kind', it has not been able to speak for and to womankind. But melodrama is a form that does not pretend to speak universally. It is clearly addressed to a particular bourgeois class and often – in works as diverse as *Pamela*, *Uncle Tom's Cabin*, or the 'woman's film' – to the particular gender of woman.

In *The Melodramatic Imagination* Peter Brooks argues that late eighteenth and nineteenth-century melodrama arose to fill the vacuum of a post-revolutionary world where traditional imperatives of truth and ethics had been violently questioned and yet in which there was still a need for truth and ethics. The aesthetic and cultural form of melodrama thus attempts to assert the ethical imperatives of a class that has lost the transcendent myth of a divinely ordained hierarchical community of common goals and values.[6]

Because the universe had lost its basic religious and moral order and its tragically divided but powerful ruler protagonists, the aesthetic form of melodrama took on the burden of rewarding the virtue and punishing the vice of undivided and comparatively powerless characters. The melodramatic mode thus took on an intense quality of wish-fulfilment, acting out the narrative resolution of conflicts derived from the economic, social, and political spheres in the private, emotionally primal sphere of home and family. Martha Vicinus notes, for example, that in much nineteenth-century stage melodrama the home is the scene of this 'reconciliation of the irreconcilable'.[7] The domestic sphere where women and children predominate as protagonists whose only power derives from virtuous suffering thus emerges as an important source of specifically female wish-fulfilment. But if women audiences and readers have long identified with the virtuous sufferers of melodrama, the liberatory or oppressive meaning of such identification has not always been clear.

Much recent feminist film criticism has divided filmic narrative into male and female forms: 'male' linear, action-packed narratives that encourage identification with predominantly male characters who 'master' their environment; and 'female' less linear narratives encouraging identification with passive, suffering heroines.[8] No doubt part of the enormous popularity of *Mildred Pierce* among feminist film critics lies with the fact that it illustrates the failure of the female subject (the film's misguided, long-suffering mother-hero who is overly infatuated with her daughter) to articulate her own point of view, even when her own voice-over introduces subjective flashbacks.[9] *Mildred Pierce* has been an important film for feminists precisely because its 'male' film noir style offers such a blatant subversion of the mother's attempt to tell the story of her relationship to her daughter.

The failure of *Mildred Pierce* to offer either its female subject or its female viewer her own understanding of the film's narrative has made it a fascinating example of the way films can construct patriarchal subject-positions that subvert their ostensible subject matter. More to the point of the mother–

daughter relation, however, is a film like *Stella Dallas*, which has recently begun to receive attention as a central work in the growing criticism of melodrama in general and maternal melodrama in particular.[10] Certainly the popularity of the original novel, of the 1925 (Henry King) and 1937 (King Vidor) film versions, and finally of the later long-running radio soap opera, suggests the special endurance of this mother–daughter love story across three decades of female audiences. But it is in its film versions in particular, especially the King Vidor version starring Barbara Stanwyck, that we encounter an interesting test case for many recent theories of the cinematic presentation of female subjectivity and the female spectator.

Since so much of what has come to be called the classical narrative cinema concerns male subjects whose vision defines and circumscribes female objects, the mere existence in *Stella Dallas* of a female 'look' as a central feature of the narrative is worthy of special scrutiny. Just what is different about the visual economy of such a film? What happens when a mother and daughter, who are so closely identified that the usual distinctions between subject and object do not apply, take one another as their primary objects of desire? What happens, in other words, when the look of desire articulates a rather different visual economy of mother–daughter possession and dispossession? What happens, finally, when the significant viewer of such a drama is also a woman? To fully answer these questions we must make a detour through some recent psychoanalytic thought on female subject formation and its relation to feminist film theory. We will then be in a better position to unravel the mother–daughter knot of this particular film. So for the time being we will abandon *Stella Dallas* to her forlorn place in the rain, gazing at her daughter through the big picture window – the enigma of the female look at, and in, the movies.

Feminist Film Theory and Theories of Motherhood
Much recent feminist film theory and criticism has been devoted to the description and analysis of Oedipal scenarios in which, as Laura Mulvey has written, woman is a passive image and man the active bearer of the look.[11] The major impetus of these forms of feminist criticism has been less concerned with the existence of female stereotypes than with their ideological, psychological, and textual means of production. To Claire Johnston, the very fact of the iconic representation of the cinematic image guarantees that women will be reduced to objects of an erotic male gaze. Johnston concludes that 'woman as woman' cannot be represented at all within the dominant representational economy.[12] A primary reason for this conclusion is the hypothesis that the visual encounter with the female body produces in the male spectator a constant need to be reassured of his own bodily unity.

It is as if the male image producer and consumer can never get past the disturbing fact of sexual difference and so constantly produces and consumes images of women designed to reassure himself of his threatened unity. In this and other ways, feminist film theory has appropriated some key concepts from Lacanian psychoanalysis in order to explain why subjectivity always seems to be the province of the male.

According to Lacan, through the recognition of the sexual difference of a female 'other' who lacks the phallus that is the symbol of patriarchal privilege, the child gains entry into the symbolic order of human culture. This culture then produces narratives which repress the figure of lack that the mother – former figure of plenitude – has become. Given this situation, the question for woman becomes, as Christine Gledhill puts it: *'Can women speak, and can images of women speak for women?'*[13] Laura Mulvey's answer, and the answer of much feminist criticism, would seem to be negative:

> Woman's desire is subjected to her image as bearer of the bleeding wound, she can exist only in relation to castration and cannot transcend it. She turns her child into the signifier of her own desire to possess a penis (the condition, she imagines, of entry into the symbolic). Either she must gracefully give way to the word, the Name of the Father and the Law, or else struggle to keep her child down with her in the half-light of the imaginary. Woman then stands in patriarchal culture as signifier for the male other, bound by a symbolic order in which man can live out his phantasies and obsessions through linguistic command by imposing them on the silent image of woman still tied to her place as bearer of meaning, not maker of meaning.[14]

This description of the 'visual pleasure of narrative cinema' delineates two avenues of escape which function to relieve the male viewer of the threat of the woman's image. Mulvey's now-familiar sketch of these two primary forms of mastery by which the male unconscious overcomes the threat of an encounter with the female body is aligned with two perverse pleasures associated with the male – the sadistic mastery of voyeurism and the more benign disavowal of fetishism. Both are ways of not-seeing, of either keeping a safe distance from, or misrecognising what there is to see of, the woman's difference.

The purpose of Mulvey's analysis is to get 'nearer to the roots' of women's oppression in order to break with those codes that cannot produce female subjectivity. Her ultimate goal is thus an avant-garde film-making practice that will break with the voyeurism and fetishism of the narrative cinema so as to 'free the look of the camera into its materiality in space and time', and the 'look of the audience into dialectics, passionate detachment'.[15] To Mulvey, only the radical destruction of the major forms of narrative pleasure so bound up in looking at women as objects can offer hope for a cinema that will be able to represent not woman as difference but the differences of women.

It has often been remarked that what is missing from Mulvey's influential analysis of visual pleasure in cinematic narrative is any discussion of the position of the female viewing subject. Although many feminist works of film criticism have pointed to this absence, very few have ventured to fill it.[16] It is an understandably easier task to reject 'dominant' or 'institutional' modes of representation altogether than to discover within these existing modes glimpses of a more 'authentic' (the term itself is indeed problematic) female subjectivity. And yet I believe that this latter is a more fruitful avenue of approach, not only as a means of identifying what pleasure there is for women spectators within the classical narrative cinema, but also as a means of developing new representational strategies that will more fully speak to women audiences. For such speech must begin in a language, that, however circumscribed within patriarchal ideology, will be recognised and understood by women. In this way, new feminist films can learn to build upon the pleasures of recognition that exist within filmic modes already familiar to women.

Instead of destroying the cinematic codes that have placed women as objects of spectacle at their centre, what is needed, and has already begun to occur, is a theoretical and practical recognition of the ways in which women actually do speak to one another within patriarchy. Christine Gledhill, for example, makes a convincing case against the tendency of much semiotic and psychoanalytic feminist film criticism to blame realist representation for an ideological complicity with the suppression of semiotic difference. Such reasoning tends to believe that the simple rejection of the forms of realist representation will perform the revolutionary act of making the viewer aware of how images are produced. Gledhill argues that this awareness is not enough: the social construction of reality and of women cannot be defined in terms of signifying practice alone. 'If a radical ideology such as feminism is to be defined as a means of providing a framework for political action, one must finally put one's finger on the scales, enter some kind of realist epistemology.'[17]

But what kind? Any attempt to construct heroines as strong and powerful leaves us vulnerable, as Gledhill notes, to the charge of male identification:

> However we try to cast our potential feminine identifications, all available positions are already constructed from the place of the patriarchal other so as to repress our 'real' difference. Thus the unspoken remains unknown, and the speakable reproduces what we know, patriarchal reality.[18]

One way out of the dilemma is 'the location of those spaces in which women, out of their socially constructed differences as women, can and do resist'.[19] These include discourses produced primarily for and (often, but not always) by women and which address the contradictions that women encounter under patriarchy: women's advice columns, magazine fiction, soap operas, and melodramatic 'women's films'. All are places where women speak to one another in languages that grow out of their specific social roles – as mothers, housekeepers, caretakers of all sorts.[20]

Gledhill's assertion that discourses about the social, economic, and emotional concerns of women are consumed by predominantly female audiences could be complemented by the further assertion that *some* of these discourses are also differently inscribed to necessitate a very different, female reading. This is what I hope to show with respect to *Stella Dallas*. My argument, then, is not only that some maternal melodramas have historically addressed female audiences about issues of primary concern to women, but that these melodramas also have reading positions structured into their texts that demand a female reading competence. This competence derives from the different way women take on their identities under patriarchy and is a direct result of the social fact of female mothering. It is thus with a view to applying the significance of the social construction of female identity to the female positions constructed by the maternal melodrama that I offer the following cursory summary of recent feminist theories of female identity and motherhood.

While Freud was forced, at least in his later writing, to abandon a theory of parallel male and female development and to acknowledge the greater importance of the girl's pre-Oedipal connection to her mother, he could only view such a situation as a deviation from the path of 'normal' (e.g., male heterosexual) separation and individuation.[21] The result was a theory that left women in an apparent state of regressive connection to their mothers.

What Freud viewed as a regrettable lack in a girl's self development, feminist theories now view with less disparagement. However else they may differ over the consequences of female mothering, most agree that it allows women not only to remain in connection with their first love objects but to extend the model of this connectedness to all other relations with the world.[22]

In *The Reproduction of Mothering* the American sociologist Nancy Chodorow attempts to account for the fact that 'women, as mothers, produce daughters with mothering capacities and the desire to mother'.[23] She shows that neither biology nor intentional role training can explain the social organisation of gender roles that consign women to the private sphere of home and family, and men to the public sphere that has permitted them dominance. The desire and ability to mother is produced, along with masculinity and femininity, within a division of labour that has already placed women in the position of primary caretakers. Superimposed on this division of labour are the two 'Oedipal asymmetries'[24] that Freud acknowledged:

that girls enter the triangular Oedipal relation later than boys: that girls have a greater continuity of pre-Oedipal symbiotic connection to the mother.

In other words, girls never entirely break with their original relationship to their mothers, because their sexual identities as women do not depend upon such a break. Boys, however, must break with their primary identification with their mothers in order to become male identified. This means that boys define themselves as males negatively, by differentiation from their primary caretaker who (in a culture that has traditionally valued women as mothers first, workers second) is female.

The boy separates from his mother to identify with his father and take on a masculine identity of greater autonomy. The girl, on the other hand, takes on her identity as a woman in a positive process of becoming like, not different than, her mother. Although she must ultimately transfer her primary object choice to her father first and then to men in general if she is to become a heterosexual woman, she still never breaks with the original bond to her mother in the same way the boy does. She merely *adds* her love for her father, and finally her love for a man (if she becomes heterosexual) to her original relation to her mother. This means that a boy develops his masculine gender identification in the *absence* of a continuous and ongoing relationship with his father, while a girl develops her feminine gender identity in the *presence* of an ongoing relationship with the specific person of her mother.

In other words, the masculine subject position is based on a rejection of a connection to the mother and the adoption of a gender role identified with a cultural stereotype, while the female subject position identifies with a specific mother. Women's relatedness and men's denial of relatedness are in turn appropriate to the social division of their roles in our culture: to the man's role as producer outside the home and the woman's role as reproducer inside it.[25]

Chodorow's analysis of the connectedness of the mother–daughter bond has pointed the way to a new value placed on the multiple and continuous female identity capable of fluidly shifting between the identity of mother and daughter.[26] Unlike Freud, she does not assume that the separation and autonomy of the male identification process is a norm from which women deviate. She assumes, rather, that the current social arrangement of exclusive female mothering has prepared men to participate in a world of often alienated work, with a limited ability to achieve intimacy.[27]

Thus Chodorow and others[28] have questioned the very standards of unity and autonomy by which human identity has typically been measured. And they have done so without recourse to a biologically determined essence of femaleness.[29]

Like Nancy Chodorow, the French feminist psychoanalyst Luce Irigaray turns to the problems of Freud's original attempt to sketch identical stages of development for both male and female. In *Speculum de l'autre femme*

Irigaray echoes Chodorow's concern with 'Oedipal asymmetries'. But what Irigaray emphasises is the *visual* nature of Freud's scenario – the fact that sexual difference is originally perceived as an absence of the male genitalia rather than the presence of female genitalia. In a chapter entitled 'Blind Spot for an Old Dream of Symmetry', the 'blind spot' consists of a male vision trapped in an 'Oedipal destiny' that cannot *see* woman's sex and can thus only represent it in terms of the masculine subject's own original complementary other: the mother.[30]

'Woman' is represented within this system as either the all-powerful (phallic) mother of the child's pre-Oedipal imaginary or as the unempowered (castrated) mother of its post-Oedipal symbolic. What is left out of such a system of representation is the whole of woman's pleasure – a pleasure that cannot be measured in phallic terms.

But what Freud devalued and repressed in the female body, Irigaray and other French feminists engaged in 'writing the female body' in an *écriture féminine*,[31] are determined to emphasise. In *Ce sexe qui n'en est pas un* (This sex which is not one) Irigaray celebrates the multiple and diffuse pleasures of a female body and a female sex that is not just one thing, but several. But when forced to enter into the 'dominant scopic economy' of visual pleasure she is immediately relegated, as Mulvey has also pointed out with respect to film, to the passive position of 'the beautiful object'.[32]

Irigaray's admittedly utopian[33] solution to the problem of how women can come to represent themselves to themselves is nevertheless important. For if women cannot establish the connection between their bodies and language, they risk either having to forego all speaking of the body – in a familiar puritanical repression of an excessive female sexuality – or they risk an essentialist celebration of a purely biological determination. Irigaray thus proposes a community of women relating to and speaking to one another outside the constraints of a masculine language that reduces everything to its own need for unity and identity – a 'female homosexuality' opposed to the reigning 'male homosexuality' that currently governs the relations between both men and men, and men and women.[34]

A 'female homosexual economy' would thus challenge the dominant order and make it possible for woman to represent herself to herself. This suggests an argument similar to that of Adrienne Rich in her article 'Compulsory Heterosexuality and Lesbian Existence'. Rich argues that lesbianism is an important alternative to the male economy of dominance. Whether or not a woman's sexual preferences are actually homosexual, the mere fact of 'lesbian existence' proves that it is possible to resist the dominating values of the male coloniser with a more nurturing and empathic relationship similar to mothering.[35] The female body is as necessary to Rich as it is to Irigaray as the place to begin.

Adrienne Rich's critique of psychoanalysis is based on the notion that its fundamental patriarchal premises foreclose the envisioning of relationships between women outside of patriarchy. Irigaray's recourse to the female body ironically echoes Rich's own but it is constructed from *within* psychoanalytic theory. The importance of both is not simply that they see lesbianism as a refuge from an oppressive phallic economy – although it certainly is that for many women – but that it is a theoretical way out of the bind of the unrepresented, and unrepresentable, female body.

The excitement generated when women get together, when they go to the market together 'to profit from their own value, to talk to each other, to desire each other', is not to be underestimated.[36] For only by learning to recognise and then to represent a difference that is not different to other women, can women begin to see themselves. The trick, however, is not to stop there; woman's recognition of herself in the bodies of other women is only a necessary first step to an understanding of the interaction of body and psyche, and the distance that separates them.[37]

Perhaps the most valuable attempt to understand this interaction is Julia Kristeva's work on the maternal body and pre-Oedipal sexuality. Like Irigaray, Kristeva attempts to speak the pre-Oedipal relations of woman to woman. But unlike Irigaray, she does so with the knowledge that such speech is never entirely authentic, never entirely free of the phallic influence of symbolic language. In other words, she stresses the necessity of positing a place from which women can speak themselves, all the while recognising that such places do not exist. That is, it cannot be conceived or represented outside of the symbolic language which defines women negatively.[38]

Thus, what Kristeva proposes is a self-conscious dialectic between two imperfect forms of language. The first is what she calls the 'emiotic': a pre-verbal, maternal language of rhythm, tone and colour linked to the body contact with the mother before the child is differentiated by entrance into the symbolic. The second is the 'symbolic' proper, characterised by logic, syntax, and a phallocratic abstraction.[39] According to Kristeva, all human subjects articulate themselves through the interaction of these two modes. The value of this conception is that we no longer find ourselves locked into an investigation of different sexual *identities*, but are freed rather into an investigation of *sexual differentiations* – subject positions that are associated with maternal or paternal functions.

Speaking from the mother's position, Kristeva shows that maternity is characterised by division. The mother is possessed of an internal heterogeneity beyond her control:

Cells fuse, split and proliferate; volumes grow, tissues stretch, and body fluids change rhythm, speeding up or slowing down. Within the body, growing as a graft, indomitable, there is an other. And no one is present, within that simultaneously dual and alien space, to signify what is going on. 'It happens, but I'm not here.'[40]

But even as she speaks from this space of the mother, Kristeva notes that it is vacant, that there is no unified subject present there. Yet she speaks anyway, consciously recognising the patriarchal illusion of the all-powerful and whole phallic mother. For Kristeva it is the dialectic of two inadequate and incomplete sexually *differentiated* subject positions that is important. The dialectic between a maternal body that is too diffuse, contradictory, and polymorphous to be represented and a paternal body that is channelled and repressed into a single representable significance makes it possible for woman to be represented at all.

So, as Jane Gallop notes, women are not so essentially and exclusively body that they must remain eternally unrepresentable.[41] But the dialectic between that which is pure body and therefore escapes representation and that which is a finished and fixed representation makes possible a different kind of representation that escapes the rigidity of fixed identity. With this notion of a dialectic between the maternal unrepresentable and the paternal already-represented we can begin to look for a way out of the theoretical bind of the representation of women in film and at the way female spectators are likely to read *Stella Dallas* and its ambivalent scene.

'Something Else Besides a Mother'

Stella's story begins with her attempts to attract the attention of the upper-class Stephen Dallas (John Boles), who has buried himself in the small town of Milhampton after a scandal in his family ruined his plans for marriage. Like any ambitious working-class girl with looks as her only resource, she attempts to improve herself by pursuing an upper-class man. To distinguish herself in his eyes, she calculatingly brings her brother lunch at the mill where Stephen is the boss, insincerely playing the role of motherly caretaker. The refinement that she brings to this role distinguishes her from her own drab, overworked, slavish mother (played by Marjorie Main, without her usual comic touch).

During their brief courtship, Stella and Stephen go to the movies. On the screen they see couples dancing in an elegant milieu followed by a happy-ending embrace. Stella is absorbed in the story and weeps at the end. Outside the theatre she tells Stephen of her desire to 'be like all the people in the movies doing everything well-bred and refined'. She imagines his whole world to be like this glamorous scene. Her story will become, in a sense, the unsuccessful attempt to place herself in the scene of the movie without losing that original spectatorial pleasure of looking on from afar.

Once married to Stephen, Stella seems about to realise this dream. In the small town that once ignored her she can now go to the 'River Club' and associate with the smart set. But motherhood intervenes, forcing her to cloister herself unhappily during the long months of pregnancy. Finally out of the hospital, she insists on a night at the country club with the smart set that has so far eluded her. (Actually many of them are a vulgar *nouveau-riche* lot of whom Stephen, upper-class snob that he is, heartily disapproves.) In her strenuous efforts to join in the fun of the wealthy, Stella makes a spectacle of herself in Stephen's eyes. He sees her for the first time as the working-class woman that she is and judges her harshly, reminding her that she once wanted to be something more than what she is. She, in turn, criticises his stiffness and asks *him* to do some of the adapting for a change.

When Stephen asks Stella to come with him to New York City for a fresh start as the properly upper-class Mrs Dallas, she refuses to leave the only world she knows. Part of her reason must be that to leave this world would also be to leave the only identity she has ever achieved, to become nobody all over again. In the little mill town where Stephen had come to forget himself, Stella can find herself by measuring the distance travelled between her working-class girlhood and upper-class wifehood. It is as if she needs to be able to measure this distance in order to possess her new self from the vantage point of the young girl she once was with Stephen at the movies. Without the memory of this former self that the town provides, she loses the already precarious possession of her own identity.

As Stephen drifts away from her, Stella plunges into another aspect of her identity: motherhood. After her initial resistance, it is a role she finds surprisingly compelling. But she never resigns herself to being *only* a mother. In Stephen's absence she continues to seek an innocent but lively pleasure – in particular with the raucous Ed Munn. As her daughter Laurel grows up, we observe a series of scenes that compromise Stella in the eyes of Stephen (during those rare moments he comes home) and the more straight-laced members of the community. In each case Stella is merely guilty of seeking a little fun – whether by playing music and drinking with Ed or playing a practical joke with itching powder on a train. Each time we are assured of Stella's primary commitment to motherhood and of her many good qualities as a mother. (She even says to Ed Munn, in response to his crude proposal: 'I don't think there's a man livin' who could get me going anymore.') But each time the repercussions of the incident are the isolation of mother and daughter from the upper-class world to which they aspire to belong but into which only Laurel fits. A particularly poignant moment is Laurel's birthday party where mother and daughter receive, one by one, the regrets of the guests. Thus the innocent daughter suffers for the 'sins' of taste and class of the mother. The end result, however, is a greater bond between the two as each sadly but nobly puts on a good face for the other and marches into the dining room to celebrate the birthday alone.

In each of the incidents of Stella's transgression of proper behaviour, there is a moment when we first see Stella's innocent point of view and then the point of view of the community or estranged husband that judges her a bad mother.[42] Their judgment rests on the fact that Stella insists on making her motherhood a pleasurable experience by sharing centre stage with her daughter. The one thing she will not do, at least until the end, is retire to the background.

One basic conflict of the film thus comes to revolve around the *excessive presence* of Stella's body and dress. She increasingly flaunts an exaggeratedly feminine presence that the offended community prefers not to see. (Barbara Stanwyck's own excessive performance contributes to this effect. I can think of no other film star of the period so willing to exceed both the bounds of good taste and sex appeal in a single performance.) But the more ruffles, feathers, furs, and clanking jewellery that Stella dons, the more she emphasises her pathetic inadequacy.

Her strategy can only backfire in the eyes of an upper-class restraint that values a streamlined and sleek ideal of femininity. To these eyes Stella is a travesty, an overdone masquerade of what it means to be a woman. At the fancy hotel to which Stella and Laurel repair for their one fling at upper-class life together, a young college man exclaims at the sight of Stella, 'That's not a woman, that's a Christmas tree!' Stella, however, could never understand such a backward economy, just as she cannot understand her upper-class husband's attempts to lessen the abrasive impact of her presence by correcting her English and toning down her dress. She counters his efforts with the defiant claim, 'I've always been known to have stacks of style!'

'Style' is the war paint she applies more thickly with each new assault on her legitimacy as a woman and a mother. One particularly affecting scene shows her sitting before the mirror of her dressing table as Laurel tells her of the 'natural' elegance and beauty of Helen Morrison, the woman who has replaced Stella in Stephen's affections. Stella's only response is to apply more cold cream. When she accidentally gets cold cream on Laurel's photo of the ideal Mrs Morrison, Laurel becomes upset and runs off to clean it. What is most moving in the scene is the emotional complicity of Laurel, who soon realises the extent to which her description has hurt her mother, and silently turns to the task of applying more peroxide to Stella's hair. The scene ends with mother and daughter before the mirror tacitly relating to one another through the medium of the feminine mask – each putting on a good face for the other, just as they did at the birthday party.

'Stacks of style', layers of make-up, clothes, and jewellery – these are, of course, the typical accoutrements of the fetishised woman. Yet such fetishisation seems out of place in a 'woman's film' addressed to a predominantly female audience. More typically, the woman's film's preoccupation with a victimised and suffering womanhood has tended, as Mary Ann Doane has shown, to repress and hystericise women's bodies in a medical discourse of the afflicted or in the paranoia of the uncanny.[43]

We might ask, then, what effect a fetishised female image has in the context of a film 'addressed' and 'possessed by' women? Certainly this is one situation in which the woman's body does not seem likely to pose the threat of castration — since the significant viewers of (and within) the film are all female. In psychoanalytic terms, the fetish is that which disavows or compensates for the woman's lack of a penis. As we have seen above, for the male viewer the successful fetish deflects attention away from what is 'really' lacking by calling attention to (over-valuing) other aspects of woman's difference. But at the same time it also inscribes the woman in a 'masquerade of femininity'[44] that forever revolves around her 'lack'. Thus, at the extreme, the entire female body becomes a fetish substitute for the phallus she doesn't possess. The beautiful (successfully fetishised) woman thus represents an eternal essence of biologically determined femininity constructed from the point of view, so to speak, of the phallus.

In *Stella Dallas*, however, the fetishisation of Stanwyck's Stella is unsuccessful; the masquerade of femininity is all too obvious; and the significant point of view on all this is female. For example, at the fancy hotel where Stella makes a 'Christmas Tree' spectacle of herself she is as oblivious as ever to the shocking effect of her appearance. But Laurel experiences the shame of her friends' scorn. The scene in which Laurel experiences this shame is a grotesque parody of Stella's fondest dream of being like all the glamorous people in the movies. Stella has put all of her energy and resources into becoming this glamorous image. But incapacitated by a cold, as she once was by pregnancy, she must remain off-scene as Laurel makes a favourable impression. When she finally makes her grand entrance on the scene, Stella is spied by Laurel and her friends in a large mirror over a soda fountain. The mirror functions as the framed screen that reflects the parody of the image of glamour to which Stella once aspired. Unwilling to acknowledge their relation, Laurel runs out. Later, she insists that they leave. On the train home, Stella overhears Laurel's friends joking about the vulgar Mrs Dallas. It is then that she decides to send Laurel to live with Stephen and Mrs Morrison and to give Laurel up for her own good. What is significant, however, is that Stella overhears the conversation at the same time Laurel does — they are in upper and lower berths of the train, each hoping that the other is asleep, each pretending to be asleep to the other. So Stella does not just experience her own humiliation; she sees for the first time the travesty she has become by sharing in her daughter's humiliation.

By seeing herself through her daughter's eyes, Stella also sees something more. For the first time Stella sees the reality of her social situation from the vantage point of her daughter's understanding, but increasingly upper-class, system of values: that she is a struggling, uneducated woman doing the best she can with the resources at her disposal. And it is *this* vision, through her daughter's sympathetic, mothering eyes – eyes that perceive, understand, and forgive the social graces Stella lacks – that determines her to perform the masquerade that will alienate Laurel forever by proving to her what the patriarchy has claimed to know all along: that it is not possible to combine womanly desire with motherly duty.

It is at this point that Stella claims, falsely, to want to be 'something else besides a mother'. The irony is not only that by now there is really nothing else she wants to be, but also that in pretending this to Laurel she must act out a painful parody of her fetishised self. She thus resurrects the persona of the 'good-times' woman she used to want to be (but never entirely was) only to convince Laurel that she is an unworthy mother. In other words, she proves her very worthiness to be a mother (her desire for her daughter's material and social welfare) by acting out a patently false scenario of narcissistic self-absorption – she pretends to ignore Laurel while lounging about in a negligee, smoking a cigarette, listening to jazz, and reading a magazine called 'Love'.

In this scene the conventional image of the fetishised woman is given a peculiar, even parodic, twist. For where the conventional masquerade of femininity can be read as an attempt to cover up supposedly biological 'lacks' with a compensatory excess of connotatively feminine gestures, clothes, and accoutrements, here fetishisation functions as a blatantly pathetic disavowal of much more pressing social lacks – of money, education, and power. The spectacle Stella stages for Laurel's eyes thus displaces the real social and economic causes of her presumed inadequacy as a mother onto a pretended desire for fulfilment as a woman – to be 'something else besides a mother'.

At the beginning of the film Stella pretended a maternal concern she did not really possess (in bringing lunch to her brother in order to flirt with Stephen) in order to find a better home. Now she pretends a lack of the same concern in order to send Laurel to a better home. Both roles are patently false. And though neither allows us to view the 'authentic' woman beneath the mask, the succession of roles ending in the final transcendent self-effacement of the window scene – in which Stella forsakes all her masks in order to become the anonymous spectator of her daughter's role as bride – permits a glimpse at the social and economic realities that have produced such roles. Stella's real offence, in the eyes of the community that so ruthlessly ostracises her, is to have attempted to play both roles at once.

Are we to conclude, then, that the film simply punishes her for these untimely resistances to her proper role? E. Ann Kaplan has argued that such is the case, and that throughout the film Stella's point of view is undercut by those of the upper-class community – Stephen, or the snooty townspeople – who disapprove of her behaviour. Kaplan notes, for example, that a scene may begin from Stella's point of view but shift, as in the case of an impromptu party with Ed Munn, to the more judgmental point of view of Stephen halfway through.[45]

I would counter, however, that these multiple, often conflicting, points of view – including Laurel's failure to see through her mother's act – prevent such a monolithic view of the female subject. Kaplan argues, for example, that the film punishes Stella for her resistances to a properly patriarchal view of motherhood by turning her first into a spectacle for a disapproving upper-class gaze and then finally into a mere spectator, locked outside the action in the final window scene that ends the film.[46]

Certainly this final scene functions to efface Stella even as it glorifies her sacrificial act of motherly love. Self-exiled from the world into which her daughter is marrying, Stella loses both her daughter and her (formerly fetishised) self to become an abstract (and absent) ideal of motherly sacrifice. Significantly, Stella appears in this scene for the first time stripped of the exaggerated marks of femininity – the excessive make-up, furs, feathers, clanking jewellery, and ruffled dresses – that have been the weapons of her defiant assertions that a woman *can* be 'something else besides a mother'.

It would be possible to stop here and take this ending as Hollywood's last word on the mother, as evidence of her ultimate unrepresentability in any but patriarchal terms. Certainly if we only remember Stella as she appears here at the end of the film, as Val in French's *The Women's Room* remembers her, then we see her only at the moment when she becomes representable in terms of a 'phallic economy' that idealises the woman as mother and in so doing, as Irigary argues, represses everything else about her. But although the final moment of the film 'resolves' the contradiction of Stella's attempt to be a woman *and* a mother by eradicating both, the 108 minutes leading up to this moment present the heroic attempt to live out the contradiction.[47] It seems likely, then, that a female spectator would be inclined to view even this ending as she has the rest of the film: from a variety of different subject positions. In other words, the female spectator tends to identify with contradiction itself – with contradictions located at the heart of the socially constructed roles of daughter, wife *and* mother – rather than with the single person of the mother.

In this connection the role of Helen Morrison, the upper-class widowed mother whom Stephen will be free to marry with Stella out of the way, takes on special importance. Helen is everything Stella is not: genteel, discreet, self-effacing, and sympathetic with everyone's problems – including Stella's. She is, for example, the only person in the film to see through Stella's ruse of alienating Laurel. And it is she who, knowing Stella's finer instincts, leaves open the drapes that permit Stella's vision of Laurel's marriage inside her elegant home.

In writing about the narrative form of daytime soap operas, Tania Modleski has noted that the predominantly female viewers of soaps do not identify with a main controlling figure the way viewers of more classic forms of narrative identify. The very form of soap opera encourages identification with multiple points of view. At one moment, female viewers identify with a woman united with her lover, at the next with the sufferings of her rival. While the effect of identifying with a single controlling protagonist is to make the spectator feel empowered, the effect of multiple identification in the diffused soap opera is to divest the spectator of power, but to increase empathy. 'The subject/spectator of soaps, it could be said, is constituted as a sort of ideal mother: a person who possesses greater wisdom than all her children, whose sympathy is large enough to encompass the conflicting claims of her family (she identifies with them all), and who has no demands or claims of her own (she identifies with no character exclusively).'[48]

In *Stella Dallas* Helen is clearly the representative of this idealised, empathic but powerless mother. Ann Kaplan has argued that female spectators learn from Helen Morrison's example that such is the proper role of the mother; that Stella has up until now illicitly hogged the screen. By the time Stella has made her sacrifice and become the mere spectator of her daughter's apotheosis, her joy in her daughter's success assures us, in Kaplan's words, of her satisfaction in being reduced to spectator.... While the cinema spectator feels a certain sadness in Stella's position, we also identify with Laurel and with her attainment of what we have all been socialised to desire; that is, romantic marriage into the upper class. We thus accede to the necessity for Stella's sacrifice.'[49]

But do we? As Kaplan herself notes, the female spectator is identified with a variety of conflicting points of view as in the TV soap opera: Stella, Laurel, Helen and Stephen cannot resolve their conflicts without someone getting hurt. Laurel loses her mother and visibly suffers from this loss; Stella loses her daughter and her identity; Helen wins Stephen but powerlessly suffers for everyone including herself (when Stella had refused to divorce Stephen). Only Stephen is entirely free from suffering at the end, but this is precisely because he is characteristically oblivious to the sufferings of others. For the film's ending to be perceived as entirely without problem, we would have to identify with this least sensitive and, therefore, least sympathetic point of view.

Instead, we identify, like the ideal mother viewer of soaps, with *all* the conflicting points of view. Because Helen is herself such a mother, she becomes an important, but not an exclusive, focus of spectatorial identification. She becomes, for example, the significant witness of Stella's sacrifice. Her one action in the entire film is to leave open the curtains – an act that helps put Stella in the same passive and powerless position of spectating that Helen is in herself. But if this relegation to the position of spectator outside the action resolves the narrative, it is a resolution not satisfactory to any of its female protagonists.

Thus, where Kaplan sees the ending of *Stella Dallas* as satisfying patriarchal demands for the repression of the active and involved aspects of the mother's role, and as teaching female spectators to take their dubious pleasures from this empathic position outside the action, I would argue that the ending is too multiply identified, too dialectical in Julia Kristeva's sense of the struggle between maternal and paternal forms of language, to encourage such a response. Certainly the film has constructed concluding images of motherhood – first the high-toned Helen and finally a toned-down Stella – for the greater power and convenience of the father. But because the father's own spectatorial empathy is so lacking – Stephen is here much as he was with Stella at the movies, present but not identified himself – *we* cannot see it that way. We see instead the contradictions between what the patriarchal resolution of the film asks us to see – the mother 'in her place' as spectator, abdicating her former position *in* the scene – and what we as empathic, identifying female spectators can't help but feel – the loss of mother to daughter and daughter to mother.

This double vision seems typical of the experience of most female spectators at the movies. One explanation for it, we might recall, is Nancy Chodorow's theory that female identity is formed through a process of double identification. The girl identifies with her primary love object – her mother – and then, without ever dropping the first identification, with her father. According to Chodorow, the woman's sense of self is based upon a continuity of relationship that ultimately prepares her for the empathic, identifying role of the mother. Unlike the male who must constantly differentiate himself from his original object of identification in order to take on a male identity, the woman's ability to identify with a variety of different subject positions makes her a very different kind of spectator.

Feminist film theorists have tended to view this multiple identificatory power of the female spectator with some misgiving. In an article on the female spectator, Mary Ann Doane has suggested that when the female spectator looks at the cinematic image of a woman, she is faced with two main possibilities: she can either over-identify (as in the masochistic dramas typical of the woman's film) with the woman on the screen and thus lose herself in the image by taking this woman as her own narcissistic object of desire; or she can temporarily identify with the position of the masculine voyeur and subject this same woman to a controlling gaze that insists on the distance and difference between them.[50] In this case she becomes, as Laura Mulvey notes, a temporary transvestite.[51] Either way, according to Doane, she loses herself.

Doane argues that the only way a female spectator can keep from losing herself in this over-identification is by negotiating a distance from the image of her like – by reading this image as a sign as opposed to an iconic image that requires no reading. When the woman spectator regards a female body enveloped in an exaggerated masquerade of femininity, she encounters a sign that requires such a reading. We have seen that throughout a good part of *Stella Dallas* this is what Stella does with respect to her own body. For Doane, then, one way out of the dilemma of female over-identification with the image on the screen is for this image to act out a masquerade of femininity that manufactures a distance between spectator and image, to 'generate a problematic within which the image is manipulable, producible, and readable by women'.[52]

In other words, Doane thinks that female spectators need to borrow some of the distance and separation from the image that male spectators experience. She suggests that numerous avant-garde practices of distanciation can produce this necessary distance. This puts us back to Mulvey's argument that narrative pleasure must be destroyed by avant-garde practices. I would argue instead that this manufacturing of distance, this female voyeurism-with-a-difference, is an aspect of *every* female spectator's gaze at the image of her like. For rather than adopting either the distance and mastery of the masculine voyeur or the over-identification of Doane's woman who loses herself in the image, the female spectator is in a constant state of juggling all positions at once.

Ruby Rich has written that women experience films much more dialectically than men. 'Brecht once described the exile as the ultimate dialectician in that the exile lives the tension of two different cultures. That's precisely the sense in which the woman spectator is an equally inevitable dialectician.'[53] The female spectator's look is thus a dialectic of two (in themselves) inadequate and incomplete (sexually and socially) differentiated subject positions. Just as Julia Kristeva has shown that it is the dialectic of a maternal body that is channelled and repressed into a single, univocal significance that makes it possible for women to be represented at all, so does a similar dialectic inform female spectatorship when a female point of view is genuinely inscribed in the text.

We have seen in *Stella Dallas* how the mediation of the mother and daughter's look at one another radically alters the representation of them both. We have also seen that the viewer cannot choose a single 'main controlling' point of identification but must alternate between a number of conflicting points of view, none of which can be satisfactorily reconciled. But the window scene at the end of the film would certainly seem to be the moment when all the above contradictions collapse into a single patriarchal vision of the mother as pure spectator (divested of her excessive bodily presence) and the daughter as the (now properly fetishised) object of vision. Although it is true that this ending, by separating mother and daughter, places each within a visual economy that defines them from the perspective of patriarchy, the female spectator's own look at each of them does not acquiesce in such a phallic visual economy of voyeurism and fetishism.

For in looking at Stella's own look at her daughter through a window that strongly resembles a movie screen,[54] the female spectator does not see and believe the same way Stella does. In this final scene, Stella is no different than the naïve spectator she was when, as a young woman, she went to the movies with Stephen. In order to justify her sacrifice, she must *believe* in the reality of the cinematic illusion she sees: bride and groom kneeling before the priest, proud father looking on. We, however, *know* the artifice and suffering behind it – Laurel's disappointment that her mother has not attended the wedding; Helen's manipulation of the scene that affords Stella her glimpse; Stella's own earlier manipulation of Laurel's view of her 'bad' motherhood. So when we look at Stella looking at the glamorous and artificial 'movie' of her daughter's life, we cannot, like Stella, naïvely believe in the reality of the happy ending, any more than we believe in the reality of the silent movements and hackneyed gestures of the glamorous movie Stella once saw.

Because the female spectator has seen the cost to both Laurel and Stella of the daughter's having entered the frame, of having become the properly fetishised image of womanhood, she cannot, like Stella, believe in happiness for either. She knows better because she has seen what each has had to give up to assume these final roles. But isn't it just such a balance of knowledge and belief (of the fetishist's contradictory phrase 'I know very well but just the same ...')[55] that has characterised the sophisticated juggling act of the ideal cinematic spectator?

The psychoanalytic model of cinematic pleasure has been based on the phenomenon of fetishistic disavowal: the contradictory gesture of *believing* in an illusion (the cinematic image, the female penis) and yet *knowing* that it is an illusion, an imaginary signifier. This model sets up a situation in which the woman becomes a kind of failed fetishist: lacking a penis she lacks the biological foundation to engage in the sophisticated game of juggling presence and absence in cinematic representation; hence her presumed over-identification, her lack of the knowledge of illusion[56] and the resulting one, two, and three handkerchief movies. But the female spectator of *Stella Dallas* finds herself balancing a very different kind of knowledge and belief than the mere existence or non-existence of the female phallus. She *knows* that women can find no genuine form of representation under patriarchal structures of voyeuristic or fetishistic viewing, because she has seen Stella lose herself as a woman and as a mother. But at the same time she *believes* that women exist outside this phallic economy, because she has glimpsed moments of resistance in which two women have been able to represent themselves to themselves through the mediation of their own gazes.

This is a very different form of disavowal. It is both a *knowing* recognition of the limitations of woman's representation in patriarchal language and a contrary *belief* in the illusion of a pre-Oedipal space between women free of the mastery and control of the male look. The contradiction is as compelling for the woman as for the male fetishist, even more so because it is not based on the presence or absence of an anatomical organ, but on the dialectic of the woman's socially constructed position under patriarchy.

It is in a very different sense, then, that the psychoanalytic concepts of voyeurism and fetishism can inform a feminist theory of cinematic spectatorship – not as inscribing woman totally on the side of the passive object who is merely seen, as Mulvey and others have so influentially argued, but by examining the contradictions that animate women's very active and fragmented ways of seeing.

I would not go so far as to argue that these contradictions operate for the female viewer in every film about relations between women. But the point of focusing on a film that both addresses female audiences and contains important structures of viewing *between* women is to suggest that it does not take a radical and consciously feminist break with patriarchal ideology to represent the contradictory aspects of the woman's position under patriarchy. It does not even take the ironic distancing devices of, for example, the Sirkian melodrama to generate the kind of active, critical response that sees the work of ideology in the film. Laura Mulvey has written that the ironic endings of Sirkian melodrama are progressive in their defiance of unity and closure:

> It is as though the fact of having a female point of view dominating the narrative produces an excess which precludes satisfaction. If the melodrama offers a fantasy escape for the identifying women in the audience, the illusion is so strongly marked by recognisable, real and familiar traps that the escape is closer to a daydream than a fairy story. The few Hollywood films made with a female audience in mind evoke contradictions rather than reconciliation, with the alternative to mute surrender to society's overt pressure lying in defeat by its unconscious laws.[57]

Although Mulvey here speaks primarily of the ironic Sirkian melodrama, her description of the contradictions encountered by the female spectator apply in a slightly different way to the very un-ironic *Stella Dallas*. I would argue that *Stella Dallas* is a progressive film not because it defies both unity and closure, but because the definitive closure of its ending produces no parallel unity in its spectator. And because the film has constructed its spectator in a female subject position locked into a primary identification with another female subject, it is possible for this spectator, like Val – the mother spectator from *The Women's Room* whose reaction to the film is quoted at the head of this article – to impose her own radical feminist reading on the film. Without such female subject positions inscribed within the text, the stereotypical self-sacrificing mother character would flatten into the mere maternal essences of so many motherly figures for melodrama.

Stella Dallas is a classic maternal melodrama played with a very straight face. Its ambivalences and contradictions are not cultivated with the intention of revealing the work of patriarchal ideology within it. But like any melodrama that offers a modicum of realism yet conforms to the 'reconciliation of the irreconcilable' proper to the genre,[58] it must necessarily produce, when dealing with conflicts among women, what Val calls a 'shock of recognition'. This shock is not the pleasurable recognition of a verisimilitude that generates naïve belief, but the shock of seeing, as Val explains, 'how they got us to consent to our own eradication'. Val and other female spectators typically do *not* consent to such eradicating resolutions. They, and we, resist the only way we can by struggling with the contradictions inherent in these images of ourselves and our situation. It is a terrible underestimation of the female viewer to presume that she is wholly seduced by a naïve belief in these masochistic images, that she has allowed these images to put her in her place the way the films themselves put their women characters in their place.

It seems, then, that Adrienne Rich's eloquent plea for works that can embody the 'essential female tragedy' of mother–daughter passion, rapture, and loss is misguided but only with respect to the mode of tragedy. I hope to have begun to show that this loss finds expression under patriarchy in the 'distorted' and 'misused' cathexes of the maternal melodrama. For unlike tragedy melodrama does not reconcile its audience to an inevitable suffering. Rather than raging against a fate that the audience has learned to accept, the female hero often accepts a fate that the audience at least partially questions.

The divided female spectator identifies with the woman whose very triumph is often in her own victimisation, but she also criticises the price of a transcendent 'eradication' which the victim-hero must pay. Thus, although melodrama's impulse towards the just 'happy ending' usually places the woman hero in a final position of subordination, the 'lesson' for female audiences is certainly not to become similarly eradicated themselves. For all its masochism, for all its frequent devaluation of the individual person of the mother (as opposed to the abstract ideal of motherhood), the maternal melodrama presents a recognisable picture of woman's ambivalent position under patriarchy that has been an important source of realistic reflections of women's lives. This may be why the most effective feminist films of recent years have been those works – like Sally Potter's *Thriller*, Michelle Citron's *Daughter Rite*, Chantal Akerman's *Jeanne Dielman...*, and even Jacques Rivette's *Céline and Julie Go Boating* – that work *within and against* the expectations of female self-sacrifice experienced in maternal melodrama.

Notes

1. *The Women's Room* (New York: Summit Books, 1977), p. 227.
2. An interesting and comprehensive introduction to this sub-genre can be found in

320

Christian Viviani's 'Who is Without Sin? The Maternal Melodrama in American Film, 1930–1939' (reprinted in this anthology, pp. 83–99).

B. Ruby Rich and I have also briefly discussed the genre of these sacrificial maternal melodramas in our efforts to identify the context of Michelle Citron's avant-garde feminist film, *Daughter Rite*. Citron's film is in many ways the flip side to the maternal melodrama, articulating the daughter's confused anger and love at the mother's sacrificial stance. 'The Right of Re-Vision: Michelle Citron's *Daughter Rite*', *Film Quarterly* 35, no. 1, Fall 1981, pp. 17–22.

3. *The Second Sex*, trans. H. M. Parshley (New York: Bantam, 1961), pp. 488–9.

4. An excellent introduction to this rapidly growing area of study is Marianne Hirsch's review essay, 'Mothers and Daughters', *Signs: Journal of Women in Culture and Society* 7, no. 1, 1981, pp. 200–22. See also Judith Kegan Gardiner, 'On Female Identity and Writing by Women', *Critical Inquiry* 8, no. 2, Winter 1981, pp. 347–61.

5. *Of Woman Born* (New York: Bantam, 1977), pp. 240, 226.

6. *The Melodramatic Imagination: Balzac, Henry James, Melodrama and the Mode of Excess* (New Haven: Yale University Press, 1976).

7. Martha Vicinus, writing about the nineteenth-century melodrama, suggests that melodrama's 'appropriate' endings offer 'a temporary reconciliation of the irreconcilable'. The concern is typically not with what is possible or actual but what is desirable. 'Helpless and Unfriended: Nineteenth-Century Domestic Melodrama', *New Literary History*, 13, no. 1, Autumn 1981, p. 132. Peter Brooks emphasises a similar quality of wish-fulfilment in melodrama, even arguing that psychoanalysis offers a systematic realisation of the basic aesthetics of the genre: 'If psychoanalysis has become the nearest modern equivalent of religion in that it is a vehicle for the cure of souls, melodrama is a way station toward this status, a first indication of how conflict, enactment, and cure must be conceived in a secularised world', p. 202.

8. Most prominent among these are Claire Johnston's 'Women's Cinema as Counter Cinema' in *Notes on Women's Cinema*, (ed.) Claire Johnston, *Screen*, Pamphlet 2 (SEFT: 1972); and Laura Mulvey's 'Visual Pleasure and Narrative Cinema', *Screen* 16, no. 3, Autumn 1975, pp. 6–18.

9. The list of feminist work on this film is impressive. It includes: Pam Cook, 'Duplicity in Mildred Pierce', in *Women in Film Noir*, (ed.) E. Ann Kaplan (London: BFI, 1978), pp. 68–82; Molly Haskell, *From Reverence to Rape: The Treatment of Women in the Movies* (NY: Holt, Rinehart and Winston, 1973), pp. 175–80; Annette Kuhn, *Women's Pictures: Feminism and Cinema* (London: Routledge and Kegan Paul, 1982), pp. 28–35; Joyce Nelson, '*Mildred Pierce* Reconsidered', *Film Reader* 2, January 1977, pp. 65–70; and Janet Walker, 'Feminist Critical Practice: Female Discourse in *Mildred Pierce*', *Film Reader* 5, 1982, pp. 164–71.

10. Molly Haskell only gave the film brief mention in her chapter on 'The Woman's Film', *From Reverence to Rape: The Treatment of Women in the Movies* (NY: Holt, Rinehart and Winston, 1973), pp. 153–88. Since then the film has been discussed by Christian Viviani (see note 2); Charles Affron in *Cinema and Sentiment* (Chicago: University of Chicago Press, 1983), pp. 74–6; Ben Brewster, 'A Scene at the Movies', *Screen* 23, no. 2, July–August 1982, pp. 4–5; and E. Ann

Kaplan, 'Theories of Melodrama: A Feminist Perspective', *Women and Perform-ance: A Journal of Feminist Theory* 1, no. 1, Spring/Summer 1983, pp. 40–48. Kaplan also has a longer article on the film, 'The Case of the Missing Mother: Maternal Issues in Vidor's *Stella Dallas*', *Heresies* 16, 1983, pp. 81–5. Laura Mulvey also mentions the film briefly in her 'Afterthoughts on "Visual Pleasure and Narrative Cinema" Inspired by *Duel in the Sun* (King Vidor, 1946)', *Framework* 15/16/17, Summer 1981, pp. 12–15 – but only in the context of Vidor's much more male-oriented western. Thus, although *Stella Dallas* keeps coming up in the context of discussions of melodrama, sentiment, motherhood, and female spectatorship, it has not been given the full scrutiny it deserves, except by Kaplan, many of whose arguments I challenge in the present work.

11. Mulvey, p. 11. See also most of the essays in *Re-vision: Essays in Feminist Film Criticism*, (eds.) Mary Ann Doane, Patricia Mellencamp, and Linda Williams (Frederick: University Publications of America, Inc., 1984).

12. Claire Johnston, for example, writes, 'Despite the enormous emphasis placed on women as spectacle in the cinema, woman as woman is largely absent.' 'Woman's Cinema as Counter-Cinema', *Notes on Women's Cinema*, p. 26.

13. Christine Gledhill, 'Developments in Feminist Film Criticism', *Re-vision: Essays in Feminist Film Criticism*, p. 31. Originally published in *Quarterly Review of Film Studies* 3, no. 4, 1978, pp. 457–93.

14. Mulvey, p. 7.

15. Mulvey, pp. 7, 18.

16. The few feminists who have begun this difficult but important work are: Mary Ann Doane, 'Film and the Masquerade: Theorizing the Female Spectator', *Screen* 23, no. 3–4, Sept.–Oct. 1982, pp. 74–87; Gertrud Koch, 'Why Women Go to the Movies', *Jump Cut* 27, July 1982, trans. Marc Silberman, pp. 51–3; Judith Mayne, 'The Woman at the Keyhole: Women's Cinema and Feminist Criticism', *Re-vision: Essays in Feminist Film Criticism*, pp. 44–66; and Mulvey herself in 'Afterthoughts on "Visual Pleasure and Narrative Cinema" Inspired by *Duel in the Sun* (King Vidor, 1946)', *Framework* 15/16/17, Summer 1981, pp. 12–15; B. Ruby Rich, in Michelle Citron et al., 'Women and Film: A Discussion of Feminist Aesthetics', *New German Critique* 13, 1978, pp. 77–107; and Tania Modleski, *Loving with a Vengeance: Mass Produced Fantasies for Women* (Hamden, CT.: Archon Books, 1982). Since I wrote this article, two important new books on women and film have appeared. Both take considerable account of the processes by which the female spectator identifies with screen images. They are: E. Ann Kaplan's *Women and Film: Both Sides of the Camera* (N.Y.: Methuen, 1983); and Teresa de Lauretis' *Alice Doesn't: Feminism, Semiotics, Cinema* (Blooming-ton: Indiana University Press, 1984).

17. Gledhill, p. 41.

18. Gledhill, p. 37.

19. Gledhill, p. 42.

20. Gledhill, pp. 44–5.

21. Freud begins this shift in the 1925 essay, 'Some Psychological Consequences of the Anatomical Distinction between the Sexes', *Standard Edition of the Complete Psychological Works* (Hogarth Press, 1953–74), vol 19. He continues it in the 1931 essay 'Female Sexuality', vol. 21.

22. Marianne Hirsch's review essay, 'Mothers and Daughters', *Signs: Journal of Women in Culture and Society* 7, no. 1, Autumn 1981, pp. 200–22, offers an excellent summary of the diverse strands of the continuing re-appraisal of the mother–daughter relation. Hirsch examines theories of this relation in Anglo-American and neo-Freudian object relations psychology (Chodorow, Miller, Dinnerstein), in Jungian myth criticism, and in the French feminist theories developing out of structuralism, post-structuralism, and Lacanian psychoanalysis. A recent study of how female connectedness affects female moral development is Carol Gilligan's *In a Different Voice* (Cambridge: Harvard Univ. Press, 1982).

23. Chodorow, *The Reproduction of Mothering: Psychoanalysis and the Sociology of Gender* (Berkeley: University of California Press, 1978), p. 7.

24. 'Oedipal asymmetries' is Chodorow's term, p. 7.

25. Chodorow, p. 178.

26. Marianne Hirsch surveys the importance of this point in her review essay 'Mothers and Daughters', p. 209. So, too, does Judith Kegan Gardiner in 'On Female Identity and Writing by Women', *Critical Inquiry: Writing and Sexual Difference* 8, no. 2, Winter 1981, pp. 347–61.

27. Chodorow, p. 188.

28. These others include: Dorothy Dinnerstein, *The Mermaid and the Minotaur: Sexual Arrangements and the Human Malaise* (New York: Harper and Row, 1976); Jessie Bernard, *The Future of Motherhood* (New York: Dial Press, 1974); and Jean Baker Miller, *Toward a New Psychology of Women* (Boston: Beacon Press, 1976).

29. This is the real advance of Chodorow's theories over those of an earlier generation of feminist psychoanalysts. Karen Horney, for example, found it necessary, as both Juliet Mitchell and Jane Gallop point out, to resort to generalising statements of women's essential, biologically determined nature, thus leaving no possibility for change. Horney, 'On the Genesis of the Castration Complex in Women', *International Journal of Psycho-Analysis*, 5, 1924, pp. 50–65.

30. Paris: Editions de Minuit, 1974.

31. Other French feminists involved in this 'feminine writing' are Hélène Cixous, Monique Wittig, Julia Kristeva, and Michèle Montrelay. A critical introduction to these writers can be found in Ann Rosalind Jones, 'Writing the Body: Toward an Understanding of L'Ecriture féminine', and Helene Vivienne Wenzel's 'The Text as Body/Politics: An Appreciation of Monique Wittig's Writings in Context', both in *Feminist Studies* 7, no. 2, Summer 1981, pp. 247–87.

32. 'Ce sexe qui n'en est pas un', trans. Claudia Reeder, *New French Feminisms*, (ed.) Elaine Marks and Isabelle de Courtivron (Amherst: University of Mass. Press, 1980), pp. 100–1.

33. Anglo-American feminists have thus been critical of the new French feminists for two different reasons: American feminists have criticised an essentialism that would seem to preclude change (see, for example, the essay by Jones referred to in note 31); British feminists have criticised their apparent failure to account for the way the female body is mediated by language (see, for example, Beverly Brown and Parveen Adams, 'The Feminine Body and Feminist Politics', *m/f*, no. 3, 1979, pp. 35–50).

34. Irigaray, pp. 106–7.

35. Rich, *Signs* 5, no. 4, Summer 1980, pp. 631–60.

36. Irigaray, p. 110.

37. Mary Ann Doane, 'Womans' Stake: Filming the Female Body', *October* 17, Summer 1981, p. 30.

38. Kristeva's work has been translated in two volumes: *Desire in Language: A Semiotic Approach to Literature and Art*, trans. Thomas Gora, Alice Jardine, Leon S. Roudiez (New York: Columbia University Press, 1980); and *About Chinese Women*, trans. Anita Barrows (New York: Horizon Books, 1977).

39. Alice Jardine, 'Theories of the Feminine: Kristeva', *enclitic* 4, no. 2, Fall 1980, p. 13.

40. Kristeva, 'Motherhood According to Giovanni Bellini', in *Desire in Language*, pp. 237–70.

41. Jane Gallop, 'The Phallic Mother: Freudian Analysis', in *The Daughter's Seduction: Feminism and Psychoanalysis* (Ithaca, New York: Cornell University Press, 1982), pp. 113–31.

42. Ann Kaplan emphasises this 'wrenching' of the filmic point of view away from Stella and towards the upper-class values and perspectives of Stephen and the townspeople. 'The Case of the Missing Mother', p. 83.

43. Doane, 'The Woman's Film: Possession and Address' (reprinted in this anthology, pp. 283–298).

44. The term – originally used by Joan Rivière – is employed in Mary Ann Doane, 'Film and the Masquerade: Theorising the Female Spectator', *Screen* 23, no. 34, September/October 1982, pp. 74–87.

45. Ann Kaplan, 'The Case of the Missing Mother', p. 83.

46. Ibid.

47. Molly Haskell notes this tendency of women audiences to come away with a memory of heroic revolt, rather than the defeat with which so many films end, in her pioneering study *From Reverence to Rape: The Treatment of Women in the Movies* (New York: Holt, Rinehart and Winston, 1973), p. 31.

48. Modleski, 'The Search for Tomorrow in Today's Soap Opera: Notes on a Feminine Narrative Form', *Film Quarterly* 33, no. 1, Fall 1979, p. 14. A longer version of this article can be found in Modleski's book *Loving with a Vengeance: Mass Produced Fantasies for Women* (Hamden, CT: Archon Books, 1982), pp. 85–109.

49. Kaplan, 'Theories of Melodrama', p. 46.

50. Doane, 'Film and the Masquerade', p. 87.

51. Mulvey, 'Afterthoughts on "Visual Pleasure and Narrative Cinema" Inspired by *Duel in the Sun* (King Vidor, 1946)', p. 13.

52. Doane, p. 87.

53. Ruby Rich, in Michelle Citron et al., 'Women and Film: A Discussion of Feminist Aesthetics', *New German Critique* 13, 1978, p. 87. Although Rich goes on to suggest that this dialectic is an either/or choice – 'to identify either with Marilyn Monroe or with the man behind me hitting the back of my seat with his knees' – I think the more proper sense of the word would be to construe it as a continuous conflict and tension that informs female viewing and which in many cases does not allow the choice of one or the other.

54. Ben Brewster has cited the many cinematic references of the original novel as an

indication of just how effective as an appeal to reality the cinematic illusion has become. 'A Scene at the Movies', *Screen* 23, no. 2, July–August 1983, pp. 4–5.

55. Freud's theory is that the little boy believes in the maternal phallus even after he knows better because he has seen evidence that it does not exist has been characterised by Octave Mannoni as a contradictory statement that both asserts and denies the mother's castration. In this 'Je sais bien mais quand même' (I know very well but just the same), the 'just the same' is the fetish disavowal. Mannoni, *Clefs pour l'imaginaire* (Paris: Seuil, 1969), pp. 9–30. Christian Metz later applied this fetishistic structure to the institution of the cinema as the creator of believable fictions of perceptually real human beings who are nevertheless absent from the scene. Thus the cinema aims all of its technical prowess at the disavowal of the lack on which its 'imaginary signifier' is based. *The Imaginary Signifier: Psychoanalysis and the Cinema*, trans. Celia Britton, Annwyl Williams, Ben Brewster, and Alfred Guzzetti (Bloomington Indiana: Indiana University Press, 1982), pp. 69–76.

56. Doane, 'Film and the Masquerade', pp. 80–1.

57. Mulvey, 'Notes on Sirk and Melodrama' (Reprinted in this anthology, pp. 75–79).

58. Vicinus, p. 132.

Time and Desire in the Woman's Film

TANIA MODLESKI

From *Cinema Journal* 23, no. 3, Spring 1984, pp. 19–30.

MAX OPHULS' 1948 film, *Letter from an Unknown Woman*, which is set in turn-of-the-century Vienna, begins late at night with the hero of the story, Stefan, returning by coach to his home and promising to fight a duel at dawn. That his attitude toward the situation is utterly frivolous is obvious from his remark as he steps out of the coach: 'Gentlemen, I don't so much mind being killed, but you know how I hate to get up in the morning.' Reaching his home, he tells his mute servant, John, that they should prepare for immediate departure since he does not intend to fight the duel. At stake here is a man's word. 'A man's word is his honour', and, as Adrienne Rich observes, this notion of honour usually has 'something to do with killing'.[1] The terms of drama seem already to have been posed with utter clarity. Stefan lives a life of ease, indulgence, and irresponsibility, unwilling to accept the values of duty and sacrifice espoused by his patriarchal society.

We might suspect, then, that the film's movement will involve Stefan's coming to repudiate the former childishness of his ways and to acknowledge the sway of patriarchal law. And indeed the final sequence of the film shows Stefan bravely setting off to keep his word and get himself killed. Thus, though the body of the film concerns the story of Lisa, the woman referred to in the title, it would appear that her story is really a story of and for the man, and, looked at this way, the film seems to provide exceptionally strong support for those critics who contend that there *is* no such thing as a woman's film, that Hollywood films are always dramas of and for the male.

When Stefan enters the house, he is given a letter which begins, 'By the time you read this, I may be dead'. It is the letter from the unknown woman who has indeed lived her life in and for Stefan, has even had a child by him, and yet has remained silent about her life-long devotion until her words, written in death's shadow, can no longer possibly bring her any benefit. At stake, then, is not only a man's word, but a woman's silence. At one point in the film, Lisa explains her radical refusal to speak about her own and their son's existence; I wanted to be the one woman you had known who never asked you for anything.' As Lisa perceives it, to speak as a woman would mean losing herself and becoming an object like the many other women in Stefan's life. However, when her own impending death releases her from her vow of silence, she only reveals how little of herself there is to know, so thoroughly has she become one with the man. Lisa's is the classic dilemma of what psychoanalysis calls the hysterical woman, caught between two equally alienating alternatives: either identifying with the man or being an object of his desire.

'Silence is the mark of hysteria', writes Hélène Cixous. 'The great hysterics have lost speech, they are aphonic, and at times they have lost more than speech. They are pushed to the point of choking, nothing gets through.'[2] It seems fair to say that many of the classic film melodramas from the 30s through the 50s are peopled by great, or near-great, hysterics – women possessed by an overwhelming desire to express themselves, to make themselves known, but continually confronting the difficulty, if not the impossibility of realising this desire. In the various film versions of *Madame X* (another title signalling the woman's anonymity), the heroine's son is defending her from criminal charges, unaware that the woman is his mother. Though she longs to reveal herself to her son, she refuses to speak, for fear of ruining his status and career. In *The Old Maid*, Bette Davis's character, who has had a child out of wedlock, masquerades as the old maid aunt to her own daughter so that the daughter may marry a suitable – rich, upper-class – man. And Stella Dallas, on becoming aware of her hopelessly lower-class life-style, pretends to be interested in having a sexual affair in order to provoke her daughter to leave her. The central truth about Stella's feelings – that she loves her daughter to the exclusion of all else – remains unexpressed to the end.

In a short but illuminating article on film melodrama, Geoffrey Nowell-Smith has theorised a close connection between melodrama and conversion hysteria. He claims that castration is always at issue in Hollywood melo-drama because 'melodrama is fundamentally concerned with the child's prob-lems of growing up into a sexual identity within the family, under the aegis of a symbolic law which the Father incarnates.'[3] Now this applies to all the aforementioned films, and perhaps most obviously to *Letter from an Unknown Woman*, in which the duel may be understood as the castration Stefan finally comes to accept. But, Nowell-Smith argues, acceptance of cas-tration never occurs without repression, and in melodrama, what is repressed at the level of the *story* often returns through the music or the *mise en scène*. Hence melodrama's resemblance to conversion hysteria, in which 'the energy attached to an idea that has been repressed returns converted into a bodily symptom.'[4] Although Nowell-Smith's argument is persuasive, he never notes that traditionally medical science and psychoanalysis have labelled *women* hysterics.[5] Yet surely we find here a clue as to why for a large period of film

327

history melodrama and the 'woman's film' have been virtually synonymous terms. If women are hysterics in patriarchal culture because, according to the feminist argument, their voice has been silenced or repressed, and if melodrama deals with the return of the repressed through a kind of conversion hysteria, perhaps women have been attached to the genre because it provides an outlet for the repressed feminine voice.

Peter Brooks argues in his book on nineteenth-century stage melodrama that melodrama may even be *defined* as a genre which works to overcome all repression in order to achieve full expressivity. In the nineteenth century, it was the beauty of moral virtue that continually sought expression over whatever attempted to silence, or negate it. Often this beauty would be conveyed in *visual* terms, in the form, say, of a tableau. Nevertheless, melodrama is *not* primarily about the problems of sight and insight – the problems, that is, of tragedy. Brooks makes this point nicely in his discussion of the special place of the mute in many melodramatic plays:

> One is tempted to speculate that the different kinds of drama have their corresponding sense deprivations: for tragedy, blindness, since tragedy is about insight and illumination; for comedy, deafness, since comedy is concerned with problems in communication, misunderstandings and their consequences; and for melodrama, muteness, since melodrama is about expression.[6]

One need only point to the importance of the mute servant John in *Letter from an Unknown Woman* to demonstrate the force of Brooks's remarks. John is melodrama's equivalent to the figure of blind Tiresias in tragedy. He is, finally, the only character who is able to recognise Lisa and to name her, filling in the signature she herself has not been able to complete at the end of her letter.

It is this essentially melodramatic preoccupation with expression and muteness that Stephen Heath misses when he characterises the entire problem of *Letter from an Unknown Woman* and of narrative cinema in general as one of '*seeing* and *knowing*'.[7] In effect, Heath is collapsing all genres into one quintessentially masculine genre: tragedy, the paradigmatic example of which is *Oedipus*, with its privileging of sight and insight. For Heath, the project of the film is to present the woman 'as a desired and untouchable image, an endless *vision*.'[8] And indeed a crucial moment of the drama occurs when Stefan, on his way to fight the duel, glances back over his shoulder and sees Lisa standing behind the glass door where he first saw her years ago. The image of the woman, forever silenced, is presented as the lost object whom Stefan may mourn and incorporate, thereby successfully taking up castration. He can now assume his place in patriarchal culture, and Lisa's image disappears from the screen.

But though Heath deplores the repression of the woman effected by turning her into a sight whose only meaning is the insight it offers the man into his life, he himself may be said to maintain this repression. As Brooks points out, melodrama cannot be fully grasped by analysing it solely in terms of seeing and knowing. To continue relying on these terms is to obliterate what may be seeking expression through the women in the films; and it is also to contribute to the hystericisation of the female *spectator*, who is offered the limited choice between identifying with the man in his active desire or identifying with the passive, apparently mute object of that desire.

But how are we to begin attempting to locate a feminine voice in texts which repress it and which, as we saw in *Letter from an Unknown Woman*, grant possession of the Word only to men? Nowell-Smith, we have seen, suggests that the repressed aspects of the script reside in the *mise en scène*. Thomas Elsaesser, in an essay on film melodrama and its historical antecedents, argues that melodrama may best be understood in terms of 'spatial and musical categories' rather than 'intellectual or literary ones'.[9] Melodrama is, after all, a hybrid form which traditionally combines music and drama. In a brief discussion of the use of fairgrounds and carousels in film melodrama, Elsaesser claims that these motifs 'underscore the main action' and at the same time take on an independent significance. 'What such devices point to', Elsaesser concludes, 'is that in melodrama the *rhythm* of experience often establishes itself against its value (moral, intellectual).'[10] As wide-ranging as Elsaesser's essay is, tracing the development of melodrama cross-culturally through many centuries, he does not address himself to women's particular attraction to the genre. However, it is possible to appropriate his insight for our purposes, and so we will begin by looking at melodrama's rhythm for meanings which are opposed to the male Word.

In *Letter from an Unknown Woman*, Lisa and Stefan enjoy one night together, and this episode occurs in the middle of the film. They dine, dance, ride in a coach, and visit an amusement park where they sit in a stationary train while on a painted backdrop the scenery of the world revolves around them. Carousel music plays as they discuss the pleasures of travel. When they run out of countries to visit, Stefan pays the attendant to begin again, saying, 'We will revisit the scenes of our youth.' For Lisa these words are prophetic: after losing Stefan for many years and finding him again, she revisits the scenes of their youth in her quest to be reunited with him – returning to the place where they had dinner, buying flowers from a vendor as they had years ago, and going back to his apartments where they once made love. Most painful of all, she revisits the train station where Stefan departed from her so many years before, and this time sends her son away from her – to his death, as it turns out. This excessive repetition characterises many film melodramas, and perhaps reaches its apotheosis in the 1932 film *Back Street*. At the end of this film the heroine, about to die, revisits in fantasy the scene of her youth when she missed meeting her lover and his mother in the park. As a result of this lost opportunity, she was not able to marry the hero and instead became his mistress, forced to reside in the back street of his life. Her final thoughts materialise on the screen as she pictures herself walking in the dazzling sunlight of the park towards the mother and son who welcome her into their family.

Unlike most Hollywood narratives, which give the impression of a progressive movement towards an end that is significantly different from the beginning, much melodrama gives the impression of a ceaseless returning to a prior state. Perhaps the effect may be compared to sitting in a train watching the world move by, and each time you reach a destination, you discover that it is the place you never really left. In this respect melodrama appears to be quite closely linked to an hysterical experience of time and place. The hysteric, in Freud's famous formulation, suffers from reminiscences. In melodrama, the important moments of the narrative are often felt as eruptions of involuntary memory, to the point where sometimes the *only* major events are repetitions of former ones. In *The Old Maid*, for example, four weddings occurring among two generations comprise the large units of the film, huge gaps in time separating some of these units. Melodrama, then, tends to be concerned with what Julia Kristeva calls the 'anterior temporal modalities', these modalities being stereotypically linked with female subjectivity in general (with the 'cycles, gestation, the eternal recurrence of a biological rhythm which conforms to that of nature').[11] As Kristeva notes, this conception of time is indissociable from space and is opposed to the idea of time most commonly recognised in Western thought: 'time as project, teleology, linear and prospective unfolding; time as departure, progression, and arrival – in other words, the time of history.'[12] The train which first carries Stefan away from Lisa and then takes her son to his death is a train that departs, progresses, and arrives, whereas the train on which Lisa prefers to travel is one which, like the woman, always stays in its place. And as the world turns, visiting inevitably becomes a revisiting.

Two conceptions of time here seem unalterably opposed: the time of repetition, which for Lisa means never entering history, but forever remaining childlike, fixated on the scenes of her youth. And the time of history which Stefan definitively enters at the end of the film when he takes his journey by coach to meet Lisa's husband and his own death. For Stefan this means, as we have already observed, that he must put away childish things and repudiate the self-indulgent life he has been leading in order to become a responsible adult. It is no mere coincidence that Stefan's entry into historical time and adulthood occurs simultaneously with his coming to accept the binding power of the word and the sway of death. For to quote Kristeva, this 'linear time is that of language considered as the enunciation of sentences ... and ... this time rests on its own stumbling block, which is also the stumbling block of that enunciation – death.'[13] And with the entry into historical time and language occurs the birth of desire: Stefan looks back at Lisa with recognition and longing only when the possibility of possessing her is forever lost. In accepting his place in language and history, he must assume a certain relation to desire: one based on an expectation destined to remain eternally unfulfilled.

But I have been a bit disingenuous in considering the antinomy between 'hysterical time' and what Kristeva calls 'obsessional time' to be based on sexual difference. Superficially it appears that in the film woman's time is hysterical time and man's time is obsessional time. Closer analysis, however, reveals that Stefan is the hysteric until the last few moments of the film, whereas Lisa adopts an altogether different relationship to time and desire which points beyond this deadly antinomy. For Stefan is the one who truly suffers from reminiscences. He cannot remember the name or the face of the woman who is the mother of his child and who is also, as the film implies, his muse. In a way, he has had a family, a career, and an entire life and never known it: the woman has lived it for him. When he sees Lisa, he struggles to overcome his forgetting and, in anguish, speaks of something which lies just over the edge of his memory. Unable to remember the woman who alone gives his life significance, Stefan is doomed to an existence of meaningless repetition, especially in relation to women, who become virtually indistinguishable to him. Moreover, it might plausibly be argued that insofar as Lisa is forced to keep repeating events, she is to a certain extent enacting *his* compulsion, for she herself has not forgotten a single moment with him.

That men may be hysterics too is an important point for feminism. Perhaps we have too quickly and unreservedly accepted theories of feminine hysteria. For if it can be said, as Lisa herself does say, that she has had no life apart from the moments with Stefan and his son, it is equally true that Stefan has had no life except the one Lisa has lived on his behalf. She has undergone all the joys and sorrows attendant on loving, possessing and losing a family while he, the father of that family, has remained oblivious. The woman and her emotional life is what Stefan has repressed and, like John Marcher in Henry James's 'The Beast in the Jungle', he is doomed to keep suffering his fate without ever having known it.

Intuitively, of course, we ally melodrama with the feminine insofar as it is a genre quintessentially concerned with emotional expression. Women in melodrama almost always suffer the pains of love and even death (as in *Dark Victory*) while husbands, lovers, and children remain partly or totally unaware of their experience. Women carry the burden of feeling for everyone. *Letter from an Unknown Woman* simply takes this situation to its furthest extreme and shows that though women are hysterics with respect to male desire, men may be hysterics with respect to feminine 'emotion'; unable to experience it directly, they gain access to it only at second hand.

Lisa's letter might be said to perform the 'talking cure' for Stefan. If women are traditionally considered hysterics because, in Catherine Clément's concise formulation, they feel in the body what comes from outside the body, we can again see how Stefan is placed in the position of hysteric, as throughout the long night it takes to read the letter the disembodied feminine voice is repeatedly shown to be speaking through the mute Stefan.[14] And just as Freud said that the hysteric is a visual type of person whose cure consists in making a ' "picture" vanish "like a ghost that has been laid to rest", ... getting rid of it by turning it into words', so too is Stefan cured when after reading Lisa's letter, he looks back at her image behind the glass door, and looks back again to find that the picture has vanished.[15] The ghost of femininity – that spectre that haunts cinema – has been laid to rest.

Stefan's trajectory represents an interesting variant on that which Laura Mulvey claims is typical of one strain of melodrama. In her 'Afterthoughts on Visual Pleasure and Narrative Cinema', she suggests that there is a kind of film in which 'a woman central protagonist is shown to be unable to achieve a stable sexual identity, torn between the deep blue sea of passive femininity and the devil of regressive masculinity.'[16] Mulvey points to Freud's theories of femininity, according to which the young girl first goes through an active masculine phase before attaining the 'correct' feminine position. In *Letter from an Unknown Woman*, it is the man who first goes through a feminine phase before reaching the active, phallic phase and thus achieving a stable sexual identity. It is possible that Stefan's experience is analogous to that undergone by the male spectator of melodrama. For it may be that insofar as films like this are appealing to men (and there is plenty of evidence to suggest that *Letter from an Unknown Woman* strongly appeals to male critics), it is because these films provide them with a vicarious, hysterical, experience of femininity which can be more definitively laid to rest for having been 'worked through'.

And it may be that one of the appeals of such a film for women is precisely its tendency to feminise the man, to complicate and destabilise his identity. There is a moment in *Letter from an Unknown Woman* when confusion in sexual identity reigns supreme – the moment when after years of separation Lisa sees Stefan again at the opera. Briefly we see a close-up of Stefan through a soft focus filter, the device typically used in filming beautiful women. The image appears against a grey background which renders its diegetic status uncertain. The cutting from Lisa to Stefan further enhances this uncertainty, as it is unclear how each is placed in relation to the other and who is looking at whom. Finally, ambiguity reaches almost vertiginous extremes when over the image of Stefan, which is strongly coded to connote what Mulvey calls 'to-be-looked-at-ness', Lisa's voice says in some panic, 'Somewhere out there were your eyes and I knew I couldn't escape them.'[17] Nowell-Smith argues that often the ' "hysterical" moment of a text [that is, the moment when the repressed element returns to find expression in a bodily symptom] can be identified as the point at which the realist representative convention breaks down.'[18] Here we find a classic example of an hysterical moment in which the possibility of feminine desire being actively aimed at the passive, eroticised male is briefly glimpsed while being explicitly denied at the verbal level. Interestingly, in Heath's discussion of this scene, he for once listens only to the words, which articulate woman's traditional position as object of the look, and completely misses the subversive element of feminine desire which is struggling for expression in the body of the text.[19]

Partly because the erotic is conventionally equated with the feminine, it is paradoxically not the virile, masculinised male, the so-called 'man's man', who elicits woman's desire in many of these films, but the feminine man: the attractive, cosmopolitan type (John Boles in *Stella Dallas, Only Yesterday,* and the first version of *Back Street*) or the well-bred, charming foreigner (Charles Boyer in the second version of *Back Street*; Louis Jourdan in *Letter from an Unknown Woman*). Moreover, the man with 'feminine' attributes frequently functions as a figure upon whom feminine desires for freedom from patriarchal authority may be projected. Here I disagree with Mulvey who claims that in classic women's films like *Stella Dallas* the masculine figure enables the heroine to postpone the power of patriarchy.[20] *Stella Dallas*, in fact, provides a clear example to the contrary.

At the beginning of the film, Stephen Dallas, played by John Boles, is the son of a failed patriarch. His father, having gone bankrupt, has committed suicide, and Stephen has retreated from the world to take a management position in a rural factory. He is frequently figured as the rather lovely though unwitting object of Stella's desirous gaze as she watches him from behind her white picket fence or stares at his photograph in a newspaper clipping. He seems to be in all ways the antithesis of Stella's harsh and repressive father, and on him Stella pins her hope of escape from this patriarch. In a stunning sequence which ends the opening section of the film, Stella's father discovers that Stella has not been home all night. He sits with his back to the camera in the foreground of the picture and bangs his fist on the table shouting that Stella must never come home again. The mother cowers in the background and Stella's brother stands arguing with his father in the middle ground. This is a scene straight out of a nineteenth-century melodrama in which the stern patriarch prepares to exile his fallen daughter into the cold, cruel world. The sound of Stella's voice interrupts the argument, and the brother opens the door to Stella and Stephen who are coming up the porch stairs announcing their marriage. As the son runs back into the house, the screen door bangs shut on the couple, still outside, and the image fades. Patriarchy and its cruelties and excesses seem to be abruptly left behind, and the next scene shows Stella, now living in the city, returning from the hospital with her new-born daughter. However, the power of patriarchy has merely been postponed, since Stephen proves to be more domineering than Stella can bear. So she relinquishes her desire for men altogether and transfers it exclusively to her daughter.

The feminised man is attractive, then, because of the freedom he seems to offer the woman: freedom to get in touch with and to act upon her own desire and freedom to reject patriarchal power. The latter point is made forcefully in *Letter from an Unknown Woman*, whose family romance involves two sets of fathers: the true fathers and the false fathers.[21] The false fathers – representative of patriarchal values and attitudes – are firstly, Lisa's stepfather, a man attached to the military who takes Lisa away from Vienna and attempts to marry her off to a stiff, boring young lieutenant; and, secondly, the stepfather of Lisa's son, a military man always prating about duty, sacrifice, and responsibility. This is the man with whom Stefan is destined to fight the duel. Stefan, the father of Lisa's child, is one of the true fathers. Although he is a womaniser, this activity paradoxically womanises *him*, for it immerses him in a sensuous existence stereotypically associated with the feminine and running counter to the life of self-denial espoused by Lisa's husband. And then there is Lisa's real father, who, though dead, is very much alive in Lisa's imagination. On the train in the amusement park Lisa tells Stefan of all the make-believe journeys she and her father took when she was a little girl, vividly evoking the pleasures and pains encountered in various climates. Lisa's father strikingly resembles the pre-Oedipal, imaginary father Julia Kristeva has theorised.[22] He is the spokesman for creativity and play and as such he represents a potential escape from the two neurotic modes of existence in which Stefan is successively trapped: the hysterical and the obsessional. If Stefan, who could be a great pianist, were to heed the message given him by Lisa through the imaginary father, he would no longer be forced to choose between a sensuous but meaningless and repetitive existence and a life given over to duty and sacrifice.

The 'pre-Oedipal' father is, I would argue, another manifestation of the feminised male who helps the woman reject the repressive father by authorising her own desire. For while Lisa appears here to be doubly an hysteric, invoking the words and activities of one man for the benefit of another, she is actually articulating a relation to the world that in the film is uniquely her own. On the train and elsewhere Lisa demonstrates an allegience to the imagination which she considers superior to lived experience.[23] Clearly this applies to her entire existence, since she has had only one brief interlude with Stefan in a lifetime of desiring him. Like the voyages she took with her father, her journey with Stefan has gone nowhere, has been an adventure mainly of consciousness.

But that it has *been* conscious makes all the difference. We have seen that *Letter from an Unknown Woman* enacts a process of mourning for the man. Stefan has forgotten everything he has had and never realised what he could have had, and therefore in reading the letter he must work through the pain of loss and nonfulfilment in order to 'lay the ghost to rest'. Lisa, however, has remained fully aware of what was and what might have been; and having buried nothing she has no need to mourn. Hélène Cixous finds in the question of mourning a difference between men and women. I would like to quote her at length because her words open up the possibility of a new way of thinking about women's experience in melodrama and women's response *to* melodrama:

> Man cannot live without resigning himself to loss. He has to mourn. It's his way of withstanding castration. He goes through castration, that is, and by sublimation incorporates the lost object. Mourning, resigning oneself to loss, means not losing. When you've lost something and the loss is a dangerous one, you refuse to admit that something of yourself might be lost in the lost object. So you 'mourn', you make haste to recover the investment made in the lost object. But I believe women *do not mourn*, and this is where the pain lies. When you've mourned it's all over after a year, there's no more suffering. Woman, though, does not mourn, does not resign herself to loss. She basically *takes up the challenge of loss* ..., seizing it, living it. Leaping. This goes with not withholding; she does not withhold. She does not withhold, hence the impression of constant return evoked by this lack of withholding. It's like a kind of open memory that ceaselessly makes way. And in the end, she will write this not withholding, this not writing; she writes of not writing, not happening.[24]

On the train which goes nowhere, Lisa describes journeys which did not happen, and the exquisite enjoyment they occasioned. In doing so, she articulates one of the basic pleasures of melodrama, which is also fundamentally about events that do not happen: the wedding that did not occur; the meeting in the park that was missed; and, above all, the word that was not spoken. Not speaking is very different from *keeping* one's word – the very phrase suggests the withholding and the resistance to loss which Cixous attributed to masculinity. Lisa resists speech not out of a need to hoard the word and not only because she wants to be different from Stefan's other women. Rather, she refuses to hold on to a man who has forgotten her, and what's more important, refuses to *hold him to* an obligation. Not seeing the relationship in terms of an investment or debt – that is, in terms of the property relations which, according to Cixous, structure masculine sexuality – she will not make him pay. So she takes up the challenge of loss and lives it. And from one point of view this challenge is more radical than the one Stefan takes up at the end of the film, resigning himself to his loss and the fate which consequently awaits him.

Cixous's words invite us to look deeper into the experience of loss which is

335

at the heart of melodrama. After all, what lingers on in our memories long after the films have ended are just those moments when the heroine relinquishes all that has mattered in her life: Lisa saying goodbye to her son at the train station, where he promises, like his father before him, to see her in two weeks; Stella Dallas standing behind an iron fence watching her daughter's wedding through the window; Bette Davis's heroine in *Dark Victory* waiting in a darkened room for death to overtake her, having cheerfully sent her husband off to a medical convention. Cixous, in a rather poetic manner, suggests that in order to understand women's experience of loss, we must go beyond the traditional psychoanalytic model based on the male's castration anxiety and his relation to the lost object. Nor do we gain in understanding by relegating woman to the position of hysteric, where film critics and theorists have been eager to place her. For though I began this paper by indicating that Lisa, the archetypal melodramatic heroine, seems to fit neatly into the psychoanalytic category of hysteric, I would now like to point to the inadequacy of this model for understanding the position of woman in the woman's film.

The experience Lisa attempts to articulate on the train to nowhere is neither obsessional nor hysterical. It is not obsessional, for it does not entail moving forward through time and space towards an ever-receding goal until one reaches the stumbling block of death. She shows that one can *be moved* without moving. And it is only superficially the experience of an hysteric. According to Freud, the hysteric, who suffers from reminiscences, is 'linked to place'.[25] Now, this would seem accurately to characterise Lisa as she sits in a train that stays in place and reminisces about past journeys with her father. But the point is that Lisa does not *suffer* from reminiscences, as Stefan does. She voluntarily and even joyfully evokes them, here as elsewhere ceaselessly gives way to them, demonstrating the possession of the 'open memory' Cixous describes. Hence the impression of constant return, which in her case has nothing compulsive about it. In his discussion of the film, Stephen Heath remarks, 'Repetition is the return to the same in order to abolish the difficult time of desire, and the resurgence in that very moment of inescapable difference.'[26] This is only partly true: it is true of Stefan, who, because he does not recognise the object of his desire, makes his experience with Lisa a mere repetition of those he has had with other women. For Lisa, however, and perhaps for all the women in melodrama constantly revisiting the scenes of their youth, repetition and return are manifestations of *another* relationship to time and space, desire and memory, and it is of this difference that the text speaks to me.[27]

Notes

1. Adrienne Rich, *On Lies, Secrets, and Silence: Selected Prose 1966–1978* (New York: Norton, 1979), p. 186.
2. Hélène Cixous, 'Castration or Decapitation?' trans. Annette Kuhn, *Signs: Journal of Women in Culture and Society* 7, no. 1, Autumn 1981, p. 49.
3. Geoffrey Nowell-Smith, 'Minnelli and Melodrama' (reprinted in this anthology, pp. 70–74).
4. Ibid., p. 73.
5. A point made in passing by Griselda Pollock in her 'Report on the Weekend School', which appears in *Screen* vol. 18, no. 2, p. 109.
6. Peter Brooks, *The Melodramatic Imagination: Balzac, Henry James, Melodrama, and the Mode of Excess* (New Haven: Yale Univ. Press, 1976), pp. 56–7.
7. Stephen Heath, 'The Question Oshima', in *Questions of Cinema* (Bloomington: Indiana University Press, 1981), p. 148.
8. Ibid., p. 146.
9. Thomas Elsaesser, 'Tales of Sound and Fury: Observations on the Family Melodrama' (reprinted in this anthology, pp. 43–69).
10. Ibid., p. 48.
11. Julia Kristeva, 'Women's Time', trans. Alice Jardine and Harry Blake, *Signs: Journal of Women in Culture and Society* 7, no. 1, Autumn 1981, p. 16.
12. Ibid., p. 17.
13. Ibid., p. 17.
14. Catherine Clément, 'Enslaved Enclave', in *New French Feminisms*, (eds.) Elaine Marks and Isabelle de Courtivron (Amherst: University of Massachusetts Press, 1980), p. 134.
15. Quoted in Joan Copjec, '*Flavit et Dissipati Sunt*', *October*, 18, Fall 1981, p. 21.
16. Laura Mulvey, 'Afterthoughts on "Visual Pleasure and Narrative Cinema" Inspired by "Duel in the Sun"', *Framework*, nos. 15/16/17, 1981, p. 12.
17. Laura Mulvey, 'Visual Pleasure and Narrative Cinema', in *Women and the Cinema*, (eds.) Karyn Kay and Gerald Peary (New York: Dutton, 1977), p. 418.
18. Nowell-Smith, 'Minnelli and Melodrama', pp. 70–74 of this anthology.
19. Heath, *Questions of Cinema*, p. 148.
20. Mulvey, 'Afterthoughts', p. 15.
21. Nowell-Smith discusses the way melodrama 'enacts, often with uncanny literalness, the "family romance" described by Freud – that is to say the imaginary scenario played out by children in relation to their paternity, the asking and answering of the question: whose child am I (or would I like to be)?' See p. 73 of this anthology.
22. Julia Kristeva, 'Woes of Love', lecture given at the Center for Twentieth Century Studies, University of Wisconsin-Milwaukee, Milwaukee, Wisconsin, 2 November 1982.
23. For example, on the way to the amusement park, Stefan remarks that he only visits it in the winter, never in the spring when it is so much more beautiful. Lisa replies that perhaps he prefers to imagine its beauties rather than to experience them.
24. Cixous, 'Castration or Decapitation?', p. 54.

25. Quoted in Kristeva, 'Women's Time', p. 15.
26. Heath, *Questions of Cinema*, p. 156.
27. I would like to thank Kathleen Woodward and the Center for Twentieth Century Studies for generously providing me with a fellowship which enabled me to research and write this essay.

Women's Genres
Melodrama, Soap Opera and Theory

ANNETTE KUHN

From *Screen* vol. 25, no. 1, 1984, pp. 18–28.

TELEVISION soap opera and film melodrama, popular narrative forms aimed at female audiences, are currently attracting a good deal of critical and theoretical attention. Not surprisingly, most of the work on these 'gyno-centric' genres is informed by various strands of feminist thought on visual representation. Less obviously, perhaps, such work has also prompted a series of questions which relate to representation and cultural production in a more wide-ranging and thoroughgoing manner than a specifically feminist interest might suggest. Not only are film melodrama (and more particularly its subtype the 'woman's picture') and soap opera directed at female audiences, they are also actually enjoyed by millions of women. What is it that sets these genres apart from representations which possess a less gender-specific mass appeal?

One of the defining generic features of the woman's picture as a textual system is its construction of narratives motivated by female desire and processes of spectator identification governed by female point-of-view. Soap opera constructs woman-centred narratives and identifications, too, but it differs textually from its cinematic counterpart in certain other respects: not only do soaps never end, but their beginnings are soon lost sight of. And whereas in the woman's picture the narrative process is characteristically governed by the enigma-retardation-resolution structure which marks the classic narrative, soap opera narratives propose

> competing and intertwining plot lines introduced as the serial progresses. Each plot ... develops at a different pace, thus preventing any clear resolution of conflict. The completion of one story generally leads into others, and ongoing plots often incorporate parts of semi-resolved conflicts.[1]

Recent work on soap opera and melodrama has drawn on existing theories, methods and perspectives in the study of film and television, including the structural analysis of narratives, textual semiotics and psychoanalysis, audience research, and the political economy of cultural institutions. At the same time, though, some of this work has exposed the limitations of existing approaches, and in consequence been forced if not actually to abandon them, at least to challenge their characteristic problematics. Indeed, it may be contended that the most significant developments in film and TV theory in general are currently taking place precisely within such areas of feminist concern as critical work on soap opera and melodrama.

In examining some of this work, I shall begin by looking at three areas in which particularly pertinent questions are being directed at theories of representation and cultural production. These are, firstly, the problem of gendered spectatorship; secondly, questions concerning the universalism as against the historical specificity of conceptualisations of gendered spectatorship; and thirdly, the relationship between film and television texts and their social, historical and institutional contexts. Each of these concerns articulates in particular ways with what seems to be the central issue here – the question of the audience, or audiences, for certain types of cinematic and televisual representation.

Film theory's appropriation to its own project of Freudian and post-Freudian psychoanalysis places the question of the relationship between text and spectator firmly on the agenda. Given the preoccupation of psychoanalysis with sexuality and gender, a move from conceptualising the spectator as a homogeneous and androgynous effect of textual operations[2] to regarding her or him as a gendered subject constituted in representation seems in retrospect inevitable. At the same time, the interests of feminist film theory and film theory in general converge at this point in a shared concern with sexual difference. Psychoanalytic accounts of the formation of gendered subjectivity raise the question, if only indirectly, of representation and feminine subjectivity. This in turn permits the spectator to be considered as a gendered subject position, masculine or feminine: and theoretical work on soap opera and the woman's picture may take this as a starting point for its inquiry into spectator–text relations. Do these 'gynocentric' forms address, or construct, a female or a feminine spectator? If so, how?

On the question of film melodrama, Laura Mulvey, commenting on King Vidor's *Duel in the Sun*,[3] argues that when, as in this film, a woman is at the centre of the narrative, the question of female desire structures the hermeneutic: 'what does *she* want?' This, says Mulvey, does not guarantee the constitution of the spectator as feminine so much as it implies a contradictory, and in the final instance impossible, 'phantasy of masculinisation' for the female spectator. This is in line with the author's earlier suggestion that cinema spectatorship involves masculine identification for spectators of either gender.[4] If cinema does thus construct a masculine subject, there can be no unproblematic feminine subject position for any spectator. Pam Cook, on the other hand, writing about a group of melodramas produced during

340

the 1940s at the Gainsborough Studios, evinces greater optimism about the possibility of a feminine subject of classic cinema. She does acknowledge, though, that in a patriarchal society female desire and female point-of-view are highly contradictory, even if they have the potential to subvert culturally dominant modes of spectator–text relation. The characteristic 'excess' of the woman's melodrama, for example, is explained by Cook in terms of the genre's tendency to '[pose] problems for itself which it can scarcely contain'.[5]

Writers on TV soap opera tend to take views on gender and spectatorship rather different from those advanced by film theorists. Tania Modleski, for example, argues with regard to soaps that their characteristic narrative patterns, their foregrounding of 'female' skills in dealing with personal and domestic crises, and the capacity of their programme formats and scheduling to key into the rhythms of women's work in the home, all address a female spectator. Furthermore, she goes as far as to argue that the textual processes of soaps are in some respects similar to those of certain 'feminine' texts which speak to a decentred subject, and so are 'not altogether at odds with … feminist aesthetics'.[6] Modleski's view is that soaps not only address female spectators, but in so doing construct feminine subject positions which transcend patriarchal modes of subjectivity.

Different though their respective approaches and conclusions might be, however, Mulvey, Cook and Modleski are all interested in the problem of gendered spectatorship. The fact, too, that this common concern is informed by a shared interest in assessing the progressive or transformative potential of soaps and melodramas is significant in light of the broad appeal of both genres to the mass audiences of women at which they are aimed.

But what precisely does it mean to say that certain representations are aimed at a female audience? However well theorised they may be, existing conceptualisations of gendered spectatorship are unable to deal with this question. This is because spectator and audience are distinct concepts which cannot – as they frequently are – be reduced to one another. Although I shall be considering some of its consequences more fully below (pp. 343–7), it is important to note a further problem for film and television theory, posed in this case by the distinction between spectator and audience. Critical work on the woman's picture and on soap opera has necessarily, and most productively, emphasised the question of gendered spectatorship. In doing this, film theory in particular has taken on board a conceptualisation of the spectator derived from psychoanalytic accounts of the formation of human subjectivity.

Such accounts, however, have been widely criticised for their universalism. Beyond, perhaps, associating certain variants of the Oedipus complex with family forms characteristic of a patriarchal society and offering a theory of the constructions of gender, psychoanalysis seems to offer little scope for theorising subjectivity in its cultural or historical specificity. Although in relation to the specific issues of spectatorship and representation there may, as I shall argue, be a way around this apparent impasse, virtually all film and TV theory — its feminist variants included — is marked by the dualism of universalism and specificity.

Nowhere is this more evident than in the gulf between textual analysis and contextual inquiry. Each is done according to different rules and procedures, distinct methods of investigation and theoretical perspectives. In bringing to the fore the question of spectator–text relations, theories deriving from psychoanalysis may claim — to the extent that the spectatorial apparatus is held to be coterminous with the cinematic or televisual institution — to address the relationship between text and context. But as soon as any attempt is made to combine textual analysis with analysis of the concrete social, historical and institutional conditions of production and reception of texts, it becomes clear that the context of the spectator/subject of psychoanalytic theory is rather different from the context of production and reception constructed by conjunctural analyses of cultural institutions.

The disparity between these two 'contexts' structures Pam Cook's article on the Gainsborough melodrama, which sets out to combine an analysis of the characteristic textual operations and modes of address of a genre with an examination of the historical conditions of a particular expression of it. Gainsborough melodrama, says Cook, emerges from a complex of determinants, including certain features of the British film industry of the 1940s, the nature of the female cinema audience in the post World War Two period, and the textual characteristics of the woman's picture itself.[7] While Cook is correct in pointing to the various levels of determination at work in this sentence, her lengthy preliminary discussion of spectator–text relations and the woman's picture rather outbalances her subsequent investigation of the social and industrial contexts of the Gainsborough melodrama. The fact, too, that analysis of the woman's picture in terms of its interpellation of a female/feminine spectator is simply placed alongside a conjunctural analysis tends to vitiate any attempt to reconcile the two approaches, and so to deal with the broader issue of universalism as against historical specificity. But although the initial problem remains, Cook's article constitutes an important intervention in the debate because, in tackling the text-context split head-on, it necessarily exposes a key weakness of current film theory.

In work on television soap opera as opposed to film melodrama, the dualism of text and context manifests itself rather differently, if only because — unlike film theory — theoretical work on television has tended to emphasise the determining character of the contextual level, particularly the structure and organisation of television institutions. Since this has often been at the expense of attention to the operation of TV texts, television theory may perhaps be regarded as innovative in the extent to which it attempts to deal specifically with texts as well as contexts. Some feminist critical work has in fact already begun to address the question of TV as text, though always with characteristic emphasis on the issue of gendered spectatorship. This emphasis constitutes a common concern of work on both TV soaps and the woman's picture, but a point of contact between text and context in either medium emerges only when the concept of social audience is considered in distinction from that of spectator.

Each term – spectator and social audience – presupposes a different set of relations to representations and to the contexts in which they are received. Looking at spectators and at audiences demands different methodologies and theoretical frameworks, distinct discourses which construct distinct subjectivities and social relations. The *spectator*, for example, is a subject constituted in signification, interpellated by the film or TV text. This does not necessarily mean that the spectator is merely an effect of the text, however, because modes of subjectivity which also operate outside spectator–text relations in film or TV are activated in the relationship between spectators and texts.

This model of the spectator/subject is useful in correcting more deterministic communication models which might, say, pose the spectator not as actively constructing meaning but simply as a receiver and decoder of pre-constituted 'messages'. In emphasising spectatorship as a set of psychic relations and focusing on the relationship between spectator and text, however, such a model does disregard the broader social implications of filmgoing or televiewing. It is the social act of going to the cinema, for instance, that makes the individual cinemagoer part of an audience. Viewing television may involve social relations rather different from filmgoing, but in its own ways TV does depend on individual viewers being part of an audience, even if its members are never in one place at the same time. A group of people seated in a single auditorium looking at a film, or scattered across thousands of homes watching the same television programme, is a *social audience*. The concept of social audience, as against that of spectator, emphasises the status of cinema and television as social and economic institutions.

Constructed by discursive practices both of cinema and TV and of social science, the social audience is a group of people who buy tickets at the box office, or who switch on their TV sets; people who can be surveyed, counted and categorised according to age, sex and socio-economic status.[8] The cost of a cinema ticket or TV licence fee, or a readiness to tolerate commercial breaks, earns audiences the right to look at films and TV programmes, and so to be spectators. Social audiences become spectators in the moment they engage in the processes and pleasures of meaning-making attendant on watching a film or TV programme. The anticipated pleasure of spectatorship is perhaps a necessary condition of existence of audiences. In taking part in the social act of consuming representations, a group of spectators becomes a social audience.

343

The consumer of representations as audience member and spectator is involved in a particular kind of psychic and social relationship: at this point, a conceptualisation of the cinematic or televisual apparatus as a regime of pleasure intersects with sociological and economic understandings of film and TV as institutions. Because each term describes a distinct set of relationships, though, it is important not to conflate social audience with spectators. At the same time, since each is necessary to the other, it is equally important to remain aware of the points of continuity between the two sets of relations.

These conceptualisations of spectator and social audience have particular implications when it comes to a consideration of popular 'gynocentric' forms such as soap opera and melodrama. Most obviously, perhaps, these centre on the issue of gender, which prompts again the question: what does 'aimed at a female audience' mean? What exactly is being signalled in this reference to a gendered audience? Are women to be understood as a subgroup of the social audience, distinguishable through discourses which construct *a priori* gender categories? Or does the reference to a female audience allude rather to gendered spectatorship, to sexual difference constructed in relations between spectators and texts? Most likely, it condenses the two meanings; but an examination of the distinction between them may nevertheless be illuminating in relation to the broader theoretical issues of texts, contexts, social audiences and spectators.

The notion of a female social audience, certainly as it is constructed in the discursive practices through which it is investigated, presupposes a group of individuals already formed as female. For the sociologist interested in such matters as gender and life-styles, certain people bring a pre-existent femaleness to their viewing or film and TV. For the business executive interested in selling commodities, TV programmes and films are marketed to individuals already constructed as female. Both, however, are interested in the same kind of woman. On one level, then, soap operas and women's melodrama address themselves to a social audience of women. But they may at the same time be regarded as speaking to a female, or a feminine, spectator. If soaps and melodramas inscribe femininity in their address, women – as well as being already formed *for* such representations – are in a sense also formed *by* them.

In making this point, however, I intend no reduction of femaleness to femininity: on the contrary, I would hold to a distinction between femaleness as social gender and femininity as subject position. For example, it is possible for a female spectator to be addressed, as it were, 'in the masculine', and the converse is presumably also true. Nevertheless, in a culturally pervasive operation of ideology, femininity is routinely identified with femaleness and masculinity with maleness. Thus, for example, an address 'in the feminine' may be regarded in ideological terms as privileging, if not necessitating, a socially constructed female gender identity.

The constitutive character of both the woman's picture and the soap opera has in fact been noted by a number of feminist commentators. Tania Modleski, for instance, suggests that the characteristic narrative structures and textual operations of soap operas both address the viewer as an 'ideal mother' – ever-understanding, ever-tolerant of the weaknesses and foibles of others – and also posit states of expectation and passivity as pleasurable:

> the narrative, by placing ever more complex obstacles between desire and fulfilment, makes anticipation of an end an end in itself.[9]

In our culture, tolerance and passivity are regarded as feminine attributes, and consequently as qualities proper in women but not in men.

Charlotte Brunsdon extends Modleski's line of argument to the extratextual level: in constructing its viewers as competent within the ideological and moral frameworks of marriage and family life, soap opera, she implies, addresses both a feminine spectator and female audience.[10] Pointing to the centrality of intuition and emotion in the construction of the woman's point-of-view, Pam Cook regards the construction of a feminine spectator as a highly problematic and contradictory process: so that in the film melo-drama's construction of female point-of-view, the validity of femininity as a subject position is necessarily laid open to question.[11]

This divergence on the question of gendered spectatorship within feminist theory is significant. Does it perhaps indicate fundamental differences be-tween film and television in the spectator–text relations privileged by each? Do soaps and melodramas really construct different relations of gendered spectatorship, with melodrama constructing contradictory identifications in ways that soap opera does not? Or do these different positions on specta-torship rather signal an unevenness of theoretical development – or, to put it less teleologically, reflect the different intellectual histories and epistemolo-gical groundings of film theory and television theory?

Any differences in the spectator–text relations proposed respectively by soap opera and by film melodrama must be contingent to some extent on more general disparities in address between television and cinema. Thus film spectatorship, it may be argued, involves the pleasures evoked by looking in a more pristine way than does watching television. Whereas in classic cinema the concentration and involvement proposed by structures of the look, identification and point-of-view tend to be paramount, television spectator-ship is more likely to be characterised by distraction and diversion.[12] This would suggest that each medium constructs sexual difference through spec-tatorship in rather different ways: cinema through the look and spectacle, and television – perhaps less evidently – through a capacity to insert its flow, its characteristic modes of address, and the textual operations of different kinds of programmes into the rhythms and routines of domestic activities and sexual divisions of labour in the household at various times of day.

It would be a mistake, however, simply to equate current thinking on spectator–text relations in each medium. This is not only because theoretical work on spectatorship as it is defined here is newer and perhaps not so developed for television as it has been for cinema, but also because conceptualisations of spectatorship in film theory and TV theory emerge from quite distinct perspectives. When feminist writers on soap opera and on film melodrama discuss spectatorship, therefore, they are usually talking about different things. This has partly to do with the different intellectual histories and methodological groundings of theoretical work on film and on television. Whereas most TV theory has until fairly recently existed under the sociological rubric of media studies, film theory has on the whole been based in the criticism-oriented tradition of literary studies. In consequence, while the one tends to privilege contexts over texts, the other usually privileges texts over contexts.

However, some recent critical work on soap opera, notably work produced within a cultural studies context, does attempt a *rapprochement* of text and context. Charlotte Brunsdon, writing about the British soap opera *Crossroads*, draws a distinction between subject positions proposed by texts and a 'social subject' who may or may not take up these positions.[13] In considering the interplay of 'social reader and social text', Brunsdon attempts to come to terms with problems posed by the universalism of the psychoanalytic model of the spectator/subject as against the descriptiveness and limited analytical scope of studies of specific instances and conjunctures. In taking up the instance of soap opera, then, one of Brunsdon's broader objectives is to resolve the dualism of text and context.

'Successful' spectatorship of a soap like *Crossroads*, it is argued, demands a certain cultural capital: familiarity with the plots and characters of a particular serial as well as with soap opera as a genre. It also demands wider cultural competence, especially in the codes of conduct of personal and family life. For Brunsdon, then, the spectator addressed by soap opera is constructed within culture rather than by representation. This, however, would indicate that such a spectator, a 'social subject', might – rather than being a subject in process of gender positioning – belong after all to a social audience already divided by gender.

The 'social subject' of this cultural model produces meaning by decoding messages or communications, an activity which is always socially situated.[14] Thus although such a model may move some way towards reconciling text and context, the balance of Brunsdon's argument remains weighted in favour of context: spectator–text relations are apparently regarded virtually as an effect of socio-cultural contexts. Is there a way in which spectator/subjects of film and television texts can be thought in a historically specific manner, or indeed a way for the social audience to be rescued from social/historical determinism?

Although none of the feminist criticism of soap opera and melodrama reviewed here has come up with any solution to these problems, it all attempts, in some degree and with greater or lesser success, to engage with them. Brunsdon's essay possibly comes closest to an answer, paradoxically because its very failure to resolve the dualism which ordains that spectators are constructed by texts while audiences have their place in contexts begins to hint at a way around the problem. Although the hybrid 'social subject' may turn out to be more a social audience member than a spectator, this concept does suggest that a move into theories of discourse could prove to be productive.

Both spectators and social audience may accordingly be regarded as discursive constructs. Representations, contexts, audiences and spectators would then be seen as a series of interconnected social discourses, certain discourses possessing greater constitutive authority at specific moments than others. Such a model permits relative autonomy for the operations of texts, readings and contexts, and also allows for contradictions, oppositional readings and varying degrees of discursive authority. Since the state of a discursive formation is not constant, it can be apprehended only by means of inquiry into specific instances or conjunctures. In attempting to deal with the text-context split and to address the relationship between spectators and social audiences, therefore, theories of representation may have to come to terms with discursive formations of the social, cultural and textual.

One of the impulses generating feminist critical and theoretical work on soap opera and the woman's picture is a desire to examine genres which are popular, and popular in particular with women. The assumption is usually that such popularity has to do mainly with the social audience: TV soaps attract large numbers of viewers, many of them women, and in its heyday the woman's picture also drew in a mass female audience. But when the nature of this appeal is sought in the texts themselves or in relations between spectators and texts, the argument becomes rather more complex. In what specific ways do soaps and melodramas address or construct female/feminine spectators?

To some extent, they offer the spectator a position of mastery: this is certainly true as regards the hermeneutic of the melodrama's classic narrative, though perhaps less obviously so in relation to the soap's infinite process of narrativity. At the same time, they also place the spectator in a masochistic position of either – in the case of the woman's picture – identifying with a female character's renunciation or, as in soap opera, forever anticipating an endlessly held-off resolution. Culturally speaking, this combination of mastery and masochism in the reading competence constructed by soaps and melodramas suggests an interplay of masculine and feminine subject positions. Culturally dominant codes inscribe the masculine, while the feminine bespeaks a 'return of the repressed' in the form of codes which may well transgress culturally dominant subject positions, though only at the expense of proposing a position of subjection for the spectator.

At the same time, it is sometimes argued on behalf of both soap opera and film melodrama that in a society whose representations of itself are governed by the masculine, these genres at least raise the possibility of female desire and female point-of-view. Pam Cook advances such a view in relation to the woman's picture, for example.[15] But how is the oppositional potential of this to be assessed? Tania Modleski suggests that soap opera is 'in the vanguard not just of TV art but of all popular narrative art'.[16] But such a statement begs the question: under what circumstances can popular narrative art itself be regarded as transgressive? Because texts do not operate in isolation from contexts, any answer to these questions must take into account the ways in which popular narratives are read, the conditions under which they are produced and consumed, and the ends to which they are appropriated. As most feminist writing on soap opera and the woman's melodrama implies, there is ample space in the articulation of these various instances for contradiction and for struggles over meaning.

The popularity of television soap opera and film melodrama with women raises the question of how it is that sizeable audiences of women relate to these representations and the institutional practices of which they form part. It provokes, too, a consideration of the continuity between women's interpellation as spectators and their status as a social audience. In turn, the distinction between social audience and spectator/subject, and attempts to explore the relationship between the two, are part of a broader theoretical endeavour: to deal in tandem with texts and contexts. The distinction between social audience and spectator must also inform debates and practices around cultural production, in which questions of context and reception are always paramount. For anyone interested in feminist cultural politics, such considerations will necessarily inform any assessment of the place and the political usefulness of popular genres aimed at, and consumed by, mass audiences of women.

Notes

1. Muriel G. Cantor and Suzanne Pingree, *The Soap Opera* (Beverly Hills, Sage Publications, 1983), p. 22. Here 'soap opera' refers to daytime (U S) or early evening (U K) serials ... not prime-time serials like *Dallas* and *Dynasty*.
2. See Jean-Louis Baudry, 'Ideological Effects of the Basic Cinematographic Apparatus', *Film Quarterly* vol. 28 no. 2, 1974–5, pp. 39–47; Christian Metz, 'The Imaginary Signifier', *Screen*, Summer 1975, vol. 16 no. 2, pp. 14–76.

3. Laura Mulvey, 'Afterthoughts on "Visual Pleasure and Narrative Cinema"', *Framework* nos. 15/16/17, 1981, pp. 12–15.

4. Laura Mulvey, 'Visual Pleasure and Narrative Cinema', *Screen*, Autumn 1975, vol. 16 no. 3, pp. 6–18.

5. Pam Cook, 'Melodrama and the Women's Picture', in Sue Aspinall and Robert Murphy, (eds.) *Gainsborough Melodrama* (London: BFI, 1983), p. 17.

6. Tania Modleski, *Loving With a Vengeance: Mass Produced Fantasies for Women* (Hamden CT: Archon Books, 1982), p. 105. See also Tania Modleski, 'The Search for Tomorrow in Today's Soap Operas', *Film Quarterly* vol. 33 no. 1, 1979, pp. 12–21.

7. Cook, 'Melodrama and the Woman's Picture'.

8. Methods and findings of social science research on the social audience for American daytime soap operas are discussed in Cantor and Pingree, *The Soap Opera*, Chapter 7.

9. Modleski, *Loving With a Vengence*, p. 88.

10. Charlotte Brunsdon, 'Crossroads: Notes on Soap Opera', *Screen*, vol. 22 no. 4, 1981, pp. 32–7.

11. Cook, 'Melodrama and the Woman's Picture', p. 19.

12. John Ellis, *Visible Fictions* (London: Routledge and Kegan Paul, 1982).

13. Brunsdon, 'Crossroads: Notes on Soap Opera', p. 32.

14. A similar model is also adopted by Dorothy Hobson in *Crossroads: the Drama of a Soap Opera* (London: Methuen, 1982).

15. Cook, 'Melodrama and the Woman's Picture'. E. Ann Kaplan takes a contrary position in 'Theories of Melodrama: a Feminist Perspective', *Women and Performance: a Journal of Feminist Theory*, vol. 1 no. 1, 1983, pp. 40–8.

16. Modleski, *Loving with a Vengeance*, p. 87.

Further Reading

Literary and Theatrical Melodrama

Althusser, Louis, 'Footnote to "The Piccolo Teatro"': Bertolazzi and Brecht', *For Marx* (Harmondsworth: Penguin, 1969).

Bailey, Peter, *Leisure and Class in Victorian England: Rational Recreation and the Contest for Control* (London: Routledge and Kegan Paul, 1978).

Bargainnier, Earl F., 'Melodrama as Formula', *Journal of Popular Culture*, vol. 9 no. 3, Winter 1975.

Bentley, Eric, *The Life of the Drama* (New York: Atheneum, 1967). Chapters on melodrama, tragedy and melodramatic acting.

Bogel, Fredric V., 'Fables of Knowing: Melodrama and Related Forms', *Genre*, vol. 11 no. 1, Spring 1978.

Booth, Michael R., *English Melodrama* (London: Herbert Jenkins, 1965). Theatrical melodrama from the eighteenth to early twentieth century.

Booth, Michael R., *Victorian Spectacular Theatre 1850–1910* (London: Routledge and Kegan Paul, 1981). The inter-relations between theatrical spectacle, melodrama, painting and other nineteenth-century visual forms.

Bradby, David; James, Louis, and Sharrat, Bernard (eds.), *Performance and Politics in Popular Drama: Aspects of Popular Entertainment in Theatre, Film and Television, 1800–1976* (Cambridge: Cambridge University Press, 1981).

Brooks, Peter, *The Melodramatic Imagination: Balzac, Henry James, Melodrama and the Mode of Excess* (New Haven: Yale University Press, 1976).

Cawelti, John G., *Adventure, Mystery and Romance: Formula Stories as Art and Popular Culture* (Chicago: University of Chicago Press, 1973).

Disher, Maurice W., *Blood and Thunder: Mid-Victorian Melodrama and its Origins* (London: Frederick Muller, 1949).

Disher, Maurice W., *Melodrama: Plots That Thrilled* (New York: Macmillan, 1954).

Gallagher, Kent G., 'Emotion in Tragedy and Melodrama', *Educational Theatre Journal*, vol. 17 no. 3, October 1965.

Grimstead, David, 'Melodrama as Echo of the Historically Voiceless', in Hareven, Tamara K. (ed.), *Anonymous Americans: Explorations in Nineteenth Century Social History* (Englewood Cliffs, New Jersey: Prentice-Hall, 1971).

Grimstead, David, *Melodrama Unveiled: American Theatre and Culture 1800–1850* (Chicago: University of Chicago Press, 1968).

Hauser, Arnold, *The Social History of Art*, vol. 3, 'Rococo, Classicism, Romanticism' (New York: Vintage, 1958). See chapter on 'The Origins of Domestic Drama'.

Heilman, Robert, *Tragedy and Melodrama: Versions of Experience* (Seattle: University of Washington Press, 1968).

James, Louis, 'Is Jerrold's Black-Eyed Susan more important than Wordsworth's Lucy? Melodrama, the Popular Ballad, and the Dramaturgy of Emotion', in Bradby et al., op. cit.

Knight, G. Wilson, 'Victorian', in *The Golden Labyrinth: A Study of British Drama* (London: Phoenix House, 1962).

Loftis, John C., *The Politics of Drama in Augustan England* (London: Oxford University Press, 1963).

Lynch, James J., *Box, Pit and Gallery: Stage and Society in Johnson's London* (Berkeley: University of California Press, 1953).

Mayer, David, 'The Music of Melodrama', in Bradby et al., op. cit.

McCormick, John, 'Joseph Bouchardy: a Melodramatist and his Public', in Bradby et al., op. cit.

Nicholson, David and Daniel, Gerould, 'Bibliography', in Daniel, Gerould (ed.), *Melodrama*, vol. 7 (New York: New York Literary Forum, 1981). Comprehensive bibliography covering 'General and Theatrical', 'Melodrama and the Novel', 'TV and Film'.

Nicoll, Allerdyce, *British Drama*, 6th rev. ed. (London: Harrap, 1978).

Rahill, Frank, *The World of Melodrama* (Philadelphia: University of Pennsylvania Press, 1967).

Reid, Douglas A., 'Popular Theatre in Victorian Birmingham', in Bradby et al., op. cit.

Smith, James L., *Melodrama*, 'The Critical Idiom' series, no. 28 (London: Methuen, 1973).

Styan, J. L., *Drama, Stage and Audience* (Cambridge: Cambridge University Press, 1975).

Sypher, Wylie, 'Aesthetic of Revolution: The Marxist Melodrama', in Corrigan, Robert W. (ed.), *Tragedy: Vision and Form* (New York: New York University Press, 1965).

Vardac, Nicholas A., *Stage to Screen: Theatrical Method from Garrick to Griffith* (Cambridge: Harvard University Press, 1949).

Williams, Raymond, *Modern Tragedy* (London: Chatto and Windus, 1966).

Williams, Raymond, 'Social Environment and Theatrical Environment: the Case of English Naturalism', in Marie Axton and Raymond Williams (eds.), *English Drama: Forms and Development* (Cambridge: Cambridge University Press, 1977).

Feminist Approaches to Theatrical Melodrama and Women's Fiction

Auerbach, Nina, *Women and the Demon: the Life of a Victorian Myth* (Cambridge: Harvard University Press, 1982).

Baym, Nina, *Women's Fiction: A Guide to Novels by and about Women in America, 1820–1870* (Ithaca: Cornell University Press, 1978).

Beauman, Nicola, *A Very Great Profession: The Woman's Novel 1914–39* (London: Virago, 1983).

Fryer, Judith, *The Faces of Eve: Women in the Nineteenth Century American Novel* (New York: Oxford University Press, 1976).

Gilbert, Sandra and Gubar, Susan, *The Madwoman in the Attic: The Woman Writer and the Nineteenth Century Literary Imagination* (New Haven: Yale University Press, 1979).

Harper, Sue, 'History with Frills: "Costume" Fiction in World War II', *Red Letters*, no. 14, 1983.

Heilbrun, Carolyn, *Reinventing Womanhood* (New York: Norton, 1979).

Light, Alison, ' "Returning to Manderley" – Romance Fiction, Female Sexuality and Class', *Feminist Review*, no. 16, April 1984.

Mitchell, Sally, 'Sentiment and Suffering: Women's Recreational Reading in the 1890s', *Victorian Studies*, vol. 21 no. 1, Autumn 1977.

Moers, Ellen, *Literary Women* (Garden City: Doubleday, 1976).

Radway, Janice A., *Reading the Romance: Women, Patriarchy, and Popular Literature* (Chapel Hill: University of North Carolina Press, 1984).

Showalter, Elaine, 'Desperate Remedies: Sensation Novels of the 1860s', *The Victorian Newsletter*, no. 49, Spring 1976.

Tompkins, Jane, *Sensational Designs: The Cultural Work of American Fiction 1790–1860s* (New York: Oxford University Press, 1985).

Vicinus, Martha, 'Helpless and Unfriended: Nineteenth Century Domestic Melodrama', *New Literary History*, vol. 13 no. 1, Autumn 1981.

Melodrama and Cinema

Aspinall, Sue and Murphy, Bob (eds.), *Gainsborough Melodrama*, Dossier no. 18 (London: BFI, 1983).

Baxter, Peter, 'On the History and Ideology of Film Lighting', *Screen*, vol. 16 no. 3, Autumn 1975. Detailed preliminary discussion of nineteenth-century theatrical lighting, including the work of Irving and Belasco.

Bogle, Donald, *Toms, Coons, Mullattoes, Mammies and Bucks* (New York: Viking, 1973). Section on Louise Beavers and Fredi Washington in *Imitation of Life* (Stahl and Sirk respectively).

Bordwell, David, 'Happily Ever After, Part Two', *The Velvet Light Trap*, no. 19, 1982.

Bourget, Jean-Loup, 'Faces of the American Melodrama: Joan Crawford', *Film Reader*, no. 3, February 1978. Argues that melodrama is defined by certain of its stars; Bill Horrigan replies in same issue.

Bourget, Jean-Loup, *Le mélodrame hollywoodien* (Paris: Stock, 1985).

Bourget, Jean-Loup, 'Sirk and the Critics', *Bright Lights*, no. 6, Winter 1977/8.

Boyd-Bowman, Susan, 'Heavy Breathing in Shropshire: The Re-Release of *Gone to Earth*', *Screen*, vol. 27 no. 6, November/December 1986.

Braun, Eric, 'A Decade of Gainsborough Melodrama: 1942–50', *Films*, vol. 4 no. 3, March 1984 and vol. 4 no. 4, April 1984.

Brewster, Ben, 'A Scene at the Movies', *Screen*, vol. 23 no. 2, July/August 1982. The development of narrative perspective in early cinema, with reference to Henry King's *Stella Dallas*.

Bright Lights, no. 6, Winter 1977/8. Special issue on Sirk.

Cadbury, William, 'Theme, Felt Life, and the Last-Minute Rescue in Griffith after *Intolerance*', *Film Quarterly*, vol. 28 no. 1, Fall 1974. Takes issue with the respectively orthodox and revisionist approaches of Alan Casty and John Dorr (see below).

Casty, Alan, 'The Films of D. W. Griffith: A Style for the Times', *Journal of Popular Film*, vol. 1 no. 2, Spring 1972.

Cook, Pam (ed.), *The Cinema Book* (London: BFI, 1985). Sections on 'History of Genre Criticism', 'Melodrama' and other genres. Also on 'Film Narrative and the Structuralist Controversy'.

Cunningham, Stuart, 'The "Force-Field" of Melodrama', *Quarterly Review of Film Studies*, vol. 6 no. 4, Fall 1981. An analysis of recent melodramas using a combination of Peter Brooks's literary with René Girard's anthropological approaches.

Cunningham, Stuart, 'Stock, Shock and Schlock', *Enclitic*, vol. 5 no. 2/vol. 6 no. 1, Fall 1981/Spring 1982. Sirk, Minnelli and *Some Came Running*.

Delgaudio, Sybil, 'The Mammy in Hollywood Film', *Jump Cut*, no. 28, 1983. Historical analysis brought to bear on Stahl and Sirk versions of *Imitation of Life*.

Dorr, John, 'The Griffith Tradition', *Film Comment*, vol. 10 no. 2, March/April 1974.

Durgnat, R. E., 'Ways of Melodrama', *Sight and Sound*, vol. 21 no. 1, August/September 1951.

Dyer, Richard, 'Minnelli's Web of Dreams', in Lloyd, Ann, *Movies of the 50s* (London: Orbis, 1982).

Eckert, Charles W., 'The Anatomy of a Proletarian Film: Warners' *Marked Woman*', *Film Quarterly*, vol. 27 no. 2, Winter 1973/4.

Eisenstein, S. M., 'Dickens, Griffith and the Film Today', *Sight and Sound*, November 1950 and *Film Form* (London: Dennis Dobson, 1963).

Fell, John L., *Film and the Narrative Tradition* (Oklahoma: University of Ohio Press, 1974).

Fell, John L., 'Motive, Mischief and Melodrama: The State of Film Narrative in 1907', *Film Quarterly*, vol. 33 no. 3, Spring 1980; reprinted in Fell, John L. (ed.), *Film Before Griffith* (Berkeley: University of California Press, 1983).

Film Criticism, vol. 9 no. 2, Winter 1984–5. Special issue on melodrama, offering analyses of *The Stranger* by R. Barton Palmer, of *Dark Passage* by J. P. Telotte, of *The Accused* by Robert Phillip Kolker and of *Stage Fright* by Richard Abel.

Flinn, Carol, 'The "Problem" of Femininity in Theories of Film Music', *Screen*, vol. 27 no. 6, Winter 1986. Analyses the function of music in classic Hollywood melodramas.

Flitterman, Sandy, '*Guest in the House*: Rupture and Reconstitution of the Bourgeois Family', *Wide Angle*, vol. 4 no. 2, 1980.

French, Brandon, *On the Verge of Revolt: Women in American Films of the Fifties* (New York: Ungar, 1978). Chapter on *All That Heaven Allows*.

Focus, no. 9, Spring/Summer 1973. Special issue on Borzage.

Gaines, Jane, '*The Scar of Shame*: Skin Color and Caste in Black Silent Melodrama', *Cinema Journal*, forthcoming.

Geduld, Harry M. (ed.), *Focus on D. W. Griffith* (Englewood Cliffs, New Jersey: Prentice Hall, 1971).

Gledhill, Christine, 'Pleasurable Negotiations', in Pribram, Deirdre (ed.), *Cinematic Pleasure and the Female Spectator* (London: Verso, forthcoming 1987). Discussion of melodrama and contemporary realist discourse in *Coma*.

Gledhill, Christine and Swanson, Gillian, 'Gender and Sexuality in Second World War Films – A Feminist Approach', in Geoff Hurd (ed.), *National Fictions: World War Two in British Films and Television* (London: BFI, 1984). Considered in relation to wartime discourses on the family and to the melodrama.

Gorbman, Claudia, 'The Drama's Melos: Max Steiner and *Mildred Pierce*', *The Velvet Light Trap*, no. 19, 1982.

Greene, Naomi, 'Coppola, Cimino: The Operatics of History', *Film Quarterly*, vol. 38 no. 2, Winter 1984–5. Examines the shift in 70s melodrama towards the subordination of narrative to spectacle.

Halliday, Jon, *Sirk on Sirk* (London: Secker and Warburg, 1972).

Handzo, Stephen, 'Intimations of Lifelessness: Sirk's Ironic Tear-jerker', *Bright Lights*, no. 6, Winter 1977/8.

Haralovich, Mary Beth, 'The Social History of Film: Heterogeneity and Mediation', *Wide Angle*, vol. 8 no. 1, 1986. With reference to *All That Heaven Allows*.

Harvey, James, 'Sirkumstantial Evidence', *Film Comment*, vol. 14 no. 4, July/August 1978.

Johnson, Albert, 'Beige, Brown or Black', *Film Quarterly*, vol. 13 no. 1, Fall 1959. Treatment of blacks in 50s Hollywood, including Sirk's *Imitation of Life*.

Journal of the University Film and Video Association, vol. 35 no. 1, Winter 1983. Special issue on melodrama.

Kehr, Dave, 'The New *Male* Melodrama', *American Film*, vol. 8 no. 6, April 1983. Deals with the new emphasis on the male in films such as *Interiors*, *Table for Five*, *Kramer vs. Kramer*, etc., and the influence of the European art movie.

Kleinhans, Chuck, 'Notes on Melodrama and the Family under Capitalism', *Film Reader*, no. 3, 1978.

Kozloff, Sarah R., 'Where Wessex Meets New England: Griffith's *Way Down East* and Hardy', *Literature and Film Quarterly*, Spring 1985.

Lippe, Richard, 'Melodrama in the 70s', *Movie*, nos. 29/30, Summer 1982.

Lopez, Ana, 'The Melodrama in Latin America: Films, *Telenovelas* and the Currency of a Popular Form', *Wide Angle*, vol. 7 no. 3, 1985.

Lloyd, Peter, 'Some Affairs to Remember: the Style of Leo McCarey , *Monogram*, no. 4, 1972.

McNiven, Roger N., 'The Middle-Class American Home of the 50s: the Use of Architecture in Nicholas Ray's *Bigger Than Life* and Sirk's *All That Heaven Allows*', *Cinema Journal*, vol. 22 no. 4, Summer 1983.

Merritt, Russell, 'Melodrama: Post-Mortem for a Phantom Genre', *Wide Angle*, vol. 5 no. 3, 1983. Supercilious attempt to disprove those who have sought to establish melodrama as a genre.

Merritt, Russell, 'Rescued from a Perilous Nest: D. W. Griffith's Escape from Theatre into Film', *Cinema Journal*, vol. 21 no. 1, Fall 1981. Well documented account of Griffith's theatre work and its influence on his use of character, gesture, props and locational detail.

Milne, Peter, *Motion Picture Directing* (New York: Falk Publishing Co., 1922) Chapter XII: 'Some Words From Frank Borzage'.

Morse, David, 'Aspects of Melodrama', *Monogram* no. 4, 1972.

Monogram, no. 4, 1972. Special issue on melodrama.

Movie, no. 29/30, Summer 1982. Special issue on melodrama.

Mulvey, Laura, '*Fear Eats the Soul*', *Spare Rib*, no. 30, December 1974. In relation to *All that Heaven Allows*.

Mulvey, Laura, 'Afterthoughts on Visual Pleasure and Narrative Cinema in relation to *Duel in the Sun*', *Framework*, nos. 15/16/17, 1981. The western, melodrama and female audiences.

Mulvey, Laura and Halliday, Jon (eds.), *Douglas Sirk* (Edinburgh Film Festival, 1972).

Neale, Steve, 'Douglas Sirk', *Framework*, vol. 11 no. 5, Winter 1976/77.

Neale, Steve, *Genre* (London: BFI, 1981). Few paragraphs on melodrama.

Neale, Steve, 'Melodrama and Tears', *Screen*, vol. 27 no. 6, November/December 1986.

Nichols, Bill, 'Revolution and Melodrama: a Marxist View of Some Recent Films', *Cinema*, vol. 6 no. 1, 1970.

Orr, Christopher, 'Closure and Containment: Marylee Hadley in *Written on the Wind*', *Wide Angle*, vol. 4 no. 2, 1980.

Pines, Jim, *Blacks in Films* (London: Studio Vista, 1975). Section on Sirk's *Imitation of Life*.

Pollock, Griselda, 'Report on the Weekend School', *Screen*, vol. 18 no. 2, Summer 1977.

Quarterly Review of Film Studies, vol. 6 no. 1, Winter 1981. Special issue on Griffith.

Renov, Michael, '*Leave Her to Heaven*: The Double Bind of the Post-War Woman', *Journal of the University Film and Video Association*, vol. 35 no. 1, Winter 1983.

Rohdie, Sam, 'Semiotic Constraints in *Now, Voyager*', *The Australian Journal of Screen Theory*, vol. 4, 1978.

Roberts, Susan, 'Melodramatic Performance Signs', *Framework*, no. 32/33, 1986.

Robinson, Casey, '*Dark Victory*', *The Australian Journal of Screen Theory*, vol. 4, 1978. Comments by the scriptwriter.

Schatz, Thomas, *Hollywood Genres* (New York: Random House, 1981). Chapter on family melodrama.

Screen, vol. 12 no. 2, Winter 1977/8. Special issue on Sirk.

Screen, vol. 25 no. 1, January/February 1984. Special issue on melodrama.

Screen, vol. 27 no. 6, November/December 1986. Special issue on melodrama.

Seiter, Ellen, 'Men, Sex and Money in Recent Family Melodramas', *Journal of the University Film and Video Association*, vol. 35 no. 1, Winter 1983.

Smith, Robert E., 'The Films of Frank Borzage', *Bright Lights*, vol. 1 no. 2, Spring 1975 and vol. 1 no. 3, Summer 1975. Authorial study of themes and style, with filmography.

Stern, Michael, *Douglas Sirk* (Boston: Twayne, 1979).

Stern, Michael, 'Patterns of Power and Potency, Repression and Violence: An Introduction to the Study of Douglas Sirk's Films of the 1950s', *The Velvet Light Trap*, no. 16, Fall 1976.

Walker, Michael, 'Melodrama and American Cinema', *Movie*, nos. 29/30, Summer 1982.

Wegner, Hart, 'Melodrama as Tragic Rondo: Douglas Sirk's *Written on the Wind*', *Literature and Film Quarterly*, vol. 10 no. 3, 1982. 'Tragic' reading of irony.

Wide Angle, vol. 4 no. 2, 1980. Special issue on melodrama.

Willemen, Paul, 'The Films of Douglas Sirk', *Screen*, vol. 12 no. 2, Winter 1977/8.

Willemen, Paul, 'Towards an Analysis of the Sirkian System', *Screen*, vol. 13 no. 4, Winter 1972/3.

Willemen, Paul, 'Frank Borzage', NFT Booklet, May/August, 1975, pp. 2–8.

Williams, Martin, *Griffith: First Artist of the Movies* (New York: Oxford University Press, 1980).

Woodward, Katherine, 'European Anti-Melodrama: Godard, Truffaut and Fassbinder', *Post Script*, vol. 3 no. 2, Winter 1984.

The Woman's Film and Woman's Melodrama

Allen, Jeanne, 'Introduction: *Now, Voyager* as Women's Film: Coming of Age Hollywood Style', in Allen (ed.), *Now, Voyager*, Wisconsin/Warner Bros Screenplay Series (Madison, Wisconsin: University of Wisconsin Press, 1984).

Aspinall, Sue, 'Sexuality in Costume Melodrama', in Aspinall and Murphy (eds.), op. cit.

Basinger, Jeanine, 'The Lure of the Gilded Cage', *Bright Lights*, no. 6, Winter 1977/8. On Douglas Sirk.

Basinger, Jeanine, 'When Women Wept', *American Film*, vol. 12 no. 10, September 1977.

Brunsdon, Charlotte, 'A Subject for the Seventies', *Screen*, vol. 23 nos. 3/4, September/October 1982. On romance and *An Unmarried Woman*.

Cinema Journal, vol. 24 no. 2, Winter 1985; vol. 25 no. 1, Fall 1985; vol. 25 no. 2, Winter 1986; vol. 25 no. 4, Summer 1986: running debate on Linda Williams' account of *Stella Dallas* and the woman's film with reference also to Tania Modleski on *Letter From an Unknown Woman* (for both essays see this volume).

Cook, Pam, 'Duplicity in *Mildred Pierce*', in Kaplan, E. Ann (ed.), *Women in Film Noir* (London: BFI, 1980).

Cook, Pam, 'Melodrama and the Woman's Picture', in Aspinall and Murphy (eds.), op. cit.

Cowie, Elizabeth, 'Fantasia', *m/f*, no. 9, 1984. Fantasy, psychoanalysis and feminism in relation to *Now, Voyager* and *The Reckless Moment*.

Creed, Barbara, 'Women in Hollywood Melodramas', *The Australian Journal of Screen Theory*, no. 4, 1978.

Doane, Mary Ann, '*Caught* and *Rebecca*: The Inscription of Femininity as Absence', *Enclitic*, vol. 5 no. 2/vol. 6 no. 1, Fall 1981/Spring 1982.

Doane, Mary Ann, *The Desire to Desire: The Woman's Film of the 1940s* (Bloomington: Indiana University Press, 1987).

Ehrenstein, David, 'Melodrama and the New Woman', *Film Comment*, vol. 14 no. 5, September/October 1978.

Fisher, Lucy, 'Two Faced Woman: the Double in Woman's Melodrama of the 1940s', *Cinema Journal*, vol. 23 no. 1, Fall 1983.

Haskell, Molly, *From Reverence To Rape: The Treatment of Women in the Movies* (Harmondsworth: Penguin, 1979). Chapter Three, 'The Woman's Film'.

Jacobs, Lea, '*Now, Voyager*: Some Problems of Enunciation and Sexual Difference', *Camera Obscura*, no. 7, 1981.

Lesage, Julia, 'The Hegemonic Female Fantasy in *An Unmarried Woman* and *Craig's Wife*', *Film Reader*, no. 5, 1982.

Modleski, Tania, *Loving with a Vengeance: Mass-Produced Fantasies for Women* (Hamden CT: Archon Books, 1982 and London: Methuen, 1985).

Modleski, Tania, 'Never To Be Thirty-Six Years Old: *Rebecca* as Female Oedipal Drama', *Wide Angle*, vol. 5 no. 1, 1982.

Palmer, R. Barton, 'The Successful Failure of Therapy in *Now, Voyager*: The Woman's Picture as Unresponsive Symptom', *Wide Angle*, vol. 8 no. 1, 1986. A 'subversive reading' in response to Mary Ann Doane and Ann Kaplan's respective accounts of the woman's film.

Waldman, Diane, ' "At last I can tell it to someone!" Feminine Point Of View and Subjectivity in the Gothic Romance Film of the 1940s', *Cinema Journal*, vol. 23 no. 2, Fall 1983.

Walsh, Andrea, *Women's Film and Female Experience* (New York: Praeger, 1984).

General

Ang, Ien, *Watching Dallas: Soap Opera and the Melodramatic Imagination* (London: Methuen, 1985).

Dyer, Richard, 'Entertainment and Utopia', *Movie*, no. 24, Spring 1977. Reprinted in Altman, Rick, *Genre: The Musical* (London: Routledge and Kegan Paul/BFI, 1981).

Ehrenreich, Barbara, *The Hearts of Men: American Dreams and the Flight from Commitment* (London: Pluto Press, 1983). Analysis of changing discourses of masculinity from the 50s to 80s.

Bordwell, David; Staiger, Janet, and Thompson, Kristin, *The Classical Hollywood Cinema: Film Style and Mode of Production to 1960* (New York: Columbia University Press, 1985).

Eckert, Charles, 'The Carole Lombard in Macy's Window', *Quarterly Review of Film Studies*, vol. 4 no. 1, Winter 1978.

Fell, John (ed.), *Film Before Griffith* (Berkeley: University of California Press, 1983).

Herzog, Charlotte Cornelia, and Gaines, Jane Marie, 'Puffed Sleeves Before Tea-Time: Joan Crawford, Adrian and Women Audiences', *Wide Angle*, vol. 6 no. 4, 1985.

Pryluck, Calvin, 'Industrialisation of Entertainment in the United States' in Austin, Bruce (ed.), *Current Research in Film*, vol. 2 (Norwood, New Jersey: Ablex Publishing Corporation, 1986).

Rajadhyaksha, Ashish, 'Neo-Traditionalism: Film as Popular Art in India', *Framework*, nos. 32/33, 1986.

Roddick, Nick, *A New Deal in Entertainment: Warner Brothers in the 1930s* (London: BFI, 1983).

Index

Home from the Hill (Vincente Minnelli, 1959)

The theatre is bigger than the playwright ... its destiny is a higher one than that of the mouthpiece for an author's theses ... plays are made for the theatre and not the theatre for plays.

HENRY IRVING

The room is lighted only by the reflection from the fireplace. The spectator's vision seems to actually penetrate the privacy of domestic life.

Contemporary reviewer on David Belasco and Henry De Mille's production of *The Wife*

Morality is a question of tracking shots.

LUC MOULLET

The curtains open. The house goes dark. A rectangle of light presently vibrates before our eyes. Soon it is invaded by gestures and sounds ... The mysterious energy which 'supports' ... the backwash of shadow and light and their foam of sound is called *mise en scène* ... The placing of the actors and objects, their movements within the frame, should express everything.

MICHEL MOURLET